SERMONS

by
John Donne

PREFACE

As THE present volume goes to press, we the editors take this opportunity to comment on two or three matters that are perhaps self-evident but that it will do no harm to emphasize.

We believe that these two initial volumes of our edition make apparent the usefulness of an attempt such as that we are making, to publish Donne's sermons in as close an approach to chronological order as the evidence will permit; since the earlier sermons, when arranged chronologically, throw fresh light on Donne's development as a preacher and a minister, in his style, his thought, and his comprehension of the functions and duties of his adopted profession. For most of the sermons, it is possible to know the exact date on which he preached them. For some, the dates can be determined only within certain limits, of months or years; such sermons we shall place at or near their latest possible dates. Some other sermons can be dated only very generally, as in his earlier or his later career as a clergyman; these we plan to include after the dated sermons for the earlier and later half of that career, respectively. A few sermons we have found it impossible to date at all; and these will be published at the end of the latest dated or approximately dated sermons, in the last volume of this edition.

We should state, furthermore, that we decided to make our notes to this edition textual, not explanatory, since our main concern is to try to establish text and chronology. General comments on the individual sermons are included in the Introductions to the separate volumes of our edition; but specific explanations of Donne's innumerable references to authorities and to the many passages in the sermons that deserve explanatory or critical consideration we leave to future scholars.

As was stated in Volume I of this edition (pages ix, 33, 327), the recently discovered Ellesmere Manuscript came to light after that first volume had gone to the publishers, and while we did consider and include in our textual notes variants from that manuscript for the only sermon appearing there that was published in our first volume, we postponed an account of the sermon texts in it and their significance. This account is now ready, and will be found as Appendix A to the present volume; also, the versions of the sermons on *Ecclesiastes* 12.1, *John* 5.22, and *John* 8.15 that appear in the Ellesmere Manuscript have been fully considered in connection with the text and notes of those sermons that appear in the present volume.

To the acknowledgments that we expressed in the Preface to Volume I we wish to add the following. We are particularly grateful anew to Dr. Geoffrey L. Keynes for his friendly help and coöperation in making the Ellesmere Manuscript available for our use. The Stanford University Press has permitted us to reproduce occasional phrases and statements from the introduction and notes to G. R. Potter's edition of the Sermon on *Psalms* 38.9, published by that Press in 1946; and we appreciate greatly its friendly courtesy in so readily giving us this permission. We are very grateful to the Masters of the Bench of the Honourable Society of Lincoln's Inn for advice and help regarding photographs and for permission to use these photographs as illustrations; also to the authorities of the British Museum for permission to reproduce part of a ground plan of Whitehall. We feel a deep and sorrowful debt of gratitude to the late Dr. F. E. Hutchinson for his kindness in lending us additional copies of the *LXXX* and *XXVI Sermons,* and also to the late Bishop of Swansea and Brecon for his extremely valuable comments on Donne's Latin. We are also deeply grateful to Professor William H. Alexander of the University of California for further help on that Latin. To Professor D. C. Simpson of Oxford University we express our sincere thanks for valuable advice regarding Hebrew words in the sermons, and to Professor Walter J. Fischel of the University of California for additional help on Hebrew. We gratefully acknowledge, too, the interest and help of Professor R. C. Bald of the University of Chicago; of A. C. Wood, Esq., Hon. Sec. of the Warwickshire Committee of the National Register of Archives; of L. Edgar Stephens, Esq., Clerk of the Warwickshire County Council and Chief Officer of the Diocesan Record Office; of J. George, Esq., of Aberdeen; and of Professor Ruth Wallerstein of the University of Wisconsin.

THE EDITORS

Table of Contents

Introduction

The five years during which Donne held the office of Divinity Reader for Lincoln's Inn must have been in many ways the pleasantest period of his clerical career. In accepting this post he returned to the scenes of early days as a student, and to renewed association with at least one of his most intimate personal friends, Christopher Brooke. Donne had entered Lincoln's Inn as a student on May 6, 1592, with Christopher Brooke as one of his two manucaptors—Brooke himself having entered on March 15, 1586/87—and the two had shared chambers. The parts that Christopher and his brother Samuel played in forwarding Donne's runaway marriage with Ann More—Samuel performing the ceremony and Christopher (quite illegally) "giving away" the bride, both of them suffering imprisonment with Donne for their shares in the escapade—are too well known to need elaboration here. Donne left Lincoln's Inn seemingly in December, 1594, and was never admitted to the bar; but in the years between that time and 1616, Christopher Brooke had continued the association with the Inn, and had risen to a place of decided importance in its government. He became a Bencher in 1610, was an active member of various committees, especially of those planning and overseeing the building of a new chapel, was intermediary on more than one occasion between the Council of the Inn and higher authorities such as the judges, the Lord Keeper (Francis Bacon), and the King, was a dependable subscriber to benevolences for the Inn, was Keeper of the Black Books for 1620–1621, and was Treasurer in 1623–1624.[1] It is at least a reasonable guess that Brooke had something to do with the choice of Donne as Divinity Reader in 1616, possibly suggested his name to the Council. Donne was chosen by the Council on October 24, 1616, under conditions that the following entry in the *Black Books* makes clear:

> Mr. Doctor Dune is at this Councell chosen to be Divinitye Reader of this House, and is to have the like entertaynement that Mr. Doctor

[1] See *The Records of the Honorable Society of Lincoln's Inn. The Black Books* (London, 1898), Vol. II, pp. 135, 181, 186, 192–193, 198–199, 206, 216, 218, 246.

Holloway had; whoe is to preach everye Sabboth Daye in the tearme, both fore-noone and after-noone, and once the Sabboth Dayes next before and after everie tearme, and on the Grand Dayes everie for-noone, and in the Reading tymes; whoe is to take place next the Double Readers that nowe have Read, or herafter shall Read, or hereafter shall fyne for theire Double Readinges.[2]

Donne was given chambers in the Inn,[3] and devoted himself to his duties during the period of his Readership except when he was abroad in the service of Viscount Doncaster from May 12, 1619, to about the first of January, 1619/20. When, on February 11, 1621/22, he resigned, to accept the Deanery of St. Paul's, the Council accepted his resignation with a tribute such as they paid to no other one of their Divinity Readers for many years previous and subsequent to this time:

Mr. Doctor Donne, being lately advaunced by the King's Majesty to the Deanry of Poule's, by reason whereof he cannot conveniently supply the place of a publick Preacher of God's Word in this House, as formerly he hath Donne,[4] in significacion of the continuance of his love to this Society, hath nowe at this Councell presented to the Masters of the Bench, as a free gift from him, six volumes of the Bible, with the comment of Lyra, etc., and the Glosse, etc. Which volumes were accordingly receaved and delivered unto Mr. Tooker, one of the Masters of the Bench, and nowe Master of the Library, there to be kept to the use of the House. And the Masters of the Bench, acknowledging this and many other the kind and loving respectes of the said Mr. Doctor Donne towardes them, whereof they have had good experience, have nowe entred into consideracion of some fitting retribucion to expresse their thankefull remembrance of him; And to th'end it may appeare that, though they are glad of his preferment, yet being loath wholly to part with him, and that he may at his pleasure and convenient leisure repaire to this House, being a worthy member thereof, and he noe stranger here, have thought fitt, and with one voice and assent have soe ordered, that the said Mr. Doctor Donne shall continue his chamber in this House which he nowe hath, as a Bencher of this

[2] *Black Books,* II, 187.

[3] *Black Books,* II, 195.

[4] W. P. Baildon, the editor of the printed selections from the Society's *Black Books,* comments justly at this point that "The capital letter and the spelling seem to show that the pun is intentional." Donne's friends could no more keep from punning on his name than could he himself, or his twentieth-century readers.

House, with such priviledges touching the same as the Masters of the Bench nowe have and ought to have for their severall and respective chambers in this House.[5]

Even the acceptance later by the Council of Donne's offer to give up this chamber is couched in friendly and complimentary language quite unusual in the Black Books for these years: "Mr. Doctour Donne, Deane of Paule's, declared by his letter his free disposicion to resign his chamber, with an expression of his humble thankes, and assurance of all readinesse to serve this Societie, or any member

[5] *Black Books,* II, 229–230. The six-volume copy of the Bible with the Gloss of Walafrid Strabo and the Commentary of Nicholas de Lyra, printed at Douay in 1617, is still preserved in the Library of Lincoln's Inn. The inscription on the flyleaf of the first volume has been reproduced many times (Gosse gives it in his *Life and Letters of John Donne,* II, 114), but is worth inserting here also since it gives interesting information on Donne's relations with Lincoln's Inn:

In Bibliotheca Hospitii Lincoln: London:
Celeberrimi in Urbe, in Orbe,
Juris Municipalis Professorum Collegii,
Reponi voluit (petit potius)
Hæc sex in universas Scripturas volumina,
Sacræ Theologiæ Professor
Sereniss^mo^ Munificentiss^mo^
REGI JACOBO
a Sacris
JOANNES DONNE,
Qui huc, in prima juventute, ad perdiscendas leges, missus,
Ad alia, tam studia, quam negotia, et peregrinationes deflectens,
Inter quæ tamen nunquam studia Theologica intermiserat,
Post multos annos, agente Spiritu S^to^, suadente Rege,
Ad Ordines Sacros evectus,
Munere suo frequenter et strenue hoc loco concionandi
Per quinque annos functus,
Novi Sacelli primis saxis sua manu positis
Et ultimis fere paratis,
Ad Decanatum Ecclesiæ Cathedr: S. Pauli, London:
A Rege (cui benedicat Dominus)
Migrare jussus est
A° L° Ætat: suæ, et sui JESU
MDCXXI

Pulpit in the Chapel of Lincoln's Inn

This pulpit, which dates from 1622, is quite certainly that from which Donne delivered the address at the dedication of the Chapel. Photograph reproduced by permission of the Masters of the Bench, of Lincoln's Inn.

thereof, with his best endevors; whose resignation was very kindly accepted by the Masters of the Bench."[6]

The Society's records, then, confirm Izaak Walton's warmly enthusiastic phrases concerning the relations between Donne and the members of the Society. "Their love to him," says Walton, "was exprest many wayes; for (besides the faire lodgings that were provided and furnisht for him) other curtesies were daily accumulated, so many, and so freely, as though they meant their gratitude (if possible) should exceed, or at least equall his merit. In this love-strife of desert and liberality, they continued for the space of three yeares; he constantly and faithfully preaching, they liberally requiting him."[7]

Donne played an active part, during these years of his Readership, in what became a major campaign carried on by the Society, for the planning, financing, and building of a new chapel. The project had been started some years before, when a resolution was made that "a fayre large Chappell, with three double chambers under the same, shalbe buylded in a place more convenient, that nowe standinge being ruynous and not sufficient for the nomber of this Howse."[8] Subscriptions were hopefully called for; but the response was totally inadequate, and the plan languished for eight years, until November 20, 1617, when consideration "for the newe erection of a Chappell" was brought up again in the Council.[9] A committee—which included Christopher Brooke—was appointed to look into the matter; on January 27, 1617/18, Brooke was requested to consult with Inigo Jones, the principal architect of the day, on a "fitt modull";[10] and thereafter the business was not again dropped, but carried on, with many vicissitudes, to its final completion. When urgent appeals for subscriptions again proved insufficient, a general tax was levied on members of the Society, strenuous efforts were made to collect the money, the site was finally determined, the plan was changed so that the new building's

[6] *Black Books,* II, 255.

[7] Walton's *Life* prefixed to Donne's *LXXX Sermons,* 1640, eighth (unnumbered) page. Walton's phrase "three years" refers to the period from 1616 to Donne's departure with Doncaster in 1619.

[8] Meeting of the Council on November 2, 1609. *Black Books,* II, 125.

[9] *Black Books,* II, 198.

[10] *Black Books,* II, 199.

ground story was not "three double chambers" but an open crypt, various older chambers were demolished to make room for the new structure, the building was started, more money was borrowed to expedite matters, and finally the building was completed and, on Ascension Day, May 22, 1623, was consecrated by the Bishop of London. Subsequently the old chapel, which was still standing after the new was built, was condemned as unfit for use, and destroyed. The "new chapel" still stands as the center of the religious life at Lincoln's Inn.

Whether Donne had anything to do with reviving this project in 1617 is not known, though one can guess that since Christopher Brooke played so prominent a part in the early negotiations, he and his old friend might have talked the matter over together earlier. At least, the evidence is clear that Donne helped campaign for subscriptions, presided at the laying of the cornerstone, and did all that he could in forwarding this dear expedience. He preached at least one whole sermon "preparing them to build their Chappell" (No. 10 in the present volume), reminded his congregation of their duty to subscribe, in various other sermons,[11] and appropriately enough was asked to and did preach the sermon at the ceremonies of consecration.[12] By this last date he had, of course, resigned his Readership and was Dean of St. Paul's. A great crowd gathered for the celebration—whether attracted by the occasion, or by Donne's popularity, or both, is uncertain—and John Chamberlain wrote to Dudley Carleton of the occasion that "there was great concourse of noblemen and gentlemen wherof two or three were endaungered and taken up dead for the time with the extreme presse and thronging. The Deane of Paules made an excellent sermon (they say) concerning dedications."[13] Donne himself in this sermon gave a pleasant and informative summary of his activities on behalf of the chapel:

[11] See, for example, in Sermon No. 6 of the present volume, p. 158.

[12] This sermon, on *John* 10.22, was separately published in 1623 under the title of *Encænia*. For bibliographical data see Vol. I of the present edition, pp. 17–18. The sermon itself will be published in its chronological place, in a later volume.

[13] *The Letters of John Chamberlain*, ed. Norman E. McClure (Philadelphia, 1939), II, 500; letter dated May 30, 1623.

This is your Dedication, that you have cheerfully pursued your first holy purposes, and deliver now into the hands of this servant of *God,* the *Right Reverend Father the Bishop of this See,* a plate to be presented to *God* for you, by him. . . . What was spent in *Salomons Temple* is not told us. . . . They gave there, till they who had the overseeing therof, complain'd of the abundance, and proclaim'd an abstinence. Yet there was one, who gave more than all they; for *Christ* sayes the poore widdow gave more then all the rest, because she gave all she had. There is a way of giving more than she gave; and I, who by your favours was no stranger to the beginning of this work, and an often refresher of it to your memories, and a poore assistant in laying the first stone, the materiall stone, as I am now, a poore assistant again in this laying of this first formall Stone, the Word and Sacrament, and shall ever desire to be so in the service of this place, I, I say, can truly testifie, that you (speaking of the whole Societie together of the publike stock, the publike treasury, the publike revenue) you gave more then the widow, who gave all, for you gave more then all. *A Stranger shall not entermeddle with our joy,* as Salomon saies: strangers shall not know, how ill we were provided for such a work, when we begun it, nor with what difficulties we have wrastled in the way; but strangers shall know to *Gods* glory, that you have perfected a work of full three times as much charge, as you proposed for it at beginning: so bountifully doth *God* blesse, and prosper intentions to his glory, with enlarging your hearts within, and opening the hearts of others, abroad.[14]

[14] *Encænia,* published 1623, pp. 20–23.

A curious tradition about Donne has been handed down, and is repeated in most of the books on Lincoln's Inn, though always tentatively and usually—as it is here—in a footnote: that is, that the bell in the southwest turret of the chapel was taken away from Cadiz when the city was captured by Essex in 1596, and that through Donne it was brought to England and presented to the Society. No evidence has ever, so far as we know, been cited for this tradition, beyond the simple and well-known fact that Donne as a young man went on that expedition and (according to Walton) "waited upon" Essex. The possibility that it is true seems rather slight. If Donne had done such a thing, it is extremely likely that somewhere in his writings he would have mentioned the fact, especially since all through his later life he was much moved by the sound of bells and refers to them again and again. The fact that nowhere in the numerous extant sermons preached at Lincoln's Inn does he even indirectly refer to the matter would be remarkable if he had been responsible for bringing to the chapel (for the bell was, so the story goes, in the old as well as the new chapel) a bell that he and his congregation must often have heard ringing. In short, our opinion on the tradition is: Not impossible, but not proved and highly unlikely.

Of the sermons Donne preached at Lincoln's Inn, twenty-three are extant.[15] These Lincoln's Inn sermons are a very interesting group; some of them are as appealing and warming to the heart as any sermons Donne ever preached, and a study of the group as a whole makes clearly apparent some of the reasons why the members of Lincoln's Inn held him in affectionate regard.

Donne must have faced a difficult task when he began his service as Reader. He had been, not too many years before, a student at the Inn and, from all indications, not one noted for any zealously religious propensities. Not only Christopher Brooke but also other men now in their middle years and high in the councils of the Inn had been resident there in Donne's student days, and acquainted with his former reputation.[16] What the members of the Inn expected of Donne when he started to preach before them, we can only guess; but it seems certain that they would have been a critical audience, open-minded and willing to be convinced of his sincerity, doubtless, but ready enough to disapprove, also, if he did not somehow make a *positively* good impression on them. That Donne was keenly aware of potential skepticism regarding him, and critical minds in his congregation, is indicated by the extant sermons, especially if one reads

[15] The list of sermons certainly, or almost certainly, preached at Lincoln's Inn is as follows: of those in the present volume, Sermons Nos. 1, 2, 3, 4, 5, 6, 10, 11, 15, 16; to be included in Vols. III, IV, and V of the present edition, the sermons on *Gen.* 18.25 (*F 80,* No. 42), *Mat.* 18.7 (two sermons on this text, *F 50,* Nos. 17 and 18), *II Cor.* 1.3 (*F 80,* No. 38), *I Pet.* 1.17 (*F 80,* No. 39), *I Cor.* 16.22 (*F 80,* No. 40), *Psalms* 2.12 (*F 80,* No. 41), *Deut.* 12.30 (*F 26,* No. 23), *Coloss.* 1.24 (*F 50,* No. 16), *Job* 19.26 (*F 50,* No. 14), *I Cor.* 15.50 (*F 50,* No. 15), *Acts* 10.44 (*F 80,* No. 33), and *John* 10.22 (separately printed under title of *Encænia,* in 1623).

[16] Even a cursory check of the names of Benchers mentioned in the *Black Books* of the Society during the years of Donne's Readership, against the records of admissions to the Society shortly before, during, and after the year 1592, when Donne was admitted as a student, brings to light at least half a dozen men who must have been associated with him during both periods; for example: Jasper Selwin (admitted November 19, 1583), William Jones (admitted July 5, 1587), Roger Owen (admitted October 7, 1589), Nicholas Ducke (admitted November 6, 1589), Anthony Herronden (admitted May 1, 1591), Anthony Irby (admitted February 12, 1593/94).

them in chronological order. He sensed a challenge; but it was the kind of challenge that he enjoyed, and he met it magnificently.

First of all, he never forgot that he was now a preacher of God's word and was responsible for the spiritual welfare of those who sat under him, whatever his former connections with Lincoln's Inn had been. He never made the mistake of treating religion or Christian morality lightly, or of seeming to apologize for the exhortations that stemmed from his priestly duty. Even when he had heavily on his mind the financial difficulties connected with the campaign to build a new chapel, he did not turn sermons into campaign speeches; material needs were always secondary in his mind to spiritual values.

Nevertheless, there are, especially in the earlier sermons of this group, many indications that he felt a personal relation to his congregation more intimate and close than that which he felt to most of the audiences to whom he preached during his clerical career. Though, as we have just said, he never implies apologies for his priestly functions, he does frequently assume a certain apologetic air concerning *himself* as an imperfect human being performing those functions. Occasionally he shows a sense that by being too long or too dull he may tire the patience of his hearers—"And of so many pieces will this exercise consist, this exercise of your *Devotion,* and perchance *Patience.*"[17] "Now I have no purpose to make you afraid of enlarging all these points: I shall onely passe through some of them, *paraphrastically,* and trust them with the rest, (for they insinuate one another) and trust your christianly meditation with them all."[18] One particularly charming passage, in a sermon that must have been preached on a warm Sunday evening, shows his friendly consideration for his hearers—"The noblest part of our work in handling this Text, falls upon . . . the application of these words to *Christ.* But for that, I shall be short, and rather leave you to *walke with God in the cool of the Evening,* to meditate of the sufferings of Christ, when you are gone, then pretend to expresse them here."[19] Donne may well have felt, as he spoke these words, that his hearers were weary; but he must have felt also that those to whom he was appealing could be

[17] P. 51 of the present volume.
[18] P. 225 of the present volume.
[19] P. 132 of the present volume.

trusted, on the evening of the Lord's Day, to be in a religious frame of mind.

He did not express often or emphatically his sense of personal unworthiness—to do so could easily have reduced his effectiveness as a spiritual leader; but on rare occasions he let something of his feelings on this matter slip out. Once in quoting St. Paul's familiar depreciation of himself as chief of sinners,[20] Donne burst out, "When I consider my infirmities (I know I might justly lay a heavier name upon them) I know I am in his other quorum, *quorum ego maximus,* sent to save sinners, of whom I am the chiefest . . ."[21]

It was not Donne's usual practice to insert stories of his personal experiences into his sermons; but his sense of intimacy with his Lincoln's Inn congregation led him occasionally into this sort of personal expression, too. One amusing memory he recounted to them, as a pat illustration for a point in his first sermon on *Psalms* 38.4:

> But whil'st we are in the consideration of this arch, this roof of separation, between God and us, by sin, there may be use in imparting to you, an observation, a passage of mine own. Lying at *Aix,* at *Aquisgrane,* a well known Town in *Germany,* and fixing there some time, for the benefit of those *Baths,* I found my self in a house, which was divided into many families, and indeed so large as it might have been a little Parish, or, at least, a great lim of a great one; But it was of no Parish: for when I ask'd who lay over my head, they told me a family of *Anabaptists;* And who over theirs? Another family of Anabaptists; and another family of *Anabaptists* over theirs; and the whole house, was a nest of these boxes; severall artificers; all *Anabaptists;* I ask'd in what room they met, for the exercise of their Religion; I was told they never met: for, though they were all *Anabaptists,* yet for some collaterall differences, they detested one another, and, though many of them, were near in bloud, and alliance to one another yet the son would excommunicate the father, in the room above him, and the Nephew the Uncle. . . . I began to think, how many roofs, how many floores of separation, were made between God and my prayers in that house.[22]

His sense of humor, which appears clearly enough in this personal reminiscence, gleams again and again in the Lincoln's Inn sermons

[20] 1 *Timothy* 1.15.

[21] The earlier version of the *Sermon of Valediction;* see the present volume, p. 388.

[22] Pp. 112–113 of the present volume.

when he wishes to make vivid a point in his interpretation of his text. Especially, and quite naturally, he liked unobtrusive legal references that must have caused smiles among his legally trained hearers, though he never made the mistake of joking so obviously as to raise a loud laugh and thus destroy the religious atmosphere in the chapel. A sick soul in a sick body shall, he says in one sermon, "not onely not make a religious *restitution,* but he shall not make a discreet *Will.* He shall suspect his wifes fidelity, and his childrens frugality, and clogge them with Executors, and them with Over-seers, and be, or be afraid hee shall bee over-seen in all."[23] In another sermon he makes—again, not obtrusively—a most unscriptural addition to a familiar Scriptural passage, that would certainly have amused any wide-awake member of his congregation of lawyers: the Fathers, he says, "scarse excuse any suite at lawe from sinne, or occasion of sinne, and they will not depart from the literall understandinge of those words of our Saviour; yf any man will sue thee at lawe for thy coate, Let him have thy cloake too, for if thine adversary have it not, thine advocate will."[24]

Other appeals to the professional interests of his hearers are serious, but still vivid and stimulating. It would not be fair to Donne to say that he loads the Lincoln's Inn sermons with legal technicalities, or that he includes so many as to suggest that he wished to parade his own legal training before this congregation; he does not become heavily technical, and does not pile legal terms or allusions together even in the sermons that contain the largest number of them. Yet his occasional appeals of this sort are vivid, and suggest to any imaginative reader the old chapel populated with the members of the Society, many of them with intelligent, keenly alive faces upturned to their Reader in Divinity in his pulpit. "This is truly to be a good Student," he says, in a Whitsunday sermon that must obviously have been preached at the Inn, "*Scrutari Scripturas,* To search the Scriptures, in which is eternall life: This is truly to be called to the Barre, to be Crucified with Christ Jesus: And to be called to the Bench, to have part in his Resurrection, and raigne in glory with him: and to be a Judge, to judge thy selfe, that thou beest not judged to condemna-

[23] Pp. 83–84 of the present volume.

[24] P. 154 of the present volume.

tion, by Christ Jesus."[25] The steps upward for a member of any of the Inns of Court are as clearly stated as in any elementary handbook for students in those institutions; yet the application to a Christian life is just as clear and explicit. "The study of our conversion to God," he says again, in another sermon, "is in this like the study of your profession, it requires a whole man for it. It is for the most part losse of time in you to divert upon other studies, and it is for the most part losse of charity in us all to divert from our selves unto the consideration of other men, to prognosticate ill for the future, upon any man."[26] Sermon No. 15 in the present volume is perhaps the most crowded of any with legal distinctions; yet even in this sermon Donne does not parade those technicalities for their own sake; rather, he exhorts his congregation to their Christian duty *through* them as illuminating comparisons familiar to his hearers. He was always conscious, as he says in that sermon, that "we are not upon a Lecture [i.e., a "Reading" such as those that were part of the instruction in the Inns of Court], but upon a Sermon."[27]

The personal touches, and the direct appeals to a legally minded audience, are particularly characteristic of the earlier sermons in the Lincoln's Inn group. Gradually the personal touches grow less—as Donne lost his first self-consciousness and feeling of insecurity—and the legal appeals more generalized. After the gap in his services to the Inn, caused by his absence of several months on the Continent in the service of Doncaster, the comparative lack of such appeals becomes marked; with the one notable exception of his last sermon (last so far as we know) to this audience, at the dedication of the new chapel, when the strong feelings raised in him by the occasion stimulated him to renewed personal and delightfully affectionate rapport with the many friends he had made through the years of his Readership.

---

[25] Sermon on *Acts* 10.44; *F 80,* No. 33, near beginning of sermon.

[26] P. 156 of the present volume. In his earlier poignant letter to his friend Sir Henry Goodyer (the relevant passage is quoted in the Introduction to the Sermons of Vol. I of the present edition, p. 128), Donne had accused himself of having been "diverted" from the study of the law by "an hydroptic, immoderate desire of human learning and languages." Probably he had himself in mind when admonishing the Lincoln's Inn students as he does in this sermon.

[27] P. 320 of the present volume.

The first six sermons included in the present volume form a group, which would seem to be part of a longer series on the Thirty-eighth Psalm. That the six sermons were preached as a series, and are not an accidental collection of separate sermons on texts taken from the same Psalm, is clearly apparent from the initial paragraphs of Nos. 4, 5, and 6, in which Donne explicitly refers to other sermons in the series. Similarly, the remark toward the end of No. 3, "And so we have done with our first part, and with all that will enter into this time," implies a series clearly enough. No one of these six sermons is dated, either in the Folio or in any of the manuscripts. Nevertheless, indications of the approximate date are fairly clear. It must have been a series preached during the spring or summer; witness the preacher's assurance to his audience that he will be short and leave his hearers to "walke with God in the cool of the Evening," in the passage quoted a few paragraphs earlier in this introduction,[28] together with the fact that that sermon *is* actually very short, and that the one just preceding it is short also. Donne would hardly have laid himself open to ridicule by referring, even with an allusion to Scripture, to "the cool of the evening" on a winter day; the two sermons must have been preached on successive Sundays—presumably in the evenings—during a warm spell of weather. The particular spring or summer is indicated by the unobtrusive yet urgent allusion to the necessity of raising funds for the new chapel, that appears in No. 6. "This is hypocriticall complement," says Donne, "to say to God or man; all's at your service; but give God some part of that, house Christ Jesus where he is harbour-lesse, helpe to beautify and build that house where his name may be glorified and his Sabbaths sanctified, cloth him where he is naked, feed him in his hunger, deliver him in his imprisonment, when he suffereth this in his afflicted members."[29] The appeal implied for contributions toward the new chapel is apparent. It is revealing

[28] Cf. *ante,* p. 9.

[29] P. 158 of the present volume. Note also the *explicit* application to the building of the chapel of this same Scriptural passage, in Sermon No. 10 of the present volume, on *Genesis* 28.16 and 17, "Preached at Lincolns Inne, preparing them to build their Chappell" (p. 216): "Now of those . . . divers exercises of charity, the particular which we are occasion'd to speak of here, is not the cloathing, nor feeding of Christ, but the *housing* of him, The providing Christ a house, a dwelling."

to contrast Donne's way of presenting the familiar idea from Scripture here with his way of doing so when the chapel was not in his mind, in a later sermon: "... if I have done any good to any of Gods servants, (or to any that hath not been Gods servant, for Gods sake) If I have but fed a hungry man, If I have but clothed a naked childe, If I have but comforted a sad soule, or instructed an ignorant soule, If I have but preached a Sermon, and then printed that Sermon, that is, first preached it, and then lived according to it, (for the subsequent life is the best printing, and the most usefull and profitable publishing of a Sermon) All those things that I have done for Gods glory, shall follow me"—etc.[80] The *Black Books* of the Society of Lincoln's Inn indicate that from the spring of 1618 to the fall of 1619 a campaign was carried on for voluntary contributions toward the building of the chapel, and that in October, 1619, a better solution to the problem was reached by levying a general tax on all members who had not by then subscribed in some reasonable way. If this is a late spring and summer series, by far the most likely year is 1618; for Donne was on the Continent from late spring, 1619, to the early days of 1620. The highly personal tone of the series, too, indicates a date before his trip to the Continent.[81]

It is a highly interesting series of sermons, concerned in the main with practical morality, excellently clear and simple in plan and structure, full of sound and shrewd observation of human nature, and also full of warm sympathy for erring and imperfect human beings. Most of Donne's observations and exhortations are as pertinent to the twentieth century as they were to the seventeenth. The best sermons of the series are, it seems to us, No. 1 and No. 6: the former for its delightfully personal beginning, in which Donne pleasantly remarks on his own lifelong fondness for epistles and poetry, and its clear-headed and subtle perception of the vagaries of our sinful humanity; the latter for its deeply appealing sympathy with the feelings of de-

---

[80] Vol. VII of the present edition, No. 9, p. 255; sermon dated November 5, 1626.

[81] Cf. *ante,* p. 6. The dating of this series in the spring and summer of 1618 was originally made, and the evidence presented, in G. R. Potter's editing of the Sermon on *Psalms* 38.9, published by Stanford University Press in 1946.

pression and despair that plague sincerely repentant souls, and for its wonderfully perceptive dealing with the thought that God sometimes does not at once relieve men's minds or take away temptation in response to their prayers and repentance. The other sermons in the series, however, have their interest also. No. 2 has some impressive and thoroughly characteristic consideration of bodily illness, its relation to the microcosm, and the general relation of the body to the soul, that reminds a reader of Donne's later meditations on those topics in his *Devotions*. No. 3 includes some pages of interesting comment on the life and conduct of David himself, whom Donne of course considers the author of the Psalm. No. 4 has one passage that expands upon the theme of our close and inescapable involvement, as individuals, with humanity as a whole[32]—a theme familiar to American and British readers today because of the fact that Ernest Hemingway adopted for his well-known novel on the Spanish civil war[33] Donne's later treatment of the theme in the seventeenth "Meditation" of the *Devotions*. There is also in this sermon an excellently clear interpretation of the now rather unpopular doctrine of "original sin."[34] No. 5 contains a passage concerning the love of man and woman that is enlightening to any reader interested in Donne's thoughts on this subject during his later life:

> It is one of Saint *Augustines* definitions of sinne, *Conversio ad creaturam,* that it is a turning, a withdrawing of man to the creature. And every such turning to the creature, let it be upon his side, to *her* whom he loves, let it be upwards, to *honour* that he affects, yet it is still down-ward, in respect of him, whom he was made by, and should direct himselfe to.... And man may not decline, and every thing, except God himself, is inferiour to man, and so, it is a *declination,* a *stooping* in man, to apply himselfe to any Creature, till he meet that Creature in God; for there, it is above him; And so, as *Beauty* and *Riches,* and *Honour* are beames that issue from God, and glasses that represent God to us, and ideas that return us into him, in our glorifying of him, by these helpes, so we may apply our selves to them; for, in this consideration, as they assist us in our way to God, they are above us, otherwise, to love them for themselves, is a *declination, a stooping* under a *burden.*[35]

---

[32] Pp. 121–122 of the present volume.
[33] *For Whom the Bell Tolls,* published in 1940.
[34] Pp. 120–121 of the present volume.
[35] P. 132 of the present volume.

This Augustinian—and Neoplatonic—way of regarding human love occupied Donne's mind a good deal in his middle and later years; witness two of his *Holy Sonnets*—the seventeenth, on Ann Donne's death,[36] in which he beautifully expresses the idea that the love of his wife led him to seek God, and the third, which expresses repentance for his earlier sinful "turning to the creature":

> O might those sighes and teares returne againe
> Into my breast and eyes, which I have spent,
> That I might in this holy discontent
> Mourne with some fruit, as I have mourn'd in vaine;
> In mine Idolatry what showres of raine
> Mine eyes did waste? what griefs my heart did rent?
> That sufferance was my sinne; now I repent;
> 'Cause I did suffer I must suffer paine....

Number 6, which never appeared in print during the seventeenth century, is clearly a sermon of this series, but appears to be separated from Nos. 1–5 by one or more sermons that have not come down to us:

> The whole psalme hath two parts, 1 a prayer and then Reasons of that prayer. The prayer hath 2 parts, 1 a deprecatory prayer in the 1 verse, and then a postulatory in the 2 last. And the reasons also are of 2 kinds, 1. intrinsecall, arisinge from consideration of himselfe, 2. extrinsecall, in the behaviour and dispositions of others towards him. The reasons of the 1 sort determine in the 10 verse, which we have handled. But this we reserved to be handled after, because we are to observe some things out of the site and place of the verse, as well as out of the words.[37]

It is, as we have remarked before, one of the two most impressive sermons we have in the series. Since it exists in four manuscripts of Donne's lifetime, it was evidently well liked by many who heard it; and the question then naturally arises, Why was it not included in some one of the Folios? The natural place for it would have been in *Fifty Sermons;* and we have given already our reasons for speculating that it may have been left out of that collection deliberately, since it

[36] Since this sonnet has already been quoted in full in the Introduction to Vol. I of the present edition, p. 135, it would seem superfluous to repeat it here.

[37] P. 144 of the present volume.

advocates the practice of auricular confession.[38] For the same reason it may have been rejected from *XXVI Sermons* also—in fact, there is at least a slight possibility that Donne's son at first included it in that 1661 publication as No. 9 (since we know it was copied at least four times, it is quite likely to have appeared in some one of the scattered manuscripts that he collected for the third Folio printing of his father's sermons) and then at the last minute decided to delete it, dividing the long sermon originally numbered 10 into two sermons, and being careless enough to leave both remaining sermons numbered as 10, with no Sermon No. 9 at all left in the volcme.[39] No one of the series shows a more kindly and personal consideration for both the souls and the human feelings of the men under Donne's pastoral care. He assumes, affectionately, their Christian faith and concern for their own salvation: "If I mistake not the measure of thy conscience, thou wilt find an infinite comfort in this particular tracinge of the Holy Ghost, and his workinge in thy soule."[40]

He sympathizes with the despondency of a repentant sinner not sure of his own salvation—a feeling he certainly had had himself, many times—and gives the congregation comfortable assurance, in terms closely related to their legal shop talk and with a touch of humor that could well have brought morbid minds into a saner and healthier state:

> Drowne that body of sinne which thou hast built up in thee, drowne that world of sinne which thou hast created . . . man is Gods creature and the sinner is mans creature, spare thy world noe more then God spared his, who drowned it with the floud, drowne thine too with repentant teares. But when that worke is religiously done, *miserere animæ tuæ,* be as mercifull to thy soule as he was to mankind, drowne it noe more, suffer it not to ly under the water of distrustfull diffidence, for soe thou mayst fall too lowe to be able to tugge up against the tide againe, soe thou mayst be swallowed in *Cains* whirlepoole, to thinke thy sinnes greater then can be forgiven. . . . When the child was dead, *David* arose from the ground and eate bread; when the sinne is dead by thy true repentance, rayse thy selfe from this sad dejection, and come and eate the bread of life, the body of thy Saviour for the seale of thy pardon. For there in this repentance and this seale, *finem litibus imponis* thou leaviest a fine upon thy sinnes,

[38] See Vol. I of the present edition, pp. 71–72.

[39] See our description of *XXVI Sermons,* in Vol. I, p. 8.

[40] See p. 159 of the present volume.

which cuts off and concludes all titles. And when God hath provided that thy sinnes shall rise noe more to thy condemnation at the last day, if thou rayse them up here to the vexation of thy conscience, thou art a litigious man to thine owne destruction.[41]

The members of Lincoln's Inn were fortunate in having at this time such an understanding, humorous, and healthy minded Christian minister.

The series on Psalm 38 is interesting also for the particularly clear and explicit statements Donne makes of one of his common methods for preaching on a Scriptural text—the consideration of the text from each of three different interpretations. This method is conventional enough; it is one of the common ways of interpreting Scripture from the Middle Ages and before, down to and past Donne's own time. Evidently, however, Donne felt a need of defining and explaining it in these sermons, perhaps for the instruction of young men, perhaps because he himself felt a need of clarifying his own point of view. He treats each text in three ways—"literally," or "historically," as in this case a poem written by David and applicable to the man who wrote it; "morally," or "by application," as God's word, sent by the Holy Ghost through the medium of David for the moral instruction of mankind; and "typically," or "by figure," as looking forward to the life, passion, and example of Christ. In Sermon No. 2 he explains that by the first interpretation David is "the *Patient,*" and is our example, by the second, the first Adam is the patient, and we in Adam, and in the third, Christ the second Adam is the patient, and is thus our physic.[42] In No. 3 he gives a clear, brief summary of the method: "First then, all these things are *literally* spoken of *David;* By *application,* of us; and by *figure,* of Christ. *Historically, David; morally,* we; *Typically,* Christ is the subject of this text,"[43]

If this repetition and reëmphasizing of the threefold method in interpreting Scripture can be considered a sign that Donne was clarifying his own mind as well as the minds of his congregation, it becomes one of a number of very interesting indications in the sermons of this period—both those preached at Lincoln's Inn, and sermons

[41] Pp. 155–156 of the present volume.
[42] P. 75 of the present volume.
[43] P. 97 of the present volume.

preached at other places as well—that Donne was still making a deliberate effort, both intellectually and emotionally, to achieve a full comprehension of his calling as a priest and his technique as a preacher. In the sermons included in Volume I of the present edition, he appears experimenting with different techniques of preaching itself, different ways of reaching the minds and hearts of his hearers. In several sermons included in the present Volume II, he shows himself to be deeply concerned with the calling itself, with the practical and the spiritual functions of a priest ministering to the needs of the souls under his care.

This concern shows itself in the first sermon of the series on Psalm 38, in at least two places. Early in the sermon, Donne in considering various Scriptural examples of men who had "such an impatience in affliction, as brings us toward a *murmuring* at Gods proceedings, and almost to a calling of God to an account," cites among others Jeremiah; but in quoting and paraphrasing that prophet, Donne merges his own personal feelings so inextricably with those of Jeremiah that it would seem an unconscious identification on his part and the result of painful broodings over his difficulties as a priest:

> *Jonas* was angry because his Prophesie was not performed; because God would not second his Prophesie in the destruction of Nineveh. *Jeremy* was angry because his Prophesie was like to be performed; he preached heavy Doctrin, and therfore his Auditory hated him; *Woe is me, my Mother,* says he, *that thou hast born me a man of strife, and a man of contention to the whole earth!* I preach but the messages of God; (and *væ mihi si non,* wo be unto me if I preach not them) I preach but the sense of Gods indignation upon mine own soul, in a conscience of mine own sins, I impute nothing to another, that I confesse not of my selfe, I call none of you to confession to me, I doe but confesse my self to God, and you, I rack no mans memory, what he did last year, last week, last night, I onely gather into my memory, and powr out in the presence of my God, and his Church, the sinfull history of mine own *youth,* and yet I am a *contentious man,* says *Jeremy,* a worm, and a burthen to every tender conscience, says he, *and I strive with the whole earth,* I am a bitter, and satyricall preacher; This is that that wearies mee, says hee, *I have neither lent on usury,* nor *men have lent me on usury,* yet, as though I were an oppressing lender, or a fraudulent borrower, *every one of them doth curse me.*[44]

[44] Pp. 52–53 of the present volume.

The passages printed in italics in the Folio are, to be sure, quoted from Jeremiah, except for the cry *"væ mihi si non"* which comes from Paul's first Epistle to the Corinthians; but what appears to be Donne's paraphrase of Jeremiah's thoughts—the statements that he imputes nothing to another that he confesses not of himself, and that he pours out to God the sinful history of his youth,—these have nothing at all to do with Jeremiah the prophet, who certainly says nothing of the sort in his prophetic writings. Donne himself—perhaps subconsciously influenced by his passing reference to St. Paul, who once called himself the chief of sinners—is imaginatively identifying himself with the prophet and justifying his own preaching against criticism, or potential criticism, that he was setting himself up as a judge over other people while a well-known sinner in his own youth. Later in the same sermon appears another remark that shows Donne's sensitiveness to criticism of a preacher: "Let a man be zealous, and fervent in reprehension of sin, and there flies out an arrow, that gives him the wound of a *Puritan*. Let a man be zealous of the house of God, and say any thing by way of moderation, for the *repairing* of *the ruines* of that house, and *making up the differences* of the Church of God, and there flies out an arrow, that gives him the wound of a Papist."[45]

Both those arrows that Donne speaks of here were arrows that he certainly had felt directed against himself, for his emphasis on sin, on the one hand, and for his occasionally expressed longing for a union among the different branches of the Christian Church, on the other (not to mention his joining in the campaign for replacing the "ruinous" old chapel with a new, which he is certainly alluding to also, indirectly).

To pass now from the sermons preached at Lincoln's Inn to other sermons included in the present volume: No. 7, described in *XXVI Sermons* as a "Lent-Sermon Preached at White-hall, February 12. 1618" (i.e., 1618/19), is particularly striking evidence of Donne's concern, at this point in his career, with the duties of a preacher and the difficulties he has to face in relation to his congregation; for it is directly and wholly on that subject. The text is *Ezekiel* 33.32: "And lo, thou art unto them as a very lovely song, of one that hath a pleasant voice, and can play well on an instrument; for they hear thy

[45] P. 58 of the present volume.

words, but they do them not." The sermon does not, as a whole, impress the reader as one of Donne's better discourses; the structure is occasionally awkward, and the style is at times so ambiguous in its grammatical structure that the editors of the present edition have wondered whether some of the flaws in style may come from careless copying—the only text we have of the sermon is in the least carefully edited of the Folios, that of 1661. They are not obvious misprints or miscopyings, however, and hence cannot be emended. But, awkward as the sermon is in some respects, it is highly interesting as an expression of Donne's ideas about preaching.

The sermon begins with a familiar phrase from *I Corinthians* that must have kept ringing in Donne's mental ears through this period, for it became one of his favorite quotations, and is repeated in sermon after sermon, all through his career: *"Væ si non,"* as he usually abbreviates the quotation, "Woe is unto me, if I preach not the gospel!" Donne then divides his exposition of the text into two main parts: first, the requirements for a preacher or "prophet," that he may do his job acceptably to God; and second, the requirements for the congregation, that they may do theirs in relation to God and the preaching of God's Word. At least half the discourse is on the first of the two main points. A preacher must be *tuba,* a trumpet, sounding continually, in season and out of season; sounding the alarm—awakening the people to their sins; sounding the battle—impelling people to fight against sin, and to wrestle with God for his mercy; sounding the "Parle"—calling men to sue for peace with God; and sounding retreat—"a safe reposing of our souls in the merit, and in the wounds of our Saviour Christ Jesus."[46] Also a preacher must be *musicum carmen,* "a very lovely song." He must be eloquent and harmonious in his speaking. (This point is highly significant for the student of Donne who is concerned with the causes behind that sharp difference between the style of Donne's verse and that of his sermons.)[47] His sermons must be carefully meditated and prepared, and he must have "a pleasant voice," not so much literally as in the sense that his voice must sound always the pleasant message to the human heart of the

---

[46] P. 170 of the present volume.

[47] For a fuller description of Donne's manner of speaking see Vol. I of the present edition, "The Literary Value of Donne's Sermons," pp. 83–103.

Scriptures and of the Holy Spirit. Finally, he must "play well on an instrument," that is, make his personal life correspond to his exhortations to others, practice what he preaches. As he sums up the matter, "God, in his promise to that Nation, prophesied upon us, that which he hath abundantly performed, a Ministry, that should first be Trumpets, and then Musick: Musick, in fitting a reverent manner, to religious matter; and Musick, in fitting an instrument to the voyce, that is, their Lives to their Doctrine."[48] Donne then develops the second main part of his text, concerning the attitude of the congregation to the preacher; and in describing both the duties of congregations and the various sorts of negligence in these duties, he expresses what must have been at this time a set of problems over which he frequently meditated and brooded.

Aside from the general interest of the whole sermon in relation to Donne's own mental development, two passages have special interest in other ways. One has been frequently quoted, as an excellent early seventeenth-century expression of the ideas of a "vital scale" and of the principle of harmony in God's universe:

> God made this whole world in such an uniformity, such a correspondency, such a concinnity of parts, as that it was an Instrument, perfectly in tune: we may say, the trebles, the highest strings were disordered first; the best understandings, Angels and Men, put this instrument out of tune. God rectified all again, by putting in a new string, *semen mulieris,* the seed of the woman, the *Messias* . . .[49]

The other passage shows an emphasis unusual for the early seventeenth century (though not, to be sure, unique)[50] on the literary qualities of Scripture:

> Religion is a serious thing, but not a sullen; Religious preaching is a grave exercise, but not a sordid, not a barbarous, not a negligent. There are not so eloquent books in the world, as the Scriptures: Accept those names of Tropes and Figures, which the Grammarians and Rhetoricians put upon us, and we may be bold to say, that in all their Authors, Greek and Latin, we cannot finde so high, and so lively examples, of those Tropes, and those Figures, as we may in the Scriptures: whatsoever hath justly delighted any man in any mans writings, is exceeded in the

[48] P. 173 of the present volume.

[49] P. 170 of the present volume.

[50] See, for instance, Sidney's *Defense of Poesy*.

Scriptures. The style of the Scriptures is a diligent, and an artificial style; and a great part thereof in a musical, in a metrical, in a measured composition, in verse.[51]

Sermon No. 8 was preached, in all probability, a little more than a week later than No. 7, before the Countess of Montgomery, and in the chapel that formed part of the Earl of Montgomery's apartments at or near Whitehall. The only date given for the sermon, in any of its several printed and manuscript texts,[52] is the impossible one that appears in *Fifty Sermons,* "Preached February 21, 1611"; impossible since Donne did not take orders until 1615. The clue to the correct date is in the fact that two of the manuscripts, the Merton and the Dobell, prefix to the sermon a dedicatory letter to the Countess.[53] In this letter Donne writes of his "going out of the kingdome, and perchance out of the World," and says that her Ladyship had been pleased to hear the sermon before he wrote it out for her at her "commandment." Plentiful evidence exists, in Donne's letters, in his "Hymn to Christ," and in the Sermon of Valediction (No. 11 of the present volume), that Donne had many apprehensions of death when contemplating his projected trip to the Continent with Doncaster. He presented a copy of the sermon to the Countess, then, at some time in

---

[51] Pp. 170–171 of the present volume.

[52] See the Textual Notes to this sermon, pp. 415 ff. of the present volume; also the Introductions "On the Manuscripts" and "On the Text," in Vol. I.

[53] We follow *M* and *Dob* in prefixing the letter to the sermon; see pp. 179 ff. of the present volume. The letter was printed in *Letters to Severall Persons of Honour* (1651), and by Gosse in his *Life and Letters of John Donne,* II, 122. Gosse had, however, for some reason unknown to us, the date of 1623 in mind for the sermon and hence did not use the clear internal evidence in the letter to fix the date of the sermon. His footnote reads: "The sermon referred to was on St. Matthew xxi.44, and was probably identical with the discourse printed, as preached on the 21st Feb. 1623, in the folio of 1649."

The arguments for our dating of this sermon were first presented by G. R. Potter in an article, "Hitherto Undescribed Manuscript Versions of Three Sermons by Donne," *Journal of English and Germanic Philology,* XLIV (1945), 31–32.

Donne's friendship with Susan, the first Countess of Montgomery, is described fully by Gosse in his *Life and Letters of John Donne.*

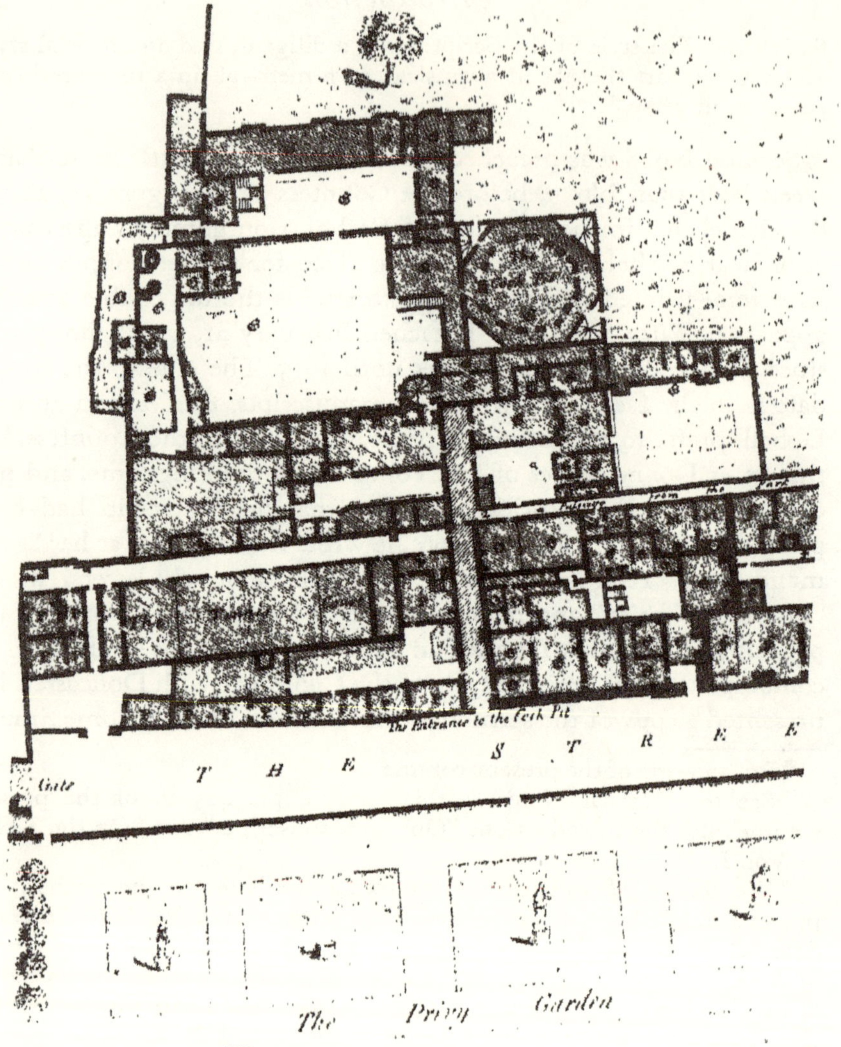

WHITEHALL: "THE COCK-PIT"

Detail from John Fisher's survey and ground plan of the Royal Palace of Whitehall, made in 1680, drawn and published by G. Vertue, London, 1747; showing the apartments known in the seventeenth century as "the Cock-pit." The letters "G," "F," "P," etc., refer to the occupants of certain apartments in 1680: the Duke of Albemarle, the Duke of Ormond, and "Captain Cook." Photographed by the Photographic Service of the British Museum.

the spring of 1619. On several occasions Donne wrote out a sermon at the request of different persons, and always not long after the sermon was preached.[54] The date of the sermon must be, then, sometime in the spring of 1619; and the most probable conclusion is that the date in *Fifty Sermons* is merely the result of a misprint of "1" for "8"; that is, that the correct date is February 21, 1618/19.

The place where Donne preached it is most fortunately given in the Merton manuscript at the end of that transcript of the sermon: "Finis of a Sermon of doctor Donns preach'd at ye Cockpit." The location is not as strange as it may appear at first sight. "The Cockpit" was the name given to a group of apartments adjacent to Whitehall, which either was on the site of a building erected by Henry VIII for cockfighting (his favorite sport) or was some adaptation of that earlier building. That the apartments included a chapel can be surmised from the fact that when Oliver Cromwell later occupied the apartments he often had a famous organist play before him there. Considering that the Earl of Montgomery lived in these apartments for many years, dying in them early in 1650, and that he was certainly residing in London during the spring of 1619, the end note in *M* becomes entirely understandable and believable.[55]

Donne's discourse preached before the Countess, on a severe, even a terrible, text is a superb example of the type of sermon often called "metaphysical," in its ingenious yet pertinent and extraordinarily suggestive elaborations and interpretations of Scripture. It is a sort of sermon to which a twentieth-century reader is not accustomed, and for that reason will probably not be among those of Donne's sermons that are most frequently read and loved today. It must, however, have pleased greatly and impressed deeply those who heard him preach it;

---

[54] Cf. Gosse, *op. cit.*, II, 160, 163, 221, 232, 247; also Keynes's Bibliography, edition of 1932, items 12, 15, 16, 19, 21, 23. Item 21 is only an apparent exception, since "24 Feb., 1625" is, by modern reckoning, 1626.

[55] Cf. *D.N.B.*, the biography of Philip Herbert, Earl of Pembroke and Montgomery; John Timbs, *Curiosities of London*, etc. (London, 1858), p. 835; C. Whitaker-Wilson, *Whitehall Palace* (London, 1934), pp. 53–54; Edward Walford, *Old and New London* (London, Paris, New York, and Melbourne, n.d.), Vol. III, p. 370; J. Henage Jesse, *Literary and Historical Memorials of London* (London, 1847), Vol. II, pp. 195–196, 228–229; etc.

and for good reasons. It is packed with unusual and yet pertinent comparisons and illustrations, from history, and from everyday life; especially with witty and highly individual applications to human morality and human experience, not only of the text itself but of many other passages from Scripture. Again and again Donne uses the device of paradox to bring out a point. And with all its ingenuity, the sermon is not crabbed or trivial, but rises to great eloquence—often in the long, arboriform sentences that are so characteristic of Donne's sermon style at its best—and deals essentially with the familiar and universal orthodox Christian doctrines of damnation and salvation; making those doctrines memorable (and at least to his seventeenth-century hearers and readers, palatable as well) by the flashing brilliance of his exposition and by the vividness and wit of his analogies and specific interpretations. A single illustration is enough for this Introduction—the whole sermon is full of passages just as pertinent and striking. In commenting on the word from his text, "*Cadere,* to fall," Donne says:

> . . . he falls as a piece of money falls into a river; we heare it fall, and we see it sink, and by and by we see it deeper, and at last we see it not at all: So no man falleth at first into any sinne, but he heares his own fall. There is a tendernesse in every Conscience at the beginning, at the entrance into a sinne, and he discerneth a while the degrees of sinking too: but at last he is out of his owne sight, till he meete this stone; (this stone is Christ) that is, till he meete some hard reprehension, some hard passage of a Sermon, some hard judgement in a Prophet, some crosse in the World, some thing from the mouth, or some thing from the hand of God, that breaks him: *He falls upon the stone and is broken.*[56]

Holy Week and Easter of the year 1619 came at a time of sorrow and anxiety throughout the kingdom, and especially in London. There was sorrow because of Queen Anne's death, which came early in March. There was anxiety in London from the prevalence of smallpox in that city throughout the winter and spring.[57] Then there was sudden and more acute anxiety throughout the kingdom for the health of King James, who later in March was seized so severely with an attack of the stone that he was for a short time thought to be in

[56] P. 191 of the present volume.

[57] See Chamberlain's correspondence through the late months of 1618 and the earlier months of 1619.

imminent danger of death, and "most of the court Lords" hurried to Newmarket to attend him in that extremity.[58] Donne was moved by these events, particularly by the danger in which he conceived his royal master to be, as well as by the normal considerations of Holy Week, when he preached Sermon No. 9 of this present volume, "To the Lords upon Easter-Day, at the Communion, the King being then dangerously sick at New-Market."

He chose as his text *Psalms* 89.48, "What man is he that liveth, and shall not see death?" It is the first, among the extant sermons, of those discourses upon death that have so much impressed later readers as to bring many of them (wrongly) to consider death as Donne's favorite topic for sermons. It is not his most impressive sermon on this subject, nor the most impressive sermon among those of this period in his career. Nevertheless, it is highly interesting in a number of respects, and is a particularly clear, simply expressed discourse. Its construction is neat, almost though not quite to the point of being artificially ingenious. The plan is not like that of the sermons on Psalm 38, a threefold interpretation of the same text; instead, Donne adds to the text of the sermon itself two other brief Scriptural passages closely allied to it, and then proceeds from the first to the second and third of the three texts: from "There is no man that lives, and shall not see death" to "It is like enough, that there are some men that live, and shall not see death," and finally to "We shall finde a man that lives, and shall not see death, our Lord, and Saviour Christ Jesus." The sermon contains a number of ideas and analogies that Donne either had developed or was to develop elsewhere more potently. For example (p. 199), we see man's life and death compared with a "flat Map," an analogy that is most familiar to Donne's readers from his later *Hymne to God my God, in my sicknesse*—

As West and East
In all flatt Maps (and I am one) are one,
So death doth touch the Resurrection.

A little later in the sermon,[59] the statement of the belief that the soul is immortal only by preservation, not by nature, recalls, to a

[58] John Chamberlain's letter to Dudley Carleton dated March 27, 1619.
[59] P. 201 of the present volume.

reader of Donne's poetry, one of his verse letters to the Countess of Bedford:

> Let the minds thoughts be but transplanted so,
> Into the body, and bastardly they grow.
> What hate could hurt our bodies like our love?
> Wee (but no forraine tyrants could) remove
> These not ingrav'd, but inborne dignities,
> Caskets of soules; Temples, and Palaces:
> For, bodies shall from death redeemed bee,
> Soules but preserv'd, not naturally free.

A sentence (pp. 202 f.) expresses an idea that Donne developed into far more beautiful form in a later sermon. In the present sermon it appears as follows: "As we could not be cloathed at first, in Paradise, till some Creatures were dead, (for we were cloathed in beasts skins) so we cannot be cloathed in Heaven, but in his garment who dyed for us."

A sermon of 1622, on *I Corinthians* 15.26,[10] applies this analogy more simply, but with a haunting beauty that makes the passage unforgettable: "As soon as we were clothed by God, our very apparell was an Embleme of death. In the skins of dead beasts, he covered the skins of dying men."

Two ideas in the earlier sermon are the embryos of ideas developed much more at length and more eloquently in his last sermon, *Deaths Duell.* One he takes from Seneca: "Wee have seene *Mortem infantiæ, pueritiam,* The death of infancy in youth; and *Pueritiæ, adolescentiam,* and the death of youth in our middle age; And at last we shall see *Mortem senectutis, mortem ipsam,* the death of age in death it selfe."[11]

Another, he used in *Deaths Duell* as an analogy upon which to build the structure of his whole discourse; in the present sermon it appears merely as an unimportant and briefly suggested comparison: "... nothing becomes a Christian better then sobriety; to make a true difference betweene problematicall, and dogmaticall points, between upper buildings, and foundations, betweene collaterall doctrines, and Doctrines in the right line ..."[12]

[10] *LXXX Sermons,* No. 15; p. 147.

[11] P. 202 of the present volume.

[12] Pp. 203–204 of the present volume.

It is particularly interesting to compare this application of the analogy of a building with the first paragraph of *Deaths Duell:* "Buildings stand by the benefit of their *foundations* that susteine and *support* them, and of their *butteresses* that comprehend and *embrace* them, and of their *contignations* that knit and *unite* them"; etc.

Much in this first of Donne's sermons on death is, then, either an echo of thoughts he had expressed earlier or an early appearance of thoughts he developed more powerfully later. At least once, however, he rose to a greater height of eloquence than in most parts of it, and in describing one kind of "death," the "death of rapture, and of extasie," achieved expression that is in itself a kind of rapture, with a musical harmony in the sound of the words that reveals a great poet speaking, with a sort of music that he strangely avoided in his own verses: "The contemplation of God, and heaven, is a kinde of buriall, and Sepulchre, and rest of the soule; and in this death of rapture, and extasie, in this death of the Contemplation of my interest in my Saviour, I shall finde my self, and all my sins enterred, and entombed in his wounds, and like a Lily in Paradise, out of red earth, I shall see my soule rise out of his blade, in a candor, and in an innocence, contracted there, acceptable in the sight of his Father."[63]

Sermon No. 10 we cannot date precisely; but we have placed it among the sermons of 1619, and before the Sermon of Valediction, because it seems probable that it was preached before Donne's departure for the Continent with Doncaster, and might have been as late as the spring of that year, though not impossibly earlier, say in the spring or summer of 1618. Its heading in *Fifty Sermons,* "Preached at Lincolns Inne, preparing them to build their Chappell," is clearly indicative of its contents. The heading might well suggest a tentative speculation that the sermon was preached on the occasion when Donne laid the cornerstone of the new building; for we know that he did preside at that occasion,[64] and presumably made an address. The beginning of the sermon itself, however, makes such a

[63] Pp. 210–211 of the present volume.

[64] Donne himself states the fact, both in the sermon he later preached at the dedication of the chapel and in an inscription he placed on the initial flyleaf of the set of books he gave the Society of Lincoln's Inn (cf. *ante,* pp. 2–3).

supposition more than doubtful, as does also the fact that no reference is made in it to the laying of the first stone.

The text, *Genesis* 28.16 and 17, is part of the account of Jacob's vision on his way to Haran, and his setting up of the stone pillar at Bethel. The application of the text to the building of a church is clear from the first sentences of the sermon: "In these verses *Jacob* is a *Surveyor;* he considers a fit place for the house of *God;* and in the very next verse, he is a *Builder,* he erects *Bethel,* the house of *God* it selfe. All was but a drowsinesse, but a sleep, till he came to this Consideration; as soon as he awoke, he took knowledge of a fit place; as soon as he found the place, he went about the work. But to that we shall not come yet."

There was a good deal of preliminary questioning and discussion of the best site for the projected new chapel at Lincoln's Inn; and the final decision to place the structure on the spot where it now stands seems not to have been made before November 19, 1618, when, say the *Black Books,* "The placinge of the Chappell in the East Court, and the modull and forme thereof," were "wholie referred to the consideracion of the Committees of the Chappell." Donne's reference to Jacob's taking knowledge of a fit place, and then going about the work, assumes interesting significance in the light of these facts. What he meant by his remark, "But to that we shall not come yet," is not too certain, for it might conceivably imply that the building of the chapel was to come later, or that a sermon on building it was to follow the present sermon. The latter supposition seems more probable; but if there was such a second sermon, no copy of it is known to exist.

Donne's discourse might well serve as a model in some respects for present-day appeals from the pulpit on behalf of a financial campaign. It is throughout relevant to such a campaign; but Donne has the good taste and insight not to descend from his proper position as a preacher of God's Word in order to plead for money from his congregation. He exhorts them to charity, but charity in the sense of affectionate help to our fellow men. He speaks beautifully of the necessity for a place to worship God; yet he emphasizes not material buildings but the necessity of sanctifying *any* place—especially within our own souls—for the fit worship of our Creator. He expounds the nature of the Church; but of the Church of God, not a material church building. The congregation at Lincoln's Inn must have been both mildly surprised and pleasantly moved by their preacher's refusal to overemphasize the obvious material needs, by his decision to prepare their minds and hearts to use their projected new chapel rightly, rather than merely to appeal for funds; and it seems quite probable that Donne's method of preparing them was more effective, even financially, than the more usual sort of appeal would have been.

A Sermon of Valediction at my going into Germany, No. 11 of the present volume, preached April 18, 1619, on the text of *Ecclesiastes* 12.1, presents several points of special interest. It was Donne's solemn farewell to the Benchers of Lincoln's Inn before he started as chaplain to the embassy which King James dispatched to the Continent of Europe in the hope of averting a war between Catholics and Protestants over the succession to the throne of Bohemia. The troubles which were to lead to the Thirty Years' War had already begun. Ferdinand of Styria, the Catholic heir to the throne, was disliked by the Protestant Bohemians, who invited the Elector Palatine, Frederick V, to become their king. Frederick was son-in-law to King James, having married James's only daughter, the Princess Elizabeth, in February, 1613.

Donne prepared for the journey with many apprehensions that he might never return. In a letter which he wrote to Sir Henry Goodyer he remarked: "We are within fourteen days of our time for going. I leave a scattered flock of wretched children, and I carry an infirme and valetudinary body, and I goe into the mouth of such adversaries, as I cannot blame for hating me, the Jesuits, and yet I go."[65] He gave voice to these fears at the close of the present sermon, where he asked the congregation for their prayers "that I, (if I may be of use for his glory, and your edification in this place) may be restored to you again," and he continues: "That if I never meet you again till we have all passed the gate of death, yet in the gates of heaven, I may meet you all . . ." It was not that Donne feared death itself, for often he had moods in which he desired it, but he did not wish to die abroad, among strange faces, and he wished, moreover, to live a while longer in order to bring up his motherless children.

[65] Letters (1651), p. 174.

There is a striking resemblance between the last page of this sermon and Donne's *Hymne to Christ, at the Authors last going into Germany:*

In what torne ship soever I embarke,
That ship shall be my embleme of thy Arke;
What sea soever swallow mee, that flood
Shall be to mee an embleme of thy blood;
Though thou with clouds of anger do disguise
Thy face; yet through that maske I know those eyes,
  Which, though they turne away sometimes,
    They never will despise.

I sacrifice this Iland unto thee,
And all whom I lov'd there, and who lov'd mee;
When I have put our seas twixt them and mee,
Put thou thy sea betwixt my sinnes and thee.
As the trees sap doth seeke the root below
In winter, in my winter now I goe,
  Where none but thee, th'Eternall root
    Of true Love I may know....

Seale then this bill of my Divorce to All,
On whom those fainter beames of love did fall;
Marry those loves, which in youth scattered bee
On Fame, Wit, Hopes (false mistresses) to thee.
Churches are best for Prayer, that have least light:
To see God only, I goe out of sight:
  And to scape stormy dayes, I chuse
    An Everlasting night.[96]

There are also less obvious links between the sermon and those earlier poems, some of which had been more notable for profanity than for piety. One such link may be found between the lurid picture of the sinner's death and Donne's early verse letter, written in 1597, on *The Storme*. In the poem Donne had described the terrific thunderstorm which forced the Earl of Essex, with Donne and Wotton among the gentlemen-adventurers in his fleet, to put back to Plymouth after setting out on his voyage to the Azores. Writing of the dense blackness of the sky, Donne had said "Lightning was all our light," and he had gone on to compare the seasick voyagers

[96] Grierson, *Poems,* I, 352–353.

peeping from their cabins to souls rising at the Day of Judgment. More than twenty years later, Donne, preparing for another voyage, this time as a divine and not as a reckless young gallant, brought together darkness and lightning and judgment in almost the same words. "He hath noe light but lightning," he said of the sinner hurried out of the world, and went on to speak of "a sodaine flash of horror" as the soul is "translated into that fire which hath noe light." Essentially Donne's imagination remains the same in both poem and sermon.

That *A Sermon of Valediction* made an immediate impression on its hearers is evident from the fact that more manuscript copies of it have been preserved than of any other sermon. The manuscript copies, none of which is in Donne's autograph, differ in many minor points among themselves, but these are of very little consequence (being mostly scribal errors) as compared with the wide differences between the manuscripts on one side and the Folio text on the other. The differences begin in the first sentence, and are found right through the sermon up to the very last clause, where the manuscripts contain four words which are not found in the Folio. We have here no slight alterations such as are found in the sermons on *Psalms* 144.15, *Hosea* 2.19, or *John* 5.22, but a complete revision of the text. There can be no doubt that the version preserved in the manuscripts is the earlier form and represents the sermon substantially as Donne delivered it. The Lothian transcript, which is certainly derived from Donne's original through several intervening MSS, is dated "Aug: 19. 1624," whereas the Folio text, published in the *XXVI Sermons* of 1661, represents a carefully thought-out revision, made by Donne at some time after he returned from the Continent, perhaps with a view to immediate publication, or perhaps in 1625 at the time of the plague epidemic when he revised a large number of his sermons.

The phrasing of the manuscript version is more vivid and dramatic in a number of places. We have already quoted, in another connection,[67] a passage from this earlier version that shows Donne's characteristic personal humility when addressing his Lincoln's Inn associates, "When I consider my infirmities (I know I might justly lay a heavier name upon them) I know I am in his other quorum, *quorum*

[67] *Ante,* p. 10.

ego maximus, sent to save sinners of whom I am the chiefest." Such an expression of penitence was suitable for Lincoln's Inn, where the Benchers had known Donne in his wild and reckless youth, but when he revised the passage for publication, he omitted the words in parentheses and toned the passage down into a more general acknowledgment of human infirmity. Again, when Donne approached the Calvinistic doctrine of predestination to hell-fire, he cried out, according to the manuscripts: "God did not make that fire for us, but much less did he make us for that fire; make us to damne us, God forbid." This is less forcible in the revised form: "God did not make the fire for us; but much less did he make us for that fire; that is, make us to damn us." Finally, the manuscript version of the closing words of the sermon runs: "It is the kingdome where we shall end, and yet begin but then, . . . where we shall live and never die, where we shall meet and never part, but here we must." These last four words, so weighty and impressive in Donne's actual leave-taking, were omitted when he revised the sermon for publication.

There are, however, a much larger number of passages in which the revised text is superior to that found in the manuscripts. Donne exercised his critical faculties to the full in pruning the sermon of many of its original digressions, and in tightening up the sentences, omitting rhetorical repetitions, and so making the main argument clearer. Here and there, with exquisite art he adjusted the rhythm of the sentences. Thus in the manuscripts we find the phrase "in the Fall, about September." In the revised draft we read "at the fall of the leaf, in the end of the year"—a sentence which by its rhythm betrays to us Donne the poet brooding over and remodeling the work of Donne the preacher.

We have decided to print the manuscript version at the end of this volume, while keeping the Folio version in the body of the work on pp. 235–249. Any scholar who cares to compare the two versions sentence by sentence will be surprised to find how often Donne has converted the loose shambling sentences of the earlier draft into well-knit vigorous sentences by striking out such padding as "It is often and well said" and by rewriting whole clauses.[68]

---

[68] Fuller examples of this rewriting are quoted by E. M. Simpson in *Donne's Sermon of Valediction* (Nonesuch Press, 1932), from which much of the foregoing criticism has been quoted or summarized.

A Sermon of Valediction has several links in thought with the sermon which Donne preached at Whitehall on St. Paul's words, "Christ Jesus came into the world to save sinners, of whom I am the chiefest," already noted as recurring in Donne's peroration of the Lincoln's Inn sermon. One of the most striking is the repetition and enlargement of the allegorical interpretation of the Six Days of Creation. In the Whitehall sermon this is briefly expressed:

> In this first creation thus presented there is a shadow, a representation of our second Creation, our Regeneration in Christ, and of the saving knowledge of God; . . . for if we consider him in his first word, . . . as he spoke from the beginning in the Old Testament, from thence we can not only see, but feel and apply a *Dixit, fiat lux,* that God hath said, *let there be light;* . . . And there we may find a *fiat firmamentum,* that there is a kind of firmament produced in us, a knowledge of a difference between Heaven and Earth; . . . So also may we find a *congregentur aquæ,* that God hath said, *Let there be a sea,* a gathering, a confluence of all such means as are necessary for the attaining of salvation; that is, that God from the beginning settled and established a Church, in which he was alwayes carefull to minister to man means of eternall happiness: The Church is that Sea, and into that Sea we launched [in] the water of Baptism.[69]

This is expanded into a lengthy digression of several pages in the manuscript version of *A Sermon of Valediction,* and although it is compressed in the Folio text, it still occupies a somewhat disproportionate amount of space in comparison with the main argument of the sermon.[70] It looks as if Donne, when composing this Lincoln's Inn Sermon, was still influenced by the reading which he had done for the Whitehall one, and as if he decided that in this discourse on *Remember now thy Creator in the days of thy youth* he might profitably develop at length the analogy between the first material Creation and the second spiritual one which he had sketched so briefly in the earlier sermon.

In spite of its personal interest, however, the sermon is by no means one of Donne's best. He was too tired and harassed to reach the heights to which he was later to ascend. Fortunately his fears for the journey were not realized, and his health improved during the slow and stately progress which the embassy made as it visited

---

[69] Vol. I, pp. 289–290.

[70] Pp. 240–243 and pp. 379–384 in the present volume.

Brussels, Cologne, Frankfort, Heidelberg, Munich, Vienna, and other cities.

Donne's appointment to Doncaster's entourage was, as Gosse long ago pointed out, probably meant by both the King and Doncaster as a means by which Donne could have a vacation from his regular duties and could recover his health and spirits. Certainly he seems to have enjoyed himself far more than he expected when he looked toward the journey apprehensively in the months preceding his departure. From these months that he spent away from England, we have three sermons—only two as they were originally preached, since the sermons on *Matthew* 4.18–20 were, according to the heading in the 1640 Folio, preached as a single discourse. Of the three sermons, Nos. 12, 13, and 14 in the present volume, only the last is of much interest to a reader looking for Donne's best eloquence; and even that last is not outstandingly impressive. Whether because he was in a vacation mood and did not muster his full energy, or because he was in unfamiliar surroundings and among foreign people and thus felt hampered, Donne was not at his best. It is somewhat surprising that he did not rise more eloquently to such occasions as called forth these sermons, for the first of them is stated to have been preached before Elizabeth, James I's daughter, who was regarded with affection by all Englishmen and for whose wedding with Frederick the Elector Palatine Donne had written an epithalamium, and the other, preached at The Hague, was rewarded by a medal that Donne treasured all his life, and must have been in response to an invitation that he felt as an honor.

No. 12, as it appears in *XXVI Sermons* (our sole source for its text), has a puzzling heading: "Two Sermons, to the Prince and Princess *Palatine,* the Lady *Elizabeth* at *Heydelberg,* when I was commanded by the King to wait upon my L. of *Doncaster* in his Embassage to *Germany. First Sermon as we went out,* June 16. 1619."

No second sermon to the Prince and Princess appears, in *XXVI Sermons* or in any other printed or manuscript source. No reference to this particular occasion or to the Prince and Princess appears in the sermon itself. Furthermore, the text is, as Donne remarks in the second sentence of the sermon, one appropriated by the Church "to the celebration of the *Advent,* before the Feast of the Birth of our

Saviour." These considerations lead a reader to wonder whether the heading may be wrongly placed before the particular sermon—such a misplacing is certainly possible in the carelessly collected and edited Folio of 1661. Nevertheless, no clear evidence makes it necessary to assume that the heading is wrong. The "I" and "we" indicate that Donne himself wrote the heading. He might quite possibly have preached to his royal auditors without addressing them or referring to them directly. Also, though the text is suitable to Advent Sunday, Donne's exposition of it makes (except for the comment just cited regarding its usual appropriation by the Church) no direct application of it to any particular season of the year. Therefore, since the burden of proof rests on any editor who believes the heading to be wrongly placed, and since the present editors have no such proof and have no suggestion as to any other more probable date or occasion, the heading and sermon are in our edition accepted as they stand, though with some misgivings.[71]

This discourse, on *Romans* 13.11, is a contrived rather than an inspired sermon; rather heavily ecclesiastical, in its elaboration of the respects in which Christians are nearer to salvation than the heathen or the Jews, and more ingenious than perceptive in the occasional analogies inserted for the purpose of making its main ideas interesting; analogies such as that of a man's looking at a house rather than living in it, or that of the superior virtues of a panacea including hundreds of ingredients over any one drug, or that of the necessity for the body to digest and assimilate its food as well as for the hand to reach for it.[72] One analogy only has any sharp appeal to the feelings; that is the unusual and characteristically Donnean description, late in the sermon, of our approach to death: "As he that travails weary, and late towards a great City, is glad when he comes to a place of execution, becaus he knows that is neer the town; so when thou comest to the gate of death, be glad of that, for it is but one step from that to thy *Jerusalem*."[73]

[71] The possibility that the second sermon to the Prince and Princess might be the one omitted from the contents of *F 26* seems to us very slight indeed, for the present sermon is No. 20 in that Folio, and the number of the missing sermon was evidently 9.

[72] Pp. 253, 256, 263 in the present volume.

[73] P. 266 in the present volume.

Another brief reference to "spirits in us, which unite body and soul,"[74] reminds a reader of a passage in Donne's great poem, *The Extasie*—

As our blood labours to beget
  Spirits, as like soules as it can,
Because such fingers need to knit
  That subtile knot, which makes us man:
So must pure lovers soules descend
  T'affections, and to faculties,
Which sense may reach and apprehend,
  Else a great Prince in prison lies.

But Donne the poet did not in this sermon very notably inspire Donne the preacher.

Sermons Nos. 13 and 14 are unusual because of the explicit and obviously autobiographical statement in the heading for No. 13, a heading that can be trusted since it appears in *LXXX Sermons,* the best and most authoritative of the Folios: "At the *Haghe* Decemb. 19. 1619. I Preached upon this Text. Since in my sicknesse at *Abrey-hatche* in Essex, 1630, revising my short notes of that Sermon, I digested them into these two."

The two sermons in *LXXX Sermons* are, then, at least in part the product of Donne's later mind in 1630 rather than of his earlier preaching in 1619. Since we have no other text, we have no means of determining what in them is revision and expansion and what the words that Donne actually preached. Such a heading as that for No. 13 may quite properly raise in a student's mind the further question, whether there may be other sermons, not explicitly stated to be expansions and revisions, that are really as much so as this. There is, of course, no evidence to disprove the supposition that there may be such; but it remains, nevertheless, very dubious. Of the considerable number of sermons for which we have earlier manuscripts and also the final form as printed in one of the Folios, only one, the Sermon of Valediction, shows evidence of a complete and thoroughgoing revision; the others showing slight changes here and there, but being essentially the same sermons in the Folio that we have in the manuscripts. Probably such a process as that which produced the present two sermons was rare enough in Donne's practice, so that he felt it

[74] P. 262 in the present volume.

necessary to comment on the matter in the heading that he attached when preparing the sermons for possible publication.

Sermons Nos. 13 and 14 are, as they stand, quite uneven in quality. No. 13 has some interest for its careful and intelligent analysis of the text, according to the literal or historical interpretation—its explanation of the facts regarding Andrew's and Peter's coming to Christ, of the nature and geographical position of the "Sea" of Galilee, of the particular sort of fishermen the two disciples were, and the contrast between their experience and that of other disciples and apostles. There is one interesting paragraph, also, that is a particularly clear expression of Donne's views regarding the Universal Catholic Church: "The Church loves the name of Catholique; and it is a glorious, and an harmonious name; Love thou those things wherein she is Catholique, and wherein she is harmonious, that is, *Quod ubique, quod semper,* Those universall, and fundamentall doctrines, which in all Christian ages, and in all Christian Churches, have beene agreed by all to be necessary to salvation; and then thou art a true Catholique."[75]

Otherwise, this first of the two sermons on *Matthew* 4.18–20 (the first part, perhaps, of the sermon Donne originally preached at The Hague) has little spark in it, little appeal to a reader's deeper feelings.

Sermon No. 14 is a good deal more interesting than No. 13. Its long exposition of the sin of pride is most impressive; and its comparison of the world to a sea and the gospel to a net is well and penetratingly developed. Yet it still lacks the quality of Donne at his best, the creative brilliance with which he often interprets Scripture. For the most part, a reader can foresee pretty well beforehand how Donne will interpret a passage; if he surprises, it is not to a sense that a new and illuminating significance is being given to a familiar Scriptural saying, but rather to a sense that the preacher is quibbling, and losing his contact with the essentials.

Sermons Nos. 15 and 16 were preached the same day, January 30, 1619/20, one in the morning and the other in the evening, and are both on texts from the Gospel according to St. John. They are interesting for a number of reasons.

First, they give us evidence of one certain and another probable

[75] P. 280 of the present volume.

series of sermons that Donne preached at Lincoln's Inn and that do not (except for these two sermons themselves) survive to us. In the first sentences of his evening sermon on *John* 8.15, Donne speaks of these two series:

> The Rivers of Paradise did not all run one way, and yet they flow'd from one head; the sentences of the Scripture flow all from one head, from the holy Ghost, and yet they seem to present divers senses, and to admit divers interpretations; In such an appearance doth this Text differ from that which I handled in the forenoon, and as heretofore I found it a usefull and acceptable labour, to employ our Evening exercises, upon the vindicating of some such places of Scripture, as our adversaries of the Roman Church had detorted in some point of controversie between them and us, and restoring those places to their true sense, (which course I held constantly for one whole year) so I think it a usefull and acceptable labour, now to employ for a time those Evening exercises to reconcile some such places of Scripture, as may at first sight seem to differ from one another . . .[76]

Just when Donne "heretofore" gave the series of evening sermons he describes seems impossible to determine precisely. Since the present two sermons were preached only a few weeks after his return from the Continent, the series must obviously date from before the summer of 1619; and if we are right in dating the series of sermons on Psalm 38 in the late spring and summer of 1618,[77] the "whole year" that Donne speaks of would have to be either sometime between his appointment as Reader in Divinity in 1616 and the late spring of 1618, or (if he were not precise in his use of the phrase "consistently for one whole year") possibly the period from late summer of 1618 to the spring of 1619. Whenever he did preach the series on Scriptural passages "detorted" by the Roman Church, the fact that he gave such a series is interesting as indicating one sort of sermon that must have become familiar to his congregation at the Inn. (It is, however, not possible to mourn too greatly over the fact that the series has not survived in print or manuscript.) Donne also, it can be seen from the passage quoted above, was inaugurating, in preaching these two sermons, a new series of evening sermons on the reconciliation of passages from Scripture that may seem to differ

---

[76] P. 325 of the present volume.

[77] See *ante*, pp. 13–14.

from one another. If he did actually go on to preach such a series, the other sermons in it are lost to us; and one might speculate that, if we had it, this second series would be more interesting than the earlier one to readers of later generations. Certainly the juxtaposition of the two sayings of Christ—"The Father judgeth no man, but hath committed all judgment unto the Son," with, "I judge no man"—suggests a paradox of the sort that constantly fascinated Donne and must have particularly interested his hearers also, considering the fact that the two sermons were copied together at least four times,[78] besides being printed later in *Six Sermons* and *Fifty Sermons.*

That the sermons were consciously directed toward an audience familiar with and interested in legal technicalities is clear, especially when one reads the first of the two, with its careful distinctions among different sorts of judgment—"Judicium detestationis," "Judicium discretionis," "Judicium retributionis," "Judicium electionis," "Judicium justificationis," and "Judicium glorificationis"—and such references to English laws as the following: "Here you are fain to supply defects of laws, that things done in one County may be tryed in another; And that in offences of high nature, transmarine offences may be inquir'd and tryed here . . ."[79]

Nevertheless, the sermons show a change from the attitude Donne took in earlier discourses to the members of Lincoln's Inn. No longer does he talk personally and intimately to his congregation; the occasional personal references, to himself or to the members of his audience, and the occasional humorous touches that light up the earlier sermons preached at the Inn are lacking in these preached shortly after his return to his preaching duties from several months of dignified leisure in the embassy headed by Doncaster. Donne still appeals to the particular interests of his hearers, but he does not speak personally or intimately to them. For example, instead of apologizing for possibly trying their patience, as he does in the sermon on *Psalms* 38.2,[80] he now simply shows concern "that we may husband our hour well."[81]

---

[78] In the Merton, Dowden, Lothian, and Ellesmere manuscripts.

[79] P. 315 of the present volume.

[80] See *ante,* p. 9.

[81] P. 319 of the present volume.

The first of the two, preached in the morning, is, at least to a reader, far more carefully considered and eloquently worded than the second. It is full of vivid, imaginative comparisons instinct with the spirit of poetry; passages such as that concerning the Garden of Eden: "When there was no more to be seen, or considered upon the whole earth but the garden of Paradise, . . . Gods delight was to be with the sons of men, and man was only there, shal we not diminish God nor speak too vulgarly of him to say, that he hovered like a Falcon over Paradise, and that from that height of heaven, the piercing eye of God, saw so little a thing, as the forbidden fruit, and what became of that, and the reaching eare of God heard the hissing of the Serpent, and the whispering of the woman, and what was concluded upon that?"[82]

Toward its end this sermon becomes rather surprisingly prosaic; but for the most part it is as full of fire and brilliance as the preceding three sermons in the present volume, those he preached abroad, are lacking in those qualities.

The evening sermon is shorter, as was fitting for a sermon preached late in the day, and is considerably less effective to read. Donne allows himself to digress, once into a polemic against the Roman Church and once again into a moral exhortation against calumny, without tying these digressions into the total structure of his sermon as skillfully as he does when he is at his best. Still, the main structure is clear, the exposition of the ways in which Christ refuses to judge man is a persuasive reconciliation of the paradox implicit in his two texts, and the poetry so noticeable in the morning sermon is not entirely absent in this evening one—as in the reference to the rivers of Paradise at the beginning (already quoted), or in this lovely figure, from the most impressive part of the sermon, the exhortation against despair: ". . . know stil, that . . . as *David* said, *By my God have I leaped over a wall,* so by thy God maist thou breake through a wall, through this wall of obduration, which thou thy selfe hast begunne to build about thy selfe. Feather thy wings againe, which even the flames of hell have touched in these beginnings of desperation, feather them againe with this text *Neminem judicat, Christ judges no man,* so as a desperate man judges himselfe . . ."[83]

Sermon No. 17 is the earliest we possess of several sermons that

[82] P. 316 of the present volume.

[83] P. 332 of the present volume.

Donne preached at marriages. The heading in *Fifty Sermons* states merely that it was preached "At a Mariage"; and there would be no means of our determining at what marriage, and when, it was preached if it were not that there is a copy of the sermon in the Merton manuscript, which has at its end the revealing note, "Finis of a Sermon preach'd by D: Donn at Sir Francis Nethersoles marriage." It can, then, be dated as preached shortly before the 12th of February, 1619/20,[84] and on an occasion that involved several of Donne's personal friends and acquaintances. John Chamberlain's comment on this wedding is worth quoting in full: "I forgat in my last that Sir Fra: Nethersole was then newly maried to Mistris Goodyeare that served the Lady of Bedford who gave her 500^{li} or 700^{li}, besides 500^{li} she bestowed upon them in gloves, which brought in a great contribution of plate to make up a portion which her father Sir Henry could not geve."

Sir Francis Nethersole had been Public Orator of the University of Cambridge till he resigned his office to become secretary to Doncaster on the same embassy with which Donne was connected. He was knighted in September, 1619, was at the same time appointed English agent to the princes of the Protestant Union and secretary to the Princess Elizabeth, Electress Palatine, and spent many years thereafter in trying to forward her cause after her husband accepted the crown of Bohemia. That Donne must have come to know Nethersole personally while they both were attending Doncaster is obvious. The bride, Lucy Goodyer, was the daughter of Donne's old and intimate friend, Sir Henry Goodyer. She was also one of the attendants upon Donne's friend and benefactress the Countess of Bedford. When Donne preached this sermon, then, it was directed to a man and woman both of whom he knew personally, and was at an occasion when his old friend Goodyer must have been present, and the Countess of Bedford probably present too.

These being the circumstances, one might expect Donne to have been at his best. For some reason he was not. The sermon is strangely flat and unattractive—certainly not one that the wedded pair could in

[84] See the quotation that follows from Chamberlain. The previous letter, to which Chamberlain refers, is dated February 12, 1619/20. Gosse (*Life and Letters of John Donne*, II, 131) dates the marriage at just before September, 1619, but gives no evidence for his date.

after years have recalled with any lift of the heart. Donne expresses rather cool approval of marriage as an institution—though, he says, virginity is also to be approved. He explains that God knew it to be good *for society* that man should not be alone and that he should have a helpmeet; but the main reason he gives for man's having a wife is for the propagation of the human race. He insists at some length that the Scripture does not imply that it is better for man's own personal good to marry, or that every individual man would be better off married. He insists even more emphatically that the woman should know her place, as the weaker vessel, and not step out of her place.[85] Even the ending of the sermon is unenthusiastic:

> To end all, there is a *Morall fitnesse,* consisting in those morall vertues, of which we have spoke enough; And there is a *Civill fitnesse,* consisting in Discretion, and accommodating her self to him; And there is a *Spirituall fitnesse,* in the unanimity of Religion, that they be not of repugnant professions that way. Of which, since we are well assured in both these, who are to be joyned now, I am not sorry, if either the houre, or the present occasion call me from speaking any thing at all, because it is a subject too mis-interpretable, and unseasonable to admit an enlarging in at this time. At this time, therefore, this be enough, for the explication and application of these words.

It is true that no sort of seventeenth-century sermon seems today more obsolete than the typical marriage sermon of that time, since the conventional belief in the inferiority of woman affects nearly all such sermons and is unattractive to those of us who live in twentieth-century England or the United States. Even granting this, however, it seems clear that Donne for some reason or reasons could not at the time express his best or deepest feelings. To guess at the reasons is

[85] It may be worth notice in a footnote that in one brief digression (p. 343) Donne inveighs against cosmetics and self-adornment as used by some women. This passage very likely reflects a happening interestingly noted in a letter of Chamberlain's dated January 25, 1619/20: "Yesterday the bishop of London called together all his Clergie about this towne, and told them he had expresse commaundment from the King to will them to inveigh vehemently and bitterly in theyre sermons against the insolence of our women, and theyre wearing of brode brimd hats, pointed dublets, theyre haire cut short or shorne, and some of them stillettaes or poinards, and such other trinckets of like moment." It is hard for us to believe, however, that a command like this would in itself have affected a whole sermon of Donne's on such a personal occasion as this wedding.

probably futile. Perhaps he was suffering from weariness and a temporary drop in emotional intensity.

Lent in this year began on March 1. On March 3, Friday of the first week in Lent, Donne preached at Whitehall an impressive sermon (No. 18 of the present volume) on a somber text from the prophecy of Amos: "Woe unto you, that desire the day of the Lord: what have yee to doe with it? the day of the Lord is darknesse and not light."[86] The "Conclusion" of the sermon makes the particular application of the text to the beginning of Lent;[87] the main body of the sermon is a clear and moving interpretation of the text historically and morally. In its implications it is a highly personal sermon, though not so on the surface. Donne never refers to himself directly, but talks to his congregation; and yet the "woes" that he calls down on those desiring "the day of the Lord," in at least two of the three moral senses he sees in the text, were certainly woes that he feared to incur himself. The sin of presumption, of "contempt, and deriding the day of the Lord, the judgements of God,"[88] is a sin that Donne dislikes to think exists in any member of his congregation, and evidently does not feel in himself: "Now if this *Woe* of this Prophet thus denounced against contemptuous scorners of the *day of the Lord,* as that day signifies afflictions in this life, have had no subject to work upon in this congregation (as by Gods grace there is none of that distemper here) it is a piece of a Sermon well lost; and God be blessed that it hath had no use, that no body needed it."[89] The sins of hypocrisy and desperation, however, of desiring the day of the Last Judgment in confidence that one will stand at God's right hand rather than fall at his left, and of desperately longing for the day of one's own individual death, are sins that Donne evidently felt to be more nearly universal because he felt the temptation toward them himself. Again and again in different sermons Donne quotes or paraphrases Paul's words, "For I am in a strait betwixt two, having a desire to depart, and to be with Christ; which is far better: Nevertheless to

[86] Donne uses for this text the wording of the Geneva Bible rather than that of the King James version. The second sentence, in the latter, reads, "To what end is it for you?" The Geneva Bible reads, "What have you to do with it?"

[87] Pp. 361 ff. of the present volume.

[88] P. 350 of the present volume.

[89] P. 355 of the present volume.

abide in the flesh is more needful to you." He prefers, too, the stronger language of the Vulgate, "Desiderium habens dissolvi, et esse cum Christo," and his favorite paraphrase is, simply, "Cupio dissolvi," "I desire to be dissolved and be with Christ." In Donne's fondness for this idea is apparent the force that both the desire for death and the desire to believe himself among God's elect had within him.

Another passage in the sermon implies still once more that Donne, though always speaking explicitly to his congregation, was implicitly talking to himself. It also is a further indication of something we have noted earlier, in our consideration of the sermons in the present volume, that is, Donne's efforts to comprehend the inner nature and functions of his position as a priest and a preacher. Early in the sermon he considers his text historically, as words spoken by Amos and rejected by the priest of Bethel, Amasiah. First he tactfully comments that there is "no *Amasiah* no mis-interpreting Priest here, (wee are farre from that, because we are far from having a *Ieroboam* to our King as he had, easie to give eare, easie to give credit to false informations) ..." But then his mind turns inward, as his mind so continually did during his whole life, and he proceeds: "... yet every man that comes with Gods Message hither, brings a little Amasiah of his owne, in his owne bosome, a little wisperer in his owne heart, that tels him, *This is the Kings Chappell, and it is the Kings Court,* and these woes and judgements, and the denouncers and proclaimers of them are not so acceptable here. But we must have our owne *Amos,* aswell as our *Amasias,* this answer to this suggestion, *I was no Prophet, and the Lord tooke me and bad me prophecy*. What shall I doe?"[60]

That Donne, called when over forty years old from a secular life by King James, and now preaching at Whitehall, was here thinking of the Amos and the Amasiah within himself is apparent enough. Even his previous tactful remark about there being no Amasiah in King James's court was at least a slight prompting of the "little Amasiah" in his own personal bosom, although he sincerely loved and admired King James. But the Amos in him was constantly struggling to overcome; and while Donne never became a completely fearless reformer like that old Hebrew prophet, he did try all through his clerical career to be honest, and to be true to his sacred calling.

[60] Pp. 348–349 of the present volume.

The Sermons

Number 1.

Preached at Lincolns Inne.

Psal. 38.2. *FOR THINE ARROWES STICK FAST IN ME, AND THY HAND PRESSETH ME SORE.*

Almost every man hath his *Appetite,* and his *tast* disposed to some kind of *meates* rather then others; He knows what dish he would choose, for his first, and for his second course. We have often the same disposition in our *spirituall Diet;* a man may have a particular love towards such or such a book of Scripture, and in such an affection, I acknowledge, that my spirituall appetite carries me still, upon the *Psalms of David,* for a first course, for the Scriptures of the Old Testament, and upon the *Epistles of Saint Paul,* for a second course, for the New: and my meditations even for these *publike exercises* to Gods Church, returne oftnest to these two. For, as a hearty entertainer offers to others, the meat which he loves best himself, so doe I oftnest present to Gods people, in these Congregations, the meditations which I feed upon at home, in those two Scriptures. If a man be asked a reason why he loves one meat better then another, where all are equally good, (as the books of Scripture are) he will at least, finde a reason in some good example, that he sees some man of good tast, and temperate withall, so do: And for my Diet, I have Saint *Augustines* protestation, that he loved the *Book of Psalms,* and Saint *Chrysostomes,* that he loved Saint *Pauls Epistles,* with a particular devotion. I may have another more particular reason, because they are Scriptures, written in such forms, as I have been most accustomed to; Saint *Pauls* being Letters, and *Davids* being Poems: for, God gives us, not onely that which is meerly necessary, but that which is convenient too; He does not onely feed us, but *feed us with marrow, and with fatnesse;* he gives us our instruction in cheerfull forms, not [Psal. 63.5] in a sowre, and sullen, and angry, and unacceptable way, but cheerfully, in *Psalms,* which is also a limited, and a restrained form; Not in an *Oration,* not in *Prose,* but in *Psalms;* which is such a form as is both curious, and requires diligence in the making, and then when it is made, can have nothing, no syllable taken from it, nor added to it: Therefore is Gods will delivered to us in *Psalms,* that we might have it the more cheerfully, and that we might have it the more certainly, because where all the words are numbred, and measured, and weighed, the whole work is the lesse subject to falsification, either by substraction or addition. God speaks to us *in oratione strictâ,* in a limited, in a diligent form; Let us [not] speak to him *in oratione solutâ;* not *pray,* not *preach,* not *hear,* slackly, suddenly, unadvisedly, extemporally, occasionally, indiligently; but let all our speech to him, be weighed, and measured in the weights of the *Sanctuary,* let us be content to preach, and to hear within the compasse of our Articles, and content to pray in those *formes* which the Church hath meditated for us, and recommended to us.

Divisio

This whole Psalm is a *Prayer,* and recommended by *David* to the Church; And a *Prayer* grounded upon *Reasons.* The *Reasons* are multiplyed, and dilated from the second to the 20. verse. But as the *Prayer* is made to him that is *Alpha,* and *Omega, first,* and *last;* so the *Prayer* is the *Alpha* and *Omega* of the Psalme; the *Prayer* possesses the first and the last verse thereof; and though the Reasons be not left out, (Christ himself settles that *Prayer,* which he recommended to our daily use, upon a Reason, *Quia tuum est Regnum, for thine is the Kingdome,*) yet *David* makes up his Circle, he begins, and ends in prayer. But our text fals within his Reasons; He prays in the first verse that God would forbear him, upon the Reasons that follow; of which some are *extrinsecall,* some arising out of the *power,* some out of the *malice,* some out of the *scorn* of other men; And some are *intrinsecall,* arising out of himself, and of his sense of Gods Judgements upon him; and our Text begins the Reasons of that last kind, which because *David* enters, with that particle, not onely of *Connexion,* but of *Argumentation* too, *For,* (*Rebuke me not O Lord, for* it stands thus and thus with me) we shall make it a first short part, to consider, how it may become a godly man, to limit God so far, as to present and oppose *Reasons* against his declared purpose, and proceedings. And then in those calamities which he presents for his Reasons in this Text, *For thine arrows stick fast in me, and thy hand presseth me sore,* we shall passe by these steps, first, we shall see in what respect, in what allusion, in what notification he cals them *arrows:* And therein first, that they are *alienæ,* they are shot from *others,* they are not in his own power; a man shoots not an arrow at himselfe; And then, that they are *Veloces,* swift in coming, he cannot give them their time; And again, they are *Vix visibiles,* though they bee not altogether invisible in their coming, yet there is required a quick eye, and an expresse diligence, and watchfulnesse to discern and avoid them; so they are arrows in the hand of another; not his own; and swift as they come, and invisible before they come. And secondly, they are *many arrows;* The victory lies not in scaping one or two; And thirdly, they *stick in him;* they finde not *David* so good proof, as to rebound back again, and imprint no sense; And *they stick fast;* Though the blow be felt, and the wound discerned, yet there is not a present cure, he cannot shake them off; *Infixæ sunt;* And then, with all this, they *stick fast in him;* that is, in *all him;* in his body, and soul; in him, in his thoughts, and actions; in him, in his sins and in his good works too; *Infixæ mihi,* there is no part of him, no faculty in him, in which they stick not: for, (which may well bee another consideration) *That hand,* which shot them, *presses* him: follows the blow, and *presses him sore,* that is, vehemently. But yet, (which will be our conclusion) *Sagittæ tuæ,* and *manus tua,* These arrows that are shot, and this hand that presses them so sore, are the *arrows,* and is the *hand* of God; and therefore, first, they must have their *Effect,* they cannot be dis-appointed; But yet they bring their comfort with them, because they are his, because no *arrows* from him, no *pressing* with his hand, comes without that *Balsamum* of mercy, to heal as fast as he wounds. And of so many pieces will this exercise consist, this exercise of your *Devotion,* and perchance *Patience.*

First then, this particle of *connexion* and *argumentation, For,* 1 Part
which begins our text, occasions us, in a first part, to consider, that such an impatience in affliction, as brings us toward a *murmuring* at Gods proceedings, and almost to a calling of God to an account, in inordinate expostulations, is a leaven so kneaded into the nature of man, so innate a tartar, so inherent a sting, so inseparable a venim

in man, as that the holyest of men have scarce avoided it in all de-
grees thereof. *Job* had Gods testimony of being an *upright man;* and
[Job] 6.8 yet *Job* bent that way, *O that I might have my request,* says *Job, and
that God would grant me the thing that I long for.* Well, if God
would, what would *Job* aske? *That God would destroy me, and cut
me off.* Had it not been as easie, and as ready, and as usefull a prayer,
[Job 6.12] *That God would deliver him? Is my strength the strength of stones,
or is my flesh of brasse?* says hee, in his impatience. What though it
bee not? Not stones, not brasse; is there no remedy, but to wish it
dust? *Moses* had Gods testimonies of a remarkable and exemplar
man, for *meeknesse.* But did God always finde it so? was it a meek
Numb. 11.11 behaviour towards God, to say, *Wherefore hast thou afflicted thy
[and 12] servant? Have I conceived all this people, have I begotten them, that
thou shouldest say unto me, Carry them in thy bosome? Elias* had
had testimonies of Gods care and providence in his behalf; and God
was not weary of preserving him, and he was weary of being pre-
1 Reg. 19.4 served; He desired that he might dye, and said, *Sufficit Domine, It
is enough O Lord, now take my soul. Jonas,* even then, when God
was expressing an act of mercy, takes occasion to be angry, and to bee
angry *at God,* and to be angry at *the mercy* of God. We may see his
fluctuation and distemper, and irresolution in that case, and his trans-
[Jon.] 4.1 portation; *He was angry,* says the text; very angry; And yet, the
text says, *He prayed,* but he prayed *angerly; O Lord take, I beseech
3 thee, my life from me; for it is better for me to dye, then to live.*
Better for *him,* that was all he considered; not what was best for the
4 service and glory of God, but best for him. God asks him, *If he doe
well to be angry?* And he will not tell him there; God gives him time
9 to vent his passion, and he askes him again after: *Doest thou well to
bee angry?* And he answers more angerly, *I doe well to be angry,
even unto death. Ieremy* was under this tentation too. *Jonas* was
angry because his Prophesie was not performed; because God would
not second his Prophesie in the destruction of Nineveh. *Jeremy* was
angry because his Prophesie was like to be performed; he preached
[Jer.] 15.10 heavy Doctrin, and therfore his Auditory hated him; *Woe is me,
my Mother,* says he, *that thou hast born me a man of strife, and a
man of contention to the whole earth!* I preach but the messages of
God; (and *væ mihi si non,* wo be unto me if I preach not them) I

preach but the sense of Gods indignation upon mine own soul, in a conscience of mine own sins, I impute nothing to another, that I confesse not of my selfe, I call none of you to confession to me, I doe but confesse my self to God, and you, I rack no mans memory, what he did last year, last week, last night, I onely gather into my memory, and powr out in the presence of my God, and his Church, the sinfull history of mine own *youth,* and yet I am a *contentious man,* says *Jeremy,* a worm, and a burthen to every tender conscience, says he, *and I strive with the whole earth,* I am a bitter, and satyricall preacher; This is that that wearies mee, says hee, *I have neither lent on usury,* nor *men have lent me on usury,* yet, as though I were an oppressing lender, or a fraudulent borrower, *every one of them doth curse me.*

This is a naturall infirmity, which the strongest men, being but men, cannot devest, that if their purposes prosper not, they are weary of their industry, weary of their lifes; But this is *Summa ingratitudo in Deum, malle non esse, quàm miserum esse:* There cannot be a greater unthankfulnesse to God then to desire to be *Nothing* at all, rather then to be that, that God would have thee to be; To desire to be out of the world, rather then to glorifie him, by thy patience in it. But when this infirmity overtakes Gods children, *Patiuntur ut homines, sustinent ut Dei amici;* They are under calamities, as they are men, but yet they come to recollect themselves and to bear those calamities, as the valiant Souldiers, as the faithfull servants, as the bosome friends of almighty God. *Si vis discere, qualis esse debeas, disce post gratiam,* says the same Father; Learn patience, not from the stupidity of Philosophers, who are but their own *statues,* men of stone, without sense, without affections, and who placed all their glory, in a *Non facies ut te dicam malum,* that no pain should make them say they were in pain; nor from the pertinacy of Heretiques, how to bear a calamity, who gave their bodies to the fire, for the establishing of their Disciples, but take out a new lesson in the times of *Grace;* Consider the Apostles there, *Gaudentes & Gloriantes,* They departed from the Councell, *rejoycing that they were counted worthy,* to suffer rebuke *for his name.* It was *Joy,* and all *Joy,* says S. *James;* It was *Glory,* and all *Glory,* says S. *Paul, Absit mihi, God forbid that I should glory, save in the Crosse of our Lord Jesus Christ;* And if

Chrysost.

Act. 5.41

[James] 1.2

Gal. 6.14

I can glory in that, (to glory in that, is to have a conscience testifying to me, that God receives glory by my use of his correction) I may come to God, reason with God, plead with God, wrastle with God, and be received and sustained by him. This was *Davids* case in our Text: therefore he doth not stray into the infirmities of these great, and good Men, *Moses, Job, Elias, Jeremy,* and *Jonah;* whose errours, it is labour better bestowed carefully to avoid, then absolutely to excuse, for that cannot be done. But *David* presents onely to God the sense of his corrections, and implies in *that,* that since the cure is wrought, since Gods purpose, which is, by corrections, to bring a sinner to *himself,* and so to *God,* is effected in him, God would now be pleased to remember all his other gracious promises too; and to admit such a zealous prayer as he doth from *Esay* after, [Isa.] 64.9 *Be not angry, O Lord, above measure;* (that is, above the measure of thy *promises* to repentant souls, or the measure of the *strength* of our bodies) *Neither remember iniquities for ever; But, loe, wee beseech thee, Behold, we are thy people.* To end this first part, (because the other extends it self in many branches) *Then* when we are come to a *sense* of Gods purpose, by his *corrections,* it is a seasonable time to flie to his *mercy,* and to pray, that he would remove them from us; and to present our *Reasons,* to spare us, *for* thy corrections have wrought upon us; *Give us this day, our daily bread,* for thou hast given us stones, and scorpions, tribulations, and afflictions, and we have *fed* upon them, found nourishment even in those tribulations and afflictions, and said thee grace for them, blessed and glorified thy name, for those tribulations, and afflictions; Give us our *Cordials* now, and our *Restoratives,* for thy physick hath evacuated all the peccant humour, and all our naturall strength; shine out in the light of thy countenance now, for this long cold night hath benum'd us; since the *drosse* is now evaporated, now withdraw thy *fire;* since thy hand hath anew *cast* us, now imprint in us anew *thine Image;* since we have not disputed against thy corrections, all this while, [Psal. 51.15] *O Lord open thou our lips now,* and accept our remembring of thee, that we have not done so; Accept our Petition, and the *Reason* of our Petition, *for thine Arrows stick fast in us, and thy hand presseth us sore.*

2 Part

David in a rectified conscience findes that he may be admitted to present *reasons* against farther corrections, And that this may be received as a reason, *That Gods Arrows are upon him;* for this is a phrase or a Metaphore, in which Gods indignation is often expressed in the Scripture. *He sent out his Arrows, and scattered them,* sayes Ps. 18.14 *David;* magnifying Gods goodness in his behalf, against his enemies. And so again, *God will ordaine his Arrowes for them that persecute* Ps. 7.13 *me. Complebo sagittas,* says God, *I will heap mischiefs upon them, and I will spend mine arrows upon them:* yea, *Inebriabo sanguine,* Deut. 32.23 *I will make mine Arrows drunk in their bloud.* It is *Idiotismus* v. 42 *Spiritus sancti,* a peculiar character of the holy Ghosts expressing Gods anger, in that Metaphore of shooting *Arrows.* In this place, some understand by these Arrows, foul and infectious *diseases,* in his body, derived by his *incontinence.* Others, the sting of *Conscience,* and that fearfull choice, which the Prophet offered him, *war, famine,* and *pestilence.* Others, his passionate *sorrow* in the *death* of *Beth-sheba's first childe;* or in the *Incest of Amnon* upon his sister, or in the *murder* upon *Amnon* by *Absolon;* or in the *death* of *Absolon* by *Joab;* or in many other occasions of sorrow, that surrounded *David* and his family, more, perchance, then any such family in the body of story. But these *Psalmes* were made, not onely to vent *Davids* present holy passion, but to serve the Church of God, to the worlds end. And therefore, change the person, and wee shall finde a whole quiver of arrows. Extend this *Man,* to all *Mankind;* carry *Davids* History up to *Adams* History, and consider us in that state, which wee inherit from *him,* and we shall see *arrows* fly about our ears, *A Deo prosequente,* the anger of God hanging over our heads, in a cloud of arrows; and *à conscientia remordente,* our own consciences shooting *poisoned arrows* of desperation into our souls; and *ab Homine Contemnente,* Men multiplying arrows of *Detraction,* and *Calumny,* and *Contumely* upon our good name, and estimation. Briefly, in that wound, as wee were all shot in *Adam,* we bled out *Impassibilitatem,* and we sucked in *Impossibilitatem;* There we lost our *Immortality,* our *Impassibility,* our assurance of Paradise, and then we lost *Possibilitatem boni,* says S. *Augustine:* all possibility of recovering any of this by our selves. So that these arrows which are lamented here, are all those miseries, which sinne hath cast upon us; *Labor,* and the childe of that, *Sicknesse,* and the off-spring of that, *Death;* And the *security* of conscience, and the *terrour* of conscience; the *searing* of the conscience, and the *over-tendernesse* of the conscience; Gods quiver, and the Devils quiver, and our own quiver, and our neighbours quiver, afford, and furnish arrows to gall, and wound us. These arrows then in our Text, proceeding from *sin,* and sin proceeding from *tentations,* and inducing *tribulations,* it shall advance your spirituall edification most, to fixe your consideration upon those *fiery darts,* as they are *tentations,* and as they are *tribulations. Origen* says, he would wish no more, for the recovery of any soul, but that she were able to see *Cicatrices suas,* those scars which these fiery darts have left in her, the deformity which every sinne imprints upon the soul, and *Contritiones suas,* the attenuating and wearing out, and consumption of the soul, by a continuall succession of more, and more wounds upon the same place. An ugly thing in a Consumption, were a fearfull spectacle, And such *Origen* imagins a soul to be, if she could see *Cicatrices,* and *Contritiones,* her ill-favourednesse, and her leannesse in the deformity, and consumption of sin. How provident, how diligent a patience did our blessed Saviour bring to his Passion, who foreseeing that that would be our case, our sicknesse, to be first wounded with *single tentations,* and then to have even the wounds of our soul wounded again, by a daily reiterating of tentations in the same kinde, would provide us physick agreeable to our Disease, Chyrurgery conformable to our wound, first to be *scourged* so, as that his holy body was torn with *wounds,* and then to have those *wounded again,* and often, with more violatings. So then these arrows, are those *tentations* and those *tribulations,* which are accompanied with these qualities of arrows shot at us, that they are *alienæ,* shot from others, not in our power; And *veloces,* swift and sudden, soon upon us; And *vix visibiles,* not discernible in their coming, but by an exact diligence.

Eph. 6.16

Alienæ

First then, these *tentations* are dangerous arrows, as they are *alienæ,* shot from *others,* and not in our own power. It was the Embleme, and Inscription, which *Darius* took for his coin, *Insculpere sagittarium,* to shew his greatnesse, that he could wound afar off, as an Archer does. And it was the way, by which God declared the deliverance of *Israel* from *Syria; Elisha* bids the King open the window East-ward, and shoot an arrow out. The King does shoot: And the Prophet says, *Sagitta salutis Domini, The arrow of the Lords deliverance:* He would deliver *Israel,* by shooting vengeance into *Syria.*

2 Reg. 13.17

One danger in our *arrows,* as they are *tentations,* is, that they come *unsuspectedly;* they come, we know not, *from whence;* from *others;* that's a danger; But in our tentations, there is a greater danger then that, for a man cannot shoot an arrow at *himself;* but we can direct *tentations* upon our selves; If we were in a wildernesse, we could sin; and where we are, we tempt temptations, and wake the Devil, when for any thing that appears, he would sleep. A certain man drew a 1 Reg. 22.34 bow at a venture, says that story; He had no determinate mark, no expresse aime, upon any one man; He drew his bow at a venture, and he hit, and he slew the King *Ahab.* A woman of tentation, *Tendit arcum in incertum,* as that story speaks; shee paints, she curls, she sings, she gazes, and is gazed upon; There's an arrow shot *at randon;* shee aim'd at no particular mark; And thou puttest thy self within shot, and meetest the arrow; Thou soughtest the tentation, the tentation sought not thee. A man is able to oppresse others; *Et* Ps. 52.1 *gloriatur in malo quia potens,* He boasts himselfe because he is able to doe mischief; and *tendit arcum in incertum,* he shoots his arrow at randon, he lets it be known, that he can prefer *them,* that second his purposes, and thou putt'st thy self within shot, and meet'st the arrow, and mak'st thy self his instrument; Thou sought'st the tentation, the tentation sought not thee; when we expose our selves to tentations, tentations hit us, that were not expresly directed, nor meant to us. And even *then,* when we begin to flie from tentations, the arrow overtakes us. *Jehoram* fled from *Jehu,* and *Jehu* shot after 2 Reg. 9.23 him, and shot him through the heart. But this was after *Jehoram* had [and 24] talk'd with him. After wee have parled with a tentation, debated whether we should embrace it or no, and entertain'd some discourse with it, though some tendernesse, some remorse, make us turn our back upon it, and depart a little from it, yet the arrow overtakes us; some *reclinations,* some *retrospects* we have, a little of *Lots wife* is in us, a little *sociablenesse,* and *conversation,* a little point of *honour,* not to be false to former promises, a little *false gratitude,* and thankfulnesse, in respect of former obligations, a little of the *compassion* and *charity* of Hell, that another should not be miserable, for want of *us,* a little of this, which is but the good nature of the *Devill,* arrests us, stops us, fixes us, till the arrow, the tentation shoot us in the back, even when wee had a purpose of departing from that sin, and kil us over again. Thus it is, when we *meet* a tentation, and put our selves in the arrows way; And thus it is when we *fly not fast enough,* nor *farre enough* from a tentation. But when we doe all *that,* and provide as safely as we can to get, and doe get quickly out of distance, Ps. 11.2 yet, *The wicked bend their bowes, that they may privily shoot at the upright in heart; In occulto;* It is a work of *Darknesse, Detraction;* and they can shoot *in the dark;* they can wound, and not be known. They can *whisper Thunder,* and passe an arrow through another mans eare, into mine heart; Let a man be zealous, and fervent in reprehension of sin, and there flies out an arrow, that gives him the wound of a *Puritan.* Let a man be zealous of the house of God, and say any thing by way of moderation, for the *repairing* of *the ruines* of that house, and *making up the differences* of the Church of God, and there flies out an arrow, that gives him the wound of a *Papist.* One shoots *East,* and another *West,* but both these arrows meet in *him,* that means well, to defame him. And this is the first misery in these arrows, these tentations, *Quia alienæ,* they are shot from others, they are not in our own quiver, nor in our own government.

Veloces

Another quality that tentations receive from the holy Ghosts Metaphore of *arrows* is, *Quia veloces,* because this captivity to sin, comes so swiftly, so impetuously upon us. Consider it first in our *making;* In the generation of *our parents,* we were *conceiv'd in sin;* that is, they sinn'd in that action; so we were conceiv'd in sinne; in *their sin.* And in *our selves,* we were submitted to sin, in that very act of generation, because then we became in part the subject of *Originall sin.* Yet, there was no arrow shot *into* us then; there was no sinne in that *substance* of which we were made; for if there had been sin in that *substance,* that substance might be damn'd, though God should never infuse a soul into it; and *that* cannot be said well then: God, whose goodnesse, and wisdome will have that substance to become a *Man,* he creates a *soul for it,* or creates a soul *in it,* (I dispute not *that*) he sends a light, or hee kindles a light, in that lanthorn; and here's no arrow shot neither; here's no sin in *that* soul, that God creates; for there God should create something that were *evill;* and that cannot be said: Here's no arrow shot from the body, no sin in the *body alone;* None from the soul, no sin in the *soul alone;* And yet, the *union* of this soul and body is so accompanied with Gods *malediction* for our first transgression, that in the instant of that *union* of life, as certainly as that *body must die,* so certainly *the whole Man* must be guilty of *Originall sin*. No man can tell me out of what *Quiver,* yet here is an arrow comes so swiftly, as that in the very first minute of our life, in our quickning in our mothers womb, wee become guilty of *Adams* sin done 6000 years before, and subject to all those arrows, *Hunger, Labour, Grief, Sicknesse,* and *Death,* which have been shot after it. This is the fearfull swiftnesse of this arrow, that *God himself* cannot get before it. In the first minute that my soul is infus'd, the Image of God is imprinted in my soul; so forward is God in my behalf, and so early does he visit me. But yet *Originall sin* is there, as soon as that Image of God is there. My soul is capable of *God,* as soon as it is capable of *sin;* and though sin doe not get the start of God, God does not get the start of sin neither. Powers, that dwell so far asunder, as *Heaven,* and *Hell, God* and the *Devill,* meet in an instant in my soul, in the minute of my quickning, and the Image of *God,* and the Image of *Adam,* Originall sin, enter into me at once, in one, and the same act. So swift is this arrow, *Originall sin,* from which, all arrows of subsequent tentations, are shot, as that God, who comes to my first minute of life, cannot come before death.

Invisibiles

And then, a third, and last danger, which we noted in our tentations, as they are represented by the holy Ghost, in this Metaphore of *arrows,* is, that they are *vix visibiles,* hardly discernible. 'Tis true, that tentations doe not light upon us, as *bullets,* that we cannot see them, till we feel them. An arrow comes not altogether so: but an arrow comes so, as that it is not discern'd, except we consider which way it comes, and watch it all the way. An arrow, that findes a man *asleep,* does not *wake* him first, and *wound* him after; A tentation that findes a man negligent, possesses him, before he sees it. *In gravissimis criminibus, confinia virtutum lædunt;* (Ambros.) This is it that undoes us, that vertues and vices are contiguous, and borderers upon one another; and very often, we can hardly tell, to which action the name of *vice,* and to which the name of *vertue* appertains. Many times, that which comes within an inch of a noble action, fals under the infamy of an odious treason; At many executions, half the company will call a man an *Heretique,* and half, a *Martyr*. How often, an excesse, makes a naturall affection, an unnaturall disorder? *Vtinam aut sororem non* (Idem) *amasset, Hamon, aut non vindicasset Absolon; Hamon* lov'd his sister *Tamar;* but a little too well; *Absolon* hated his brothers incest, but a little too ill. Though *love* be good, and *hate* be good, respectively, yet, says S. *Ambrose,* I would neither that love, nor that hate had gone so far. 1 Sam. 20 [21, 22] The contract between *Jonathan* and *David,* was, *If I say, The arrow* [is] *on this side of thee, all is wel; If I say, The arrow is beyond thee, thou art in an ill case.* If the arrow, the tentation, be yet on this side of thee, if it have not lighted upon thee, thou art well; God hath directed thy face to it, and thou may'st, if thou wilt, continue thy diligence, watch it, and avoid it. But if the arrow be beyond thee, and thou have cast it at thy back, in a forgetfulnesse, in a security of thy sin, thy case is dangerous. In all these respects, are these arrows, these infirmities, deriv'd from the sin of *Adam,* dangerous, as they are *alienæ,* in the hand of others, as they are *veloces,* swift in seising us, and as they are *vix visibiles,* hardly discern'd to be such; And these considerations fell within this first branch of this second part, *Thine arrows, tentations,* as they are arrows, *stick fast in me.*

Plures

These dangers are in them, as they are *sagittæ, arrows;* and would be so, if they were but *single* arrows; any *one* tentation would endanger us, any one tribulation would encumber us; but they are *plurall, arrows,* and *many arrows.* A man is not safe, because one arrow hath mist him; nor though he be free from *one* sin. Ios. 7.25 In the execution of *Achan,* all *Israel* threw stones at him, and stoned him. If *Achan* had had some brother, or cousin amongst them, that would have flung over, or short, or weakly, what good had that done him, when he must stand the mark for all the rest? All *Israel* must stone him. A little disposition towards some one vertue, may keep thee from some one tentation; Thou mayst think it pity to corrupt a chast soul, and forbear soliciting her; pity to oppresse a submitting wretch, and forbear to vex him; and yet practise, and that with hunger and thirst, other sins, or those sins upon other persons. But all *Israel* stones thee; arrows flie from every corner; and thy measure is not, [Luke 18.11] *to thank God, that thou art not as the Publican, as some other man,* but thy measure is, *to be pure and holy, as thy father in heaven is pure, and holy,* and to conform thy self in some measure, to thy pattern, Christ Jesus. Against him it is noted, that the Jews took up stones twice to stone him. Joh. 8.59 Once, when they did it, *He went away and hid himself.*

Our way to scape these arrows, these tentations, is to goe out of the way, to abandon all occasions, and conversation, that may lead into tentation. In the other place, Christ stands to it, and disputes it out [John] 10.31 with them, and puts them from it by the *scriptum est;* and that's our [–39] safe shield, since we must necessarily live in the way of tentations, (for *coluber in via,* there is a snake in every path, tentation in every [Gen. 49.17] calling) still to receive all these arrowes, upon the *shield of faith,* still to oppose the *scriptum est,* the faithfull promises of God, that he will give us the issue with the tentation, when we cannot avoid the tentation it self. Otherwise, these arrows are so many, as would tire, and wear out, all the diligence, and all the constancy of the best morall man. Wee finde many mentions in the Scriptures of filling of *quivers,* and emptying of *quivers,* and *arrows,* and *arrows,* still in the *plurall, many arrows.* But in all the Bible, I think, we finde not this word, (as it signifies tentation, or tribulation) in the *singular, one arrow,* any where, but once, where *David* cals it, *The arrow that flies by* Psal. 91.5 *day;* And is seen, that is, known by every man; for, for that, the Fathers, and Ancients runne upon that Exposition, that that one arrow common to all, that day-arrow visible to all, is the *naturall death;* (so the Chalde paraphrase calls it there expresly, *Sagitta mortis,* The arrow of death) which every man knows to belong to every man; (for, as clearly as he sees the Sunne set, he sees his death before his eyes.) Therefore it is such an arrow, as the Prophet does not say, *Thou shalt not feel,* but, *Thou shalt not feare the arrow that flies by day.* The arrow, the *singular* arrow that flies by day, is that arrow that fals upon every man, *death.* But every where in the Scriptures, but this one place, they are *plurall, many,* so many, as that we know not *whence,* nor *what* they are. Nor ever does any man receive one arrow alone, any one tentation, but that he receives another tentation, to hide that, though with another, and another sin. And the use of arrows in the war, was not so much to *kill,* as to *rout,* and *disorder* a battail; and upon that routing, followed *execution.* Every tentation, every tribulation is not *deadly.* But their multiplicity disorders us, discomposes us, unsettles us, and so hazards us. Not onely every *periodicall* variation of our years, *youth* and *age,* but every day hath a divers arrow, every houre of the day, a divers tentation. An old man wonders then, how an arrow from an eye could wound him, when he was young, and how *love* could make him doe those things which hee did *then;* And an arrow from the tongue of inferiour people, that which we make shift to call *honour,* wounds him deeper now; and *ambition* makes him doe as strange things now, as *love* did then; A fair day shoots arrows of *visits,* and *comedies,* and *conversation,* and so wee goe abroad: and a foul day shoots arrows of *gaming,* or *chambering,* and *wantonnesse,* and so we stay at home. Nay, the same sin shoots arrows of *presumption* in God, before it be committed, and of *distrust* and *diffidence* in God after; we doe not *fear* before, and we cannot *hope* after: And this is that misery from this *plurality,* and *multiplicity* of these arrows, these manifold tentations, which *David* intends here, and as often as he speaks in the same phrase of plurality, *vituli multi,* many buls, *canes multi,* many dogs, and *bellantes multi,* many warlike enemies, and *aquæ multæ,* many deep waters compasse me. For as it is said of the spirit of wisdome, that it is *unicus multiplex, manifoldly one, plurally singular:* so the spirit of tentation in every soul is *unicus multiplex,* singularly plurall, *rooted* in some *one* beloved sin, but derived into infinite branches of tentation.

Ps. 22.12, 16 [12, 16 : 13, 17 *F* as in Vulg.]

Wisd. 7.22

Fixæ

And then, these arrows *stick in us;* the raine fals, but that cold sweat hangs not upon us; Hail beats us, but it leaves no pock-holes in our skin. These arrows doe not so fall about us, as that they misse us; nor so hit us, as they rebound back without hurting us; But we complain with *Jeremy, The sons of his quiver are entred into our reins.* The Roman Translation reads that *filias, The daughters of his quiver;* If it were but so, *daughters,* we might limit these arrows in the signification of *tentations,* by the many occasions of tentation, arising from *that sex.* But the Originall hath it *filios,* the sons of his quiver, and therefore we consider these arrows in a stronger signification, *tribulations,* as well as *tentations; They stick in us.* Consider it but in one kinde, *diseases,* sicknesses. They stick to us so, as that we are not sure, that any old diseases mentioned in Physicians books are worn out, but that every year produces *new,* of which they have no mention, we are sure. We can scarce expresse the number, scarce sound the names of the diseases of mans body; 6000 year hath scarce taught us what they are, how they affect us, how they shall be cur'd in us, nothing, on this side the *Resurrection,* can teach us. They stick to us so, as that they passe by *inheritance,* and last more generations

Lam. 3.13

in families, then the inheritance it self does; and when no land, no Manor, when no title, no honour descends upon the heir, the stone, or the gout descends upon him. And as though our bodies had not *naturally diseases,* and infirmities enow, we contract more, inflict more, (and that, out of necessity too) in *mortifications,* and *macerations,* and *Disciplines* of this rebellious flesh. I must have this body with me to heaven, or else salvation it self is not perfect; And yet I cannot have this body thither, except as S. *Paul* did his, *I beat down this body,* attenuate this body by mortification; *Wretched man that I am, who shall deliver me from this body of death?* I have not body enough for my body, and I have too much body for my soul; not body enough, not bloud enough, not strength enough, to sustain my self in *health,* and yet body enough to destroy my soul, and frustrate the grace of God in that miserable, perplexed, riddling condition of man; sin makes the body of man miserable, and the remedy of sin, *mortification,* makes it miserable too; If we enjoy the good things of this world, *Duriorem carcerem præparamus,* wee doe but carry an other wall about our prison, an other story of unwieldy flesh about our souls; and if wee give our selves as much *mortification* as our body needs, we live a life of *Fridays,* and see no *Sabbath,* we make up our years of *Lents,* and see no other *Easters,* and whereas God meant us *Paradise,* we make all the world a *wildernesse.* Sin hath cast a curse upon all the creatures of the world, they are all worse then they were at first, and yet we dare not receive so much blessing, as is left in the creature, we dare not eat or drink, and enjoy them. The *daughters* of Gods quiver, and the *sons* of his quiver, the arrows of *tentation,* and the arrows of *tribulation,* doe so stick in us, that as he lives miserably, that lives in *sicknes,* and he as miserably, that lives in *physick:* so *plenty* is a misery, and *mortification* is a misery too; plenty, if we consider it in the *effects,* is a *disease,* a continuall sicknes, for it breeds diseases; And *mortification,* if we should consider it without the *effects,* is a disease too, a continuall hunger, and fasting; and if we consider it at best, and in the effects, mortification is but a *continuall physick,* which is misery enough.

1 Cor. 9 *ult.*

[Rom. 7.24]

Basil

They stick, and they *stick fast; altè infixæ;* every syllable aggravates our misery. Now for the most part, experimentally, we know not whether they stick fast or no, for we never goe about to pull them

Altè Infixæ

out: these arrows, these tentations, come, and welcome: we are so far from offering to pull them out, that we fix them faster and faster in us; we assist our tentations: yea, we take preparatives and fomentations, we supple our selves by *provocations,* lest our flesh should be of proof against these arrows, that death may enter the surer, and the deeper into us by them. And he that does in some measure, soberly and religiously, goe about to draw out these arrows, yet never consummates, never perfects his own work; He pulls back the arrow a little way, and he sees *blood,* and he feels *spirit* to goe out with it, and he lets it alone: He forbears his sinfull companions, a little while, and he feels a *melancholy* take hold of him, the spirit and life of his life decays, and he falls to those companions again. Perchance he rushes out the arrow with a sudden, and a resolved vehemence, and he leaves the head in his body: He forces a divorce from that sinne, he removes himself out of distance of that tentation; and yet he surfets upon cold meat, upon the sinfull remembrance of former sins, which is a dangerous rumination, and an unwholesome chawing of the cud; It is not an ill derivation of repentance, that *pœnitere* is *pœnam tenere;* that's true repentance, when we continue in those means, which may advance our repentance. When *Joash* the King of *Israel* came to visit *Elisha* upon his sick bed, and to consult with him about his war, *Elisha* bids the King smite the ground, and he smites it thrice, and ceases: Then the man of God was angry, and said, *Thou shouldst have smitten five or sixe times, and so thou shouldst have smitten thine enemies, till thou hadst consumed them.* Now, how much hast thou to doe, that hast not pull'd at this arrow at all yet? Thou must pull thrice and more, before thou get it out; Thou must *doe,* and *leave undone* many things, before thou deliver thy selfe of that arrow, that sinne that transports thee. One of these arrows was shot into Saint *Paul* himselfe, and it stuck, and stuck fast; whether an arrow of *tentation,* or an arrow of *tribulation,* the Fathers cannot tell; And therefore, wee doe now, (not inconveniently) all our way, in this exercise, mingle these two considerations, of tentation, and tribulation. Howsoever Saint *Paul* pull'd thrice at this arrow, and could not get it out; *I besought the Lord thrice,* says he, *that it might depart from mee.* But yet, *Joash* his thrice striking of the ground, brought him some victory; Saint *Pauls* thrice praying,

2 Reg. 13.18, 19

2 Cor. 12.7

brought him in that provision of *Grace,* which God cals *sufficient for him.* Once pulling at these arrows, a slight consideration of thy sins will doe no good. Do it *thrice;* testifie some true desire by such a diligence; Doe it now as thou sitt'st, doe it again at the *Table,* doe it again in thy *bed;* Doe it *thrice,* doe it in thy *purpose,* do it in thine *actions,* doe it in thy *constancy;* Doe it thrice, within the wals of thy *flesh,* in thy self, within the wals of thy *house* in thy family, and in a holy and *exemplar conversation* abroad, and God will accomplish *thy work,* which is *his work* in thee; And though the arrow be not utterly pull'd out, yet it shall not fester, it shall not *gangrene;* Thou shalt not be cut off from the body of Christ, in his Church here, nor in the Triumphant Church hereafter, how fast soever these arrows did stick upon thee before. God did not refuse *Israel* for her wounds, Esa. 1.6
and bruises, and putrefying sores, though from the sole of the foot, to the crown of the head, but because those wounds were not closed, nor bound up, nor suppled with ointments, therefore he refused her. God shall not refuse any soul, because it hath been shot with these arrows; Alas, God himself hath set us up *for a mark,* says *Job,* and [Job 7.20;
so says *Jeremy, against these arrows.* But that soul that can pour out 16.12]
floods of tears, for the losse, or for the absence, or for the unkindnes, Lam. 3.12
or imagination of an unkindness of a friend, mis-beloved, beloved a wrong way, and not afford one drop, one tear, to wash the wounds of these arrows, that soul that can squeaze the wound of Christ Jesus, and spit out his bloud in these blasphemous execrations, and shed no drop of this bloud upon the wounds of these arrows; that soul, and only that soul, that refuses a cure, does God refuse; not because they fell upon it, and stook, and stook fast, and stook long, but because they never, never went about to pull them out; never resisted a tentation, never lamented a transgression, never repented a recidivation.

Now this is more put home to us in the next addition, *Infixæ mihi,* *Mihi*
they stick, and stick fast, *in mee,* that is, *in all mee.* That that sins must be sav'd or damn'd; That's not the soul alone, nor body alone, but *all,* the whole man. God is the God of *Abraham,* as he is the God of the living; Therefore *Abraham* is alive; And *Abraham* is not alive, if his body be not alive; Alive *actually* in the person of *Christ;* alive in an *infallible assurance* of a particular resurrection. Whatsoever belongs to *thee,* belongs to thy *body* and *soul;* and these arrows stick

fast *in thee;* In *both*. Consider it in both; in things belonging to the body and to the soul; We need clothing; Baptisme is Gods Wardrobe; there *Induimur Christo;* In Baptisme we put on Christ; there we are invested, apparell'd in Christ; And there comes an arrow, that cuts off

2 Sam. 10.4

half our garment, (as *Hanon* did *Davids* servants) A tentation that makes us think, it is enough to be *baptized,* to professe the name of Christ; for *Papist,* or *Protestant,* it is but the *train* of the garment, matter of *civility,* and *policy,* and *government,* and may be cut off, and the garment remain still. So we need *meat, sustenance,* and then an arrow comes, a tentation meets us, *Edite, & bibite, Eat and drink, to morrow you shall die;* That there is no life, but this life, no blessednesse but in worldly abundances. If we need *physick,* and God offer us his physick, medicinall corrections, there flies an arrow, a tentation, *Medice cura*

[Luke 4.23]

teipsum, that hee whom wee make our Physician, died himselfe, of an infamous disease, that Christ Jesus from whom we attend our salvation, could not save himself. In our clothing, in our diet, in our physick, things which carry our consideration upon the *body,* these arrowes stick fast in us, in that part of us. So in the more spirituall actions of our souls too. In our *alms* there are *trumpets* blowne, there's an arrow of *vaine-glory;* In our *fastings,* there are *disfigurings,* there's an arrow of *Hypocrisie;* In our *purity,* there is contempt of others, there's an arrow of *pride;* In our *coming* to Church, there is *custome* and *formality;* In *hearing Sermons,* there is *affection* to the parts of the Preacher. In our sinfull actions these arrows abound; In our best actions they lie hid; And as thy soul is in every part of thy body; so these arrows are in every part of thee, body, and soul; they stick, and stick fast, in thee, in all thee.

Manus

And yet there is another weight upon us, in the Text, there is still a *Hand* that follows the blow, and presses it, *Thy hand presses me sore;* so the Vulgat read it, *Confirmasti super me manum tuam, Thy hand is settled upon mee;* and the Chalde paraphrase carries it farther then, to *Mansit super me vulnus manus tuæ;* Thy hand hath wounded mee, and that hand keeps the wound open. And in this sense the Apostle says, *It is a fearfull thing to fall into the hands of*

Heb. 10.31

the living God. But as God leaves not his children without *correction,* so he leaves them not without *comfort,* and therefore it behoves us to consider his hand upon these arrows, more then one way.

Tua ut afflictio

First, because his hand is upon the arrow, it shall certainly hit the mark; Gods purpose cannot be disappointed. If men, and such men, *left-handed men,* and so many, 700 left-handed men, and so many of *one Tribe,* 700 *Benjamites,* could sling stones at a hairs breadth, and Iud. 20.16 not fail, God is a better *Mark-man* then the left-handed Benjamites; his arrows alwayes hit as he intends them. Take them then for *tribulation,* his hand is upon them; Though they come from the *malice* of *men,* his hand is upon them. S. *Ambrose* observes, that in afflictions, Gods hand, and the Devils are but one hand. *Stretch out thy hand,* [Job 1.11–12] says Satan to God, concerning *Job;* And, *all that he hath is in thy* [Job 2.5–6] *hand,* says God to Satan. *Stretch out thy hand, and touch his bones,* says Satan again to God; And again, God to Satan, *He is in thy hand, but touch not his life.* A difference may be, that when Gods purpose is but to punish, as he did *Pharaoh,* in those severall premonitory plagues, there it is *Digitus Dei;* It was but a *finger,* and Exod. 8.19 Gods finger. When *Balshazzar* was absolutely to be destroyed, there Dan. 5.5 were *Digiti,* and *Manus hominis,* mens fingers, and upon a mans hand. The arrows of men are ordinarily more venimous, and more piercing, then the arrows of God. But as it is in that story of *Elisha,* 2 Reg. 13. [16,] 17 and *Joash,* The Prophet bade the King shoot, but *Elisha* laid his hand upon the Kings hand; So from what instrument of Satan soever, thy affliction come, Gods hand is upon *their hand* that shoot it, and though it may *hit* the mark according to *their* purpose, yet it hath the *effect,* and it *works* according to *his.*

Yea, let this arrow be considered as a *tentation,* yet *his* hand is upon *Tua ut Peccatum* it; at least God *sees* the shooting of it, and yet *lets* it flie. Either hee *tries* us by these arrows, what proof we are; Or he *punishes* us by those arrows of new sins, for our former sins; and so, when he hath lost one arrow, he shoots another. He shoots a *sermon,* and that arrow is lost; He shoots a *sicknesse,* and that arrow is lost; He shoots a *sin;* not that *he* is *authour* of any sin, as *sin;* but as *sin is a punishment* of sin, he *concurs* with it. And so he shoots arrow after arrow, permits sin after sin, that at last some sin, that draws affliction with it, might bring us to understanding; for that word, in which the Prophet here expresses this sticking, and this fast sticking of these arrows, which is *Nachath,* is here, (as the Grammarians in that language call it) in *Niphal, figere factæ,* they were made to stick; Gods hand is upon them, the *work* is his, the *arrows* are his, and the *sticking* of them is his, whatsoever, and whosesoever they be.

Tua ut Medicamenta

His hand shoots the arrow, as it is a *tribulation*, he *limits* it, whosoever inflict it. His hand shoots it, as it is a *tentation;* He *permits* it, and he orders it, whosoever offer it. But it is especially from his hand, as it hath a *medicinall nature* in it; for in every *tentation*, and every *tribulation*, there is a *Catechisme*, and *Instruction;* nay, there is a *Canticle*, a *love-song*, an *Epithalamion*, a *mariage song* of God, to our souls, wrapped up, if wee would open it, and read it, and learn that new tune, that musique of God; So when thou hear'st *Nathans* words

2 Sam. 12.14

to *David, The child that is born unto thee, shall surely die*, (let that signifie, the children of thy labour, and industry, thy *fortune*, thy *state* shall perish) so when thou hear'st Gods word to *David, Choose*

2 Sam. 24. [12, 13]

famine, or war, or pestilence, for the people, (let that signifie, those that depend upon thee, shal perish) so when thou hear'st *Esays* words

Esa. 38.[1]

to *Hezekiah, Put thy house in order, for thou shalt die*, (let that signifie, thou thy self in person shalt perish) so when thou hear'st all the judgements of God, as they lie in the body of the Scriptures, so the applications of those judgements, by Gods Ministers, in these services, upon emergent occasions, all these are arrows shot by the hand of God, and that child of God, that is accustomed to the voice, and to the ear of God, to speak with him in *prayer*, when God speaks to him, in any such voice here, as that to *David*, or *Hezekiah*, though

Job 41.28 [28 : 19 *F* as in Vulg.]

this be a shooting of arrows, *Non fugabit eum vir sagittarius, The arrow*, (as we read it) *The Archer*, (as the Romane Edition reades it) cannot make that child of God afraid, afraid with a distrustfull fear, or make him loth to come hither again to hear more, how close soever Gods arrow, and Gods archer, that is, his word in his servants mouth, come to that Conscience now, nor make him mis-interpret that which he does hear, or call that *passion* in the Preacher, in which the Preacher is but *sagittarius Dei*, the deliverer of Gods arrows; for Gods arrows, are *sagittæ Compunctionis*, arrows that draw bloud from the eyes; Tears of repentance from *Mary Magdalen*, and from

Confess. l. 9, c. 2

Peter; And when from thee? There is a *probatum est* in S. *Augustine*, *Sagittaveras cor meum*, Thou hast shot at my heart; and how wrought that? To the withdrawing of his tongue, *à nundinis loquacitatis*, from that market in which I sold my self, (for S. *Augustine* at that time taught *Rhetorique*) to turn the stream of his eloquence, and all his other good parts, upon the service of God in his Church. You may have read, or heard that answer of a *Generall,* who was threatned with that danger, that his enemies arrows were so many, as that they would cover the Sun from him; *In umbra pugnabimus;* All the better, says he, for then we shall fight in the shadow. Consider all the arrows of *tribulation,* even of *tentation,* to be directed by the hand of God, and never doubt to fight it out with God, to lay violent hands upon heaven, to wrastle with God for a blessing, to charge and presse God upon his contracts and promises, for *in umbra pugnabis,* though the clouds of these arrows may hide all suns of worldly comforts from thee, yet thou art still *under the shadow of his wings.* Nay, thou are still, for all this shadow, in the light of his countenance. To which purpose there is an excellent use of this Metaphor of arrows, *Habakkuk* 3. 11. where it is said, that *Gods servants shall have the light of his arrows, and the shining of his glittering spear:* that is, the light of his presence, in all the instruments, and actions of his corrections.

Christus

To end all, and to dismisse you with such a re-collection, as you may carry away with you; literally, primarily, this text concerns *David:* He by *tentations* to sin, by *tribulations* for sin, by *comminations,* and *increpations* upon sin, was bodily, and ghostly become a quiver of arrows of all sorts; they *stook,* and stook *fast,* and stook *full* in him, in *all* him. The Psalm hath a *retrospect* too, it looks back to *Adam,* and to every particular man in his loines, and so, *Davids* case is our case, and all these arrowes stick in all us. But the Psalm and the text hath also a *prospect,* and hath a *propheticall* relation from *David* to our Saviour Christ Jesus. And of him, and of the multiplicity of these arrows upon him in the exinanition, and evacuation of himself, in this world for us, have many of the *Ancients* interpreted these words literally, and as in their first and primary signification; Turne we therefore to *him,* before we goe, and he shall return home with us. How our first part of this text is applyable to *him,* that our prayers to God, for ease in afflictions, may be grounded upon reasons, out of the sense of those afflictions, Saint *Basil* tels us, that Christ therefore prays to his Father now in heaven, to spare mankinde, because man had suffered so much, and drunk so deep of the bitter cup of his anger, in his person and passion before: It is an avoidable plea, from Christ in heaven, for us, *Spare them O Lord in themselves, since thou didst not spare them in me.* And how far he was from sparing thee, we see in all those severall weights which have aggravated his hand, and these arrowes upon us: If they be heavy upon us, much more was their weight upon *thee,* every *dram* upon us was a *Talent* [Lam. 1.12] upon thee, *Non dolor sicut dolor tuus,* take *Rachel* weeping for her children, *Mary* weeping for her brother *Lazarus, Hezekiah* for his health, *Peter* for his sins, *Non est dolor sicut dolor tuus.* The arrows *Alienæ* that were shot at thee, were *Alienæ,* Afflictions that belonged to *others;* and did not onely come from *others,* as ours doe; but they were *alienæ* so, as that they should have fallen upon others; And *all* that should have fallen upon all others, were shot at *thee,* and lighted upon thee. Lord, though we be not capable of sustaining that part, this *passion for* others, give us *that,* which we may receive, *Compas-* *Veloces* *sion with* others. They were *veloces,* these arrows met swiftly upon thee; from the sin of *Adam* that induced *death,* to the sin of the last man, that shall not sleep, but be changed, when thy hour came they came all upon thee, in that hour. Lord put this swiftnesse into our sins, that in this one minute, in which our eyes are open towards thee, and thine eares towards us, our sins, all our sins, even from the *impertinent frowardnesse of our childhood,* to the *unsufferable frowardnesse of our age,* may meet in our present *confessions,* and *repentances,* and never appear more. They were (as ours are too) *Invisibiles* *Invisibiles;* Those arrows which fell upon thee, were so *invisible,* so undiscernible, as that to this day, thy Church, thy School cannot see, what kinde of arrow thou tookest into thy soul, what kinde of [Mat. 26.37, 38; Mark 14.33, 34] affliction it was, that made thy *soul heavy unto death,* or dissolved thee into a gelly of blood in thine agony. Be thou O Lord, a Father of Lights unto us, in all our ways and works of darkenes; manifest unto us, whatsoever is necessary for us to know, and be a light of *understanding* and *grace* before, and a light of *comfort* and *mercy* after any sin hath benighted us. These arrows were, as *ours* are also, *Plures* *plures,* plurall, many, infinite; they were the sins of some that shall never thank thee, never know that thou borest their sins, never know that they had any such sins to bee born. Lord teach us to number thy corrections upon us, so, as still to see thy torments suffered for us, and our own sins to be infinitely more that occasioned those torments, then those corrections that thou layst upon us. Thine arrows *stook* and *stook fast in thee;* the weight of thy torments, thou wouldest not cast off, nor lessen, when at thy execution they offered thee, that stupefying drink, (which was the civill charity of those times to condemned persons, to give them an easier passage, in the agonies of death) thou wouldest not tast of that cup of ease. Deliver us, O Lord, in all our tribulations, from turning to the miserable comforters of this world, or from wishing or accepting any other deliverance, then may improve and make better our Resurrection. These arrows were in *thee,* in *all thee:* from thy *Head* torn with thorns, to thy *feet* pierced with nayls; and in thy *soul* so as we know not how, so as to extort a *Si possibile, If it be possible let this cup passe,* and an *Vt quid dereliquisti, My God, my God, why hast thou forsaken me?* Lord, whilest we remain entire here, in body and soul, make us, and receive us an entire sacrifice to thee, in directing body and soul to thy glory, and when thou shalt be pleased to take us in pieces by death, receive our souls to thee, and lay up our bodies for thee, in consecrated ground, and in a *Christian buryall.* And lastly, thine arrows were followed, and *pressed with the hand of God; The hand of God pressed upon thee,* in that *eternall decree,* in that *irrevocable contract,* between thy *Father* and *thee,* in that *Oportuit pati, That all that thou must suffer, and so enter into thy glory.* Establish us, O Lord, in all occasions of diffidences here; and when thy hand presses our arrows upon us, enable us to see, that *that* very hand, hath from all eternity written, and written in thine own blood, a *decree* of the *issue,* as well, and as soon, as of the *tentation.* In which confidence of which decree, as men, in the virtue thereof already in possession of heaven, we joyn with that Quire in that service, in that *Anthem, Blessing, and glory, and wisdome, and thanksgiving, and honour, and power, and might, be unto our God for ever, and ever,* Amen.

Fixæ

Mar. 15.23

[Mat. 26.39]

[Mat. 27.46; Mark 15.34]

[Luke 24.46]

Apoc. 7.11, 12

Number 2.

Preached at Lincolns Inne.

PSAL. 38.3. *THERE IS NO SOUNDNESSE IN MY FLESH, BECAUSE OF THINE ANGER, NEITHER IS THERE ANY REST IN MY BONES, BECAUSE OF MY SINNE.*

IN THAT which is often reported to you, out of Saint *Hierome, Titulus clavis,* that the title of the Psalme, is the key of the Psalm, there is this good use, That the book of Psalms is a *mysterious* book; and, if we had not a lock, every man would thrust in, and if we had not a key, we could not get in our selves. Our lock is the *analogy* of the *Christian faith;* That wee admit no other sense, of any place in any Psalm, then may consist with the *articles* of the *Christian faith;* for so, no *Heretique,* no *Schismatique,* shall get in by any countenance of any place in the Psalms: and then our key is, that intimation which we receive in the *title* of the Psalm, what *duty* that Psalm is principally directed upon; and so we get into the understanding of the Psalm, and profiting by the Psalm. Our key in this Psalm, given us in the title thereof, is, that it is *Psalmus ad Recordationem,* a Psalm of Remembrance; The faculty that is awakened here, is our *Memory.* That plurall word *nos,* which was used by God, in the making of Man, when God said *Faciamus, Let us, us make man, according to our image,* as it intimates a plurality, a concurrence of all the Trinity in our making, so doth it also a *plurality in that image of God,* which was then imprinted in us; As God, one *God* created us, so wee have a soul, *one soul,* that represents, and is some image of that one God; As the three Persons of the *Trinity* created us, so we have, in our one soul, a *threefold impression* of that image, and, as Saint *Bernard* calls it, *A trinity from the Trinity,* in those *three*

[Gen. 1.26]

faculties of the soul, the *Vnderstanding,* the *Will,* and the *Memory.* God calls often upon the first faculty, *O that this people would but understand;* But understand? *Inscrutabilia judicia tua; Thy judgements are unsearchable, and thy ways past finding out;* [Rom. 11.33] And, *oh that this people would not goe about to understand those unrevealed decrees, and secrets of God.* God calls often upon the other faculty, the *Will* too, and complaines of the stiffe perversnesse, and opposition of *that.* Through all the Prophets runs that charge, *Noluerunt,* and *Noluerunt, they would not, they refused me. Noluerunt audire,* says God in *Esay; They are rebellious children, that will not hear.* [Isa.] 30.9 *Domus Israel noluit,* says God to *Ezekiel, The house of Israel will not hear* [Ezek.] 3.7 *thee;* not *Thee,* not the *minister;* That's no marvail; it is added by God there, *Noluit me, they will not hear me. Noluerunt erubescere,* [Jer.] 3.3 says God to *Ieremy, They will not be ashamed of their former ways,* And therefore *Noluerunt reverti, They will not return to better ways:* [Jer.] 5.3 Hee that is past shame of sin, is past recovery from sin. So Christ continues that practise, and that complaint in the Gospel too, He Mat. 22.3 sends forth his servants, (*us*) to call them, that were bidden, *Et noluerunt venire,* and they would not come upon their call; Hee [Mat.] 23.37 comes *himself,* and would *gather them, as a hen her chickens, and they would not;* Their fault is not laid in this, that they had no such faculty, as a *will,* (for then their not coming were not their fault) but that they perverted that will. Of our perversenesse in both faculties, *understanding,* and *will,* God may complain, but as much of our *memory;* for, for the rectifying of the *will,* the *understanding* must be rectified; and that implies great difficulty: But the *memory* is so familiar, and so present, and so ready a faculty, as will always answer, if we will but speak to it, and aske it, *what God hath done for us, or for others.* The art of *salvation,* is but the art of *memory.* When God gave his people the *Law,* he proposes nothing to them, but by that way, to their memory; *I am the Lord your God, which brought you* Exod. 20.[2] *out of the land of Egypt;* Remember but that. And when we expresse Gods mercy to us, we attribute but that faculty to God, that he *remembers* us; *Lord, what is man, that thou art mindfull of him?* Ps. 8.4 And when God works so upon us, as that *He makes his wonderfull* [Ps.] 111.4 *works to be had in remembrance,* it is as great a mercy, as the very doing of those wonderfull works was before. It was a *seal* upon a *seal,*

a seal of *confirmation*, it was a *sacrament* upon a *sacrament*, when in instituting the *sacrament* of his *body and his bloud*, Christ presented
Luc 22.19
it so, *Doe this in remembrance of me. Memorare novissima*, remember the *last* things, and *fear* will keep thee from sinning; *Memorare præterita*, remember the *first* things, what God hath done for thee, and *love*, (love, which, mis-placed, hath transported thee upon many sins) love will keep thee from sinning. *Plato* plac'd *all learning* in the memory; wee may place *all Religion* in the memory too: All knowledge, that seems new to day, says *Plato*, is but a remembring of *that*, which your soul knew before. All instruction, which we can give you to day, is but the remembring you of the mercies of God, which have been *new every morning*. Nay, he that hears no Sermons, he that reads no Scriptures, hath the Bible without book; He hath a *Genesis* in his *memory*; he cannot forget his *Creation*; he hath an *Exodus* in his memory; he cannot forget that God hath delivered him, from some kind of *Egypt*, from some oppression; He hath a *Leviticus* in his memory; hee cannot forget, that God hath proposed to him some Law, some rules to be observed. He hath *all* in his memory, even to the *Revelation*; God hath *revealed* to him, *even at midnight alone*, what shall be his portion, in the next world; And if he dare but remember that nights communication between God and him, he is well-near learned enough. There may be enough in *remembring our selves*; but sometimes, that's the hardest of all; many times we are farthest off from our selves; most forgetfull of our selves. It was a narrow enlargement, it was an addition that diminish'd the sense, when our former Translators added that word, *themselves; All the*
Ps. 22.27
world shall remember themselves; there is no such particularity, as *themselves*, in that text; But it is onely, as our later Translators have left it, *All the world shall remember*, and no more; Let them remember what they will, what they can, let them but remember thoroughly, and then as it follows there, *They shall turn unto the Lord, and all the kindreds of the Nations shall worship him*. Therefore *David* makes *that* the key into this Psalme; *Psalmus ad Recordationem*, A *Psalm for Remembrance*. Being lock'd up in a close prison, of multiplied calamities, this turns the key, this opens the door, this restores him to liberty, if he can *remember*. *Non est sanitas, there is no soundnesse, no health in my flesh*; Doest thou wonder at *that*? Remember

thy selfe, and thou wilt see, that thy case is worse then so; *That there is no rest in thy bones.* That's true too; But doest thou wonder at *that?* Remember thy self, and thou wilt see the cause of all that, *The Lord is angry with thee;* Find'st thou *that* true, and wondrest *why* the Lord should be angry with thee? Remember thy self well, and thou wilt see, it is *because of thy sins, There is no soundnesse in my flesh, because of thine anger, neither is there any rest in my bones, because of my sinne.* So have I let you in, into the whole Psalm, by this key, by awaking your memory, that it is a *Psalm for Remembrance:* And *that* that you are to remember, is, that all calamities, that fall upon you, fall not from the malice or power of man, but from the anger of God; And then, that Gods anger fals not upon you, from his *Hate,* or his *Decree,* but from *your sins, There is no soundnesse in my flesh, because of thine anger, neither is there any rest in my bones, because of my sinne.*

Divisio

Which words we shall first consider, as they are our present object, as they are historically, and literally to be understood of *David;* And secondly, in their *retrospect,* as they look back upon the first *Adam,* and so concern *Mankind collectively,* and so *you,* and *I,* and all have our portion in these calamities; And thirdly, we shall consider them in their *prospect,* in their future relation to the *second Adam,* in *Christ Jesus,* in whom also all mankinde was collected, and the calamities of all men had their *Ocean* and their confluence, and the cause of them, the anger of God was more declared, and the cause of that anger, that is sin, did more abound, for the sins of all the world were *his,* by imputation; for this Psalm, some of our Expositors take to be a *historicall,* and *personall* Psalm, determin'd in *David;* some, a *Catholique,* and *universall* Psalm, extended to the whole condition of *man;* and some a *Propheticall,* and *Evangelicall* Psalm, directed upon *Christ.* None of them inconveniently; for we receive help and health, from every one of these acceptations; first, *Adam* was the *Patient,* and so, his promise, the promise that he received of a *Messiah,* is our *physick;* And then *David* was the *Patient,* and there, his *Example* is our *physick;* And lastly, *Christ Jesus* was the *Patient,* and so, his *blood* is our physick. In *Adam* we shall finde the *Scriptum est,* the medicine is in our books, an assurance of a Messiah there is; In *David* we shall find the *Probatum est,* that this medicine wrought upon *David;* and in *Christ* we finde the receit it self; Thus you may take this physick, thus you may apply it to your selves. In every acceptation, as we consider it in *David,* in *our selves,* in *Christ,* we shall consider first, That specification of humane misery and calamity, expressed here, *sicknesse,* and an *universall sicknesse; No soundnesse in the flesh:* And more then that, *trouble,* and an *universall trouble; No peace, no rest, not in the bones.* And then in a second branch, we shall see, that those calamities proceed from the *anger of God;* we cannot discharge them, upon *Nature,* or *Fortune,* or *Power,* or *Malice* of *Men* or *Times;* They are from the *anger of God,* and they are, as the Originall Text hath it, *à facie iræ Dei,* from the face of the anger of God, from that anger of God that hath a *face,* that looks upon *something in us,* and growes not out of a *hate* in God, or *decree* of God against us. And then lastly, this that Gods anger lookes upon is *sin;* God is not angry till he see sin; nor with *me,* till it come to be *my sinne;* and though *Originall sinne* be my *sinne,* and *sicknesse,* and *death* would follow, though there were no more but *Originall sinne,* yet God comes not to this, *Non sanitas, No soundnesse in my flesh,* nor to this, *Non pax, No rest in my bones,* till I have made sinne, *my sinne,* by *act,* and *habit* too, by *doing* it, and *using to doe it.* But then, though it bee but *Peccatum* in the singular, (so the Text hath it) *One sinne,* yet for that *one beloved sinne,* especially when that my *sinne* comes to have a *face,* (for so, the Originall phrase is in this place too, *à facie peccati,* from the face of my sinne) when my sin looks bigge, and justifies it self, then come these calamities, *No soundnesse in the flesh, no rest in the bones,* to their heighth, because the anger of God which exalts them, is in the exaltation: *There is no soundnesse in my flesh, because of thine anger, neither any rest in my bones, because of my sin.*

1. Part

All these particulars will best arise to us in our second consideration, when wee consider, *Humanitatem,* not *Hominem,* our humane condition, as we are all kneaded up in *Adam,* and not this one person *David.* But because we are in the consideration of *health,* and consequently of *physick,* (for the true and proper use of physick, is to *preserve* health, and, but by accident to restore it) we embrace that Rule, *Medicorum theoria experientia est, Practise is a Physicians study;* and he concludes out of events: for, says he, He that professes

Paracels.

himself a Physician, without experience, *Chronica de futuro scribit,* He undertakes to write a Chronicle of things before they are done, which is an irregular, and a perverse way. Therefore, in this spirituall physick of the soul, we will deal upon *Experience* too, and see first, how this wrought upon this *particular person,* upon *David.*

David durst not presume, that God could not, or would not bee angry. Anger is not always a *Defect,* nor an *inordinatenesse in man; Be angry, and sin not:* anger is not utterly to be rooted out of our Ephes. 4.26 *ground,* and cast away, but *transplanted;* A Gardiner does wel to grub up thornes in his garden; there they would hinder good herbes from growing; but he does well to plant those thorns in his hedges, there they keep bad neighbours from entring. In many cases, where there is no *anger,* there is not much *zeal. David* himself came to a high exaltation in this passion of *anger.* He was ordinarily so meek, as that that which we translate *afflictions,* the Vulgat Edition translates *meeknesse,* and *patience* in his afflictions. *Remember David and all his afflictions,* says our translation; and *Memento David & omnis* Psal. 132.1 *mansuetudinis ejus,* say they, *Remember David, and all his mildnesse.* How mildly he endured *Ioabs* insultation? *Thou lovest,* says *Ioab,* 2 Sam. 19.6 *thine enemies, and thou hatest thy friends;* Bitterly spoken; *Come* [and 7] *out, and speak comfortably,* says *Ioab,* or, *I swear by the Lord, there will not tarry a man with thee this night;* Seditiously spoken; And *David* obeyed him. How mildly he endured *Shimei's* cursing? He 2 Sam. 16.5 cast stones at him, and at all his servants; He charges him with murder; and, that which is heaviest of all, he cals *Absolons rebellion, a judgement of God;* and *David* accepts it so, and says, *The Lord hath bidden him to curse David.* And yet this exemplar mild man, *David* himself, upon a scorn offered to him by *Hanun* in the abuse of his Ambassadours, goes himself in person, into a dangerous war, against the Ammonites, assisted with 32000 chariots of their neighbours the 2 Sam. 10 Aramites, and there he destroys those great numbers, which are mentioned in that story: and after this defeat, in cold blood, he goes out 1 Chron. 20 against them, that had assisted them; He takes the City *Rabbah,* and the people he cuts with Saws, and with Harrows of iron, and with Axes; *David* saw that a mild man can grow angry, and that a fire that is long kindling, burns most vehemently. That which is an Adage, and Proverb now, was ever true in substance, *Ab inimico flegmatico libera me Domine;* from him that is long before hee be angry, for he is long before hee be reconciled again. Gods goodnesse hath that disposition, to bee long suffering; mans ilnesse and abuse of that, is able to inflame God. So *Davids* sin had inflamed him; and the fire of Gods anger produced the calamities of this text upon him: which our Expositors ordinarily take to have been historically this, 2 Sam. 24.17 that when *David* had provoked God, with that sinfull confidence in *numbring his people,* when Gods anger was executed in that *devouring plague,* and *David* saw the persecuting Angel, then *à facie iræ Domini,* from that face, that manifestation of Gods anger, he fell into 1 Reg. 1.[1] that dampe, and dead cold, that howsoever they covered him, they could never get heat in him: And this was the sin, say our Expositors, and this was the *anger,* and this was the *manifestation,* and this was the *disease* that *David* complains of here. And be this enough of the personall acceptation of these words; *There is no soundness in my flesh, because of thine anger, neither is there rest in my bones, because of my sinne;* for in their second acceptation as they are referred to the miserable condition of all *mankinde* by sinne, the particulars which we laid down before, will fall into more particular consideration.

2. Part *Miseria* In this second part, first we contemplate *man,* as the Receptacle, the Ocean of all misery. Fire and Aire, Water and Earth, are not the Elements of man; Inward decay, and outward violence, bodily pain, and sorrow of heart may be rather styled his Elements; And though he be destroyed by these, yet he consists of nothing but these. As the good qualities of all creatures are not for their own use, (for the *Sun* sees not his own glory, nor the *Rose* smells not her own breath: but all their good is for *man*) so the ill conditions of the creature, are not directed upon themselves, (the Toad poisons not it selfe, nor does the Viper bite it self) but all their ill powrs down upon *man.* As though man could be a *Microcosm,* a world in himself, no other way, except all the misery of the world fell upon him. *Adam* was able to decypher the nature of every Creature in the *name* thereof, and the Holy Ghost hath decyphered his in his *name* too; In all those names that the Holy Ghost hath given man, he hath declared him miserable, Gen. 5.2 for, *Adam,* (by which name God calls him, and *Eve* too) signifies but *Redness,* but a *Blushing:* and whether we consider their low

materials, as it was but *earth,* or the *redness* of that earth, as they stained it with their own blood, and the blood of all their posterity, and as they drew another more precious blood, the blood of the Messias upon it, every way *both* may be *Adam,* both may *blush.* So God called that pair, our first Parents, man in that root, *Adam:* But the first name, by which God called man in generall, *mankinde,* is *Ish, Therefore shall a man leave his Father, &c.* And *Ish,* is but *à sonitu,* (Gen. 2.24) *à rugitu:* Man hath his name from *crying,* and the occasion of *crying, misery,* testified in his entrance into the world, for he is *born crying;* and our very Laws presume, that if he be alive, he will cry, and if he be not heard cry, conclude him to be born dead. And where man is called *Gheber,* (as he is often) which is derived from *Greatness,* man is but great so, as that word signifies; It signifies a Giant, an *oppressour,* Great in power, and in a delight to doe great mischiefs upon others, or *Great,* as he is a *Great mark,* and easily hit by others. But man hath a fourth name too in Scripture, *Enosh,* and that signifies nothing but *misery.* When *David* says, *Put them in fear O Lord,* (Psal. 9.20) *that the Nations may know they are but men;* there's that name *Enosh,* that they are but miserable things. *Adam* is *Blushing, Ish* is *lamenting, Geber* is *oppressing, Enosh* is *all* that; but especially that, which is especially notified for the misery in our Text, *Enosh* is *Homo æger,* a man miserable, in particular, by the misery of *sicknesse,* which is our next step, *Non sanitas, There is no soundnesse, no health in me.*

God created man in health, but health continued but a *few hours,* (*Morbus*) and sicknesse hath had the Dominion 6000 years. But was man impassible before the fall? Had there been no sicknesse, if there had been no sinne? *Secundum passiones perfectivas,* we acknowledge in (Aquin.) the School, man was passible before: Every *alteration* is in a degree a *passion,* a *suffering;* and so, in those things which conduced to his *well-being, eating,* and *sleeping,* and other such, man was *passible:* that is, subject to *alteration;* But, *Secundum passiones destructivas,* to such sufferings, as might frustrate the end for which he was made, which was *Immortality,* he was not subject, and so, not to sicknesse. Now he is; and put all the miseries, that man is subject to, together, *sicknesse* is more then all. It is the *immediate* sword of God. *Phalaris* could invent a Bull; and others have invented Wheels and Racks; but no persecutor could ever invent a *sicknesse* or a way to inflict a *sicknesse* upon a condemned man: To a *galley* he can send him, and to the *gallows,* and command execution that hour; but to a *quartane fever,* or to a *gout,* hee cannot condemn him. In *poverty* I lack but other things; In *banishment* I lack but other men; But in *sicknesse,* I lack my *self.* And, as the greatest misery of war, is, when our own Country is made the seat of the war; so is it of *affliction,* when *mine own Body* is made the subject thereof. How shall I put a just value upon Gods great *blessings* of *Wine,* and *Oyle,* and *Milke,* and *Honey,* when my tast is gone, or of *Liberty,* when the *gout* fetters my feet? The King may release me, and say, *Let him goe whither he will,* but God says, *He shall not goe till I will.* God hath wrapped up all misery, in that condemnation, *Morte morietur,* That the sinner shall *die twice:* But if the *second death* did not follow, the *first death* were an ease, and a blessing in many sicknesses. And no sicknesse can be worse, then that which is intended here, for it is all over, *Non sanitas, no soundnesse,* no health in any part.

[Mat. 15.4; Mark 7.10; Gen. 26.11; etc.]

Non sanitas

This consideration arises not onely from the Physicians Rule, that the best state of Mans body is but a *Neutrality,* neither well nor ill, but *Nulla sanitas,* a state of true and exquisit health, say they, no man hath. But not onely out of this strictnesse of *Art,* but out of an acknowledgment of *Nature,* we must say, *sanitas hujus vitæ, bene intelligentibus, sanitas non est;* It is but our mistaking, when we call any thing *Health.* But why so? *fames naturalis morbus est;* Hunger is a sicknesse; And that's naturally in us all. *Medicamentum famis cibus, & potus sitis, & fatigationis somnus;* when *I eate,* I doe but take Physique for *Hunger,* and for *thirst,* when I *drink,* and so is sleep my physique for *wearinesse. Detrahe medicamentum, & interficient;* forbeare but these Physiques, and these diseases, *Hunger,* and *thirst,* and *wearinesse,* will kill thee. And as this sickness is upon us *all,* and so *non sanitas,* there is no Health, in *none* of us, so it is upon us all, *at all times,* and so *Non sanitas,* there is *never* any soundness in us: for, *semper deficimus;* we are *Borne* in a *Consumption,* and as *little* as we are then, we grow less from that time. *Vita cursus ad mortem;* Before we can craule, we runne to meet death; *& urgemur omnes pari passu:* Though some are cast forward to death, by the use, which others have of their ruine, and so throw them, through

Augustin

Augustin

Discontents, into desperate enterprises; and some are drawn forward to death, by false *Markes,* which they have set up to their own Ambitions; and some are spurred forward to death, by sharp *Diseases* contracted by their own intemperance, and licentiousness; and some are whip'd forward to death, by the *Miseries,* and *penuries* of this life: take away all these accidentall furtherances to death, this drawing, and driving, and spurring, and whipping, *pari passu urgemur omnes,* we bring all with us into the world, that which carries us out of the world, a naturall, unnaturall consuming of that radicall vertue, which sustaines our life. *Non sanitas,* there is no health in *any,* so universall is sickness; nor at *any time* in any, so universall; and so universall too, as that *not in any part* of any man, at any time. As the King was but sick in his feet, and yet it killed him: It was but in his *feet,* yet it flew up into his *head,* it affected his head; as our former translation observed it in their margin; that the disease did not onely grow to a great height in the disease, but to the highest parts of the body: It was at first but in the *feet,* but it was presently *all over. Iosiah* the King was shot with an arrow at the battail of *Megiddo;* One book that reports the story says he was carried out of the field alive and dyed at *Ierusalem,* and another, that he was carried out of the field dead. Deadly wounds and deadly sicknesses spread themselvs all over, so fast, as that the holy Ghost, in relating it, makes it all one, to tell the beginning, and the end thereof. If a man doe but prick a finger, and binde it above that part, so that the Spirits, or that which they call the *Balsamum* of the body, cannot descend, by reason of that ligature, to that part, it will *gangrene;* And, (which is an argument, and an evidence, that mischiefes are more operative, more insinuating, more penetrative, more diligent, then *Remedies* against *mischiefes* are) when the *Spirits,* and *Balsamum* of the body cannot passe by that ligature to that wound, yet the *Gangrene* will passe from that wound, by that ligature, to the body, to the Heart, and destroy. In every part of the body death can finde a door, or make a breach; Mortall diseases breed in every part. But when every part at once is diseased, death does not *besiege* him, but *inhabit* him. *In the day, when the keepers of the house shall tremble, and the strong men shall bow themselves, and the grinders cease, because they are few, and those that look out at the windows, be darkned,* when age of

2 Chron. 16.12

2 Chron. 35.24

2 Reg. 23.30

Eccles. 12.3

Gods making, age grown by *many years,* or age of the Devills making, age grown by *many sinnes,* hath spred an universall debility upon me, that all sicknesses are in me, and have all lost their names, as all simples have in *Triacle,* I am sick of *sicknesse,* and not of a *Fever,* or any *particular distemper,* then is the misery of this Text fallen upon me, *Non sanitas,* no health, none at any time, none in any part, *non in Carne, not in my flesh,* not in my whole substance, which is also another circumstance of exaltation in humane misery.

Non in carne

Numb.27.16

[Gen. 1.28]

Take *flesh* in the largest extent and signification, that may be, as *Moses* calls God, *The* God *of the spirits of all flesh,* that is, of the *Beeing* of all Creatures, and take all these Creatures to be ours in that Donation, *Subjicite & dominamini, Subdue, and rule all Creatures,* yet there is no soundnesse in our flesh, for, all these Creatures are corrupted, and become worse then they were, (to us) by the sinne of *Adam.* Bring *flesh* to a nearer signification, to our *own,* there was *Caro juxta naturam,* and there is *Caro juxta culpam.* That flesh which was naturall to man, that which God gave man at first, that had health and soundnesse in it; but yet not such a degree of soundnesse, as that it needed no more, then it then had. That had been naturally enough, (if that had been preserved) to carry that flesh it selfe to heaven; but even *that flesh* if it had not sinned, though it had an *Immortality* in it self, yet must have received a *glorification* in heaven; as well, (though in another measure) as those bodies, which shall be alive at the last day, and shall be but changed, and not dissolved in the dust, must receive a glorification there, besides that preservation from dissolution. Now this *Caro juxta culpam,* sinfull flesh, is farther from that Glorification; Our naturall flesh, when it was at best, had some thing to put on; but our sinfull flesh hath also something to put off, before it can receive glory. So then, for flesh in generall, the body of Creatures, though that flesh be our flesh, because all Creatures are ours, in *that* flesh there is no soundnesse, because they are become worse; for *that* flesh, which we call naturall, *Adams first flesh,* besides that it was never capable of glory in *it selfe,* but must have *received* that, by receiving the light of Gods presence, there is none of that flesh remaining now; now *universa caro,* all flesh is corrupted; and that curse is gone upon it, *The glory of Iacob shall be empoverished, and the fatnesse of his flesh shall be made leane.*

Gregor.

Esay 17.4

Gregory

Quia elatum sumpsimus spiritum, because we have raised our spirits in pride, higher then God would, *Ecce defluens quotidie portamus lutum,* Behold God hath walled us with mud walls, and wet mud walls, that waste away faster, then God meant at first, they should. And by sinnes, this flesh, that is but the loame and plaster of thy Tabernacle, thy body, *that, all* that, *that* in the intire substance is corrupted. Those Gummes, and spices, which should embalme thy flesh, when thou art dead, are spent upon that diseased body whilest thou art alive: Thou seemest, in the eye of the world, to walk in *silks,* and thou doest but walke in *searcloth;* Thou hast a desire to please some *eyes,* when thou hast much to do, not to displease every *Nose;* and thou wilt solicite an adulterous entrance into their beds, who, if they should but see thee goe into thine own bed, would need no other mortification, nor answer to thy solicitation. Thou pursuest the works of the flesh, and hast none, for thy flesh is but dust held together by plaisters; Dissolution and putrefaction is gone over thee alive; Thou has over liv'd thine own death, and art become thine own ghost, and thine own hell; *No soundnesse in all thy flesh;* and yet beyond all these, beyond the generall miserable condition of man, and the highest of humane miseries, sicknesse, and sicknesse over all the parts, and so over them all, as that it hath putrefied them all, there is another degree, which followes in our Text, and *David* calls *Trouble, There is no soundnesse in my flesh, nor rest in my bones.*

Non Pax

That which such a sicke man most needs, this sick soule shall not have, *Rest.* The Physician goes out, and says, hee hath left him to *Rest,* but hee hath left no *Rest* to him. The anguish of the disease, nay, the officiousnesse of visitors, will not let him rest. Such send to see him as would faine heare hee were dead, and such weep about his sick-bed, as would not weep at his grave.

Psal. 41.5

Mine enemies speake evill of mee, (says *David*) and say, *When shall hee die, and his name perish?* And yet these evill-speaking enemies come there to see him.

ver. 8

They say, an evill disease cleaveth fast unto him; and that they say is true, but they say it not out of compassion, for they adde, *And now that hee lyeth, let him rise no more.* Hee shall not get to that good trouble, to that holy disquiet of a conscientious consideration, how his state was got; and, it shall bee a greater trouble then hee can overcome, how to dispose it: He shall not onely not make a religious *restitution,* but he shall not make a discreet *Will.* He shall suspect his wifes fidelity, and his childrens frugality, and clogge them with Executors, and them with Over-seers, and be, or be afraid hee shall bee over-seen in all. And yet a farther trouble then all this, is intended in the other word, which is the last and highest of these vexations, *Non in ossibus, no rest in my bones.*

In ossibus

Grego.

Gal. 5.20

[Luke 12.20]

Saint *Basil* will needs have us leave the obvious, and the naturall signification of this, *Bones;* for, *Habet & anima ossa sua,* says he, The soule hath Bones, as well as the body, and there shall be no Rest in those Bones. Such a signification is applyable to the Flesh, as well as the Bones; The flesh may signifie the *lower faculties* of the soule, or the weaker works of the higher faculties thereof; There may bee a Carnality in the understanding; a concupiscence of disputation, and controversie in unnecessary points. *Requirit quod sibi respondere nequit,* The mind of a curious man delights to examine it selfe upon Interrogatories, which, upon the Racke, it cannot answer, and to vexe it selfe with such doubts as it cannot resolve. *Sub eo ignara deficit, quod prudenter requirit;* Wee will needs shew wit in moving subtile questions, and the more ignorance, in not being able to give our selves satisfaction. But not onely *seditions,* and *contentions,* but *Heresies* too, are called workes of the *flesh;* howsoever men thinke themselves wittie, and subtile, and spirituall in these wranglings, yet they have carnall respects, they are of the flesh, and there is no soundnes in them. But beyond this carnality in matters of Opinions, in points of a higher nature, this diseased man in our Text, comes to trouble in his Bones, S. *Basils spirituall bones:* Hee shall suspect his Religion, suspect his Repentance, suspect the Comforts of the Minister, suspect the efficacy of the Sacrament, suspect the mercy of God himselfe. Every fit of an Ague is an Earth-quake that swallows him, every fainting of the knee, is a step to Hell; every lying down at night is a funerall; and every quaking is a rising to judgment; every bell that distinguishes times, is a passing-bell, and every passing-bell, his own; every singing in the ear, is an Angels Trumpet; at every dimnesse of the candle, he heares that voice, *Fool, this night they will fetch away thy soul;* and in every judgement denounced against sin, he hears an *Ito maledicte* upon himselfe, *Goe thou accursed into hell fire.* And whereas such meditations as these, might sustaine a rectified soule, as Bones, in this sinner, *despaire* shall have suck'd out all the marrow of these Bones, and so there shall bee no *soundnesse in his flesh, no rest in his bones.* And so have you this sicke sinner dissected and anatomized; Hee hath not onely his portion in misery that lies upon all mankinde, which was our first branch, but in the heavyest of all, sickenesse, which was a second, and then a third sicknesse spread over all, *no soundnesse,* nor rest in that sicknesse, which was a fourth consideration, *No soundnesse in his flesh,* in his weaker faculties and operations, *No rest in his bones,* no acquiescence in his best actions, with which we end this first part. In which, wee consider sinfull man, in *himself,* and so all is desperate; But in the second, where we find him upon the consideration of the cause of all these distresses, That it is from the Contemplation of the anger of God, *There is no soundnesse in my flesh, because of thine Anger,* there wee shall finde a way offered to him, that may, if hee pursue it aright, bring him to a Reparation, to a Redintegration; for, if hee look upon the Anger of God in a right line, it will shew him, that as that Anger is the cause of his Calamities, so his sinnes are the cause of that Anger.

Ira Dei

May wee not piously apply that Proverbiall speech, *Corruptio optimi pessima,* (that when good things take in another nature then their own, they take it in the highest exaltation) thus, that when God, who is all mercy, growes angry, he becomes all anger? The Holy Ghost himselfe seemes to have given us leave to make that application, when expressing God in the height of his anger, hee calls God then, in that anger, a *Dove;* wee read it the *fiercenesse of an oppressour,* but Saint *Hierome* reads it, *The anger of a Dove.* And truly there is no other word then that, in that tongue, (the word is *Ionah,*) that signifies a *Dove,* and that word does signifie a *Dove,* in many other places of Scripture; And that Prophet which made his flight from God, when hee sent him to Nineveh, is called by that name, *Ionah,* a *Dove;* And the Fathers of the Latine Church, have read, and interpreted it so, of a *Dove.* Some of them take *Nebuchadnezzar* to be this angry *Dove,* because hee left his owne *Dove-coat* to feed abroad, to prey upon them; and some, because the *Dove* was the Armes and Ensigne of the Assyrians from the time of *Semiramis;* But the rest take this Dove to bee God himselfe, and that the sinnes of men had put a *Gall into a Dove,* Anger into God. And then, to

Ier. 25. *ult.*

what height that anger growes, is expressed in the Prophet *Hosea;* [Hos.] 13.8 *I will meet them,* says God, (when hee is pleased, he says, *hee will wait for them*) as a *Bear,* (no longer a *Dove*) as a *Bear robbed of her whelpes,* (sensible of his injuries) and *I will rent the caule of their hearts,* (shiver them in peeces with a dispersion, with a discerption) *And I will devour them as with a Lyon,* (nothing shall re-unite them Ier. 19.11 again But *I will break them as a Potters vessell, that cannot be made whole again.*) Honour not the malice of thine enemy so much, as to say, thy misery comes from him: Dishonour not the complexion of the times so much, as to say, thy misery comes from them; justifie not the *Deity* of Fortune so much, as to say, thy misery comes from her; Finde God pleased with thee, and thou hast a hook in the *nostrils* of every *Leviathan,* power cannot shake thee, Thou hast a wood to cast into the waters of *Marah,* the bitternesse of the times cannot hurt thee, thou hast a Rock to dwell upon, and the dream of a *Fortunes wheel,* can not overturn thee. But if the Lord be angry, he needs no Trumpets to call in Armies, if he doe but *sibilare muscam,* hisse and whisper for the flye, and the Bee, there is nothing so little in his hand, as cannot discomfort thee, discomfit thee, dissolve and powr out, attenuate and annihilate the very marrow of thy soul. Every thing is His, and therefore every thing is Hee; thy sicknesse is his sword, and therefore it is Hee that strikes thee with it, still turne upon that consideration, the *Lord is angry;* But then look that anger *in the face,* take it in the right line, as the Originall phrase in this text directs, *à facie iræ Dei, There is no soundnesse in my flesh, from the face of thine anger.*

Iob 41.1, 2
Exod. 15.23
[25]

A facie iræ

As there is a *Manifestation* of Gods anger in this phrase, *The face of Gods anger,* so there is a *Multiplication,* a plurality too, for it is indeed, *Mippenei, à faciebus,* the faces, the divers manifestations of Gods anger; for, the face of God, (and so of every thing proceeding from God) is that, by which God, or that work of God is manifested to us. And therefore since God manifests his anger so many usefull, and medicinall ways unto thee, take heed of looking upon his anger, where his anger hath no face, no manifestation; take heed of imagining an anger in God, amounting to thy *Damnation,* in any such Decree, as that God should be angry with thee in that height, without looking upon thy sinnes, or without any declaration why hee is

Aug.

angry. Hee opens his face to thee in his Law, he manifests himself to thee in the Conditions, by which he hath made thy *salvation possible,* and till he see thee, in the transgression of them, he is not angry. And when he is angry so, be glad he shews it in his face, in his outward *declarations;* that fire smothered, would consume all; Gods anger reserved till the last day, will last as long as that day, as that undeterminable day, for ever. When should we goe about to quench that fire, that never bursts out, or to seek reconciliation, before a hostility be declared? Therefore Saint *Bernard* begs this anger at Gods hands, *Irascaris mihi Domine,* O Lord, be angry with me; And therefore *David* thanks God, in the behalf of that people, for his anger, *Thou forgavest them, though thou tookest vengeance of their inventions.* (Psalm 99.8) The fires of hell, in their place, in hell, have no light; But any degrees of the fires of Hell, that can break out in this life, have, in Gods own purpose, so much light, as that through the darkest smother of obduration, or desperation, God would have us see him. Therefore Saint *Hierome* makes this milder use of this phrase, that God shewes *faciem iræ,* but *non iram,* that his face of anger is rather a telling us, that hee will bee angry, then that hee is angry yet; the corrections that God inflicts to reduce us, if wee profit not by them, were anger *Ab initio,* wee shall suffer for the sinnes, from which those corrections should have reduced us, and for that particular sinne, of not being reduced by them; but if they have their effect, there was not a drop of gall, there was not a dramme of anger in the anger. Now that that God intends in them is, that as wee apprehend our calamities to proceed from Gods anger, and to discharge Destiny, and Fortune, so wee apprehend that anger to proceed from our own sinnes, and so discharge *God* himselfe; *There is no rest in my bones because of my sin.*

3. Part
Peccatum

As we are the sons of *Dust,* (worse, the sonnes of *Death*) we must say to *Corruption, Thou art my Father, and to the worm, Thou art my Mother,* (Iob 17.14) so we may say to the *anger* of God, it is our *grandfather,* that begot these miseries, but wee must say too, to our sinne, Thou art my *great-grandfather,* that begot Gods anger upon us: and here is our wofull *pedegree,* howsoever wee be otherwise descended. (Gregor.) 'Tis true, there is no soundnesse, there is misery enough upon thee; and true, that God is angry, vehemently angry; But, *Expone justitiam iræ Dei,* deal clearly with the world, and clear God, and confesse it Gen. 4.[13] is because of thy sinne. When *Cain* says, *My sin is greater then can be forgiven,* that word *Gnavon* is ambiguous, it may bee sinne, it may bee punishment, and wee know not whether his impatience grew out of the horrour of his sinne, or the weight of his punishment. But here wee are directed by a word that hath no ambiguity; *Kata* signifies sin, and nothing but sinne; Here the holy Ghost hath fixed thee upon a word, that will not suffer thee to consider the punishment, nor *the cause of the punishment,* the anger, but *the cause of that anger,* and all, the sin. Wee see that the bodily sicknesse, and the death of many is attributed to one kind of sinne, to the negligent receiving of the 1 Cor. 11.30 Sacrament, *For this cause many are weak and sick amongst you, and many sleep.* Ambrose *Imaginem judicii ostenderat,* God had given a representation of the day of Judgement in that proceeding of his, for then we shall see many men condemned for sinnes, for which we never suspected them: so wee thinke men dye of *Fevers,* whom we met lately at the Sacrament, and God hath cut them off perhaps for that sin of their unworthy receiving the Sacrament. My miseries are the *fruits* of this Tree; Gods anger is the arms that spreads it; but the root is sin. My *sin,* which is another consideration.

Meum

We say of a Possession, *Transit cum onere,* It passes to me, with the burthen that my Father laid upon it; his debt is my debt: so does it, with the sin too; his sin, by which he got that possession, *is my sin,* if I know it: and, perchance, the punishment mine, though I know not the sin. *Adams* sin, 6000 years agoe, is my sin; and their sin, that shall sinne by occasion of any wanton *writings* of mine, will be my sin, though they come after. Wofull riddle; sin is but a privation, and yet there is not such another positive possession: sin is nothing, and yet there is nothing else; I sinned in the first man that ever *was;* and, but for the mercy of God, in something that I have said or done, might sin, that is, occasion sin, in the last man that ever *shall be.* But that sin that is called *my sinne* in this text, is that that is become mine by an *habituall practise,* or mine by a *wilfull relapse* into it. And so *my sin* may kindle the anger of God, though it bee but a *single sinne, One sinne,* as it is delivered here in the singular, and no farther, *Because of my sinne.*

Singulare

Every man may find in himself, *Peccatum complicatum,* sinne wrapped up in sinne, a body of sin. We bring Elements of our own; earth of Covetousnesse, water of unsteadfastnesse, ayre of putrefaction, and fire of licentiousnesse; and of these elements we make a body of sinne; as the Apostle says of the Naturall body, *There are* (1 Cor. 12.20) *many members, but one body,* so we may say of our sin, it hath a wanton eye, a griping hand, an itching ear, an insatiable heart, and feet swift to shed blood, and yet it is but one body of sin; It is all, and yet it is but One. But let it be simply, and singularly but One, (which is a miracle in sin, truly I think an impossibility in sin, to be single, to be but One) (for that unclean Spirit, which possessed the man that dwelt amongst the tombs, carryed it at first, as though he had been a single Devill, and he alone in that man, *I, I adjure thee,* (Mar. 5.[7]) says he to Christ, and *torment not me, not me,* so far in the *singular,* but when Christ puts him to it, he confesses, *we are many, and my name is legion:* So though thy sinne, slightly examined, may seem but One, yet if thou dare presse it, it will confesse a plurality, a *legion*) if it be but One, yet if that One be made thine, by an *habituall love* to it, as the *plague* needs not the help of a Consumption to kill thee, so neither does *Adultery* need the help of Murder to damn thee. For this making of any One sin, thine, thine, by an habituall *love* thereof, will grow up to the last and heaviest waight, intimated in that phrase, which is also in this clause of the Text, *In facie peccati;* that this sin will have a *face,* that is, a *confidence,* and a devesting of all bashfulnes or disguises.

Facies peccati

There cannot bee a heavier punishment laid upon any sinne, then Christ lays upon *scandall: It were better for him a mil-stone were hanged about his neck, and hee drowned in the Sea.* (Luke 17.2) If something worse, then such a death, belong to him, surely it is eternall Death. And this, this eternall death, is interminated by Christ, in cases, where there is not always sinne, in the action which wee doe, but if we doe any action, so, as that it may scandalize another, or occasion sin in him; we are bound to study, and favour the weaknesse of other men, and not to doe such things, as they may think sins. We must prevent the mis-interpretation, yea the malice of other men; for though the *fire* be theirs, the *fewell,* or at least, the *bellows,* is ours; The uncharitablenesse, the malice is in them, but the awaking, and the stirring thereof, is in our carelesnesse, who were not watchfull upon our actions. But when an action comes to be sin indeed, and not onely *occasionally* sin, because it scandalizes another, but *really* sin in it selfe, then even the Poet tels you, *Maxima debetur pueris reverentia, si quid Turpe paras,* Take heed of doing any sinne, in the sight of thy Child: for, if we break through that wall, we shall come quickly to that, *faciem Sacerdotis non erubuerunt,* they will not be afraid, nor Lam. 4.16 ashamed in the presence of the Priest, they will look him in the face, nay receive at his hands, and yet sin their sinne, that minute, in their hearts; and to that also, *faciem seniorum non erubuerunt,* they will not be afraid, nor ashamed of the Office of the Magistrate; but sin for [Isa. 3.9] *nothing,* or *sin at a price, bear out,* or *buy out* all their sins. *They sin as Sodom, and hide it not,* is the highest charge that the Holy Ghost Psal. 12.4 could lay upon the sinner. When they come to say, *Our lips are ours, who is Lord over us?* They will say so of their hands, and of all their bodies, *They are ours, who shall forbid us, to doe what wee will with them?* And what lack these open sinnners of the last judgement, and the condemnation thereof? That judgement is, that men shall stand naked in the sight of one another, and all their sinnes shall be made manifest to all; and this open sinner, does so, and chuses to doe so, Psal. 19.12 even in this world. When *David* prays so devoutly, *to be cleansed* 2 Cor. 4.2 *from his secret sins;* and Saint *Paul* glories so devoutly, in having *renounced the hidden things of dishonesty,* how great a burthen is there, in these open and avowed sins; sins that have put on so brasen a face, as to out-face the Minister, and out-face the Magistrate, and call the very Power, and Justice of God in question, whether he do hate or can punish a sinne? for, they doe what they can to remove that opinion out of mens hearts. Truly, as an Hypocrite at Church, may doe more good, then a devout man in his Chamber at home, because the Hypocrites outward piety, though counterfeit, imprints a good example upon them, who doe not know it to bee counterfeit, and wee cannot know, that he that is absent from Church now, is now at his prayers in his Chamber: so a lesser sinne done with an open avowment, and confidence, may more prejudice the Kingdome of God, then greater in secret. And this is that which may be principally intended, or, at least, usefully raised out of this phrase of the Holy Ghost in *David, A facie peccati,* that the habituall sinner comes to sin, not onely with a negligence, who know it, but with a glorious desire, that all the world might know it; and with a shame, that any such *Judge as feared not God nor regarded man,* should be more Luke 18.2 feareless of God, or regardless of man, then he.

But now, beloved, when we have laid man thus low, *Miserable,* because *Man,* and then *Diseased,* and that *all over,* without *any soundnesse,* even in his whole substance, *in his flesh,* and in the height of this disease, *Restlesse* too, and *Restlesse even in his bones, diffident* in his strongest assurances; And when we have laid him lower then *that,* made him see the *Cause* of all this misery to be the *Anger* of God, the inevitable anger of an incensed God, and such an anger of God as hath a *face,* a manifestation, a reality, and not that God was angry with him in a *Decree,* before he shewed man *his face* in the *Law,* and saw *Mans face* in the transgression of the law; And laid him lower then *that* too, made him see the cause of this anger, as it is *sinne,* so to be *his sinne,* sinne made *his* by an *habituall love* thereof, which, though it may be but *one,* yet is become an *out-facing* sinne, a sinne in *Contempt* and *confidence,* when we have laid *Man,* laid *you,* thus low, in your own eyes, we returne to the Canon and rule of *that Physician* whom they call *Evangelistam medicinæ,* the Mesues Evangelist of Physique, *Sit intentio prima in omni medicina comfortare,* whether the physician purge, or lance, or sear, his principall care, and his end, is to comfort and strengthen: so though we have insisted upon *Humane misery,* and the cause of *that, the anger of God,* and the cause of *that* anger, *sinne* in that excesse, yet we shall dismisse you with that *Consolation,* which was first in our intention, and shall be our conclusion, that as this Text hath a *personall* aspect upon *David* alone, and therefore we gave you *his case,* and then a *generall retrospect* upon *Adam,* and *all in him,* and therefore we gave you your *own* case, so it hath also an *Evangelicall prospect* upon *Christ,* and therefore, for your comfort, and as a bundle of Myrrhe in your bosomes, we shall give you *his case* too, to whom these words belong, as well as to *Adam,* or *David,* or *you; There is no soundnesse in my flesh, because of thine anger, neither is there any rest in my bones, because of my sinne.*

Christus

If you will see the miseries of Man, in their exaltation, and in their accumulation too, in their weight, and in their number, take them in the *Ecce homo,* when Christ was presented from *Pilate,* scourged and [Joh. 19.5]

scorned. *Ecce homo,* behold man, in *that* man, in the *Prophets;* They
Psal. 89.51 *have reproched the footsteps of thine Anointed,* says *David,* slandred
his actions, and conversation; *He hath no form, nor comlinesse, nor*
[Isa.] 53.2 *beauty, that we should desire to see him,* says *Esay;* Despised, rejected
[and 3] of men; *A man of sorrows, and acquainted with griefes.* And *Ecce*
homo, behold man, in *that* man, in the whole history of the *Gospell.*
That which is said of us, of sinfull men, is true in *him,* the salvation
Esay 1.6 of men, *from the sole of the foot, even unto the Head, there is no*
soundnesse, but wounds, and bruises, and putrefying sores. That
question will never receive answer, which Christ askes, *Is there any*
Lam 1.12 *sorrow like unto my sorrow?* Never *was,* never *will* there be any
sorrow like unto his sorrow, because there can never be such a person,
[Mat. 26.37, to suffer sorrow. Affliction was upon *him,* and upon *all him;* for, *His*
38; Mark *soule was heavy unto death;* Even upon his *Bones; fire was sent into*
14.33, 34] *his bones, and it prevailed against him.* And the highest cause of this
[Lam. 1] affliction was upon him, the *anger of God; The Lord had afflicted*
ver. 13 *him, in the day of his fierce anger.* The height of Gods anger, is *Dere-*
[Lam. 1] *liction;* and he was brought to his *Vt quid dereliquisti, My God, my*
ver. 12 *God why hast thou forsaken me? We did esteem him striken of the*
[Mat. 27.46; *Lord,* says *Esay;* And we were not deceived in it; *Percutiam pas-*
Mark 15.34] *torem,* says Christ himselfe of *himselfe,* out of the *Prophet, I will smite*
[Isa.] 53.4 *the shepheard, and the sheep of the flock shall be scattered;* And then,
Mat. 26.31 the cause of this anger, *sinne,* was so upon him, as that, though in
Zech. 13.7 one consideration, the raine was upon all the world, and onely this
fleece of *Gedeon* dry, all the world surrounded with sinne, and onely
Iud. *He innocent,* yet in another line we finde all the world dry, and onely
6.[36–40] *Gedeons* fleece wet, all the *world innocent,* and onely *Christ guilty.*
Esay 53.4, 5 But, as there is a *Verè tulit,* and a *Verè portavit,* surely he bore those
griefes, and surely he carried those sorrows, so they were *Verè nostri,*
surely he hath borne *our griefes,* and carried *our sorrows, he was*
wounded for our transgressions, and bruised for our iniquities; The
Chastisement of our peace was upon him; and therefore it must
necessarily follow, (as it does follow there) *with his stripes wee were*
healed; for, God will not exact a debt twice; of Christ for *me,* and of
Ezek. *me* too. And therefore, *Quare moriemini Domus Israel?* since I have
18.[31] made ye of the houshold of *Israel,* why will ye die? since ye are
recovered of your former sicknesses, why will ye die of a new disease,

of a suspicion, or jealousie, that this recovery, this redemption in *Christ Jesus* belongs not to you? Will ye say, *It is a fearfull thing to fall into the hands, Dei viventis, of the living God?* 'Tis so; a fearfull thing; But if *Deus mortuus,* the God of life bee but *dead* for mee, be fallen into my hands, applied to mee, made mine, it is no fearefull thing to fall into the hands of the living God. *Non satis est medicum fecisse suum officium, nisi ægrotus, & adstantes sua;* It is not enough for Christ Jesus to have prepared you the balm of his bloud, not enough for us, to minister it to you, except every one of you help himself, in a faithfull application, and help one another, in a holy and exemplar conversation. *Quàm exactè, & accuratè usus dictionibus?* How exact and curious was the holy Ghost, in *David,* in choice of words? He does not say, *Non sanitas mihi, sed non in carne;* not that there is no health *for me,* but none *in me; non in carne mea, not in my flesh,* but *in carne ejus,* in the flesh and bloud of my Saviour, there is health, and salvation. *In ossibus ejus,* in *his bones,* in the strength of *his merits,* there is rest, and peace, *à facie peccati,* what face soever my sins have had, in my former *presumptions,* or what face soever they put on now, in my declination to *desperation. The Lord waiteth that he may have mercy upon you;* He stays your leisure; *and therefore will he be exalted,* (says that Prophet there) that hee may have mercy upon you; He hath chosen *that* for his way of honour, of exaltation, *that he may have mercy upon you.* And then, *Quare moriemini?* If God bee so *respective* towards you, as to wait for you, if God be so *ambitious* of you, as to affect a kingdome in you, why will ye die? since *he* will not let ye die of *Covetousnesse,* of *adultery,* of *ambition,* of *prophanenesse* in your selves, why will yee die of *jealousie,* of *suspition in him?* It was a mercifull voice of *David; Is there yet any man left of the house of* Saul, *that I may shew mercy for* Jonathans *sake?* It is the voice of God to you all, *Is there yet any man of the house of Adam, that I may shew mercy for Christ Jesus sake?* that takes Christ Jesus in his arms, and interposes *him,* between his sins, and mine indignation, and *non morietur,* that man shall not die. We have done; *Est ars sanandorum morborum medicina, non rhetorica;* Our physick is not eloquence, not directed upon your *affections,* but upon your *consciences;* To *that* wee present this for physick, *The whole need not*

Heb. 10.[31]
Hippocrates
Chrysost.
Esa. 30.18
2 Sam. 9.1
Paracels.
[Mat. 9.12; Mark 2.17; Luke 5.31]

a Physician, but the sick doe. If you mistake your selves to be *well,* or think you have physick enough at home, knowledge enough, divinity enough, to save you *without us,* you need no Physician; that is, a Physician can doe you no good; but then is this Gods physick, and Gods Physician welcome unto you, if you be come to a remorse-full sense, and to an humble, and penitent acknowledgement, that you are sick, and that *there is no soundnesse in your flesh, because of his anger, nor any rest in your bones, because of your sins,* till you turn upon *him,* in whom this anger is appeas'd, and in whom these sins are forgiven, the Son of his love, the Son of his right hand, at his right hand Christ Jesus. And to this glorious Sonne of God, &c.

Number 3.

Preached at Lincolns Inne.

PSALME 38.4. *FOR MINE INIQUITIES ARE GONE OVER MY HEAD, AS A HEAVY BURDEN, THEY ARE TOO HEAVY FOR MEE.*

DAVID having in the former verses of this Psalm assign'd a reason, why he was bound to pray, because he was in misery, (*O Lord rebuke me not in thine anger, for thine arrows stick fast in mee*) And a reason why hee should be in misery, because God was angry, (*Thy hand presseth me sore, v.* 2. And, *there is no soundnesse in my flesh, because of thine anger, v.* 3.) And a reason, why God should be angry, because he had sinn'd, (*There is no rest in my bones, because of my sin,* in the same verse) He proceeds to a reason, why this prayer of his must be vehement, why these miseries of his are so *violent,* and why Gods anger is *permanent,* and he findes all this to be, because in his sins, all these venimous qualities, *vehemence, violence,* and *continuance,* were complicated, and enwrapp'd; for, hee had sinn'd vehemently, in the rage of lust, and violently, in the effusion of bloud, and permanently, in a long, and senslesse security. They are all contracted in this *Text,* into two kinds, which will be our two parts, in handling these words; first, the *supergressæ super, Mine iniquities are gone over my head,* there's the *multiplicity,* the number, the succession, and so the continuation of his sin: and then, the *Gravatæ super, My sins are as a heavy burden, too heavy for me,* there's the greatnesse, the weight, the insupportablenesse of his sin. S. *Augustine* cals these two distinctions, or considerations of sin, *Ignorantiam, & Difficultatem;* first, that *David* was ignorant, that he saw not the Tide, as it swell'd up upon him, *Abyssus Abyssum,* Depth call'd upon Depth; and, *all thy waters,* and all thy billows are Ps. 42.7

gone over me, (says he, in another place) hee perceiv'd them not coming till they were over him, he discern'd not his particular sins, then when he committed them, till they came to the *supergressæ super,* to that height, that he was overflowed, surrounded, *his iniquities were gone over his head,* and in that S. *Augustine* notes *Ignorantiam,* his in-observance, his inconsideration of his own case; and then he notes *Difficultatem,* the hardnesse of recovering, because he that is under water, hath no aire to see by, no aire to hear by, he hath nothing to reach to, he touches not ground, to push him up, he feels no bough to pull him up, and therein that Father notes *Difficultatem,* the hardnesse of recovering. Now *Moses* expresses these two miseries together, in the destruction of the *Egyptians,* in his song, after *Israels* deliverance, and the *Egyptians* submersion, *The Depths have covered them,* (there's the *supergressæ super,* their iniquities, in that punishment of their iniquities, were gone over their heads) And then, *They sank into the bottome as a stone* (says *Moses*) there's the *gravatæ super,* they depressed them, suppressed them, oppressed them, they were under them, and there they must lie.

Exod. 15.5

The *Egyptians* had, *David* had, we have too many sins, to swim above water, and too great sins to get above water again, when we are sunk; The number of sins then, and the greatnesse of sin, will be our two parts; the dangers are equall, to multiply many lesser sins, or to commit a few, more hainous: except the danger be greater, (as indeed it may justly seem to be) in the multiplication, and custome, and habit of lesser sins; but how great is the danger then, how desperate is our state, when our sins are great in themselves, and multiplied too?

Divisio

In his *many* sins, we shall touch thus many circumstances: First, they were *peccata,* sins, iniquities; and then *peccata sua,* his sins, his iniquities, which intimates *actuall sins;* for though God inflict miseries for originall sin, (*death,* and that, that induces it, *sicknesse,* and the like) yet those are miseries common to all, because the sin is so too; But these, are his punishments, personall calamities, and the sins are *his own* sins; And then, (which is a third circumstance) they are sins in the *plurall,* God is not thus angry for *one* sin; And again, they are such sins, as have been long in going, and are now got over, *supergressæ sunt,* they are gone, gone over; And then lastly, for that first part, *supergressæ Caput,* they are gone over my head, In which exaltation, is intimated all this; first, *sicut tectum, sicut fornix,* they are over his head, as a roofe, as a cieling, as an Arch, they have made a wall of separation, betwixt God and us, so they are above our head; And then *sicut clamor,* they are ascended as a noise, they are got up to heaven, and cry to God for vengeance, so they are above our head; And again *sicut aquæ,* they are risen and swollen as waters, they compass us, they smother us, they blinde us, they stupefie us, so they are above our head; But lastly and principally, *sicut Dominus,* they are got above us, as a Tyran, and an usurper, for so they are above our head too: And in these we shall determine our first part. When from thence we come to our second part, in which, (as in this we shall have done their *number*) we shall consider their *greatnesse,* we finde them first *heavy,* sinne is no light matter; And then, they are *too heavy,* a little weight would but ballast us, this sinkes us; Too heavy for *me,* even for a man equall to *David;* and where is he? when is that man? for, says our text, they are as heavy, as a heavy *Burden;* And the nature, and inconvenience of a Burden is, first to *Crooken,* and bend us downward from our naturall posture, which is erect, for this incurvation implies a declination in the inordinate love of the Creature, *Incurvat.* And then the nature of a burden is, to *Tyre* us; our very sinne becomes fulsome, and wearisome to us, *fatigat;* and it hath this inconvenience too, *ut retardet,* it slackens our pace, in our right course, though we be not tired, yet we cannot goe so fast, as we should in any way towards godliness; and lastly, this is the inconvenience of a burden too, *ut præcipitet,* it makes us still apt and ready to stumble, and to fall under it: It crookens us, it deprives us of our *rectitude;* it tires us, extinguishes our alacrity; It slackens us, enfeebles and intepidates our zeale; It occasions our stumbling, opens and submits us, to every emergent tentation. And these be the dangers, and the mischievous inconveniences, notified to us, in those two Elegancies of the holy Ghost, the *supergressæ,* the multiplicity of sinnes, *They are gone over my head,* and the *gravatæ, They are a heavy burden, too heavy for me.*

First then, all these things are *literally* spoken of *David;* By *application,* of us; and by *figure,* of Christ. *Historically, David; morally,* we; *Typically,* Christ is the subject of this text. In *Davids* David person, we shal insist no longer upon them, but onely to look upon the two generall parts, the *multiplicity* of his sinne, and the *weight* and *greatnesse* thereof: And that onely in the *matter of Vriah,* as the I Reg. 15.5 *Holy Ghost,* (without reproching the *adultery* or the murder, after *Davids* repentance) vouchsafes to mollifie his manifold, and his hainous sinne. First; he did wrong to a loyall and a faithfull servant; and who can hope to be well served, that does so? He corrupted that woman, who for ought appearing to the contrary, had otherwise preserved her honour, and her Conscience entire; It is a sinne, Psal. 50.18 *To runne with a theife when thou seest him, or to have thy portion with them that are adulterers already;* to accompany them in their sinne, who have an inclination to that sinne before, is a sinne; but to solicite them, who have no such inclination, nor, but for thy solicitation, would have had, is much more inexcusable. In *Davids* sinne, there was thus much more, he defrauded some, to whom his love was due, in dividing himselfe with a strange woman. To steale from another man, though it be to give to the poor, and to such poor, as would otherwise sterve, if that had not been stollen, is injustice, is a sinne. To divide that heart, which is intirely given to a wife, in mariage, with another woman, is a sinne, though she, to whom it is so given, pretend, or might truly suffer much torment and anguish if it were not done. *Davids* sinne flew up to a higher spheare; He drew the enemy to blaspheme the name of *God,* in the victory over *Israel,* where *Vriah* was slaine: God hates nothing more in great persons, then that prevarication, to pretend to assist his cause, and promove his Religion, and yet underhand give the enemies of that Religion, way to grow greater. His sinnes, indeed, were too many to be numbred; too great too, to be weighed in comparison with others. *Vriah* was innocent towards him, and faithfull in his imployment, and, at that time, in an actuall, and in a dangerous service, for his person, for the State, for the Church. Him *David* betrays in his letter to *Joab;* Him *David* makes the instrument of his own death, by carrying those letters, the warrants of his own execution; And he makes *Joab,* a man of honour, his instrument for a murder to cover an adultery. Thus many sinnes, and these heavy degrees of sin, were in this one; I Chron. 21.1 and how many, and how weighty, were in that, of *numbring of his people,* wee know not. We know, that *Satan* provoked him to doe it;

and we know, that *Joab,* who seconded and accomplished his desire ver. 3
in the murder of *Vriah,* did yet disswade, and dis-counsell this numbring of the people, and not out of *reason of State,* but as an expresse sin. Put all together, and lesse then all, we are sure *David* belied not himself, *His iniquities were gone over his head, and as a heavy burden, they were too heavy for him;* Though this will be a good rule, for the most part, in all *Davids* confessions and lamentations, that though that be always literally true of himself, for the *sinne,* or for the *punishment,* which he says, *personally David* did suffer, that which he complains of in the *Psalms,* in a great measure, yet *David* speaks *prophetically,* as well as *personally,* and to us, who exceed him in his sins, the exaltation of those miseries, which we finde so often in this book, are especially intended; That which *David* relates to have been his own case, he foresees will be ours too, in a higher degree. And that's our second, and our principall object of all those circumstances, in the *multiplicity,* and in the *hainousnesse* of sin; And therefore, to that second part, these considerations in our selves, we make thus much hast.

First then, they were *peccata, sins, iniquities.* And we must not think to ease our selves in that subtilty of the School, *Peccatum nihil;* That sin is nothing, because sinne had no creation, sin hath no reality, sin is but a deflection from, but a privation of the rectitude required in our actions; that's true; 'tis true, that is said by *Catarinus, Let* Eph. 5.2
wives be subject to their husbands in omnibus, in every thing, omnium appellatione, in Scripturis, nunquam venit malum, wheresoever the Scripture says all things, it never means any ill thing, *quia malum, ut malum, defectio est, nihil est,* because, says hee, ill things, are no things, ill, considered as ill, is nothing; for, whatsoever is any thing, was made by God, and ill, sin, is no creature of his making. This is true; but that will not ease my soul, no more then it will ease my body, that *sicknesse* is nothing, and *death* is nothing: for, death hath no reality, no creation, death is but a privation, and *damnation,* as it is the everlasting losse of the sight and presence of God, is but a privation. And therefore as we fear death, and fear damnation, though in discourse, and in disputation, we can make a school-shift, to call them *nothing,* and but privations, so let us fear sin too, for all this imaginary *nothingnesse,* which the heat of the School hath smoak'd it withall.

Vniversality of sin

Sin is so far from being nothing, as that there is nothing else but sin in us: sin hath not onely a place, but a Palace, a Throne, not onely a beeing, but a dominion, even in our best actions: and if every action of ours must needs be denominated from the degrees of good, or of bad, that are in it, howsoever there may be some tincture of some morall goodnesse, in some actions, every action will prove a sin, that is, vitiated and depraved with more ill, then rectified with good conditions.

Treason of sin

And then, every sin will prove *læsio Dei,* a violence, a wound inflicted upon God himselfe, and therefore it is not nothing.

Coster

It is strangely said in the *Roman Church,* for the establishing of their kind of *veniall* sin, that every sin is not *læsio Dei,* a violation, and a wounding of God, because God is charity, and charity is not extinguished by every sin. The *Priest* and the *Levite* neglected the man, that lay in his bloud, in the way to *Jericho;* but they did not argue so, Tush this man is not hurt, for we see him breathe, and move. Out of the *Civill Law,* we assigne divers *Diminutiones Capitis,* many things, that are called capitall, and yet doe not take away mans life; And it were strangely concluded, that a man were not hurt in his head, because he was not beheaded. Yet so they conclude, that say, a veniall sin is not *læsio Dei,* not a violation of God, who is charity, because it does not extinguish charity: so that, at the last, nothing shall be sin with them, except it *kill God;* that is, nothing. And indeed they have brought it too near to that, when they have left no sin, which may not be bought out after, no sin, to which, by some just consequence, and inference upon some points of their doctrine, a man may not be encouraged before.

August.

Turpis omnis pars suo universo non consentiens; Every lim that is not proportionable to the whole body, deforms the body.

Deformity of sin

God made a body of goodnesse; all good; and he that enters an ill action, a sin, deforms this body of God, defaces this work of his making.

Leo

Mentis principatus in peccato obliviscimur; we resigne, we disavow that *soveraignty,* which God hath given us, when we sin.

Slavery of sin

God spake not onely of the beasts of the forest, but of those beasts, that is, those brutish affections, that are in us, when he said, *Subjicite & dominamini,* subdue, and govern the world; and in sinning we lose this dominion over our selves, and forfeit our dominion over the creature too.

Clem. Alex.

Qui peccat, quatenus peccat, seipso deterior; Every

Debility of sin

August.

Facility of sin

sin leaves us worse, then it found us, and we rise poorer, ignobler, weaker, for every nights sin, then we lay down. *Plerumque non implemus bonum propositum, ne offendamus eos quibuscum vivimus;* If any good purpose arise in us, we dare not pursue it, for fear of displeasing those, with whom we live, and to whom we have a relation, and a dependence upon them. We sin, and sin, and sin, lest our abstinence from sin, should work as an increpation, as a rebuke upon them that doe sin; for this they will call an ambition in us, that being their *inferiours,* we goe about to be their *betters,* if wee will needs be *better,* that is, less vicious then they. First then, personally in himselfe, prophetically in us, *David* laments our state, *quia peccata,* because we are under sin, sin which is a depravation of man in himself, and a deprivation of God from man. And then our next cause of lamentation is, the *propriety in sin,* that they are *nostra, our own, iniquitates meæ,* says *David, My sins, Mine iniquities* are gone over my head.

Sua

We are not all *Davids, amabiles,* lovely and beloved in that measure that *David* was, *men according to Gods heart:* But we are all *Adams, terrestres,* and *lutosi,* earth, and durty earth, red, and bloudy earth, and therefore in our selves, as deriv'd from him, let us finde, and lament all these *numbers,* and all these *weights* of sin. Here we are all born to a patrimony, to an inheritance; an inheritance, a patrimony of sin; and we are all good husbands, and thrive too fast upon that stock, upon the encrease of sin, even to the treasuring up of sin, and the wrath of God for sin. How naked soever we came out of our mothers wombe, otherwise, thus we came all apparell'd, apparell'd and invested in sin; And we multiply this wardrobe, with new *habits,* habits of customary sins, every day. Every man hath an answer to that question of the Apostle, *What hast thou, that thou hast not received from God?* [1 Cor. 4.7] Every man must say, I have pride in my heart, wantonnesse in mine eyes, oppression in my hands; and that I never receiv'd from God. Our sins are our *own;* and we have a covetousnesse of more; a way, to make other mens sins ours too, by drawing them to a fellowship in our sins. I must be beholden to the loyalty and honesty of my *wife,* whether my children be mine own, or no; for, he whose eye waiteth for the evening, the adulterer, may rob me of that propriety. I must be beholden to the protection of the *Law,*

whether my goods shall be mine, or no; A potent adversary, a corrupt Judge may rob me of that propriety. I must be beholden to my *Physician,* whether my health, and strength shal be mine, or no; A garment negligently left off, a disorderly meal may rob me of that propriety. But without asking any man leave, my sins will be mine own. When the presumptuous men say, *Our lips are our own, and*
Ps. 12.[4] *our tongues are our own,* the Lord threatens to cut off those lips and those tongues. But except we doe come to say, *Our sins are our own,* God will never cut up that root in us, God will never blot out the memory in himself, of those sins. Nothing can make them none of ours, but the avowing of them, the confessing of them to be ours. Onely in this way, I am a holy lier, and in this the God of truth will reward my lie; for, if I say my sins are mine own, they are none of mine, but, by that confessing and appropriating of those sins to my selfe, they are made the sins of him, who hath suffered enough for all, my blessed Lord and Saviour, *Christ Jesus.* Therefore that servant of God, S. *Augustine* confesses those sins, which he never did, to be his sins, and to have been forgiven him: *Peccata mihi dimissa fateor, & quæ mea sponte feci, & quæ te duce non feci;* Those sins which I have done, and those, which, but for thy grace, I should have done, are all, my sins. Alas, I may die here, and die under an everlasting condemnation of fornication with that *woman,* that lives, and dies a Virgin, and be damn'd for a murderer of that man, that outlives me, and for a robbery, and oppression, where no man is damnified, nor any penny lost. The sin that I have done, the sin that I *would* have done, is my sin. We must not therefore transfer our sins upon any other. Wee must not think to discharge our selves upon a
Non patris *Peccata Patris;* To come to say, My father thriv'd well in this course, why should not I proceed in it? My father was of this Religion, why should not I continue in it? How often is it said in the Scriptures, of evill Kings, he did evill in the sight of the Lord, and walk'd *in via Patris,* in the way of his *father?* father in the *singular;* It is never said *plurally, In via Patrum;* in the way of his *fathers.* Gods blessings in this world, are express'd so, in the plurall, thou gavest this land
1 Reg. 8.48 *patribus,* to their fathers, says *Solomon,* in the dedication of the
v. 53 Temple; And, thou brought'st *Patres,* our *Fathers* out of *Egypt;* And
v. 57 again, Be with us, Lord, as thou wast with our *Fathers;* So, in

Ezekiel, where your *Fathers* dwelt, you, their children, shall dwell [Ezek.]
too, and your children, and their childrens children for ever. His 37.25
blessings upon his Saints, his holy ones in this world, are expressed
so, *plurally,* and so is the transmigration of his Saints out of this
world also; Thou shalt sleep *cum patribus,* with thy *fathers,* says Deut. 31.16
God to *Moses;* And *David* slept *cum patribus,* with his *fathers;* And 1 Reg. 2.10
Jacob had that care of himselfe, as of that in which consisted, or in
which was testified, the blessing of God, I will lie *cum patribus,* with
my *fathers,* and be buried in their burying place, says *Jacob* to his son Gen. 47.30
Joseph: Good ways, and good ends are in the *plurall,* and have many
examples; else they are not good; but sins are in the *singular,* He
[that] walk'd in the way of his *father,* is in an ill way: But carry our
manners, or carry our Religion high enough, and we shall finde a
good rule in our fathers: *Stand in the way,* says God in *Jeremy, and* [Jer.] 6.16
ask for the old way, which is the good way. We must put off *veterem*
hominem, but not *antiquum;* Wee may put off that Religion which
we think old, because it is a little elder then our selves, and not rely
upon that, it *was the Religion of my Father.* But *Antiquissimum* [Dan. 7.22]
dierum, Him, whose name is, *He that is, and was, and is for ever,* [Apoc. 1.4]
and so involves, and enwraps in himself all the Fathers, him we must
put on. Be that our issue with our adversaries at *Rome, By the*
Fathers, the Fathers in the *plurall,* when those fathers unanimely
deliver any thing dogmatically, for matter of faith, we are content
to be tried by the Fathers, the Fathers in that plurall. But by that
one Father, who begets his children, not upon the true mother, *the*
Church, but upon the *Court,* and so produces articles of faith, accord-
ing as State businesses, and civill occasions invite him, by that *father*
we must refuse to be tried: for, to limit it in particular, to my father,
we must say with *Nehemiah, Ego & domus patris mei,* If I make my Nehem. 1.[6]
fathers house my Church, my father my Bishop, I, and my fathers
house have sinned, says he; and with *Mordecai* to *Esther, Thou, and* [Esther]
thy fathers house shall be destroyed. 4.14

They are not *peccata patris,* I cannot excuse my sins, upon the ex- *Non*
ample of my father: nor are they *peccata Temporis,* I cannot dis- *temporis*
charge my sins upon the *Times,* and upon the present ill disposition
that reigns in men now, and doe ill, because every body else does so;
To say, there is a rot, and therefore the sheep must perish; Corrup-

tions in Religion are crept in, and work in every corner, and therefore Gods sheep, simple souls, must be content to admit the infection of this rot; That there is a murrain, and therefore cattell must die; superstition practis'd in many places, and therefore the strong servants of God, must come to sacrifice their obedience to it, or their bloud for it. There is no such rot, no such murrain, no such corruption of times, as can lay a *necessity,* or can afford an excuse to them who are corrupted with the times. As it is not *pax temporis,* such a *State-peace,* as takes away honour, that secures a Nation, nor such a *Church-peace,* as takes away *zeal,* that secures a conscience, so neither is it *peccatum temporis,* an observation what other men incline to, but what truth, what integrity thou declin'st from, that appertains to thy consideration.

Non ætatis

[Mat. 19.20; Mark 10.20; Luke 18.21]

2 Tim. 2.22

Ps. 25.7

Eccles. 12.1

It is not *peccatum ætatis;* not the sin of thy father, not the sin of the *times,* not the sin of thine own *years.* That thou shouldst say in thy old *age,* in excuse of thy *covetousnesse, All these things have I observed from my youth,* I have lived temperately, continently all my life, and therefore may be allowed one sin for mine ease in mine age. Or, that thou shouldest say in thy *youth,* I will retire my self in mine age, and live contentedly with a little then, but now, how vain were it to goe about to keep out a tide, or to quench the heats, and impetuous violence of youth? But *fuge juvenilia desideria, fly also youthfull lusts;* And lest God hear not thee at last, when thou comest with that petition, *Remember not the sins of my youth; Remember* thou *thy Creator, now in the days of thy youth:* for, if thou think it enough to say, I have but liv'd, as other men have liv'd, wantonly, thou wilt finde some examples to die by too; and die, as other old men, old in years, and old in sins, have died too, negligently, or fearfully; without any sense at all, or all their sense turned into fearfull apprehensions, and desperation.

Non artis

Esa. 44.13 [also 14–17]

They are not *peccata ætatis,* such sins, as men of that age must needs commit, nor *peccata artis,* such sins as men of thy *calling,* or thy *profession,* cannot avoid; that thou should'st say, I shall not be beleeved to understand my profession, as well as other men, if I live not by it, as well as other men doe. Is there no being a *Carpenter,* but that after he hath warmed him by the chips, and baked, and roasted by it, hee must needs make an *idoll* of his wood, and worship it? Is there no being a *Silver-smith,* but he must needs make shrines for *Diana* of the *Ephesians,* as *Demetrius* did? No being a *Lawyer,* without serving the passion of the Client? no being a *Divine,* without sowing pillows under great mens elbows? It is not the sin of thy Calling that oppresses thee; As a man may commit a massacre, in a single murder, and kill many in one man, if he kill one, upon whom many depended, so is that man a generall libeller, that defames a lawfull Calling, by his abusing thereof; that lives so scandalously in the *Ministery,* as to defame the Ministery it self, or so imperiously in the *Magistracy,* as to defame the Magistracy it self, as though it were but an engine, and instrument of oppression, or so unjustly in any Calling, as his abuse dishonours the Calling it self. God hath instituted Callings, for the conservation of order in generall, not for the justification of disorders in any particular. For he that justifies his faults by his calling, hath not yet received that calling from above, whereby he must be justified, and sanctified in the way, and glorified in the end. There is no lawfull calling, in which, a man may not be an honest man.

Acts 19.24

Non Magistratus

It is not *peccatum Magistratus,* thou canst not excuse thy selfe upon the unjust command of thy superiour; that's the blinde and implicite obedience practised in the *Church* of *Rome;* Nor *peccatum Pastoris,* the ill example of thy Pastor, whose life counter-preaches his doctrine, for, that shall aggravate his, but not excuse thy sinne; Nor *Peccata Cœli,* the influence of Stars, concluding a fatality, amongst the *Gentiles,* or such a working of a necessary, and inevitable, and unconditioned *Decree* of God, as may shut up the ways of a Religious walking in this life, or a happy resting in the life to come; It is none of these, not the sinne of thy *Father*, not the sinne of the present *times,* not the sin of thy *years,* and age, nor of thy *calling,* nor of the *Magistrate,* nor of thy *Pastor,* nor of *Destiny,* nor of *decrees,* but it is *peccatum tuum,* thy sin, thy own sin. And not onely thy sin so, as *Adams* sin is communicated to thee, by propagation of *Originall* sin; for, so thou mightest have some colour to discharge thy selfe upon *him,* as he did upon *Eve,* and *Eve* upon the *Serpent;* Though in truth it make no difference, in this spirituall debt, of that sin, *who is first in the bond: Adam* may stand first, but yet thou art no surety but a Principall, and for thy selfe; and he, and thou are equally subject to the penalty. For though *Saint Augustine* confesse, that there are many things concerning *Originall* sin, of which he is utterly ignorant, yet of this he would have no man ignorant, that to the guiltinesse of originall sin, our own wills concurre as well as to any actuall sin: An involuntary act, cannot be a sinfull act; and though our will work not now, in the admitting of originall sin, which enters with our soule in our conception, or in our inanimation and quickening, yet, at first,

August.

Sicut omnium natura, ita omnium voluntates erant in Adam, as every man was in *Adam,* so every *faculty* of every man, and consequently the will of every man concurred to that sin, which therefore lies upon every man now: So that that debt, *Originall* sin, is as much *thine* as *his;* And for the other debts, which grow out of this debt, (as nothing is so generative, so multiplying, as debts are, especially spirituall debts, sins) for *actuall sins,* they are thine, out of thine own choice; Thou mightest have left them undone, and wouldest needs doe them; for God never induces any man into a perplexity, that is, into a necessity of doing any particular sin. Thou couldest have disswaded a Son, or a friend, or a servant, from that sin, which thou hast embraced thy selfe: Thou hast been so farre from having been *forced* to those sins, which thou hast done, as that thou hast been sorry, thou

Chrysost.

couldest not doe them, in a greater measure. They are thine, thine own, so, as that thou canst not discharge thy selfe upon the *Devill;* but art, by the habit of sin, become *Spontaneus Dæmon,* a Devill to thy selfe, and wouldest minister tentations to thy selfe, though there were no other Devill. And this is our *propriety* in sin; *They are our own.*

Plural

This is the propriety of thy sin; The next is the *Plurality,* the *multiplicity, iniquitates;* Not onely the committing of one sin *often;* and yet, he deceives himselfe in his account dangerously, that reckons but upon *one* sin, because he is guilty but of *one kinde* of sin. Would a man say he had but one wound, if he were shot seven times in the same place? Could the *Jews* deny, that they flead Christ, with their second or third or twentieth blow, because they had torne skin, and flesh, with their former scourges, and had left nothing but bones to wound? But it is not onely that, the repeating of the same sin often, but it is the multiplicity of *divers kinds* of sins, that is here lamented in all our behalfes. It is not when the conscience is tender, and afraid of every sin, and every appearance of sin. When *Naaman* desired pardon of God by the Prophet, for sustaining the King upon his knees, in the house of *Rimmon,* the Idol, and the Prophet bad him *goe in peace,* it is not that he allows him any peace under the conscience, and guiltinesse of a sin; That was indispensable. Neither is there any dispensation in *Naamans* case, but onely a rectifying of a tender and timorous conscience, that thought *that* to be a sin, which was not, if it went no further, but to the exhibiting of a *Civill duty* to his Master, in what place soever, Religious, or prophane, that service of kneeling were to be done. *Naamans* service was truely no sin; but it had been a sin in him to have done it, when *he thought* it to be a sin. And therefore the Prophets phrase, *Goe in peace,* may well be interpreted so, set thy minde at rest; for all that, that thou requirest, may be done without sin. Now that tendernesse of conscience is not in our case in the Text. He that proceeds so, to examine all his actions, may meet scruples all the way, that may give him some anxiety, and vexation, but he shall never come to that overflowing of sin, intended in this *plurality,* and *multiplicity* here. For, this plurality, this multiplicity of sin, hath found first a spunginesse in the soul, an aptnesse to receive any liquor, to embrace any sin, that is offered to it; and after a while, a hunger and thirst in the soul, to hunt, and pant and draw after a tentation, and not to be able to endure any *vacuum,* any discontinuance, or intermission of sinne: and hee will come to think it a melancholique thing, still to stand in fear of Hell; a sordid, a *yeomanly* thing, still to be plowing, and weeding, and worming a conscience; a mechanicall thing, still to be removing logs, or filing iron, still to be busied in removing occasions of tentation, or filing and clearing particular actions: and, at last he will come to that case, which S. *Augustine* out of an abundant ingenuity, and tendernesse, and compunction, confesses of himself, *Ne vituperarer, vitiosior fiebam,* I was fain to sin, lest I should lose my credit, and be under-valued; *Et ubi non suberat, quo admisso, æquarer perditis,* when I had no means to doe some sins, whereby I might be equall to my fellow, *Fingebam me fecisse quod non feceram, ne viderer abjectior, quo innocentior,* I would bely my self, and say I had done that, which I never did, lest I should be under-valued for not having done it. *Audiebam eos exaltantes flagitia,* sayes that tender blessed Father, I

2 Reg. 5.[18, 19]

saw it was thought wit, to make Sonnets of their own sinnes, *Et libebat facere, non libidine facti, sed libidine laudis,* I sinn'd, not for the pleasure I had in the sin, but for the pride that I had to write feelingly of it. O what a *Leviathan* is sin, how vast, how immense a body! And then, what a spawner, how numerous! Between these two, the *denying* of sins, which we have done, and the *bragging* of sins, which we have not done, what a space, what a compasse is there, for millions of millions of sins! And so have you the *nature* of sin, which was our first; The *propriety of sin,* which was our second; and the *plurality,* the multiplicity of sin, which was our third branch; And follows next, the *exaltation* thereof; *supergressæ sunt, My sins are gone over my head.*

Supergressae sunt
1 Reg. 18.43–45

They are, that is, they are *already* got above us; for in that case we consider this plurall, this manifold sinner, that he hath slipt his time of preventing, or resisting his sins; His habits of sins are got, already got above him. *Elijah* bids his man look towards the Sea, and he saw nothing; He bids him look again, and again to a seventh time, and he saw nothing. After all, he sees but a little cloud, like a mans hand; and yet, upon that little appearance, the Prophet warns the King, to get him into his Chariot, and make good hast away, lest the rain stopp'd his passage, for, instantly the heaven was black, with clouds, and rain. The sinner will see nothing, till he can see nothing; and, when he sees any thing, (as to the blindest conscience something will appear) he thinks it but a little cloud, but a melancholique fit, and, in an instant, (for 7 years make but an instant to that man, that thinks of himself, but once in 7 years) *Supergressæ sunt,* his sins are got above him, and his way out is stopp'd. The Sun is got over us now, though we saw none of his motions, and so are our sins, though we saw not their steps. You know how confident our adversaries are in that argument, *Why doe ye oppugne our doctrine of prayer for the dead,* or *of Invocation of Saints,* or *of the fire of Purgatory,* since you cannot assigne us a time, when these doctrines came into the Church, or that they were opposed or contradicted, when they entred? When a conscience comes to that inquisition, to an *iniquitates supergressæ,* to consider that our sins are gone over our head in any of those ways, which we have spoken of, if we offer to awaken that conscience farther, it startles, and it answers us drowsily, or frowardly, like a new wak'd man, Can you remember when you sin'd this sin first, or did you resist it then, or since? whence comes this troublesome singularity now? pray let me sleep still, says this startled conscience. Beloved, if we fear not the wetting of our foot in sin, it will be too late, when we are over head and ears. Gods deliverance of his children, was *sicco pede,* hee made the sea dry land, and *they wet not their foot.* Exod. 14. [16, 22, 29] At first, in the creation, *subjecit omnia sub pedibus,* God put all things under their feet; Ps. 8.6 In mans wayes, in this world, his Angels beare us up in their hands; why? *Ne impingamus pedem,* that we should not hurt our foot against a stone, [Psal. 91.12] but have a care of every step we make. If thou have defiled thy feet, (strayed into any unclean ways) wash them again, and stop there, and that will bring thee to the consideration of the Spouse, *I have washed my feet, how shall I then defile them again?* Cant. 5.3 I have found mercy for my former sins, how shal I dare to provoke God with more? stil God appoints us a permanent means to tread sin under our feet here, in this life; The woman, that is, the Church, hath the Moon, that is, all transitory things, (and so, all tentations) under her feet; Apoc. 12.[1] As Christ himself expressed his care of *Peter,* to consist in that, *That if his feet were washed, all was clean;* [John 13.10] And as in his own person he admitted nails in his feet, as wel as in his hands, so crucifie thy hands, abstain from unjust actions, but crucifie thy feet too, make not one step towards the way of Idolaters, or other sinners. If we watch not the *ingressus sum,* we shall be insensible of the *supergressæ sunt;* If we look not to a sin, when it comes towards us, we shal not be able to look towards it, when it is got over us: for, if a man come to walk in the counsel of the ungodly, he wil come to sit in the seat of the scornful; for, that's the sinners progress, in the first warning that *David* gives in the beginning of his First *Psalm.* If he give himself leave to enter into sinful ways, he wil sit and sin at ease, and make a jest of sin; and he that loveth danger, shal perish therein. So have you then the nature of sin; it was sin that oppressed him; and the propriety of sin, it was his sin, actuall sin; and the plurality of sin, habituall, customary sin; and the victory of sin, they had been long climing, and were now got up to a height; and this height and exaltation of theirs, is expressed thus, *super caput, Mine iniquities are got above my head.*

Super caput

S. *Augustine,* (who truly had either never true copy of the Bible, or else cited sometimes, as the words were in his memory, and not as they were in the Text) he reads not these words so, *supergressæ super caput,* but thus, *sustulerunt caput;* And so he interprets the words, not that his sins had got over his head, and depressed his head, subdued and subjugated his head, but that they had extoll'd his head, made him lift his head high, and say, *Who is the Lord? Sursum tollitur,* says he upon this place, *cui erigitur caput contra Deum,* his head is exalted, who is set against God. And certainly, that's a desperate state in sin, when a man thinks himself the wiser, or the better, or the more powerfull for his sin; That he can the better stand upon his own legs, or the lesse needs the assistance of God, because he hath prosper'd in the world, by the ways of sin. S. *Augustine's* is an useful mistaking, but it is a mistaking. But to pursue the right word, and the true meaning of this metaphoricall expressing, *supergressæ caput,* My sins are got above my head, sin may be got to our foot, and yet not to the eye. A man may stray into company of tentations, and yet not be tempted; A man *may make a covenant with his eye, that he will not see a maid.* Sin may come to the eye, and yet the hand be above water; we may look, and lust, and yet, by Gods watchfull goodnes, and studious mercy, escape action. But if it be above our head, then the brain is drown'd, that is, our reason, and *understanding,* which should dispute against it, and make us asham'd of it, or afraid of it; And our *memory* is drown'd, we have forgot that there belongs a repentance to our sins, perchance forgot that there is such a sin in us; forgot that those actions are sins, forgot that we have done those actions; and forgot that there is a law, even in our own hearts, by which we might try, whether our actions were sins, or no. If they be above our heads, they are so, in many dangerous acceptations. Of which, the first is, that they cover our heads *sicut tectum, sicut fornix,* as a roof, as an arch, as a separation between God and us.

Job [31.1]

Tectum

Esa. 59.2

Your *iniquities have separated between you and your God,* says the Prophet. A wall of separation between man and man, even in the service of God, there was always; a wall of Gods making; that is, the *Ceremoniall Law,* by which God enclos'd the *Jews* from the *Gentiles.* But this was but a side wall, and Christ threw it down; *He is our peace,* says the Apostle, and hath made *of both one, and hath broken the stop of the partition wall;* This he did when he

Eph. 2.14

opened the *Gentiles* a way into his religion. This wall was the distinction between the *Jew,* and *Gentile,* when the *Jew* call'd them ignominiously *Incircumcisos,* uncircumcised, and they call'd the *Jews,* with as much scorn, *Recutitos,* and *Apellas;* when the *Jew* wondred at the *Gentiles* eating of unclean things, and the *Gentiles* wondred to hear them call things, of as good nourishment, as their clean meats, uncleane; when the *Jew* placed his holinesse in singularity, and ceremonies of distinction, and the *Gentiles* call'd that but a pride in them, and a scornefull detestation of their neighbours. And truly it is a lamentable thing, when ceremoniall things in matter of discipline, or problematicall things in matter of doctrine, come so farre, as to separate us from one another, in giving ill names to one another. *Zeal* is directed upon God, and charity upon our brethren; but God will not be seen, but by that spectacle; nor accept any thing for an act of zeal to himself, that violates charity towards our brethren, by the way. Neither should we call any man *Lutheran,* or *Calvinist,* or by any other name, ignominiously, but for such things, as had been condemned in *Luther,* or *Calvin,* and condemned by such, as are competent Judges between them, and us; that is, by the universall, or by our own Church. This wall then, between the *Jew* and *Gentile,* (as it was the ceremony it self, and not the abuse of it) God built, and Christ threw downe. There are outward things, Ceremoniall things, in the worship of God, that are temporary, and they did serve God that brought them in, and they doe serve God also, that have driven them out of the Church, because their undeniable abuse had clog'd them with an impossibility of being restor'd to that good use, which they were at first ordained for; of which, the brazen serpent is evidence enough. God set up a wall, which God himself meant should be demolish'd again. Such another wal, (as well as the Devil can imitate Gods workmanship) the Devil hath built now in the Christian Church; and hath morter'd it in the brains and bloud of men, in the sharp and virulent contentions arisen, and fomented in matters of Religion. But yet, says the Spouse, *My well beloved stands* Cant. 2.9
behind the wall, shewing himself through the grates: he may be seen on both sides. For all this separation, Christ Jesus is amongst us all, and in his time, will break downe this wall too, these differences amongst Christians, and make us all glad of that name, the name

of Christians, without affecting in our selves, or inflicting upon others, other names of envy, and subdivision. But besides this wall of Gods making, the *Ceremoniall law,* and this wall of the Devils making, *dissention* in Christian Churches, there is a wall of our own making, a roof, an arch above our heads, by which our continuall sins have separated God and us. God had covered himself with a cloud, so that *prayer* could not passe thorough; That was the misery of *Ierusalem.* But in the acts and habits of sin, we cover our selves, with a roof, with an arch, which nothing can shake, nor remove, but Thunder, and Earthquakes, that is, the execution of Gods fiercest judgments; And whether in that fall of the roof, that is, in the weight of Gods judgments upon us, the stones shall not brain us, overwhelm and smother, and bury us, God only knows. How his Thunders, and his Earthquakes, when we put him to that, will work upon us, he onely knows, whether to our amendment, or to our destruction. But whil'st we are in the consideration of this arch, this roof of separation, between God and us, by sin, there may be use in imparting to you, an observation, a passage of mine own. Lying at *Aix,* at *Aquisgrane,* a well known Town in *Germany,* and fixing there some time, for the benefit of those *Baths,* I found my self in a house, which was divided into many families, and indeed so large as it might have been a little Parish, or, at least, a great lim of a great one; But it was of no Parish: for when I ask'd who lay over my head, they told me a family of *Anabaptists;* And who over theirs? Another family of *Anabaptists;* and another family of *Anabaptists* over theirs; and the whole house, was a nest of these boxes; severall artificers; all *Anabaptists;* I ask'd in what room they met, for the exercise of their Religion; I was told they never met: for, though they were all *Anabaptists,* yet for some collaterall differences, they detested one another, and, though many of them, were near in bloud, and alliance to one another, yet the son would excommunicate the father, in the room above him, and the Nephew the Uncle. As S. *John* is said to have quitted that *Bath,* into which *Cerinthus* the Heretique came, so did I this house; I remembred that *Hezekiah* in his sicknesse, turn'd himself in his bed, to pray *towards that wall,* that look'd to *Ierusalem;* And that *Daniel* in *Babylon,* when he pray'd in his chamber, opened those windows that look'd *towards Ierusalem;* for, in the first dedication of the

Lam. 3.44

[2 Kings 20.2; Isa. 38.2]

[Dan. 6.10]

Temple, at *Ierusalem,* there is a promise annext to the prayers made *towards the Temple:* [1 Kings 8.38, 39; 9.3] And I began to think, how many roofs, how many floores of separation, were made between God and my prayers in that house. And such is this multiplicity of sins, which we consider to be got over us, as a roof, as an arch, many arches, many roofs: for, though these habituall sins, be so of kin, as that they grow from one another, and yet for all this kindred excommunicate one another, (for covetousnesse will not be in the same roome with prodigality) yet it is but going up another stair, and there's the tother *Anabaptist;* it is but living a few years, and then the prodigall becomes covetous. All the way, they separate us from God, as a roof, as an arch; and then, an arch will bear any weight; An habituall sin got over our head as an arch will stand under any sicknesse, any dishonour, any judgement of God, and never sink towards any humiliation.

Clamor

They are above our heads, *sicut tectum,* as a roofe, as an arch, and they are so too *sicut clamor,* as a voice ascending, and not stopping, till they come to God. *O my God, I am confounded and ashamed to lift up mine eyes to thee, O my God;* (Ezra 9.6) why not thine eyes? there is a cloud, a clamour in the way; for as it follows, *Our iniquities are encreased over our heads, and our trespasse is grown up to the heaven.* I think to retain a learned man of my counsell, and one that is sure to be heard in the Court, and when I come to instruct him, I finde mine adversaries name in his book before, and he is all ready for the other party. I think to finde an Advocate in heaven, when I will, and my sin is in heaven before mee. The voice of *Abels* bloud, and so, of *Cains* sin, was there: The voice of *Sodomes transgression* was there. Bring down that sin again from heaven to earth: Bring that voice that cries in heaven, to speake to Christ here in his Church, upon earth, by way of *confession;* bring that clamorous sin to his bloud, to be washed in the Sacrament, for, as long as thy sin cries in heaven, thy prayers cannot be heard there. Bring thy sinne under Christs feet there, when hee walks amongst the Candlesticks, [Apoc. 1.12, 13] in the light, and power of his Ordinances in the Church, and then, thine absolution will be upon thy head, in those seals which he hath instituted, and ordained there, and thy cry will be silenced. Till then, *supergressæ caput,* thine iniquities will be over thy head, as a roof, as a cry, and, in the next place, *sicut aquæ,* as the overflowing of waters.

Aquæ

We consider this plurality, this multiplicity of habituall sinnes, to bee got over our heads, as waters, especially in this, that they have stupefied us, and taken from us all sense of reparation of our sinfull condition. The Organ that God hath given the naturall man, is the *eye;* he sees God in the creature. The Organ that God hath given the Christian, is the *ear;* he hears God in his Word. But when we are under water, both senses, both Organs are vitiated, and depraved, if not defeated. The habituall, and manifold sinner, sees nothing aright; Hee sees a *judgement,* and cals it an *accident.* He hears nothing aright; He hears the Ordinance of *Preaching* for salvation in the next world, and he cals it an invention of the State, for subjection in this world. And as under water, every thing seems distorted and crooked, to man, so does man himself to God, who sees not his own Image in that man, in that form as he made it. When *man hath drunk* Job. 15.16 *iniquity like water,* then, *The flouds of wickednesse shall make him* Ps. 18.4 *afraid;* The water that he hath swum in, the sin that he hath delighted in, shall appear with horrour unto him. As God threatens the pride of *Tyrus, I shall bring the deep upon thee, and great waters* Ezek. 26.19 *shall cover thee,* That, God will execute upon this sinner; And then, upon every drop of that water, upon every affliction, every tribulation, he shall come to that fearfulnesse, Lam. 3.54 *Waters flowed over my head;* then said I, *I am cut off;* Either he shall see nothing, or see no remedy, no deliverance from desperation. Keep low these waters, as waters signifie *sin,* and God shall keep them low, as they signifie Gen. 8.8 [also 9–11] *punishments;* And his Dove shall return to the Ark with an Olive leaf, to shew thee that the waters are abated; he shall give thee a testimony of the return of his love, in his Oyle, and Wine, and Milk, and Honey, in the temporall abundances of this life. And, Joh. 2.7 [also 8–10] *si impleat Hydrias aqua,* if he doe fill all your vessels with water, with water of bitternesse, that is, fill and exercise all your patience, and all your faculties with his corrections, yet he shall doe that, but to *change your water into wine,* as he did there, he shall make his very Judgements, Sacraments, conveyances and seals of his mercy to you, though those manifold sins be got over your heads, as a roof, as a noise, as an overflowing of waters: And, that, which is the heaviest of all, and

Dominus

our last consideration, *sicut Dominus,* as a Lord, as a Tyran, as an Usurper.

Pretio redempti estis, nolite fieri servi, says the Apostle; you are bought with a price, therefore glorifie God. There he shews you, your own value; and then, *Ne dominetur peccatum,* Let not sin have dominion over you; there he shews you the insolency of that Tyran. You shall know the truth, and the truth shall make you *free,* says Christ to the *Jews.* Well; They stood not much upon the truth; but for the *freedome,* We were *Abrahams* seed, and were never bound to any; but Christ replies, *Whosoever committeth sin, is the servant of sin;* And, *of whomsoever a man is overcome, to the same he is in bondage.* Now we are slaves to sin, not onely as we have been overcome by sin (for he that is said to be overcome by sin, is presumed to have made some resistance) but as we have sold our selves to sin, which is a worse, and a more voluntary act. There was none *like him,* like *Ahab;* (says the holy Ghost) *wherein* was his singularity above all? He *had sold himself, to work wickednesse,* in the sight of the Lord. Now, how are we sold to sin? By *Adam?* That's true; *Ejus prævaricatione, & ut ita dicam, Negotiatione, damnoso, & fraudulento commercio venditi sumus:* Wee were all sold under hand, fraudulently sold, and sold under foot, cheaply sold by *Adam.* But thus, wee might seem to be sold by others; so *Joseph* was, and no fault in himself; But we have sold our selves since. Did not *Adam* sell himself too? Did God sell him by any *secret Decree*, or contract, between the Devil and him? Was God of counsel in that bargain? God forbid. Thus saith the Lord, *Where is the bill of your mothers divorce, whom I have put away? or, which of my creditours is it, to whom I have sold you? Behold, for your iniquities you have sold your selves, and for your transgressions, is your mother put away.* In *Adam* we were sold in *grosse;* in our selves we are sold by *retail;* In the first, and generall sale, we all pass'd, even the best of us. We know *the Law is spirituall, but I am carnall, sold under sin,* says the Apostle, even of himselfe. But when does the Apostle say this? in what state was hee, when he accuses himselfe of this mancipation, and sale under sin? Says he this onely with relation to his former times, when he was a *Jew,* and under the Law? Or, but then when he was newly come to the light of the Gospel, and not to a clear sight of it? It is true, that most of the *Eastern Fathers,* and it is true, that S. *Augustine* himselfe was of that opinion, that S. *Paul* said of himselfe, *that he was sold under*

1 Cor. 6.20 [also 7.23]
Joh. 8.32 [also 33]
2 Pet. 2.19
1 Reg. 21.20
Cassian
Esa. 50.1
Rom. 7.14

sin, respecting himself before his regeneration. *Non qui vult esse sapiens, statim fit sapiens,* says *Origen;* A man is not presently learned, because he hath a good desire to be learned; nor hath he that hath begun a conversion, presently accomplished his regeneration; nor is he discharged of his bargain of being sold under sin, as soon as hee sees that he hath made an ill bargain. But when he growes up in grace, (say they) as S. *Paul* had done, when hee said this, then he is discharged. But, as S. *Augustine* ingenuously retracts that opinion, which, (as he says) he had held, when he was a *young Priest* at *Carthage,* so is there nothing clearer, by the whole purpose of the Apostle in that place, then that he in his best state, was still sold under sin. As *David* speaks of himself being then regenerated, *In thy sight shall no man living be justified,* So S. *Paul* speaks of himself in his best state, still he *was sold under sin,* because still, that *concupiscence,* under which he was sold in *Adam,* remains in him. And that concupiscence is sin, *Quia inest ei inobedientia contra dominatum mentis.* Because it is a rebellion against that soveraignty which God hath instituted in the soul of man, and an ambition of setting up another Prince; so it is *peccatum,* sin in it self; And it is *pœna peccati,* says that Father, *Quia reddita est meritis inobedientis;* Because it is laid upon us for that disobedience, it hath also the nature of a punishment of sin, as well as of sin it self; And then it is *Causa peccati* too, *Defectione consentientis,* because man is so enfeebled by this inherence, and invisceration of Originall sin, as that thereby he is exposed to every emergent tentation, to any actuall sin. So, *Originall sinne,* is called by many of the Ancients, the cause of sin, and the effect of sin, but not so, *exclusively,* as that it is not sin, really sin in it self too. Now, as Originall sin causes Actuall, in that consideration (as we sell our selves over again in our acts of recognition, in ratifying our first sale, by our manifold sins here) so is *sin gone over our heads,* by this dominion, as a Tyran, as an usurper. *Hoc lex posuit, Non concupisces;* This is the Law, Thou shalt not covet: *Non quod sic valeamus, sed ad quod perficiendo tendamus;* Not that we can perform that Law, but that that Law might be a rule to direct our endevours: *Multum boni facit, qui facit quod scriptum est, Post concupiscentias tuas non eas;* He does well, and well in a fair meaure, that fulfils that Commandement, *Thou shalt not walk in the con-*

Retract. 1. c. 23

[Psal. 143.2]

August.

August.

[Ecclus. 18.30]

cupiscences of thine own heart; sed non perficit, quia non implet quod scriptum est, Non concupisces, But yet, says he, hee does not all that is commanded, because he is commanded not to covet at all: *Vt sciat, quò debeat in hac mortalitate conari,* That that commandement might teach him, what he should labour for in this life, *Et quò possit in illa immortalitate pervenire,* to what perfection wee shall come in the life to come, but not till then. Though therefore we did our best, yet we were *sold under sin,* that is, sold by *Adam;* but because we doe not but consent to that first sale, in our sinfull acts, and habits, wee have *sold our selves* too, and so sin is gone over our heads, in a dominion, and in a tyrannicall exercise of that dominion. If we would goe about to expresse, by what customes of sin this dominion is established, we should be put to a necessity of entring into every profession, and every conscience. And the morall man Seneca says usefully, *Si tantum irasci vis sapientem, quantum exigit indignitas scelerum,* (we will translate it in the Church tongue, and make his morality divinity) If we would have a *zealous Preacher,* cry out as fast, or as loud, as sins are committed, *non irascendum, sed insaniendum,* says he, you would not call that man an angry man, but a mad man, you would not call that Preacher, a zealous preacher, but a *Puritan.* Touch we but upon one of his reprehensions, because that may have the best use now; he considers the iniquities, and injustices, admitted, and committed in *Courts of justice;* and he says, *Turpes lites, turpiores Advocati;* Ill sutes are set on foot, and worse advocates defend them. *Delator est criminis qui manifestior reus,* even in criminall matters, he informes against another, that should be but defendant in that crime; And (as he carries it higher) *Iudex damnaturus quæ fecit, eligitur,* the Judge himself condemns a man for that, which himselfe is farre more guilty of, then the prisoner. *Nullus nisi ex alieno damno quæstus,* and one man growes rich, by the empoverishing of many. But then it is so in all other professions too. And this Tyranny, and dominion is justly permitted by God upon us, *ut qui noluit superiori obedire, nec ei obediat inferior caro,* we have been rebellious to our Soveraigne, to God, and therefore our subject, the flesh, is first rebellious against us, and then Tyrannicall over us. *But he that leadeth into captivity shall goe into captivity;* Revel. 13.10
yea, Christ hath led *captivity* it selfe *captive,* and *given gifts to men;* Ephes. 4.8

that is, he hath established his Church, where, by a good use of those meanes which God hath ordained for it, the most oppressed soule, may raise it selfe above those exaltations, and supergressions of sin; And so we have done with our first part, and with all that will enter into this time, where *David* in his humble spirit feels in himselfe, but much more in his propheticall spirit, foresees, and foretells in others, the infectious *nature* of sin; It is a mortall wound, and in a strange consideration; for, it is a wound upon God, and mortall upon man; And then the *propriety* of sin, that sin is not at all from God, nor it is not all from the Devill, but our sin is our own; Our sins in a *Plurality;* our sins of one kind, determine not in one sin, we sin the same sin often, and then we determine not in one kinde, but slide into many. And after this multiplication of sin, the *continuation* thereof, to an irrecoverablenesse, *supergressæ sunt,* we thinke not of them, till it be too late to think of them, till they produce no thought but despair; for *supergressæ Caput,* they are got above our *Heads,* above our strongest faculties; Above us, in the nature of an arched *roof,* they keep Gods grace in a separation from us, and our prayers from him, so they have the nature of a roof, and then, they feel no weight, they bend not under any judgement, which he lays upon us, so they have the nature of an *Arch.* Above us, as a *voice,* as a *cry;* Their voice is in possession of God, and so prevents our prayers; above us as *waters,* they disable our eyes, and our eares, from right conceiving all apprehensions; And above us, as *Lords,* and *Tyrans,* that came in by conquest, and so put what Laws they list upon us. And these instructions have arisen from this first, the *Multiplicity, Mine iniquities are gone over my Head,* and more will from the other, the *weight* and *burden, They are as a heavy burden, too heavy for me.*

Number 4.

Preached at Lincolns Inne.

Second Sermon on

Psal. 38.4. *FOR MINE INIQUITIES ARE GONE OVER MY HEAD, AS A HEAVY BURDEN, THEY ARE TOO HEAVY FOR ME.*

As the Philosopher says, if a man could see *vertue,* he would *love it,* so if a man could see *sin,* he would *hate* it. But as the *eye* sees every thing but *it selfe,* so does *sinne,* too. It sees *Beauty,* and *Honour,* and *Riches,* but it sees not it selfe, not the sinfull coveting, and compassing of all these. To make, though not sin, yet the *sinner* to see himselfe, for the explication, and application of these words, we brought you these two lights; first, the *Multiplicity* of sin, in that elegancy of the holy Ghost, *supergressæ sunt, Mine iniquities are gone over my head,* and the *weight,* and *oppression* of sin, in that, *Gravatæ nimis, As a heavy burden they are too heavy for me;* In the first, how *numerous,* how manifold they are, in the other, how grievous, how insupportable; first, how many hands, then how fast hold sinne lays upon me. The first of these two, was our exercise the last day, when we proposed and proceeded in these words, in which we presented to you, the dangerous multiplicity of sinne, in those pieces, which constituted that part. But because, as men, how many soever, make but a Multitude, or a Throng, and not an Army, if they be unarmed, so sin, how manifold, and multiform so ever, might seem a passable thing, if it might be easily shaked off, we come now to imprint in you a sense of the *weight* and *oppression* thereof, *As a heavy burthen, they are too heavy for mee;* The particular degrees whereof, we laid down the last day, in our generall division of the whole Text, and shall now pursue them, according to our order proposed then.

Gravatæ

First then, sinne is *heavy*. Does not the sinner finde it so? No marvail, nothing is heavy in his proper place, in his own Sphear, in his own Center, when it is where it would be, nothing is heavy. He that lies under water finds no burthen of all that water that lies upon him; but if he were out of it, how heavy would a small quantity of that water seem to him, if he were to carry it in a vessell? An *habituall sinner* is the naturall place, the Center of sinne, and he feels no weight in it, but if the grace of God raise him out of it, that he come to walke, and walke in the ways of godlinesse, not onely his watery Tympanies, and his dropsies, those waters which by actuall and habituall sinnes he hath contracted, but that water, of which he is properly made, the water that is in him naturally, infused from his parents, *Originall sinne,* will be sensible to him, and oppresse him. Scarce any man considers the weight of Originall sinne; And yet, as the strongest tentations fall upon us when wee are weakest, in our *death-bed,* so the heavyest sinne seises us, when wee are weakest; as soon as wee are any thing, we are sinners, and there, where there can be no more tentations ministred to us, then was to the Angels that fell in heaven, that is, in *our mothers womb,* when no world, nor flesh, nor Devill could present a provocation to sinne to us, when no faculty of ours is able to embrace, or second a provocation to sin, yet there, in that weaknesse, we are under the weight of Originall sin. And truly, if at this time, God would vouchsafe mee my choice, whether hee should pardon me all those actuall and habituall sins, which I have committed in my life, or extinguish Originall sinne in me, I should chuse to be delivered from Originall sin, because, though I be delivered from the *imputation* thereof, by *Baptism,* so that I shall not fall under a condemnation for Originall sin onely, yet it still remains in me, and practises upon me, and occasions all the other sins, that I commit: now, for all my actuall and habituall sins, I know God hath instituted meanes in his Church, the *Word,* and the *Sacraments,* for my reparation; But with what a holy alacrity, with what a heavenly joy, with what a cheerfull peace, should I come to the participation of these meanes and seals of my reconciliation, and pardon of all my sins, if I knew my selfe to be delivered from Originall sinne, from that snake in my bosome, from that poyson in my blood, from that leaven and tartar in all my actions, that casts me into Relapses of those sins which I have repented? And what a cloud upon the best serenity of my conscience, what an interruption, what a dis-continuance from the sincerity and integrity of that joy, which belongs to a man truly reconciled to God, in the pardon of his former sins, must it needs be still to know, and to know by lamentable experiences, that though I wash my selfe with Soap, and Nitre, and Snow-water, mine own cloathes will defile me again, though I have washed my selfe in the tears of Repentance, and in the blood of my Saviour, though I have no guiltinesse of any former sin upon me at that present, yet I have a sense of a *root* of sin, that is not grub'd up, of *Originall sinne,* that will cast me back again. Scarce any man considers the weight, the oppression of Originall sinne. No man can say, that an Akorn weighs as much as an Oak; yet in truth, there is an Oak in that Akorn: no man considers that Originall sinne weighs as much as Actuall, or Habituall, yet in truth, all our Actuall and Habituall sins are in Originall. Therefore Saint *Pauls* vehement, and frequent prayer to God, to that purpose, could not deliver him from Originall sin, and that *stimulus carnis,* that provocation of the flesh, that *Messenger of Satan,* which rises out of that, God would give him *sufficient grace,* it should not worke to his destruction, but yet he should have it: Nay, the infinite merit of Christ Jesus himself, that works so upon all actuall and habituall sins, as that after that merit is applyed to them, those sins are no sins, works not so upon Originall sin, but that, though I be eased in the *Dominion,* and *Imputation* thereof, yet the same Originall sin is in me still; and though God doe deliver me from eternall death, due to mine actuall and habituall sins, yet from the temporall death, due to Originall sin, he delivers not his dearest Saints.

[Job 9.31]

[2 Cor. 12.7]

Thus sin is heavy in the *seed,* in the *grain,* in the *akorn,* how much more when it is a *field* of Corn, a *barn* of grain, a *forest* of Oaks, in the multiplication, and complication of sin in sin? And yet wee consider the weight of sin another way too, for as Christ feels all the afflictions of his children, so his children will feel all the wounds that are inflicted upon him; even the sins of other men; as *Lots* righteous soule was grieved with sins of others. If others sin by my example and provocation, or by my connivence and permission, when I have authority, their sin lies heavyer upon me, then upon themselves; for they have but the *weight of their own sinne;* and I have *mine,* and *theirs* upon me; and though I cannot have *two souls* to suffer, and though there cannot be two *everlastingnesses* in the torments of hell, yet I shall have two measures of those unmeasurable torments upon my soul. But if I have no interest in the sins of other men, by any occasion ministred by me, yet I cannot chuse but feel a weight, a burthen of a holy anguish, and compassion and indignation, because every one of these sins inflict a new wound upon my Saviour, when my Saviour says to him, that does but injure me, *Why persecutest thou me,* [Acts 9.4] and feels the blow upon himselfe, shall not I say to him that wounds my Saviour, *Why woundest thou me,* and groane under the weight of my brothers sin, and my Fathers, my Makers, my Saviours wound? If a man of my blood, or allyance, doe a shamefull act, I am affected with it; If a man of my calling, or *profession,* doe a scandalous act, I feel my self concerned in his fault; God hath made all *mankinde* of *one blood,* and all *Christians* of *one calling,* and the sins of every man concern every man, both in that respect, that *I,* that is, *This nature,* is in that man that sins that sin; and *I,* that is, *This nature,* is in that Christ, who is wounded by that sin. The weight of sin, were it but Originall sin, were it but the sins of other men, is an insupportable weight.

But if a sinner will take a true balance, and try the right weight of sin, let him goe about to leave his sin, and then he shall see how close, and how heavily it stook to him. Then one sin will lay the weight, of *seelinesse,* of *falshood,* of *inconstancy,* of *dishonour,* of *ill nature,* if you goe about to leave it: and another sin will lay the weight of *poverty,* of *disestimation* upon you, if you goe about to leave it. One sin will lay your *pleasures* upon you, another your *profit,* another your *Honour,* another your *Duty* to wife and children, and weigh you down with these. Goe but out of the water, goe but about to leave a sin, and you will finde the weight of it, and the hardnesse to cast it off. *Gravatæ sunt, Mine iniquities are heavy,* (that was our first) and *gravatæ nimis,* they are *too heavy,* which is a second circumstance.

Nimis

Some weight, some *balast* is necessary to make a ship goe steady; we are not without advantage, in having *some sinne;* some *concupiscence,* some *tentation* is not too heavy for us. The greatest sins that ever were committed, were committed by them, who had *no former sinne,* to push them on to that sin: The first *Angels* sin, and the sin *of Adam* are noted to be the most desperate and the most irrecoverable sins, and they were committed, when they had no former sin in them. The *Angels* punishment is pardoned in *no part; Adams* punishment is pardoned in *no man,* in this world. Now such sins as those, that is, sins that are never pardoned, no man commits now; not now, when he hath the weight of former sins to push him on. Though there be a heavy guiltinesse in *Originall sin,* yet I have an argument, a plea for mercy out of that, *Lord, my strength is not the* Iob 6.12 *strength of stones, nor my flesh brasse; Lord, no man can bring a clean thing out of uncleannesse; Lord, no man can say after, I have cleansed my heart, I am free from sinne,* I could not be borne cleane, I could not cleanse my selfe since. It magnifies Gods glory, it amplifies mans happinesse, that he is subject to tentation. If man had been made *impeccable,* that he could not have sinned, he had not been so happy; for then, he could onely have enjoyed that state, in which he was created, and not have risen to any *better;* because that better estate, is a reward of our willing obedience to God, in such things, as we might have disobeyed him in. Therefore when the Apostle was in danger, of growing too light, *lest he should be exalted out of measure,* 2 Cor. 12.7 *through the abundance of revelation,* (says that Scripture) he had a weight hung upon him; There was something *given him,* therefore it was a benefit, *a gift;* And it was *Angelus, an Angel,* that was given him; But it was not a good Angel, a Tutelar, a Gardian Angel, to present *good motions* unto him, but it was *Angelus Satanæ, a messenger of Satan, sent,* as he says, *to buffet him;* and yet this hostile Angel, this *messenger of Satan* was a benefit, a *gift,* and a fore-runner, and some kind of *Inducer* of that *Grace,* which was *sufficient for him;* and it would not have appeared to us, no nor to himselfe, that he had had so much of that grace, if he had not had this tentation. God is as powerfull upon us when he delivers us *from* tentation, that it doe not overtake us; but not so apparent, so evident, so manifest, as when he delivers us *in* a tentation, that it doe not overcome us: some weight does but *ballast* us, as some enemies never doe us more harme, but occasion us, to arme and to stand upon our gard. Therefore, this weight that is complained of here, is not *In carne,* in our naturall flesh; (though in *that* be no *goodnesse*) it is nothing that God from the beginning hath imprinted in our nature, not that *peccability,* and *possibility* of sinning; nor it is not *in stimulo carnis,* in these accessary tentations, and provocations which awaken, and provoke the malignity of this flesh, and put a sting into it; we doe not consider this heavy weight to be the *naturall possibility* which was in man, *before Originall sinne* entred, nor to be that naturall pronenesse to sinne, which is *originall sinne it selfe.* But it is, when we our selves whet that sting, when we labour to breake hedges, and to steale wood, and gather up a stick out of one sin, and a stick out of another, and to make a fagot to load us, in this life, and burne us in the next, in multiplying sins, and aggravating circumstances, so it is *Heavy,* so it is *too heavy, It is too heavy for me,* (for that's also another circumstance) *for David himselfe,* for any man even in *Davids* state.

Mihi

Though this consideration might be enlarged, and usefully carried into this expostulation, can sin be too heavy for *me,* any burden of sin sink *me* into a dejection of spirit, that am wrapped up in the *Covenant,* borne of *Christian Parents,* that am bred up in an *Orthodox,* in a *Reformed Church,* that can perswade my selfe sometimes, that I am of the *number of the elect;* Can any sin be too heavy for *me,* can I doubt of the execution of his *first purpose* upon me, or doubt of the efficacy of his *ordinances* here in the Church, what sin soever I commit, can any sins be too heavy for me? yet it is enough that in this Sea, God holds no man up by the chin so, but that if he sin in confidence of that sustentation, he shall sink. But in this personall respect in our text, we consider onely with what weights *David* weighed his sins, when hee found here that they were too heavy for him. He weighed his sin with his punishment, and in his punishment hee saw the anger, and *indignation of God,* and when we see sin through that spectacle, through an *angry God,* it appears great, and red, and fearefull unto us; when *David* came to see himselfe in his infirmity, in his deformity, when his body could not bear the punishment here in this world, he considered how insupportable a weight the sin, and the anger of God upon that sin, would be in the world to come. For *me* that rise to preferment by my sin, for *me* that come to satisfie my *carnall appetites* by my sin, my sin is not too heavy; But for *me* that suffer *penury* in the bottome of a plentifull state exhausted by my sin, for *me* that languish under *diseases* and putrefaction contracted by my sin, for *me* upon whom the hand of God lies heavy in any *affliction* for my sin, for *me,* my sins are too heavy. Till I come to hear that voice, *Come unto me all you that labour, and* Mat. 11.[28] *are heavy laden, and I will refresh you,* till I come to consider my sin in the mercy of God, and not onely in his justice, in his punishments, my sins will be too heavy for me; for, though that be a good way, to consider the justice of God, yet it is not a good *end;* I must *stop,* but not *stay* at it, I must consider my sin in his justice, how *powerfull* a God I have provoked; but I must passe through his justice to his mercy; his justice is my *way,* but his mercy is my *lodging;* for wee cannot tell by the construction and origination of the words, whether *Cain* said, *My sin is greater then can bee par-* [Gen. 4.13] *doned,* or, *my punishment is greater then can bee borne:* But it needes not bee disputed; for it is all one; He that considers *onely* the anger of God in the *punishment,* will thinke his sin unpardonable, *his sinne will be too heavy for him.* But as a *feaver* is well spent, when the patient is fit to take physick, so if God give me physick, if I take his corrections as *medicines,* and not as *punishments,* then my disease is well spent, my danger is well overcome; If I have buryed my sins in the wounds of my Saviour, they cannot be too heavy for me, for they are not upon me at all; But if I take them out again, by relapsing into them, or imagine them to rise again, by a suspicion and jealousie in God, that he hath not forgiven them, because his hand lies still upon me, in some afflictions, so, in such a relapse, so, in such a jealous *mis-interpretation* of Gods proceeding with me, *my sins are too heavy for me;* for *me,* because I do not sustain my self by those helps that God puts into my hands.

It is *heavy, too heavy, too heavy for me,* says *David;* if you con- *Onus* sider the *elect themselves,* their election will not beare them out in their sins. But here we consider the insupportablenesse, in that, wherein the holy Ghost hath presented it, *Quia onus,* because it lies upon me, in the nature and quality of a *Burden, Mine iniquities are as a burden, too heavy for me.* When all this is packed up upon me, that I am first under a *Calamity,* a *sicknesse,* a *scorne,* an *imprisonment,* a *penury,* and then upon that calamity, there is laid the *anger* and *indignation of God,* and then upon that, the *weight* of *mine own sinnes;* this is too much to settle me, it is enough to sinke me, it is a burden, in which the danger arises from the last addition, in that, which is last laid on: for, as the *sceptique Philosopher* pleases himselfe in that argumentation, that either a penny makes a man rich, or he can never be rich, for says he, if he be not rich yet, the addition of a penny more would make him rich: or if not that penny, yet another, or another, so that at last it is the *addition of a penny* that makes him rich; so without any such fallacious or facetious circumvention in our case, it is the last addition, that that we look on last, that makes our burden insupportable, when upon our calamity we see the anger of God piled up, and upon that, *our sin,* when I come to see my sin, in that glasse, not in a Saviour bleeding for me, but in a Judge frowning upon mee; when my sins are so far off from me, as that they are the *last thing* that I see; for, if I would look upon my sins, first, with a remorsefull, a tearfull, a repentant eye, either I should see no anger, no calamity; or it would not seem strange to me, that God should bee angry, nor strange, that I should suffer calamities, when God is angry; Therefore is sin heavy as a burden, because it is the last thing that I lay upon my selfe, and feel not that till a heavy load of calamity and anger be upon me before. But then, as when we come to be unloaded of a burden, that that was last laid on, is first taken off, so when we come, by any meanes, though by the sense of a calamity, or of the anger of God, to a sense of our sin, before the calamity it selfe be taken off, the sin is forgiven. When the Prophet found *David* in this state, the first act that the Prophet came to was the *Transtulit peccatum, God hath taken away thy sinne,* but the calamity was not yet taken away. The *child* begot in sin *shall surely die,* though the sin be pardoned. The *fruit* of the tree may be preserved and kept, after the tree it selfe is cut down and burnt; The fruit, and off-spring of our sin, calamity, may continue upon us, after God hath removed the guiltinesse of the sin from us. In the course of civility, our parents goe out before us, in the course of Mortality, our parents die before us; In the course of Gods mercy, it is so too; The sin that begot the calamity, is dead, and gone, the calamity, the child, and off-spring of that sin, is alive and powerfull upon us. But for the most part, as if I would lift *an iron chain* from the ground, if I take but the first linke, and draw up that, the whole chain follows, so if by my repentance, I remove the uppermost weight of my

[2 Sam. 12.13, 14]

load, *my sin,* all the rest, the declaration of the anger of God, and the calamities that I suffer, will follow my sin, and depart from me. But still our first care must be to take off the last weight, the last that comes to our sense, *The sin.*

You have met, I am sure, in old *Apophthegms,* an answer of a Philosopher celebrated, that being asked, *what was the heaviest thing in the world,* answered, *Senex Tyrannus, An old Tyran;* For a Tyran, at first, dares not proceed so severely; but when he is established, and hath continued *long,* he prescribes in his injuries, and those injuries become *Laws.* As sin is a *Tyran,* so he is got *over our head, in Dominio,* as we shewed you in the *supergressæ sunt,* in our former part; As he is an *old Tyran,* so he is *the heaviest burden* that can be imagined; An inveterate sin, is an inveterate sore, we may hold out with it, but hardly cure it; we may slumber it, but hardly kill it. Weigh sin in *heaven;* heaven could not *beare* it, in the *Angels;* They fell: In the *waters;* The Sea could not *beare* it in *Jonas;* He was cast [Jonah 1] in: In the *earth;* That could not *beare* it in *Dathan,* and *Abiram;* [Num. 16] They were swallowed: And because all the inhabitants of the earth are sin it selfe, *The earth it selfe shall reel to and fro, as a Drunkard,* Esay 24.20 *and shall be removed like a Cottage, and the transgression thereof shall be heavy upon it, and it shall fall and not rise againe;* There's the totall, the finall fall, proper to the wicked; they shall *fall;* so shall the godly; And *fall every day;* and fall *seven times a day;* but they shall *rise againe* and *stand in judgement; The wicked shall not doe so;* They shall *rise,* rise to judgement; and they shall stand, *stand for* Psal. 1.[5] judgement, stand *to receive* judgement; and then, *not fall,* but *be cast out,* out of the presence of God, and *cast down,* down into an impossibility of rising, for ever, for ever, for ever. There is a lively expressing of this deadly weight, this burden in the Prophet *Zechary.* First, there was a certaine vessell, a measure shewed, and the Angel said, *Hic est oculus, This is the sight,* (says our first translation) *This* [Zech.] 5.6 *is the resemblance through all the earth,* (says our second) That is, to this measure, and to that that is figured in it, every man must look, this every man must take into his consideration; what is it? In this measure sate *a woman whose name was Wickednesse;* At first, this woman, this wickednesse, *sate up* in this vessell, she had not filled the measure, she was not laid securely in it, she was not prostrate, not groveling, but her nobler part, *her head,* was yet out of danger, *she sate up in it.* But before the Vision departs, she is plunged wholly into that measure; (into *darknesse,* into *blindnesse*) and not for a time; for, then, *there was a cover,* (says the text) and *a great cover,* and *a great cover of Lead put upon that vessell;* and so, a perpetuall imprisonment, no hope to get out; and *heavy fetters,* no ease to be had within; Hard ground to tread upon, and heavy burdens to carry; first a *cover,* that is, an *excuse; a great cover,* that is, a *defence,* and a *glory;* at last, *of Lead;* all determines in *Desperation.* This is when the multiplicity and indifferencie to lesser sins, and the habituall custome of some particular sin, meet in the aggravating of the burden: Iob 6.3 for then, they are *heavyer then the sand of the Sea,* says the holy Ghost: where he expresses the greatest weight by the least thing; Nothing lesse then a graine of *sand,* nothing *heavyer then the sands of the Sea,* nothing easier to resist then a *first tentation,* or a *single sinne* in it selfe, nothing heavyer, nor harder to devest, then *sinnes complicated* in one another, or then *an old Tyran,* and *custome* in any one sin. And therefore it was evermore a familiar phrase with the *Prophets,* when they were to declare the sins, or to denounce the punishments of those sins upon the people, to call it by this word, *Onus visionis, Onus Babylonis, Onus Ninives, O the burden of Babylon, the burden of Niniveh.* And because some of those *woes,* those *Iudgements,* those *burdens,* did not always fall upon that people presently, they came to mock the Prophets, and say to them, Ier. 23.33 *Now, what is the burden of the Lord, What Burden have you to preach to us,* and to talke of now? Say unto them, says God to the Prophet there; *This is the Burden of the Lord, I will even forsake you.* And, ver. 36 as it is elegantly, emphatically, vehemently added, *Every mans word shall be his burden;* That which he *says,* shall be that that shall be laid to his charge; His *scorning,* his idle questioning of the Prophet, *What burden now, what plague, what famine, what warre* now? *Is not all well for all your crying* The burden of the Lord? *Every mans word shall be his burden,* the *deriding* of Gods Ordinance, and of the denouncing of his Judgements in that Ordinance, shall be their burden, that is, aggravate those Judgements upon them. Nay, there ver. 38 is a heavyer weight then that, added; *Ye shall say no more* (says God to the Prophet) *the burden of the Lord,* that is, you shall not bestow so much care upon this people, as to tell them, that the Lord threatens them. Gods presence in anger, and in punishments, is a heavy, but Gods absence, and dereliction, a much heavyer burden; As (if extremes will admit comparison) the everlasting losse of the sight of God in hell, is a greater torment, then any lakes of inextinguishable Brimstone, then any gnawing of the incessant worme, then any gnashing of teeth can present unto us.

Now, let no man ease himself upon that fallacy, *sin cannot be,* nor sin cannot induce such burdens as you talk of, for many men are come to *wealth,* and by that *wealth,* to *honour,* who, if they had admitted a tendernesse in their consciences, and forborn some sins, had lost both; for, are they without burden, because they have *wealth,* and *honour?* In the Originall language, the same word, that is here, a *burden, Chabad,* signifies *honour,* and *wealth,* as well as a *burden.* And therefore says the Prophet, *Woe unto him that loadeth himselfe* Habak. 2.6
with thick clay. Non densantur nisi per laborem; There goes much Gregor.
pains to the laying of it thus thick upon us; The multiplying of riches is a laborious thing; and then it is a new pain to bleed out those riches for a *new office,* or a *new title; Et tamen lutum,* says that Father, when all is done, we are but roughcast with durt; All those *Riches,* all those *Honours* are a *Burden,* upon the *just* man, they are but a multiplying of *fears,* that they shall lose them; upon the *securest* man, they are but a multiplying of *duties* and *obligations;* for the more they have, the more they have to answer; and upon the *unjust,* they are a multiplying of everlasting torments. *They possess months* Iob 7.3
of vanity, and wearisom nights are appointed them. Men are as weary of the *day,* upon *Carpets* and *Cushions,* as at the plough. And the labourers wearinesse, is to a good end; but for these men, *They* Ier. 9.5
weary themselves to commit iniquity. Some doe, and some doe not; All doe. *The labour of the foolish wearieth every one of them;* Why? *Because he knows not how to goe to the City.* He that directs not his Eccles. 10.15
labours to the right end, the glory of God, he goes not to Jerusalem, the City of holy peace, but his sinfull labours shall bee a burden to him; and his Riches, and his Office, and his Honour hee shall not be able to put off, then when he puts off his body in his death-bed; He shall not have that happinesse, which he, till then, thought a misery, *To carry nothing out of this world,* for his Riches, his Office, his [1 Tim. 6.7]

Honour shall follow him into the next world, and clog his soule there. But we proposed this consideration of this Metaphor, *That sinne is a burden,* (as there is an infinite sweetnesse, and infinite latitude in every Metaphor, in every elegancy of the Scripture, and therefore I may have leave to be loath to depart from it) in some particular inconveniences, that a *burden* brings, and it is time to come to them.

Number 5.

Preached at Lincolns Inne.

The Third Sermon on

Psal. 38.4. *FOR MINE INIQUITIES ARE GONE OVER MY HEAD, AS A HEAVY BURDEN, THEY ARE TOO HEAVY FOR MEE.*

As a *Torch* that hath been lighted, and used *before,* is easier lighted then a *new torch,* so are the branches, and parts of this Text, the easier reduced to your memory, by having heard former distributions thereof. But as a *Torch* that hath been lighted and us'd before, will not last so long as a new one, so perchance your *patience* which hath already been twice exercised with the handling of these words, may be too near the bottom to afford much. And therefore much I have determined not to need. God did his greatest work upon the *last day,* and yet gave over work betimes. In that day he made man, and, (as the context leades us, most probably, to thinke) he made Paradise, and placed man in Paradise that day. For the variety of opinions amongst our Expositors, about the time when God made Paradise, arises from one errour, an errour in the *Vulgat Edition,* in the translation of the Roman Church, that reads it *Plantaverat, God had planted a garden,* as though God had *done it before.* Therefore some state it before the Creation, which Saint *Hierome* follows, or at least relates, without disapproving it; and others place it, upon the *third day,* when the whole earth received her accomplishment; but if any had looked over this place with the same ingenuity as their own great man *Tyr:* (an active man in the *Councell of Trent*) hath done over the *Book of Psalms,* in which one Book he hath confessed 6000 places, in which their translation differs from the Originall, they would have seen this difference in this place, that it is not *Plantaverat,* but *Plantavit,* not that God *had before,* but

Gen. 2.8

that he *did then, then* when hee had made man, make a Paradise for man. And yet God made an end of all this days work betimes; in that day, *He walked in the garden in the cool of the Evening.* The noblest part of our work in handling this Text, falls upon the conclusion, reserved for this day; which is, the application of these words to *Christ.* But for that, I shall be short, and rather leave you to *walke with God in the cool of the Evening,* to meditate of the sufferings of Christ, when you are gone, then pretend to expresse them here. The *passion* of Christ Jesus is rather an amazement, an astonishment, an extasie, a consternation, then an instruction. Therefore, though something we shall say of that anone, first, we pursue that which lies upon our selves, the *Burden,* in those four mischievous inconveniences wrapped up in that Metaphor.

[Gen. 3.8]

Inclinat

Of them, the first was, *Inclinat;* That a Burden *sinkes* a man, *declines* him, *crookens* him, makes him *stoop.* So does sin. It is one of Saint *Augustines* definitions of sinne, *Conversio ad creaturam,* that it is a turning, a withdrawing of man to the creature. And every such turning to the creature, let it be upon his side, to *her* whom he loves, let it be upwards, to *honour* that he affects, yet it is still down-ward, in respect of him, whom he was made by, and should direct himselfe to. Every inordinate love of the Creature is a descent from the dignity of our Creation, and a disavowing, a disclaiming of that Charter, *Subjicite & dominamini, subdue, and govern the Creature. Est quoddam bonum, quod si diligat anima rationalis, peccat.* There are good things in the world, which it is a sin for man to love, *Quia infra illum ordinantur,* because though they *be good,* they are not *so good* as man; And man may not decline, and every thing, except God himself, is inferiour to man, and so, it is a *declination,* a *stooping* in man, to apply himselfe to any Creature, till he meet that Creature in God; for there, it is above him; And so, as *Beauty* and *Riches,* and *Honour* are beames that issue from God, and glasses that represent God to us, and ideas that return us into him, in our glorifying of him, by these helpes, so we may apply our selves to them; for, in this consideration, as they assist us in our way to God, they are above us, otherwise, to love them for themselves, is a *declination, a stooping* under a *burden;* And this *declination,* this incurvation, this descent of man, in the *inordinate love of the Creature,* may very justly seem to be forbidden

[Gen. 1.28]

August. De ver. relig. c. 20

in that Commandement, that forbids *Idolatry, Thou shalt not bow down to them, nor worship them;* If we bow down to them, we doe worship them; for it is in the love of all Creatures, as it is in money; *Covetousnesse,* that is, the love of money, is *Idolatry,* says the Apostle; and so is all other inordinate love of any, Idolatry. And then, as we have seen some grow crooked, by a long sitting, a lying in one posture, so, by an easie resting in these descents and declination of the soule, it comes to bee a fashion to stoop, and it seemes a comely thing to be crooked; and we become, *infruniti,* that is, *quibus nemo frui velit,* such as no body cares for our conversation, or company, except we be ill company, sociable in other sinnes, *Et viliores quò castiores,* if we affect Chastity, or any other vertue, we disaffect and distast other men; for one mans vertue chides, and reproaches a whole vicious company. But if he will needs bee in fashion, *Cum perverso perverti,* to grow crooked with the crooked, *His iniquities shall take him, and hee shall be holden with the cords of his sinne;* that is, in that posture that he puts himself, he shall be kept; kept all his life; and then, (as it follows there) *He shall die without instruction;* Die in a place, where he can have no *Absolution,* no *Sacrament,* or die, in a disposition, that he shall receive no benefit by them, though he receive them. He hath packed a burden upon himself, in *habituall sinne,* he hath chosen to stoop under this burden, in an *Idolatrous love* of those sinnes, and nothing shall be able to erect him again, not *Preaching,* not *Sacraments,* no not *judgements.* And this is the first inconvenience, and mischief, implyed in this Metaphor which the holy Ghost hath chosen, *Mine iniquities are as a burden, Inclinant,* they bend down my soule, created streight, to an incurvation, to a crookednesse.

[Exod. 20.5]

[Eph. 5.5; Col. 3.5]

August.

Prov. 5.22

Fatigat

A second inconvenience intimated in this Metaphore, a *burden,* is the *fatigat,* a burden *wearies* us, tires us: and so does our sinne, and our best beloved sinne. It hath wearied us, and yet we cannot devest it. We would leave that sin, and yet there is *one talent* more to be added, *one childe* more to be provided for, *one office,* or *one title* more to be compassed, *one tentation* more to be satisfied. Though we grumble, not out of remorse of *conscience,* but out of a bodily wearinesse of the sinne, yet wee proceed in it. How often men goe to *Westminster,* how often to the *Exchange,* called by unjust suits or called by corrupt bargaines to those places, when their ease, or their health perswades them to stay at home? How many go to forbidden beds, then when they had rather stay at home, if they were not afraid [Jer. 9.5] of an unkind interpretation? *We have wearied our selves in the ways of wickednesse; Plus miles in uno torneamento, quàm sanctus Monachus in decem annis,* says our *Holkot,* upon that place, a soldier suffers more in one expedition, then a Monk does in ten years, says he; and perchance he says true, and yet no commendation to his Monke neither; for that soldier may doe even the cause of God, more good, in that one expedition, then that Monke in ten years: But it is true as *Holkot* intended it, (though perchance his example doe not much strengthen it) vicious men are put to more pains, and to doe more things against their own mindes, then the Saints of God are in the ways of holinesse. *We have wearied our selves in the ways of wickednesse,* says he, that is, in doing as other wicked men have done, in ways which have been beaten out to us, by the frequent practise of other men; but he addes more, *We have gone thorough Deserts, where there lay no way;* that is, through sins, in which, wee had no example, no precedent, the inventions of our hearts. The covetous man lies still, and attends his *quarter days,* and studies the endorsements of his bonds, and he wonders that the ambitious man can endure the shufflings and thrustings of Courts, and can measure his happinesse by the smile of a greater man: And, he that does so, wonders as much, that this covetous man can date his happinesse by an *Almanack,* and such revolutions, and though he have quick returns of receipt, yet scarce affords himself bread to live till that day come, and though all his joy be in his bonds, yet denies himself a candles end to look upon them. *Hilly ways* are wearisome ways, and tire the ambitious man; Carnall pleasures are *dirty ways,* and tire the licentious man; Desires of gain, are *thorny ways,* and tire the covetous man; Æmulations of higher men, are *dark* and *blinde ways,* and tire the envious man; Every way, that is out of the way, wearies us; But, Lam. 5.5 *lassati sumus; sed lassis non datur requies; we labour, and have no rest,* when we have done; we are wearied with our sins, and have no satisfaction in them; we goe to bed to night, weary of our sinfull labours, and we will rise freshly to morrow, to the same sinfull labours again; And when a sinner does so little remember *yesterday,* how little does he consider *to morrow?* He that forgets what he hath *done,* foresees not what he shall suffer: so sin is a burden; it crookens us, it wearies us; And those are the two first inconveniences.

And then a third is *Retardat.* Though a man can stand under a burden, that he doe not sink, but be able to make some steps, yet his burden slackens his pace, and he goes not so fast, as without that burden he could have gone. So it is in *habituall sinnes;* though we doe not sinke into *desperation,* and *stupefaction,* though we doe come to the participation of outward means, and have some sense, some feeling thereof, yet, as long as any one beloved and habituall sin hangs upon us, it slackens our pace in all the ways of godlinesse. And we come not to such an appropriation of the promises of the Gospel, in *hearing Sermons,* nor to such a *re-incarnation,* and invisceration of Christ and his merits into our selves, in the *Sacrament,* as if wee were altogether devested of that sin, and not onely at that time, we should doe. *Quis ascendet,* says *David; who shall ascend unto the hill of the Lord?* It is a painfull clambring; up a hill. And Saint *Augustine* makes use of the answer, *Innocens manibus, He that hath clean hands;* first, he must have *hands,* as well as *feet;* He must *doe* something for himself; And then, *Innocent* hands; such as doe no harme to others; such as hold, and carry no hurtfull thing to himself; Either he must have the first Innocence, *Abstinence* from ill getting, or the second Innocence, *Restitution* of that which was ill gotten, or he shall never get up that hill; for, it is a steep hill; and there is no walking up; but he must crawle, *hand and foot.* Therefore, says the Apostle, *Deponamus pondus, Let us lay aside every weight;* He does not say, sin in *generall,* but *every weight, every circumstance* that may aggravate our sin, every conversation that may occasion our sin; And, (as hee addes, particularly and emphatically) *The sin, that does so easily beset us; Easily,* because *customarily,* habitually; And then, says that Apostle, in that place, *Let us run;* when we have laid down *the sin, that does so easily beset us,* our beloved and habituall sinne, and laid down *every weight,* every circumstance that aggravates that sin; then we may be able to run, to proceed with a holy chearfulnesse and proficiency in the wayes of *sanctification;* but till that we cannot, how due observers soever we be of all outward means; for, sin is a burden, in *perverting* us, in *tyring* us, in *retarding* us.

Retardat

Ps. 24.3

[Heb. 12.1]

Præcipitat

And last of all, it is a burden, *quatenus præcipitat,* as it gives him ever new occasion of *stumbling;* He that hath not been accustomed to a sin, but exercised in resisting it, will finde many *tentations,* but as a *wash way* that he can *trot* thorough, and goe forward religiously in his Calling for all them; (for though there be *coluber in via, A snake in every way, tentations* in every calling, yet, *In Christo omnia possumus, In Christ, we can doe all things,* and therefore, in him, we can *bruise the Serpents head*) and spurn a tentation out of his way. But he that hath been long under the custome of a sin, evermore meets with stones to stumble at, and bogges to plunge in. It is S. *Chrysostomes* application; He that hath had a *fever,* though he have cast it off, yet he walks weakly, and he hath an inclination to the beds side, or to a chaire, at every turn that he makes about his chamber. So hath he to *relapses,* that hath been under the *custome* of an habituall sin, though he have discontinued the practise of that sin. And these be the inconveniences, the mischiefs, represented to us in this metaphore, *A burden, Mine iniquities are as a burden too heavy for me,* Because they *sink me down,* from the Creator to the creature; Because they *tire* and *weary* me, and yet I must bear them; Because when they doe not absolutely tire me, yet they *slacken my pace;* And because, though I could lay off that burden, leave off that sin, for the present practise, yet the former habit hath so weakned me, that I am always apt to stumble, and fall into *relapses.*

[Gen. 49.17]
[Phil. 4.13]
[Gen. 3.15]

Conclusio Christus

Thus have you the mischievous inconveniences of habituall sin laid open to you, in these two elegancies of the holy Ghost, *supergressæ, Mine iniquities are gone over my head,* and the *gravatæ, As a burden they are too heavy for me.* But as a good Emperour received that commendation, that no man went ever out of his presence discontented, so our gracious God never admits us to his presence in this his Ordinance, but with a purpose to dismisse us in heart, and in comfort; for, his Almoner, he that distributeth his mercies to Congregations, is the *God of comfort,* of *all comfort,* the holy Ghost himself. Nay, they whom he admits to his presence here, goe not out of his presence, when they goe from hence; He is with them, whilst they stay here, and hee goes home with them, when they goe home. Princes out of their Royall care call *Parliaments,* and graciously deliver themselves over to that Representative Body; God out of his Fatherly love calls *Congregations,* and does not onely deliver himself over, in his *Ordinance,* to that Representative Body, the whole *Church* there, but when every man is become a private man again, when the Congregation is dissolv'd, and every man restored to his own house, God, in his Spirit, is within the doores, within the bosomes of every man that receiv'd him here. Therefore we have reserved for the conclusion of all, the application of this Text to our *blessed Saviour;* for so our most ancient Expositors direct our meditations, first, *historically,* and *literally,* upon *David,* and that we did at first; Then *morally,* and by just application to our selves, and that we have most particularly insisted upon; And lastly, upon our Saviour *Christ Jesus* himself; and that remains for our conclusion and consolation; for, even from him, groaning under our burden, we may hear these words, *Mine iniquities are gone over my head, &c.*

Peccatum

First then, that that lay upon Christ, was *sin,* properly *sin.* Nothing could estrange God from man, but *sin;* and even from this *Son of man,* though he were the *Son of God* too, was God far estranged; therefore God saw *sin* in him. *Non novit peccatum, He knew no sin;* (2 Cor. 5.21) not by any *experimentall* knowledge, not by any perpetration; for, *Non fecit peccatum, He did no sin,* he committed no sin. (1 Pet. 2.22) What though? we have sin upon us, sin to condemnation, *Originall sin* before we *know sin,* before we have committed any sinne. *They esteemed him stricken, and smitten of God;* (Esa. 53.4) and they mistook not in *that;* He was stricken and smitten of God; It pleased the Lord *to bruise him, and to put him to grief;* (v. 10) And the Lord proceeds not thus, where he sees no sin. Therefore the Apostle carries it to a very high expression, *God made him to be sin for our sakes;* (2 Cor. 5.21) not onely *sinfull,* but *sin* it self. And as one cruell Emperour wished all mankinde in one man, that hee might have beheaded mankinde at one blow, so God gathered the whole nature of sinne into one Christ, that by one *action,* one *passion, sin,* all *sin,* the whole nature of sinne might bee overcome. It was sin that was upon Christ, else God could not have been angry with him, nor pleased with us.

Sua

It was sin, and *his own sin; Mine iniquities,* says Christ, in his *Type,* and *figure, David;* and in his *body,* the *Church;* and, (we may be bold to adde) in his *very person; Mine iniquities.* Many Heretiques denied his body, to be *his Body,* they said it was but an *airy,* an *imaginary,* an *illusory Body;* and denied *his Soul* to be *his Soul,* they said he had no *humane soul,* but that his divine nature supplied that, and wrought all the operations of the soul. But we that have learnt Christ better, know, that hee could not have redeemed *man,* by that way that was contracted betweene him and his Father, that is, by way of *satisfaction,* except he had taken the very body, and the very soul of man: And as verily as his *humane nature,* his *body* and *soul* were *his, his sins* were *his* too. As my mortality, and my hunger, and thirst, and wearinesse, and all my *naturall infirmities* are his, so *my sins* are his sins. And now when my sins are by him thus made *his* sins, no Hell-Devill, not *Satan,* no Earth-Devill, no *Calumniator,* can any more make those sins *my* sins, then he can make *his divinity, mine.* As by the *spirit of Adoption,* I am made the *childe of God, the seed of God,* the *same Spirit with God,* but yet I am not made *God,* so by Christs taking my sins, I am made a *servant of my God,* a *Beads-man* of my God, a *vassall,* a *Tributary* debtor to God, but I am no sinner in the sight of God, no sinner so, as that man or the Devill can impute that sin unto me, then when my Saviour hath made my sins *his.* As a *Soldier* would not part with his *scars,* Christ would not.

Plura

They were *sins,* that lay upon him, †part with† *our sins;* And *his sins;* and, as it follows in his Type, *David,* sins in a *plurality, many sins.* I know nothing in the world so manifold, so plurall, so numerous, as my sins; And my Saviour had *all* those. But, if every other man have not so many sins, *as I,* he owes that to *Gods grace,* and not to the Devils forbearance, for the Devill saw no such parts, nor no such power in me to advance or hinder his kingdome, no such *birth,* no such *education,* no such *place* in the *State* or *Church,* as that he should be gladder of me, then of other men. He ministers tentations to *all;* and all are overcome by his tentations; And all these sins, in all men, were upon Christ at once. All *twice over;* In the *root,* and in the *fruit* too; In the *bullein,* and in the *coin* too; In *grosse,* and in *retail;* In *Originall,* and in *Actuall sin.* And, howsoever the sins of *former ages,* the sins of all men for 4000 years before, which were all upon him, when he was upon the Crosse, might possibly be numbred, (as things that are *past,* may easilier fall within a possibility of such an imagination) yet all those sinnes, which were to come after, he himself could not number; for, hee, *as the Sonne of man,* though hee know how long the world *hath lasted,* knowes not how long this sinfull world *shall last,* and when the day of Judgement shall be; And all those *future sins,* were his sins before they were committed; They were *his* before they were *theirs* that doe them. And lest *this world* should not afford him sins enow, he took upon him the sins of *heaven* it self; not *their* sins, who were *fallen* from heaven, and fallen into an absolute incapacity of reconciliation, but their sins, which *remained* in heaven; Those sins, which the Angels that stand, *would* fall into, if they had not received a *confirmation,* given them in contemplation of the death and merits of *Christ,* Christ took upon him, for all things, in *Earth,* and *Heaven* too, *were reconciled to God by him:* for, if there had been as *many worlds,* as there are *men* in this, (which is a large multiplication) or as many worlds, as there are *sins* in this, (which is an infinite multiplication) his merit had been sufficient to *all.* [Col. 1.19, 20]

Supergressæ

They were *sins, his sins, many sinnes,* the *sinnes of the world;* and then, as in his Type, *David, Supergressæ,* his sins, these sins *were got above him.* And not as *Davids,* or *ours,* by an insensible growth, and swelling of a Tide in course of time, but this inundation of all the sins of all places, and times, and persons, was upon him in an instant, in a minute; in such a point as admits, and requires a subtile, and a serious consideration; for it is *eternity;* which though it doe infinitely exceed all *time,* yet is in this consideration, lesse then any part of time, that it is *indivisible,* eternity is so; and though it last for ever, is all at once, eternity is so. And from this point, this *timelesse time,* time that is all *time,* time that is no *time,* from all eternity, all the sins of the world were gone over him.

Caput

And, in that consideration, *supergressæ caput,* they were *gone over his head.* Let his *head* bee his *Divine nature,* yet they were gone over his *head:* for, though there bee nothing more *voluntary,* then the *love of God* to man, (for, he loves us, not onely for *his own* sake, or for *his own glories* sake, but he loves us *for his loves sake,* he loves us, and *loves his love of us,* and had rather want some of his glory, then *wee* should not have, nay, then *he* should not have so much love towards us) though this love of *his* be an act simply voluntary, yet in that act of expressing this love, in the sending a *Saviour,* there was a kinde of necessity contracted on Christs part; such a contract had passed between him and his Father, that as himself says, there was an

Luc. 24.[26] *oportuit pati,* a necessity that he should *suffer* all that he suffered, and so enter into glory, when he was come; so there was an *oportuit venire,* a necessity, (a necessity induced by that contract) that he should *come* in that humiliation, and smother, and suppresse the glory of the divine nature, under a cloud of humane, of passible, of inglorious flesh.

Tectum

So, be his *divine* nature this head, his sins, all our sins made *his,* were gone *above his head;* And *over his head,* all those ways, that we considered before, in our selves; *Sicut tectum, sicut fornix,* as a *roof,* as an *arch,* that had separated between God, and *him,* in that he

[Mat. 26.39]

prayed, and was not *heard;* when in that *Transeat Calix, Father, if it be possible, let this cup passe from me,* the Cup was not onely not taken out of his hands, but filled up again as fast, as he, in obedience to his Father, dranke of it, more and worse miseries succeeding, and exceeding those which hee had born before. They were above him *in*

Clamor [Luke 23.34] *Aquæ*

clamore, in that voice, in that clamour which was got up to heaven, and in possession of his Fathers ears, before his prayer came, *Father, forgive them,* for they are not forgiven *that* sinne of crucifying the Lord of life, *yet.* They were above his head, *tanquam aquæ,* as an

[Luke 22.44; John 19.34]

inundation of waters, then when he *swet water and bloud,* in the Agony, when hee, who had formerly passed his *Israel* thorough the *Red Sea,* as though that had not been *love* large enough, was now himself overflowed with a *Red Sea* of his owne bloud, for his *Israel*

Dominum

again. And they were over his head *in Dominio,* in a Lordship, in a Tyranny, then when those marks of soveraign honour, a *robe,* and a *scepter,* and a *Crown of thorns* were added to his other afflictions. And so is our first part of this Text, the *supergressæ sunt,* the *multiplicity* of sin, appliable to Christ, as well as to his Type, to *David,* and to us, the members of his body.

Graves

And so is the last part, that which we handled to day, too, the *gravatæ sunt,* the weight and insupportablenesse of sin. They were heavy, they weighed him down from his Fathers bosome, they made *God Man.* That *one* sin could make an *Angel* a *Devill,* is a strange consideration; but that all the sins of the world, could make *God*

Nimis

Man, is stranger. Yet sinne was so heavy; *Too heavy,* sayes the Text. It did not onely make *God Man,* in investing our nature by his *birth,* but it made him *no Man,* by devesting that body, by *death;* and, (but for the vertue, and benefit of a former *Decree*) submitting that body, to the corruption, and putrefaction of the grave; But this was the peculiar, the miraculous glory of Christ Jesus. He had *sin, all* our sin, and yet never felt *worme of conscience;* He lay dead in the grave, and yet never felt *worm of corruption.* Sin was *heavy;* It made *God Man;* Too *heavy;* It made *Man* no *Man;* Too heavy *for him,* even *for him,* who was God and Man together; for, even that person, so composed, had certain *velleitates,* (as wee say in the *School*) certain motions arising sometimes in him, which required a *veruntamen,* a review, a re-consideration, *Not my will, O Father, but thine be done;* and such, as in us, who are pushed on by *Originall sinne,* and drawn on by sinfull concupiscences in our selves, would become sins, though in Christ they were farre from it. Sin was heavy, even upon *him,* in all those inconveniences, which wee noted in a burden; *Incurvando,* when he was bowed down, and gave his back to their scourges; *Fatigando,* when *his soul was heavy unto death; Retardando,* when they brought him to think it long, *Vtquid dereliquisti, Why hast thou forsaken mee?* And then, *præcipitando,* to make that haste to the *Consummatum est,* to the finishing of all, as to die before his fellows that were crucified with him, died; to *bow down his head,* and to *give up his soul,* before they extorted it from him.

Mihi

[Mat. 26.39; Mark 14.36; Luke 22.42]

Onus

[Mat. 26.37, 38]

[Mat. 27.46; Mark 15.34]

[John 19.30]

Thus we burdned him; And thus he unburdned us; *Et cum exonerat nos onerat,* when he unburdens us, he burdens us even in that unburdening: *Onerat beneficio, cum exonerat peccato.* He hath taken off the obligation of *sinne,* but he hath laid upon us, the obligation of *thankfulnesse,* and *Retribution. Quid retribuam? What shall I render to the Lord, for all his benefits to me?* is *vox onerati,* a voyce that grones under the burden, though not of *sinne,* yet of *debt,* to that Saviour, that hath taken away that sinne. *Exi à me Domine,* that which Saint *Peter* said to *Christ, Lord depart from me, for I am a sinfull man,* is, says that Father, *vox onerati,* the voyce of one oppressed with the blessings and benefits of God, and desirous to spare, and to husband that treasure of Gods benefits, as though he were better able to stand without the support of some of those benefits, then stand under the debt, which so many, so great benefits laid upon him: Truly he that considers seriously, what his sins have put the Son of God to, cannot but say, *Lord lay some of my sinnes upon me,*

Bernard

Ps. 116.12

Luke 5.8

rather then thy Sonne should beare all this; that devotion, that says after, *Spare thy people, whom thou hast redeemed with thy most precious bloud,* would say before, spare that Son, that must die, spare that precious bloud, that must be shed to redeeme us. And rather then Christ should truely, *really* beare the torments of *hell,* in his *soule,* (which torments cannot be severed from *obduration,* nor from *everlastingness*) I would, I should desire, that my sins might return to me, and those punishments for those sins; I should be ashamed to [Exod. be so farre exceeded in zeal, by *Moses,* who would have been *blotted* 32.32] *out of the book of life,* or by *Paul,* who would have been *separated* [Rom. 9.3] *from Christ for his brethren,* as that I would not undertake as much, *to redeem my redeemer,* and suffer the torments of Hell my selfe, rather then *hee* should; But it is an insupportable burden of *debt,* that he hath laid upon me, by suffering that which he suffered, with- John 5.6 out the torments of Hell. Those words, *Vis sanus fieri, hast thou a desire to be well,* and *a faith* that I can make thee well? are *vox exonerantis,* the words of him that would take *off* our burden; But [John 5.8] then, the *Tolle grabatum & ambula, Take up thy bed and walke,* this is *vox onerantis,* the voyce of Christ, as he lays a new burden upon us; *ut quod prius suave, jam onerosum sit,* that bed which he had ease in before, must now be born with pain; that sin which was forgotten with pleasure, must now be remembred with *Contrition;* Christ speaks not of a *vacuity,* nor of a *levity;* when he takes off one burden, he lays on another; nay, two for one. He takes off the burden, of *Irremediablenesse,* of *irrecoverablenesse,* and he reaches out his hand, in his Ordinances, in his Word and Sacraments, by which we may be disburdened of all our sins; but then he lays upon us, *Onus resipiscentiæ,* the burden *of Repentance* for our selves, and *Onus gratitudinis,* the burden of retribution, and thankfulnesse to *him,* in *them* who are *his,* by our relieving of them, in whom he suffers. The end of all, (that we may end all in endlesse comfort) is, That our word, in the originall, in which the *holy Ghost* spoake, is *Jikkebedu,* which is not altogether, as we read them, *graves sunt,* but *graves fieri;* not that they *are,* but that *they were as a burden, too heavy for me;* till I could lay hold upon a *Saviour* to sustaine me, Psal. 18.29 *they were too heavy for me:* And *by him, I can runne through a troop* (through the multiplicity of my sins,) *and by my God I can leap over a wall;* Though *mine iniquities be got over my head,* as a wall of separation, yet *in Christo omnia possum, In Christ I can doe all things;* [Phil. 4.13] Mine iniquities are got *over my head;* but my *head is Christ;* and in *him,* I can doe whatsoever *hee* hath done, by applying his sufferings to my soule for all; my sins are *his,* and all *his* merit is mine: And all my sins shall no more hinder my ascending into heaven, nor my sitting at the right hand of God, in mine own person, then they hindered *him,* who bore them all in *his* person, mine onely Lord and Saviour Christ Jesus, blessed for ever.

Number 6.

Preached at Lincoln's Inne.

Psalme 38.9. *LORD ALL MY DESIRE IS BEFORE THEE, AND MY GRONINGE IS NOT HID FROM THEE.*

Oratio et ratio

THE WHOLE psalme hath two parts, 1 a prayer and then Reasons of that prayer. The prayer hath 2 parts, 1 a deprecatory prayer in the 1 verse, and then a postulatory in the 2 last. And the reasons also are of 2 kinds, 1. intrinsecall, arisinge from consideration of himselfe, 2. extrinsecall, in the behaviour and dispositions of others towards him. The reasons of the 1 sort determine in the 10 verse, which we have handled. But this we reserved to be handled after, because we are to observe some things out of the site and place of the verse, as well as out of the words. First out of the place, this: that *David* having presented the intrinsecall reasons of his deprecatory prayer, Lord correct me not for I have suffered these and these corrections already, and nowe presentinge his humble referringe of all to Almighty God, *Domine omne desiderium,* Lord all my desire is before thee, this comforts me, this confirmes me, this establishes me, that all is knowne unto thee, yet for all this sufferinge and this willinge sufferinge, for all this passion and all this patience, God doth not presently take of his hand, nor end his misery, but (as we see) all the extrinsecall occasions of his misery, the scornes and the reall injuries of other men followe and fall upon him after all this affliction, and all this submission. This consideration arises out of the place of this text, that though afflictions bringe the godly to prayer for deliverance, yet that prayer does not presently bringe deliverance: and that wilbe our first part. For a 2 part we shall take the wordes alltogether in theire whole frame, and thereby consider the generall doctrine arisinge out of them, that all thinges are present to God, *videt omnia;* and then if he see all thinges as God, he did ever see all

v. 1, 2

thinges, for he was ever God, *prævidit omnia;* and if he foresawe all thinges, he foresawe our sinnes, and there we shall have occasion to see howe farre our sinnes are necessary and howe farre God is any cause of our sinnes; and these wilbe the branches of our second part. In the third we shall descend to a more particular consideration of the wordes, and see *Davids* profession, that, first, *desideria,* the first internall motions of his heart, and then *Gemitus,* the first externall motions of his sorrowe are knowne to God. And if our thoughts be knowne, much more our actions, if our sighes and groanes be knowne, much more our prayers, our confessions, our conferences, our devotions, our more manifest and evident wayes of seekinge and establishinge our reconciliation with God. But then these which *David* considered, are *desideria sua,* and *sui gemitus,* he reveales not, he enquires not after other mens sinnes, nor sorrowes, nor judges upon their actions, nor censures their repentances: he is his owne Library, he studyes himselfe. Nowe these desires and these groaninges, they are, sayes hee, *ante te,* not only as they are desires and groaninges, but as they are mine, and therefore I have brought them before thee, I have opened them, I have presented them to thee, by way of confession, the matter is brought before thee, the cause depends before thee; soe they are *ante te;* thou couldst see them without me, but yet I have brought them to thy sight too, and they are soe brought before thee, *Ut nihil absconditum,* my sinnefull desires are not hid from thee, though I have laboured sometimes to cover them, and my sorrowfull repentance is not hid from thee, though my unworthiness and the abhomination of my foulenes might have drawne a curtaine, yea built a wall of separation betweene thee and me, yet nothinge is hid from thee, nay nothinge is hid by me. For all this that I have done, all the sinnes that I have committed, and all this repentance that I have begunne and proceeded in is *ante te, Domine,* it is *ante te,* for my sinnes are only against thee, and my confession belongs only to thee, but yet *ad te Dominum,* to thee as thou art Lord and hast a dominion, and exercisest a government, to thee that art Lord of a spiritual kingdome, of a visible and establisht Church; and soe many considerations the particular words will minister unto us in the third part.

First then, out of the site and place of these words, as they stand 1 part betweene the narration of miseries of 2 kinds, some before it, some after it, we collected that God does not allwayes put an end to our miseries, assoone as we take knowledge of his purpose upon us by those miseries, we pray and yet are not delivered. Gregor. It is true, *omne desiderium in pœnam convertitur, si non cito evenerit quod optatur,* when Gods corrections have brought us to a relligious desire of beinge delivered, then not to be delivered is a newe, and the greatest correction, Idem yea the most dangerous temptation of all. *Cupiditati ipsa celeritas tarda est.* When I pray to be delivered, and beginne to thinke that God hath bound himselfe by his promise to give me the issue Job 5.18, 19 with the temptation, that he maketh the wound and bindeth up, he smiteth, and his hand maketh whole, that he will deliver me in sixe troubles, but in the seaventh the evill shall not touch me, that he will preserve me from despayre in all the afflictions of my life, but in the seaventh, that is when I am come to my Sabbath, to my rest and confidence in his mercy, that then it shall not touch me, it shall passe away presently; when I beginne to come to these meditations, *ipsa celeritas tarda est,* though God deliver me sooner then I deserve, yet it seemes longe in doinge, yf it be not assoone as I have conceived that which appeares to me to be so religious a desire. 2 Pet. 3.9 But the Lord is not slacke concerning his promise as some men count slackenes. In that place of the Apostle his promise is, judgment, punishment for sinne; and yf God be not slacke in that promise, much lesse is he slacke in the dispensinge of his mercyes, and removinge those judgments againe. The mistakinge rises out of the different computations betweene Hieron: God and us, *annos centum æternitatem putamus,* we never reckon beyond a 100 yeares, because that is the longest life, we thinke there is noe more, noe other life but that. But with God one daye is as 1000 yeares, and 1000 yeares as one day. Whenesoever he comes to judgment, he comes soone to thee, yf he come before thou beest prepared, and whensoever he comes in mercy, he comes soone to thee too, consideringe how farre thou wast runne away from him. It is all one when that fire beginnes that shall never goe out. If the torments of hell must take hold of thee, they beginne soone yf they beginne in thy desperation upon thy death-bed, and yf thy tribulations end upon thy death-bed they end soone, consideringe howe much rust and drosse there was to be burnt off of thy soule.

It was longe in the *Romane* state before they came to a distinction of houres; all their reckoninge for some hundreds of yeares was, *ab ortu solis ad occasum,* this was done after the risinge, and this after the settinge of the sunne; but the distinction of hours in the degrees of the ascendinge or descendinge of the sunne they had not: We reckon all thinges soe too; we reckon from the risinge of the sunne, when any greate fortune fell upon us, when we came to yeares, when the father dyes and leaves the estate, when the mother dyes and leaves the joynture, when the predecessor dyes and leaves the office; and we reckon from the settinge of the sunne, when any greate calamity falls upon us, when a decree passed against us and swept away such a Mannor, when a shipwracke impoverishd us, when a fire, a rott, a murraine, a feaver overthrewe our bodyes or our estates. The risinge and settinge of the sunne, height of prosperity, depth of adversity we observe, but we observe not the degrees of the ascendinge of this sunne, howe God hath led us every step and preserved us in many particular dangers in our risinge, nor the degrees of the descendinge of this sunne we observe not, we observe not that God would shewe us in the losse of our children, the sinnefull wantonness in which they were begotten and conceived, in the losse of health, the sinnefull voluptuousnes in which the Bodye was pamperd, in the losse of goods, the sinnefull extortion in which they were gathered, we consider sometimes in generall *Jobs nudus egressus,* that we came naked [Job 1.21] out of our mothers wombe, that we rose of nothinge, and in generall *Jobs nudus revertar,* that we shall returne naked againe, that we shall carry away noe more then we brought, but we consider not in particular that *Dominus dedit,* and *Dominus abstulit,* that it is the Lord that gave and the Lord that takes away, and thereupon blesse the name of the Lord for it, in all his stepps and degrees of our risinge and fallinge. God hath not only given thee a naturall day, from period to period to consider thy birth and thy death, this thou wast borne to, and this thou dyest worth, but he hath given thee an artificiall day, and a day which he hath distinguished into houres by continuall benefits, and a day which thou hast distinguished into houres by continuall sinnes. And he would have thee remember those houres when and howe and by what degrees, by what meanes he raised thee, and humbled thee againe, and at what time and place, with what actions thou hast provoked his anger; and then thou wilt [Gen. 3.8] find that it was in the coole of the eveninge, it was late before God Psal. 90.14 came to correct *Adam,* but he hath filled us with mercy in the morninge that we might be glad and rejoyce all the day.

God is not slacke in his promises sayes the Apostle there, for he, 2 Pet. 3.9 as it is sayd there in the Originall ὁ κύριος τῆς ἐπαγγελίας, *Dominus promissionis,* it is not only the Lord is not slacke of his promise, but the Lord of his promise is not slacke; he is Lord of his promise, and in that sense we are sure that he can and may bee sure that he will performe his promise. Delayes in Courts of Princes, and in Courts of Justice, proceede out of this, that men are not Lords of 2 Cor. 7.5 their promises maisters of their words, *foris pugnæ, intus timores* may welbe applyed here, there are afflictions within, and feares of offendinge without, Letters from above, kindred from within, money from both sides, which keepes them from beinge *Domini promissionis* Lords of their promises, masters of their words; either they thinke that if they dispatch a suitor too soone, ther's an end of his observance, of his attendance, of his respect, he undervalewes the favor, if it be so soone shewed, and so ther's a delay out of state, to give a dignity a majesty to the busines; or else they see that when there is an end a dispatch of the cause, there is an end of the profitt too, that Mine is exhausted, that veine is dryed up, that Cow gives noe more milke, and therefore by references and conferences, they keepe open that which howsoever it be an udder to them, is a wound to them that beare it, and heer's a delay to keep a way open to extortion and bribery. Perchance abundance of wealth (or els of honour and command if not of wealth) may make them over indulgent to their owne ease, and heer's a delay out of lazines; perchance corrupt meanes have brought an insufficient man to the place, and then he must putt of busines, till he be better inform'd, till he have consulted with more sufficient men and heere's a delay out of ignorance; (to contract this) every man hath made a promise to God and to the state to doe the dutyes of his place, and either for feare, or love, or money, for state, for ease, or ignorance he is not *Dominus promissionis* Lord of that promise, Master of that word, he is not able to performe it. God only [2 Pet. 3.9] is soe; and therefore *non tardat* (sayth the Apostle) whatsoever thou Augustine countest slackenes, yet as that is *natura rei quam indidit Deus* (soe that if God would imprint a cold quality in fire, the nature of fire were cold) soe that's the time for thy deliverance which God hath appointed. If thou pray for deliverance and beest not delivered, doe not thinke that thou art not heard, nay doe not thinke that thou art not delivered for God delivers thee by continuinge thee in that calamity from some greater. When mans sinne extorts judgments from God, that it concerns him for his glory, or for the edification of his Church, to inflict those judgments, if *Noah* and *Daniel* and *Job* were amongst Ezech. 14.14 them, they should not deliver them from those judgments, but yet (says the prophet there) there shalbe a remnant in whome ye shalbe [Ezek. comforted. 14.22] Though the hand of God ly heavy upon thee, yet there shalbe a remnant to wrap up the wound of thy heart, the seede of God, the balme of God, an humble confidence in him shall still preserve thee. St. *Paul* prayed and prayed thrice that that *stimulus carnis* [2 Cor. might be removed from him, and it was not, God did not give him 12.7–10] that, but he gave him as good a suite, an equivalent thinge, *gratia mea sufficit:* St. *Paul* desired peace, God saw it to conduce more to his glory to make him able to hold out the warre, and therefore he removed not the enemy, his concupiscence, but assisted him with grace against that enemy. Thus St. *Paul* prayed longe for one thinge [Gen. and had another. 18.23–33] *Abraham* prayed and seemed to have all that he asked, and yet had nothinge; he prayed in the behalfe and favour of the citty of *Sodome,* and he had courage to goe on in his prayer, for he found that he wonne and gayned upon God in every petition, that he bated much of Gods first price, and that he beate that holy bargayne from 50. to 10., and yet when all was done nothing was done, he rescued none, the judgment was executed upon the citty. Limit not God therefore in his wayes or times, but yf you would be heard by him, heare him, yf you would have him graunt your prayers, doe his will. We pray you in Christs steed that you would be reconciled to God; and are you reconciled? durst you heare the trumpet nowe? Christ Jesus prayes for you nowe to his Father in heaven, that you might be converted and are you converted? If the prayers of the Church militant and the Church triumphant and the head of both Churches Christ Jesus, be not yet heard effectually on your behalfe, yet they shalbe in his time, his eternall election shall infallibly worke upon you. Soe if your owne prayers for your deliverance in any temporall or spirituall affliction be not presently heard, persevere for youre selves, as the Churches and the heade of them persevere in your behalfe, and God will certainly deliver you in his time, and strengthen you to fight out his battle all the way.

2 Part
Videt

We passe nowe from the occasion, taken justly by the place of these words, to the words themselves; and firste, takinge them alltogether to that generall doctrine, *Videt omnia,* for since he made all thinges, he hath a care of all thinges, a providence which (in such perfection as becomes us to ascribe to God) he could not have, except he sawe all thinges. Our seeinge of God hereafter is the blessednes we hope for, and our comfort in the way to that, is, that he sees us, for soe we never are, never shalbe out of syght of one another. If any sinner can conceite that wish, that God did not see him, he should loose more by it then he should get. Though he would be glad not to be seene by him in his sinnefull pleasures, yet he would be sorry not to be seene by him in his miseries and afflictions, and the miseries the afflictions of this life are more then the pleasures in the most habituall sinner. A man that would be glad that God sawe not his extortions, his oppressions, his grindinge of the poore by color of an office, would yet be sorry that God sawe not those privy whisperinges, those machinations and plotts and *nequitias in cœlestibus* (as we may call them) practises above in high places to traduce him, to defame him, to supplant him and wringe his office from him, perchance for thinges he never did, though he hath done as ill: and then we make our selves supervisors, overseers of God, yf we will appoint, soe farre as in our wishes, what he should see and what not. You knowe howe certaine and howe speedy a conviction it is, yf a man be taken in the manner, and you knowe howe heavily the fault is aggravated which is done in the face of the Court. All our actions are soe *in facie Judicis,* and there needs noe evidence, we are deprehended in the manner, in corners where nothing sees us, God sees us, and in hell where wee shall see nothinge, he shall see us too, *Videt omnia.*

Prævidet
Ro: 4.17
Ecclus. 23.20

And *praevidet omnia.* He sees as God and therefore he allwayes sawe all. He calleth those things which be not, as though they were, sayes the Apostle, he looketh upon all things after they bee brought to passe, sayes the wise man, and he knewe them er ever they were made. You would thinke him a weake lawyer that cold not foresee what would be the yssue of a cause, which depended wholly upon the lawe, without relation to the opinion of the judge, or to the affection of the Jury; and a weake Astrologer that cold not foresee Eclipses and positions of the heavens; and a weake Councell that cold not foresee the good or ill of such a warr, or such a peace, or such a marriage; and shall the sight and knowledge of God depend upon our actions? Omniscience is an attribute of his, as well as omnipotence, God can be noe more ignorant of a thinge then impotent in it; and whatsoever is his attribute was allwayes soe; was not God omnipotent, had he not all power till I was made, upon whome he exerciseth part of that power, which he did not before I was? Was he not omniscient, did he not knowe all thinges before those thinges were produced into action and execution? God ever knewe all thinges that were, that are, and that shalbee, and that may be, and that may not be, because he will not have them be, for if he would, they should be. He knowes them otherwise then they are, for he knowes future thinges as present, and he knowes contingent thinges as certaine and necessary. It is true, he shall say at the last day to Hypocrits, *nescio vos* I doe not knowe you, I never did knowe you. [Mat. 25.12; Luke 13.25] But this is that knowledge of which St. *Gregory* speakes, *scire Dei est approbare,* soe God never knewe the Hypocrits, nor ever shall, as to accept them, to allowe them, to approve them. And soe also it is said of Christ *non nosse peccatum;* he who knewe no sinne was made sinne for us. [2 Cor. 5.21] Experimentally, actually, personally he knewe noe sinne, but in his eternall knowledge he ever knew all our particular sinnes, and he knewe the generall roote of all, the sinne of *Adam,* before that sinne was, or before that man was. But was this knowledge or foreknowledge the cause of it? God forbid! *Detestanda, abominanda opinio quæ Deum facit cuiusquam malæ Voluntatis autorem,* Aug: the opinion is detestable, abhominable, *nefas est ascribere Deo causas peccatorum,* sayes the same Father, and therefore let us be afraid of cominge soe neere this detestable and abhominable opinion as to expresse our selves in misinterpretable termes, and phrases too bold and too different from the modest and sober use of the ancient doctors and Fathers, that there is in God an effectuall and an actuall, and a positive and a consulted and a deliberat reprobation of certaine men, before their sinnes, yea before their creation was considered, or that there is in man a necessary damnation, which he was made for and created to; Gods knoweledge of sinne prints not a necessity of sinne. An Astrologers knowledge of an Eclipse causes not that Eclipse; my knowledge that he that will fall from a steeple will breake his bones, did not thrust him downe, nor precipitate him to that ruine. But God myght have preserved him from sinne, and soe cannot an Astrologer worke upon an Eclipse, nor I upon a desperate man that will cast himself downe. It is true, God might have preserved him from sinne, by makinge him better, and soe he myght by makinge him worse too; He might have preserved him by makinge him an angell in a confirmed estate, and he might have preserved him, by makinge him a beast without a reasonable soule, for then he cold not have sinned, and he had byn the better for it. Augustine But Gods will (*cuius qui quærit rationem aliquid maius Deo quærit*) was to make him a man, and as a man he finds the reason of his sinne to be the perversenes of his owne will. Who perverts that? Did God? *Abominandum, detestandum*. But God myght have prevented this perversnes, he myght have made him soe stronge as that he cold not have perverted himselfe. But then God had not made him man. God did abundantly ynough in makinge him good, and able to continue soe; and he does abundantly ynough in givinge us those generall declarations of his desire, that we should all returne to that goodnes, that he would [2 Pet. 3.9] have noe man to perish, but that all men should come to repentance. He sees all thinges, even sinnes, and foresees them, but yet his foresight is noe cause of them.

3 Part We are come nowe to the third part, the particular consideration of the words. God sees and foresees 1 *Desideria* the desires and all desires, for *David* does not speake this by way of discomfort, as though God did only watch our ill desires to punish them, and not our obedience to cherish and reward that. It is true as the prophet [Jer. 2.22] *Jeremy* testifyes, Our iniquity is marked before the Lord, but it is Psal. 56.8 also true which *David* sayes, that our teares are put into his bottle, and into his Register, soe that (as St. *Ambrose* enlarges this desire) it Psal. 84.2 may be *Davids* desire, *concupiscit et deficit anima mea,* my soule longeth and fainteth for the Courts of the Lord, a desire to live in 1 Pet. 2.2 the Church of God, and it may be the Apostles desire, *concupiscite lac,* as newe borne babes desire the milke of the word, a desire to be

fed with such knowledge in the Church as is fit and proportionable
to my capacitye and understanding. Consider *desiderium beatorum,*
the desire of the blessed saints in heaven, who though they be in full
possession of happines, have yet a further desire of a consummation
and re-union of body and soule. Consider *desiderium iustorum,* the
desire of the righteous: the desire of the righteous is only good (sayth Pro. 11.23
Solomon) it is good, as it is a desire to knowe God. My heart breaketh Ps. 119.20
for the desire to thy judgments allwaies. And it is good as it is a
desire to propagate this their knowledge of God to others by instruc-
tion or at least by good example. For God hath given every man a Ecclus. 17.14
commandement concerning his neighbour. And it is good, as it is a
desire to be united to God; as *Simeon* expressed it in his *Nunc dimit-* [Luke 2.29]
tis, Lord nowe lettest thou thy servant depart in peace, and St. *Paul*
in his *cupio dissolui,* I desire to be dissolved and to be with Christ. [Phil. 1.23]
Consider it lastly as *desiderium peccatorum,* the divers and contrary
desires of sinners, every way, every desire, *Davids* desire to live in
the Church, the Apostles desire to be satisfied with thinges necessary
in the Church, the desire of the saints in heaven for the consumma-
tion, the desire of the saints in earth to knowe God, to make him
knowne to others, and to be united to him, and the desire of sinne-
full men too, all these meete in the Center, in the eye of God; All
our desires are before him. But principally this is intended of cor-
rupt and sinnefull desires, for though it be *omne desiderium,* yet all
the imaginations of the thoughts of our hearts are only evill contin- Gen. 6.5
ually; The Imaginations, *ipsa figmenta,* as the originall word *Jetzer*
imports, before it come to be a formall and debated thought; and then
the thoughts themselves, when I have discovered them, debated them,
and in my heart at home seriously, not only in tentations presented
to my fancy or senses. These imaginations and all these imaginations
they are evill. If any good be mingled with them, yet it is soe little,
as that *denominantur à maiori,* they are evill, because they are evill
for the most part, but it is worse then soe, for they are only evil, noe
dramme, noe tincture of good in them; all evill and only evill and
this continually, evill in the roote, in the first concupiscence, and
evill in the fruite, in the growth and in the perseverance. Soe that
Desideria heere are most properly *figmenta,* the first Imaginations,
and they are evill and their sinnefull affection is in the sight of God.

But soe are *gemitus,* our groaninges too, hee sees them, and what is good or evill in them, as well as in our desires.

Gemitus

First then, as *David* had expressed it before in the verse precedent, It is *gemitus cordis,* the groaninge of the heart, *cordis non carnis,* as St. *Austin* makes the difference, a hearty groaninge and not merely sensuall. *Abstulit Deus filium et uxorem,* sayth that Father: God hath beaten downe thy greene fruite from thy beloved tree, God hath hewen downe the beloved tree it selfe, the young children and the mother of those children he hath taken from thee, *grandinata vinea,* (as he enlarges this consideration) thy Vine is stroken with the haile, the raine hath drown'd thy meadowes, now thou lackest heate to make thy hay, and then heate takes hold of it in the stacke, and setts it on fire, and then thou lackest water to quench it; unseasonable weather, negligence of servants, casuall accidents, Violence of theives, greatnes of neighbours, all concurre to thine impoverishinge, and then thou comest *ad gemitum,* to a groaning, but it is *Carnis non Cordis,* it is a meere sensuall groaning, not from the heart, or not from the heart soe disposed towards God as it should be. It must then first be *cordis* and not *carnis,* and it must be *gemitus* not *rugitus,* a groaninge not a roaringe, the voice of a Turtle not of a Lyon. If we take it heere for the voyce of sorrowe in worldly crosses, we must not presently roare out in petitions, in suites, in complaints for every *1 Cor. 6.7* such crosse. There is a fault amongst you (sayth the Apostle) because you goe to Lawe with one another. Why rather suffer ye not wronge, why rather sustayne ye not harme? The Apostle would not call it expressely a sinne but he calls it a fault, and in a word which signifies weakenes and imperfection. The streame of the Fathers runnes somewhat vehemently in this point, for they scarse excuse any suite at lawe from sinne, or occasion of sinne, and they will not depart from the literall understandinge of those words of our Saviour; *Mat. 5.40* yf any man will sue thee at lawe for thy coate, Let him have thy cloake too, for if thine adversary have it not, thine advocate will. Howsoever, every man feeles in his owne conscience whether he be not the lesse disposed to charity, the lesse fit to come worthily to the Sacrament, and the more apt to corrupt and bribe an officer, and *offic. l. 1 c. 41* to delude and circumvent a Judge, by havinge suits in lawe than otherwise. And at last, as St. *Ambrose* reports the words and behavior of St. *Laurence* at his martirdome, that he came to that constancy to say to the persecutor *assatum satis, versa et manduca,* soe the Devill will allwayes have his martyrs too, who out of a desperate impatience after longe delayes will come to that desperate yssue towards the adversary or the Councell or the Judge, you have taken my livinge, take my life too. To end this, for every damage, every trespasse, every injurious word to call one another with the Kings letter, the Kinges writt, this is *rugitus Leonis* (for the voyce of the [Prov. Kinge is like the roaringe of a lyon) whereas *gemitus columbæ,* such 19.12; 20.2] a mild complaint as might referre it to men of lesse quality, but more [Isa. 59.11] leasure, would make a better end. Soe then if we consider this groaninge to be the voyce of sorrowe for worldly losses, it must not be *rugitus,* a vociferation, a cryinge out, as though we were undone, as though we cold not be happy except we were rich, and as though we cold not be rich except we had just soe much; It is not an immoderate complayninge for worldly losses to the magistrate for remedy for every petty injury, it must be but *gemitus* both these wayes. And take it, as it is most properly to be taken, for the voyce of spirituall sorrowe, a sorrowe for our sinnes, soe it must be but *gemitus* neyther, it must not be an immoderate sorrowe that terrifyes, or argues a distrust in Gods goodnes. Drowne that body of sinne which thou hast built up in thee, drowne that world of sinne which thou hast created (for we have a creation as well as God) *hominem fecit* Augustine *Deus, pecatorem homo,* man is Gods creature and the sinner is mans creature, spare thy world noe more then God spared his, who drowned it with the floud, drowne thine too with repentant teares. But when that worke is religiously done, *miserere animæ tuæ,* be as mercifull to thy soule as he was to mankind, drowne it noe more, [Gen. 9.11] suffer it not to ly under the water of distrustfull diffidence, for soe thou mayst fall too lowe to be able to tugge up against the tide againe, soe thou mayst be swallowed in *Cains* whirlepoole, to thinke thy [Gen. 4.13] sinnes greater then can be forgiven. God deales with us as he did with *Ezechias, Vidit lachrimas,* yea as it is in the Original, *vidit* [2 Kings *lachrymam* in the singular, God sees every teare, our first teare, and 20.5] is affected with that. When the child was dead, *David* arose from the [2 Sam. ground and eate bread; when the sinne is dead by thy true repent- 12.18–20] ance, rayse thy selfe from this sad dejection, and come and eate the bread of life, the body of thy Saviour for the seale of thy pardon. For there in this repentance and this seale, *finem litibus imponis* thou leaviest a fine upon thy sinnes, which cuts off and concludes all titles. And when God hath provided that thy sinnes shall rise noe more to thy condemnation at the last day, if thou rayse them up here to the vexation of thy conscience, thou art a litigious man to thine owne destruction. This was then *Davids* comfort, and is ours; *Desideria et gemitus,* the beginninge of our sinnefull concupiscences and the beginninge of our repentance are seene by God, and God of his mercy stoppes those desires at the beginninge, eyther he keeps away the August: Devill or the woman, he takes away *stimulum* or *obiectum,* eyther my lust to that sinne, or the occasion and opportunitye for the sinne. In his mercy he stops me at the beginninge of my desire, and in his mercy he perfitts the beginninges of my repentance, he sees *desideria* and *gemitus.*

Sua Nowe these desires and these groanes they are *sua,* his; the study of our conversion to God, is in this like the study of your profession, it requires a whole man for it. It is for the most part losse of time in you to divert upon other studies, and it is for the most part losse of charity in us all to divert from our selves unto the consideration of other men, to prognosticate ill for the future, upon any man, I see his covetous desires, I see his carnall desires, I see his sinnefull courses, this man can never repente; or to collect ill from that which is past, I see his repentance his sadnes, his dejection of Countenance and spirit, his approach towards desperation; surely this man is a more greivous sinner then we tooke him for. To prognosticate thus, to collect thus upon others is an intrusion an usurpation upon them and a dangerous dereliction and abandoninge of our selves. When John 9.[2–5] the disciples of Christ would needs call into question the sinnes of that man which was borne blind, rather then let them goe on in that, although no punishment be inflicted without sinne preceding, yet Christ sayes there, neyther this man nor his parents have sinned, not that he or they were simply without sinne, but he would drawe his disciples from that which concerned not them, the sinnes of another, to that which concerned them more, the contemplation of his omnipotence who would recover that man of his blindness in their Luke 13.[4–5] sight. Thinke you, (sayes Christe) that those 18 upon whom the tower of *Siloe* fell, were the greatest sinners in *Hierusalem?* No; Christ had a care to deliver them from that misinterpretation then, and the Holy Ghost hath not suffered the names nor the sinnes of those men soe slayne to come to our knowledge. In all the Evangelists, in all the other histories of the *Jewish* nation and affaires there is no mention, noe word, noe record of the death of those men nor of the fall of this Tower. God would not have posterity knowe their names nor theyr sinnes soe particularly, after he had inflicted that extraordinary punishment upon them. Bee thine owne text then, and bee thine owne comment, watch thine owne desires, and God shall stop them, and thine owne groanes, and God shall perfitt them with his unexpresseable comfort.

Ante te Aug:

But all this must be *Ante te,* before God, in his presence and soe before him, *ut nihil absconditum,* that nothinge be hid from him; Nowe *quale desiderium debet esse quod ante Deum? Oras ut moriantur inimici,* is that thy desire, that thine enemies might come to confusion? And is that a fitt desire for the presence of God? Is this a writinge after thy coppy, after thy master Christ? His coppy is, *Pater ignosce,* Father forgive them, for they knowe not what they [Luke 23.34] doe. Or is it after his usher, his disciple *Stephen?* His copy is, *Domine ne statuas illis,* O Lord lay not this sinne to their charge. [Acts 7.60] If thou wilt needes pray for thine enemies death, the same Father teaches thee a good way, *ora ut corrigantur, et moriuntur inimici,* pray for their amendment, and the enemy is dead, when the enmity is dead. But this phrase of *David* heere, that all this is *ante te,* imports not only Gods seeinge of it, but it implyes our bringinge of our desires and groanings into his sight. Lord thou hast heard the desires of the poore, [Ps. 10.17] says *David,* but howe? Thou preparest their heart, and thou bendest thine eare to heere them; first Gods preventinge grace prepares, enables us, and then he bends downe with a farther supply of concurringe grace, but that is to heere us. For yf we doe nothinge then, yf we speake not then, he departs from us. He hath looked downe from the height of his sanctuary, sayth he in another place, [Ps. 102.19–20] heer's his first grace, that he lookes towards us, and then he heares the mourninge of the prisoner, and he delivers the child of Death. But firste the prisoner must knowe himselfe to be in prison, and send forth a voyce of mourninge. He sawe and succoured *Ezechias,* but not till he sawe his teares, he lookes for outward demonstrations of our sorrowe, for confession and amendment of life. It is one thinge in a Judge to knowe, another to knowe soe, as he may take knowledge and Judge upon it. God knowes thy desires and thy groanes, but he will not take knowledge of them to thy comfort to stop thy desires, to perfect thy repentance, except thou bringe them Judicially before him; thy desires by way of confession, and thy groanes by way of thankfullnes. It is nothinge for a rich man to say in generall, Lord all I have is from thee, and if thou wilt have it againe, I am ready to part with it. This is hypocriticall complement to say to God or man; all's at your service; but give God some part of that, house Christ Jesus where he is harbour-lesse, helpe to beautify and build that house where his name may be glorified and his Sabbaths sanctified, cloth him where he is naked, feed him in his hunger, deliver him in his imprisonment, when he suffereth this in his afflicted members. All your recognitions to God without Subsidyes without benevolences, without releivinge him in his distressed children, are but ceremoniall, but hypocriticall complements. So thy tellinge to God that he knowes all thy desires and all thy groanes, this is an easy matter for any man, it is a word soone sayd. But bringe all these before him, shewe him where and howe when by neglectinge his grace thou hast strayed into these and these desires, and where and howe and when thou hast taken light at his visitation to returne towards him, and then he shall overthrowe thy worke, and build up his owne, extinguish thy desires, and perfect thy repentance.

[Mat. 25.34–46]

Non absconditus

This *David* intends in that word *ante te,* and more fully in the next *non absconditus*. For I may be content to bringe some things before God, and yet hide others, or hide circumstances that may aggravate, yea that may alter the very nature of the fact. We must not hide our desires under our groanes, nor hide our grones under our desires; Not our desires under our groanes, by wrappinge up all our sinnes in a sadnes, in a dejection, in a stupidity, soe that I never see my sinnes in a true proportion as they ly upon Christs shoulders and not upon my soule, nor in their true apparell as they are clothed with Christs righteousnes, and not with my corruption, nor with their true weight as they are weighed downe with Christs merits, but as they weigh downe my soule into desperation. This is a hidinge of our desires in our groaninges, our sins in our dejection; And the hidinge of our groaninges in our desires is to wrap up all sorrowe for sinne in a verball confession and enumeration of our sinnes, without any particular contrition for the sinne, or detestation of it. We must hide neither; but anatomize our soule in both, and find every sinnewe, and fiber, every lineament and ligament of this body of sinne, and then every breath of that newe spirit, every drop of that newe bloud that must restore and repayre us. Study all the history, and write all the progres of the Holy Ghost in thy selfe. Take not the grace of God, or the mercy of God as a meddall, or a wedge of gold to be layd up, but change thy meddall or thy wedge into currant money, find this grace and this mercy applyed to this end this action. For though the meritt of Christ be a sea, yet be thou content to take it in drop after drop, and to acknowledge in the presence of God, that at such a time (by reducinge them to thy memory and contemplation his Agony) thou wast brought to a sense of thy miserable estate, and after (by consideringe the ministeringe of the angells to him there) [Luke 22.43] thou tookest a confidence of receiving succour from him; That at such a particular time, the memory of his fastinge rescued thee from a voluptuous and riotous meetinge, and the memory of his proceedinge and behaviour in his tentations brought thee also to deliver thy selfe by applyinge his word and the promises of the Gospell from those dangerous attempts of the tempter. Hide nothinge from God, neyther the diseases thou wast in, nor the degrees of health that thou art come to, nor the wayes of thy fallinge or risinge; for *Dominus fecit, et erit mirabile.* [Psal. 118.23; Mat. 21.42; Mark 12.11] If I mistake not the measure of thy conscience, thou wilt find an infinite comfort in this particular tracinge of the Holy Ghost, and his workinge in thy soule.

This is the layinge open and not hidinge, but all this is limited, *ante te,* and *tibi,* before God and to God. For why should I open my sinnes to man? He cannot releive me by way of pardon. Or why should I open my groanings to man? He will not releive me soe much as by compassion. *Recedit gemitus servorum Dei ab auribus hominum, sed ante Deum semper.* Aug. There therefore they are only well placed, from whence they never part. But yet consider to whome all this is directed. It is *ante te,* and it is *tibi,* but *tibi Domine.* Nowe there are two names of God which are ordinarily in the Scriptures translated by this word Dominus, the Lord. One name is *Jehovah,* and the other is *Adonai.* And *Jehovah* signifies essence, beinge, *Adonai* signifies properly basis, *fundamentum,* that upon which some buildinge rests, and in this place thats the word, *Adonai.* Soe that this is an openinge of our desires and groanings, of the wounds and scruples of our consciences to God, as God is the Lord, and such a Lord as is the basis and foundation, the corner-stone, and the piller of our buildinge, and that buildinge is the Church. All power of remission of sinnes is in the Lord, but in the Lord in his Church. And therefore since that Church in which God hath sealed thee to him in both sacraments, accordinge to the direction of the Holy Ghost, hath ordayned that sick persons shall make a speciall confession, yf they feele their consciences troubled with any weighty matter, and that after that confession, the priest shall absolve them, let noe man thinke himselfe wiser then the Church, and for the abuse of a thinge in a corrupt Church, goe forward in an ignorance of what the true Church holds in that point, or defraude himselfe of nourishment out of a false feare of poysons and fumes, when there are none. Let noe man thinke himselfe out of the presence of God, by puttinge himselfe into the presence of his minister, nor doubt but that, that confession is *ante Dominum,* and that absolution is *a Domino,* and from that Lord who is presented heere not as *Jehovah* the Lord of essence and beinge, and so in his generall providence and sustayninge of all creatures, but as *Adonai,* a Lord that is the basis and foundation of his Church. And let noe man deale so niggardly soe penuriously with his owne soule, as to contract this ease and discharge of his conscience only to the point of Death because it is not literally expressly appointed to others, but let us all thinke ourselves deadly sicke, whensoever we are under the burden of any deadly sinne. I am not upon that frivolous and yet impious doctrine of the *Romane* Church of Veniall and deadly sinne, as though there were any sinne which deserved not death, or might be washed out by our selves without the application of the merits of Christ; but agreeable to the modesty and sobriety of the Ancients, I call that deadly sinne, which is *peccatum vastans conscientiam,* such as if they be not rooted out, destroy the conscience, and in their owne nature oppose the workinge of Gods grace in us, as longe as they are in us. To end this, God knewe where

Adam was, and yet he asks him, *Adam ubi es,* he would fayne have [Gen. 3.9] knowne it from himselfe. God knew that the *Sodomites* had done accordinge to the cry which was come up, and yet he would come downe and see. [Gen. 18.20–21] God knowes our desires and our gronings in heaven as God, he would knowe them upon earth in his Church too, as Lord.

Nowe the conclusion of all, accordinge to our custome held in the parts of this psalme, shalbe a short application of some of the most important passages to the person of Christ, of whome many ancient expositors have understood this psalme to have byn principally intended. First then, he in the dayes of his flesh offered up prayers and supplications with stronge cryings and teares unto him that was able to save him from death; and was also heard in that which he feared. [Heb. 5.7] He was heard, but when? First, when prayed he that vehement prayer? All agree that that place of the Apostle hath relation to Christs prayer in his Agony in the garden, *quando non contentus lachrimis oculorum, totius corporis sanguineis lachrimis lachrimavit,* [Ambrose] when besides his tears of water, he opened as many eyes as he had pores in his body, and wept out bloud at every one of those eyes. And they agree that that place of the Apostle hath relation to his vehement prayer upon the Crosse, *Eli, Eli,* My God, my God etc. That when his Father *non solvit unionem, sed subtrahit extentione,* [Aug.] soe that Christ prayed in his affliction, and yet prayed againe, that which was *Davids* case and is ours, was his case too, he was heard, but not at the first prayinge. After his first prayer, of *transeat calix,* he was put to his expostulation, *quare dereliquisti?* [Mat. 26.39; 27.46] The Father was allwayes with him, and is with us, but our deliverance is in his time, and not in ours, which was the doctrine raysed out of the first part of the Text.

For the second, the knowledge and fore knowledge of God, it is true, that God who sees all, and foresees all, foresawe all the malignity of the *Jewes* in crucifyinge of Christ, but yet he was noe cause of it. St. *Augustine* presents that passion pathetically before our eyes, [Aug:] *propinator fontium potatur aceto, mellis dator cibatur felle, flagellatur remissio, et condemnatur venia: illuditur maiestas et irridetur virtus, et perfunditur dator imbrium sputis.* And all this and more then this, even the sheddinge of his bloud was foreseene, for he was *agnus occisus ab origine,* and all this was done too *ut im-* [Apoc. 13.8; Mark 14.49] [margin: ıt. 26.54] *plerentur Scripturæ,* and, as *Matthew* expresses it, howe els should the Scriptures be fulfilled, which say, that it must be soe. But were these prophecyes the cause of it? No; the prophecyes were longe before the execution, but the foreknowledge of God was longe before the prophecyes. This foreknowledge was the cause of this prophecy, but neyther the foreknowledge nor the prophecy was any cause of the sinnefull part of their fact. And thats as much as is appliable to Christ in the 2d part.

In the 3d part, (to passe speedily through some of the principall words) first for *Desideria,* himselfe tells us, as *Chrysostome* observes [margin: Luk. 22.[15]] it, what his desire was, *Desiderio desideravi comedere pascha hoc.* Other passovers he had eate with them before, but this passover, (which was to be a memoriall not of their departinge out of *Egypt,* but of his departinge out of this world by a bitter and ignominious death for their salvation) he had a desire to institute and celebrate, and to commend to their desires in imitation and commemoration of him.

When we consider the next, *gemitus,* his mourninges, they were vehement, but yet still they ended in a calme. At first in the *tristis anima* and *si possibile,* there appeare some gusts, some beginning of a storme, but all becalmed presently in the *veruntamen,* yet not my will, but thy will be done. Soe at first in the *Quare dereliquisti?* there appeares a gust, but in *In Manus tuas,* a calme againe. We doe not call that an immoderate nor over-passionate sorrowe for sinne, which sees day, and apprehends the presence of God, in that dejection of spirit. But exclamations upon destiny, imputations upon necessity, aspersions upon the Decrees of God himselfe, (as yf any thinge but the perversnes of my will were the cause of my sinne) those are *rugitus Leonis,* the roaringe of that Lyon, that seekes whome he may devoure, and not *Gemitus columbæ,* the voyce of that Dove that comes to the Arke with an Olive branch, settles in the Church with the testimonies of peace and reconciliation which are there. Moreover Christ was to be glorified with the glory which he had before, and nowe he longed till that was accomplished, but yet all was, *ante Patrem,* his meate was to doe his Fathers will, and till his time was come, *nondum venit hora mea,* sayes Christ, my hower is not yet come.

Conclusio

To end all; he proposed all *ante Patrem,* but *ante Patrem Dominum,* to his Father soe, as his Father had a Church upon earth, and therefore, though there were a newe Church to be erected by him, yet he yeilded all obedience to that which was formerly erected; In that he was circumcised, and presented; and in that his Mother was purified accordinge to the Lawe, and in that he sent his owne disciples to be instructed by the scribes and *Pharises.* And to conclude, all refractory persons, by his example: in that Church he honoured with his presence the feast of the dedication, which was an Anniversary feast, and a feast not of divine Institution, but ordained by the Church.

[Luke 2.21, 22]
[Mat. 23.1–2]
Jo. 10. [22–23]

Number 7.

A Lent-Sermon Preached at White-hall, February 12. 1618. [*1618/19*]

EZEK. 33.32. *AND LO, THOU ART UNTO THEM AS A VERY LOVELY SONG, OF ONE THAT HATH A PLEASANT VOYCE, AND CAN PLAY WELL ON AN INSTRUMENT; FOR THEY HEAR THY WORDS, BUT THEY DOE THEM NOT.*

[1 Cor. 9.16]

AS THERE lies alwayes upon Gods Minister, a *væ si non,* Wo be unto me, if I preach not the Gospel, if I apply not the comfortable promises of the Gospel, to all that grone under the burden of their sins; so there is *Onus visionis,* (which we finde mentioned in the Prophets) it was a pain, a burden to them, to be put to the denunciation of Gods heavy judgements upon the people: but yet those judgements, they must denounce, as well as propose those mercies: wo be unto us, if we bind not up the broken hearted; but wo be unto us too, if we break not that heart that is stubborn: wo be unto us, if we settle not, establish not the timorous and trembling, the scattered, and fluid, and distracted soul, that cannot yet attain, intirely and intensely, and confidently and constantly, to fix it self upon the Merits and Mercies of Christ Jesus; but wo be unto us much more, if we do not shake, and shiver, and throw down the refractory and rebellious soul, whose incredulity will not admit the History, and whose security in presumptuous sins will not admit the working and application of those Merits and Mercies which are proposed to him. To this purpose, therefore, God makes his Ministers *speculatores;* I have set thee for their watchman, saies God to this Prophet; that so they might see and discern the highest sins of the highest

Ezek. 33.7]

persons, in the highest places: they are not onely to look down towards the streets, and lanes, and alleys, and cellars, and reprehend the abuses and excesses of persons of lower quality there, all their service lies not below staires; nor onely to look into the chamber, and reprehend the wantonnesses and licentiousnesse of both sexes there; nor onely unto the house top and tarras, and reprehend the ambitious machinations and practises to get thither; but still they are *speculatores,* men placed upon a watchtower, to look higher then all this, to look upon sins of a higher nature then these, to note and reprehend those sins, which are done so much more immediately towards God, as they are done upon colour and pretence of Religion: and upon that station, upon the Execution of that Commission, is our Prophet in this Text, *Thou art unto them a very lovely Song, &c. for they shall heare thy words, but they do them not.* Through this whole chapter, he presents matter of that nature, either of too confident, or too diffident a behaviour towards God. In the tenth verse, he reprehends their diffidence and distrust in God: This they say (sayes the Prophet) *If our transgressions and our sins be upon us, and we pine away in them, how should we live?* How should you live? sayes the Prophet: thus you should live, by hearing what the Lord of Life hath said, *As I live, saith the Lord God, I have no pleasure in the death of the wicked.* In the 25 verse he reprehends their confidence; they say, *Abraham* was one, and he inherited this land; we are many, this land is given us for our inheritance: but say unto them, sayes God to the Prophet there, *You lift up your eyes to Idols, and you shed blood, and shall you possess the land? Ye defile one anothers wife, and ye stand upon the sword, and shall ye possess the land?* We were but one, and are many; 'tis true: God hath testified his love, in multiplying Inhabitants, and in uniting Kingdomes; but if there be a lifting up of eyes towards Idols, a declination towards an Idolatrous Religion; if there be a defiling of one anothers wife, and then standing upon the sword, that it must be matter of displeasure, or of quarrel, if one will not betray his wife, or sister, to the lust of the greatest person; shall we possess the land? shall we have a continuance of Gods blessing upon us? we shall not. And as he thus represents their over-confident behaviour towards God; God is bound by his promise, and therefore we may be secure: And their over-diffident behaviour; God hath begun to shew his anger upon us, and therefore there is no recovery: he reprehends also that distemper, which ordinarily accompanies this behaviour towards God, that is, an Expostulation, and a Disputing with God, and a censuring of his actions: in the 20 verse they come to say, *The way of the Lord is not equal;* that is, we know not how to deal with him, we know not where to find him; he promises Mercies, and layes Afflictions upon us; he threatens judgements upon the wicked, and yet the wicked prosper most of all; *The ways of the Lord are [not] equal.* But, to this also God says by the Prophet, *I will judge every one of you after his own ways. The ways of the Lord are unsearchable;* [Rom. 11.33] look ye to your own ways, for according to them, shall God judge you. And then after these several reprehensions, this watchman raises himself to the highest pinacle of all, to discover the greatest sin of all, treason within doors, contemning of God in his own house, and in his presence; that is, a coming to Church to hear the word of God preached, a pretence of cheerfulness and alacrity, in the outward service of God, yea a true sense and feeling of a delight in hearing of the word; and yet for all this, an unprofitable barrenness, and (upon the whole matter) a despiteful and a contumelious neglecting of Gods purpose and intention, in his Ordinance: for, Our voice is unto them but as a song to an instrument; they hear our words, but they do them not.

Though then some Expositors take these words to be an increpation upon the people, that they esteemed Gods ablest Ministers, indued with the best parts, to be but as musique, as a jest, as a song, as an entertainment; that they under-valued and disesteemed the whole service of God in the function of the Ministery, and thought it either nothing, or but matter of State and Government, as a civil ordinance for civil order, and no more: yet I take this increpation to reach to a sin of another nature; that the people should attribute reverence enough, attention enough, credit enough to the preacher, and to his preachings, but yet when all that is done, nothing is done: they should hear willingly, but they do nothing of that which they had heard.

Divisio

First then, God for his own glory promises here, that his Prophet, his Minister shall be *Tuba,* as is said in the beginning of this Chapter, a Trumpet, to awaken with terror. But then, he shall become *Carmen musicum,* a musical and harmonious charmer, to settle and compose the soul again in a reposed confidence, and in a delight in God: he shall be *musicum carmen,* musick, harmony to the soul in his matter; he shall preach harmonious peace to the conscience: and he shall be *musicum carmen,* musick and harmony in his manner; he shall not present the messages of God rudely, barbarously, extemporally; but with such meditation and preparation as appertains to so great an imployment, from such a King as God, to such a State as his Church: so he shall be *musicum carmen,* musicke, harmony, *in re & modo,* in matter and in manner: And then *musicum* so much farther (as the text adds) as that he shall have a pleasant voice, that is, to preach first sincerely (for a preaching to serve turns and humors, cannot, at least should not please any) but then it is to preach acceptably, seasonably, with a spiritual delight, to a discreet and rectified congregation, that by the way of such a holy delight, they may receive the more profit. And then he shall play well on an instrument; which we do not take here to be the working upon the understanding and affections of the Auditory, that the congregation shall be his instrument; but as S. *Basil* says, *Corpus hominis, Organum Dei,* when the person acts that which the song says; when the words become works, this is a song to an instrument: for, as S. *Augustine* pursues the same purpose, *Psallere est ex preceptis Dei agere;* to sing, and to sing to an instrument, is to perform that holy duty in action, which we speak of in discourse: And God shall send his people preachers furnished with all these abilities, to be *Tubæ,* Trumpets to awaken them; and then to be *carmen musicum,* to sing Gods mercies in their ears, in reverent, but yet in a diligent, and thereby a delightful manner; and so to be musick in their preaching, and musick in their example, in a holy conversation: *Eris,* says God to this prophet, such a one thou shalt be, thou shalt be such a one in thy self; and then *eris illis,* thou shalt be so to them, to the people: To them thou shalt be *Tuba,* a Trumpet, Thy preaching shall awaken them, and so bring them to some sence of their sins: To them thou shalt be *carmen musicum,* musick and harmony; both *in re,* in thy matter, they shall conceive an apprehension or an offer of Gods mercy through thee; and *in modo,* in the manner; they shall confess, that thy labors work upon them, and move them, and affect them, and that that unpremeditated, and drowsie, and cold manner of preaching, agrees not with the dignity of Gods service: they shall acknowledge (says God to this Prophet) thy pleasant voice; confesse thy doctrine to be good, and confesse thy playing upon an Instrument, acknowledge thy life to be good too; for, in testimony of all this, *Audient* (saies the text) They shall hear this. Now, every one that might come, does not so; businesses, nay less then businesses, vanities, keep many from hence; less then vanities, nothing; many, that have nothing to do, yet are not here: All are not come that might come; nor are all that are here, come hither; penalty of law, observation of absences, invitation of company, affection to a particular preacher, collateral respects, draw men; and they that are drawn so, do not come; neither do all that are come, hear; they sleep, or they talk: but *Audient,* says our text, They shall be here, they shall come, they shall hear; they shall press to hear: every one that would come, if he might sit at ease, will not be troubled for a Sermon: but our case is better, *Audient,* they shall rise earlier then their fellows, come hither sooner, indure more pains, hearken more diligently, and conceive more delight then their fellows: *Audient,* they will hear: but then, after all (which is the height of the malediction, or increpation) *Non facient,* they will not do it; *Non facient quæ dixeris,* They will do nothing of that which thou hast said to them; nay, *non facient quæ dixerunt,* they will do nothing of that, which during the time of the Sermons, they had said to their own souls, they would do; so little hold shall Gods best means, and by his best instruments, take of them; *They shall hear thy words, and shall not do them.*

These then are our parts that make up this increpation: First, the Prophet shall do his part fully: Secondly, the people shall do some of theirs: But then lastly, they shall fail in the principal, and so make all uneffectual. First, God will send them Prophets that shall be *Tubæ,* Trumpets; and not onely that, but *speculatores;* not onely Trumpets which sound according to the measure of breath that is blown into them, but they themselves are the watchmen that are to sound them: not Trumpets to sound out what airs the occasion of the present time, or what airs the affections of great persons infuse into them; for so they are only Trumpets, and not Trumpetors; but God hath made them both: And, as in civil matters, *Angusta inno-*

Seneca

centia est, ad legem bonum esse, That's but a narrow, but a faint honesty, to be no honester then a man must needs be, no honester then the law, or then his bodily sickness constrains him to be; so are these Trumpets short-winded Trumpets, if they sound no oftner then the Canons enjoyn them to sound; for, they must preach in [2 Tim. 4.2] season and out of season: If the Canonical season be but once a month, the preaching between, is not so unseasonable, but that it is within the Apostles precept too. If that be done, if the watchman sound the Trumpet, says the beginning of this Chapter (when you see it is the watchman himself that sounds, and not another to sound him; he is neither to be an instrument of others, nor is he to sound always by others, and spare his own breath) but if the watchman do duly sound, then there is an *Euge bone serve,* belongs to him; *Well* [Mat. 25.21, 23] *done good and faithful servant, enter into thy Masters joy:* And if he be not heard, or be not followed, then there is a *væ Betsaida,* a wo [Mat. 11.21–24; Luke 10.13] belonging to that City, and to that house; for, if those works had been done in *Sodom,* if all this preaching had been at *Rome, Rome* would have repented in sackcloth and ashes. I set watchmen over Jer. 6.17 you, says God in another Prophet, *Et dixi, Audite,* I said unto you, Hearken to them: so far God addresses himself to them, speaks personally to them, *super vos,* and *Audite vos;* I sent to you, and hear you: but when they would not hear, then he changes the person, *Et dixerunt,* says that text, And they said, We will not hear: after this stubbornness, God does not so much as speak to them: it is not *Dixistis,* you said it; God will have no more to do with them; but it is *Dixerunt,* they said it; God speaks of them as of strangers. But this is not altogether the case in our text: God shall send Prophets, Trumpets, and Trumpetors, that is, preachers of his word, and not the word of men; and they shall be heard willingly too; for as they are *Tubæ,* Trumpets, so they shall be *musicum carmen,* acceptable musick to them that hear them.

In Re

They shall be so, first *In re,* in their matter, in the doctrine which they preach. The same trumpet that sounds the alarm (that is, that awakens us from our security) and that sounds the Battail (that is, that puts us into a colluctation with our selves, with this world, with powers and principalities, yea into a wrastling with God himself and his Justice) the same trumpet sounds the Parle too, calls us to hearken to God in his word, and to speak to God in our prayers, and so to come to treaties and capitulations for peace; and the same trumpet sounds a retreat too, that is, a safe reposing of our souls in the merit, and in the wounds of our Saviour Christ Jesus. And in this voice they are *musicum carmen,* a love-song (as the text speaks) in proposing the love of God to man, wherein he loved him so, as that he gave his onely begotten Son for him. God made this whole world in such an uniformity, such a correspondency, such a concinnity of parts, as that it was an Instrument, perfectly in tune: we may say, the trebles, the highest strings were disordered first; the best understandings, Angels and Men, put this instrument out of tune. God rectified all again, by putting in a new string, *semen mulieris,* the seed of the woman, the *Messias:* And onely by sounding that string in your ears, become we *musicum carmen,* true musick, true harmony, true peace to you. If we shall say, that Gods first string in this instrument, was Reprobation, that Gods first intention, was, for his glory to damn man; and that then he put in another string, of creating Man, that so he might have some body to damn; and then another of enforcing him to sin, that so he might have a just cause to damne him; and then another, of disabling him to lay hold upon any means of recovery: there's no musick in all this, no harmony, no peace in such preaching. But if we take this instrument, when Gods hand tun'd it the second time, in the promise of a *Messias,* and offer of the love and mercy of God to all that will receive it in him; then we are truly *musicum carmen,* as a love-song, when we present the love of God to you, and raise you to the love of God in Christ Jesus: for, for the musick of the Sphears, whatsoever it be, we cannot hear it; for the decrees of God in heaven, we cannot say we have seen them; our musick is onely that salvation which is declared in the Gospel to all them, and to them onely, who take God by the right hand, as he delivers himself in Christ.

So they shall be musick *in re,* in their matter, in their doctrine; and they shall be also *in modo,* in their manner of presenting that doctrine. Religion is a serious thing, but not a sullen; Religious preaching is a grave exercise, but not a sordid, not a barbarous, not a negligent. There are not so eloquent books in the world, as the Scriptures: Accept those names of Tropes and Figures, which the Grammarians and Rhetoricians put upon us, and we may be bold to say, that in all their Authors, Greek and Latin, we cannot finde so high, and so lively examples, of those Tropes, and those Figures, as we may in the Scriptures: whatsoever hath justly delighted any man in any mans writings, is exceeded in the Scriptures. The style of the Scriptures is a diligent, and an artificial style; and a great part thereof in a musical, in a metrical, in a measured composition, in verse. The greatest mystery of our Religion, indeed the whole body of our Religion, the coming, and the Kingdome of a *Messias,* of a Saviour, of Christ, is conveyed in a Song, in the third chapter of *Habakkuk:* and therefore the Jews say, that that Song cannot yet be understood, because they say the *Messiah* is not yet come. His greatest work, when he was come, which was his union and marriage with the Church, and with our souls, he hath also delivered in a piece of a curious frame, *Solomons* Song of Songs. And so likewise, long before, when God had given all the Law, he provided, as himself sayes, a safer way, which was to give them a heavenly Song of his owne making: for that Song, he sayes there, he was sure they would remember. So the Holy Ghost hath spoken in those Instruments, whom he chose for the penning of the Scriptures, and so he would in those whom he sends for the preaching thereof: he would put in them a care of delivering God's messages, with consideration, with meditation, with preparation; and not barbarously, not suddenly, not occasionally, not extemporarily, which might derogate from the dignity of so great a service. That Ambassadour should open himself to a shrewd danger and surprisall, that should defer the thinking upon his Oration, till the Prince, to whom he was sent, were reading his letters of Credit: And it is a late time of meditation for a Sermon, when the Psalm is singing. *Loquere Domine,* sayes the Prophet; speak, O Lord: But it was when he was able to say, *Ecce paratus,* Behold I am prepared for thee to speak in me: If God shall be believed, to speak in us, in our ordinary Ministry, it must be, when we have, so as we can, fitted our selves, for his presence. To end this, then are we *Musicum carmen in modo,* musick to the soul, in the manner of our preaching, when in delivering points of Divinity, we content our selves with that language, and that phrase of speech, which the Holy Ghost hath expressed himself in, in the Scriptures: for to delight in the new and

Deut. 31.[19–22]

bold termes of Hereticks, furthers the Doctrine of Hereticks too. And then also, are we *Musicum carmen,* when, according to the example of men inspired by the Holy Ghost, in writing the Scriptures, we deliver the messages of God, with such diligence, and such preparation, as appertains to the dignity of that employment.

Vox suavis

Now these two, to be Musick both these wayes, in matter and in manner, concur and meet in the next, which is, to have a pleasant voyce: *Thou art a lovely song of one that hath a pleasant voyce.* First, A Voyce they must have, they must be heard: if they silence themselves, by their ignorance, or by their laziness; if they occasion themselves to be silenced, by their contempt and contumacy, both wayes they are inexcusable; for a voyce is essentiall to them, that denominates them: *John Baptist* hath other great names; even the name of *Baptist,* is a great name, when we consider whom he baptized; him, who baptized the Baptist himself, and all us, in his own blood. So is his name of *Preacher,* the fore-runner of Christ (for in that name he came before him, who was before the world;) so is his *Propheta,* [Mat. 11.9, 11] that he was a Prophet, and then, more then a Prophet; and then, the greatest among the sons of women; these were great names, but yet the name that he chose, is *Vox clamantis, The voyce of him that cryes in the wilderness.* [John 1.23] What names and titles soever we receive in the School, or in the Church, or in the State; if we lose our voice, we lose our proper name, our Christian name. But then, *John Baptists* name is not A voyce, Any voyce, but The voyce: in the Prophesie of *Esay,* in all the four Evangelists, constantly, The voyce. Christ is *verbum,* [John 1.1] The word; not A word, but The word: the Minister is *Vox,* voyce; not A voyce, but The voyce, the voyce of that word, and no other; and so, he is a pleasing voyce, because he pleases him that sent him, in a faithfull executing of his Commission, and speaking according to his dictate; and pleasing to them to whom he is sent, by bringing the Gospel of Peace and Reparation to all wounded, and scattered, and contrite Spirits.

Instrumentum

They shall be Musick both wayes, in matter, and in manner; and pleasing both wayes, to God, and to men: but yet to none of these, except the Musick be perfect, except it be to an Instrument, that is, as we said at first, out of S. *Basil,* and S. *Augustine,* except the Doctrine be express'd in the life too: Who will believe me when I speak, if by my life they see I do not believe my self? how shall I be believed to speak heartily against Ambition and Bribery in temporall and civil places, if one in the Congregation be able to jogge him that sits next him, and tell him, That man offered me money for spirituall preferment? To what a dangerous scorn shall I open my selfe, and the service of God, if I shall declaime against Usury, and look him in the face that hath my money at use? One such witness in the Congregation, shall out-preach the Preacher: and God shall use his tongue (perchance his malice) to make the service of that Preacher uneffectual. *Quam speciosi pedes Evangelizantium!* sayes S. Paul, (and he sayes that out of *Esay,* and out of *Nahum* too, as though the Holy Ghost had delighted himself with that phrase in expressing it) How beautifull are the feet of them that preach the Gospel! Men look most to our feet, to our wayes: the power that makes men admire, may lie in our tongues; but the beauty that makes men love, lies in our feet, in our actions. And so we have done with all the pieces that constitute our first part: God, in his promise to that Nation, prophesied upon us, that which he hath abundantly performed, a Ministry, that should first be Trumpets, and then Musick: Musick, in fitting a reverent manner, to religious matter; and Musick, in fitting an instrument to the voyce, that is, their Lives to their Doctrine. *Eris,* said God here, to this Prophet, *All this thou shalt be:* and that leads us into our second part.

Rom. 10.[15] [Isa. 52.7; Nahum 1.15]

Part II *Eris illis*

Now, in this second part, there is more; for it is not onely *Eris,* thou shalt be so in thy self, and as thou art employed by me; but *Eris illis,* thou shalt be so unto them, they shall receive thee for such, acknowledge thee to be such: God provides a great measure of ability in the Prophet, and some measure of good inclination in the people. *Eris illis Tuba,* thou shalt be to them, they shall feel thee to be a Trumpet: they shall not say in their hearts, *There is no God;* they shall not say, *Tush, the Lord sees us not,* or he is a blind, or an indifferent God, or, the Lord is like one of us, he loves peace, and will be at quiet; but they shall acknowledge, that he is *Dominus Exercituum,* the Lord of Hosts, and that the Prophet is his Trumpet, to raise them up to a spiritual battel. *Eris illis Tuba,* thou shalt be to them a Trumpet, they shall not be secure in their sins; and *Eris illis carmen musicum,* by thy preaching they shall come to confess, *That God is a God*

[Psal. 53.1] [Ezek. 8:12; 9.9]

of harmony, and not of discord; of order, and not of confusion; and that, as he made, so he governs all things, in weight, and number, and measure; that he hath a Succession, and a Hierarchy in his Church; that it is a household of the Faithfull, and a Kingdome of Saints, and therefore regularly governed, and by order, and that in this government no man can give himself Orders, no man can baptize himselfe, nor give himself the Body and Blood of Christ Jesus, nor preach to himself, nor absolve himself; and therefore they shall come to thee, whom they shall confess to be appointed by God, to convey these graces unto them: *Eris illis carmen musicum:* from thee they shall accept that musick, the orderly application of Gods mercies, by visible and outward meanes in thy Ministry in the Church. *Eris illis vox suavis,* they shall confess thou preachest true Doctrine, and appliest it powerfully to their consciences; and *Eris illis vox ad Citharam,* thou shalt be a voyce to an Instrument: they shall acknowledge thy life to be agreeable to thy Doctrine; they shall quarrel thee, challenge thee in neither, not in Doctrine, not in Manners.

Audient

Such as God appoints thee to be, *Eris,* thou shalt be; and *Eris illis,* they shall respect thee as such, and reward thee as such: and they shall express that, in that which followes, *Audient,* they shall hear thy word. The worldly man, though it trouble him to hear thee, though it put thorns and brambles into his conscience, yet though it be but to beget an opinion of holiness in others, *Audiet,* he will hear thee. The fashionall man, that will do as he sees great men do, if their devotion, or their curiosity, or their service and attendance, draw him hither, *Audiet,* he will come with them, and he will hear. He that is disaffected in his heart, to the Doctrine of our Church, rather then incur penalties of Statutes and Canons, *Audiet,* he will come, and hear: yea, there is more then that, intended, *Audient,* they shall hear willingly; and more then that too, *Audient,* they shall hear cheerfully, desirously. Here is none of that action which was in S. *Stephens* persecutors, *Continuerunt aures,* they withheld their eares, they withdrew themselves from hearing, they kept themselves out of distance; here is no such Recusancy intended; neither is there any of their actions, *Qui obturant aures,* as the Psalmist sayes, the Serpent does, who (as the Fathers note often) stops one ear with

Act. 7.57

Psal. 58.[4]

laying it close to the ground, and the other with covering it with his tail: here is none of their action, *Qui indurant,* nor *qui declinant;* [Jer. 7.26] none that turneth away his ear (for even his prayer shall be an [Prov. 28.9] abomination, sayes *Solomon;* his very being here is a sin) here, in our case, in our Text, is none of these indispositions; but here is a ready, a willing, and (in appearance) a religious coming to hear: Expectation, Acceptation, Acclamation, Congratulation, Remuneration, in a fair proportion; we complain of no want in any of these now. *Sumus,* God hath authoriz'd us, and God hath exalted us, in some measure, to deliver his messages; and *Sumus vobis,* you do not deny us to be such; you do not refuse, but you receive us, and his messages by us; you do hear our words. And that's all that belonged to our second part.

Part III *Non facient*

Now in both these former parts, who can discern, who would suspect any foundation to be laid for an Increpation, any preparation for a Malediction or Curse? God will send good Preachers to the people, and the people shall love their preaching; and yet, as he said to *Samuel,* he will do a thing, at which, both the ears of him that [1 Sam. 3.11] hears it shall tingle. Now, what is that in our case? This; he will aggravate their condemnation, therefore, because they have been so diligent herein, *Et non fecerunt,* they have done nothing of that which they have heard. As our very Repentance contracts the nature of sin, if we persevere not in that holy purpose; but, as though we had then made even with God, sin on again upon a new score: so this hearing it self is a sin, that is, such an aggravating circumstance, as changes the very nature of the sin, to them that hear so much, and doe nothing. This is not a preparation of that curse in *Ezekiel;* [[Ezek.] 2.5] whether they will hear or forbear, yet they shall know, that a Prophet hath been among them; that is, heare, or heare not, subsequent judgements shall bring them to see, that they might have heard: but here God accompanies them with a stronger grace, then so; *Audient,* they will hear. There are Vipers in the Psalm that will not hear, how [[Psal.] 58.[5]] wisely soever the charmers charm; But there is a Generation of Vipers which do hear, and yet depart with none of their viperous [Mat. 3.7] nature: *O generation of vipers, who hath warned you to flee from the wrath to come!* sayes *John Baptist,* there to the Pharisees and Sadduces, that came to his baptism. They had apprehended *Tubam,* a warning, and they did come; but when they were come, he found [Mat. 3] them in their *Non faciunt,* without any purpose of bringing forth ver. 8 fruits worthy of repentance.

Quæ dixeris

Here then is S. *Paul's Judæus in abscondito,* a Jew inwardly. Here Rom 2.29 is the true Recusant, and the true Non-conformitan; *Audiunt, sed non faciunt:* he comes to hear, but never comes to doe; there's Recusancy: he confesses that he hath received good instruction, but he refuses to conform himself unto it; there's Non-conformity. First, *Non facient quæ dixeris,* they will not doe those things which thou hast said; and yet, that's strange, since they confess thou saist true: but yet that's not so strange; for they may be *Duri sermones;* though it be true that we say, it may be hard, and it may trouble them, and perchance damnifie them in their Profit, or mortifie them in their Pleasures. It may be we may say, that thy relapsing into a sin formerly repented, submits thee again to all the punishment due to the former sin; and that's *Durus sermo,* a hard saying: It may be we may say, that a repentance which hath all other formall parts of a true repentance, if it reach not to all the branches, and to all the specifying differences and circumstance of thy sins, so far as a diligent examination of thy conscience can carry thee, is a voyd repentance; and that's *Durus sermo,* a hard saying. It may be we may say, That though thou hast truly and intirely repented, though thou do leave the practice of the sin, yet if thou doe not also leave that which thou hast corruptly got by the wayes of that sin, the sin it selfe lies upon thee still; and that's *Durus sermo,* a hard saying: And Christs own Dis- John 6.60 ciples forsook him, and forsook him for ever, *Quia durus sermo,* because that which Christ said, seemed to them a hard saying. This we may say; and they may come to hear, and come to say we say true, and yet *Non facient quæ dixeris,* never do any of that which we say, *Quia duri sermones,* because we presse things hardly upon them.

Quæ dixerint

But yet that's not so strange, as *Non facere quæ dixerint,* not to do those things which they have said themselves. That when, as the [2 Cor. 3.2] Apostle sayes of the *Corinthians, Vos estis,* you are our Epistle, not written with ink, but with the spirit of the living God: so a man, by hearing, is become *Evangelium sibi,* a Gospel to himself; and by the [John 8.11] preaching of the Gospel, is come to say, *Non amplius,* I will go, and sin no more, lest a worse thing fall unto me: yet he goes and sins again, fall what will, or can fall; and *Non facit quæ dixerit,* he does not perform his own promise to himself. He is affected with some particular passage in a Sermon, and then he comes to *David*'s *Secundum innocentiam; O Lord, deale with me according to my* [Psal. 7.8—7.9 in Vulg.] *future innocence; shew thy mercy to me, as I keep my selfe from that sin hereafter;* and then, *abominantur eum vestimenta ejus,* his old [Job 9.31] clothes defile him again, his old rags cast vermin upon him, his old habits of sin throw new dirt upon him. He goes out of the Church as that mans son went from his father, who sent him to work in the Vineyard, with that word in his mouth, *Eo Domine,* Sir, I go; but [Matth. 21.30] he never went, he turns another way, *Non facit quæ dixerat,* he keeps not his own word, with his own soul: when he is gone out of his right way, a Sickness, a Disgrace, a Loss, overtakes him, the arrowes of the Almighty stick in him, and the venome thereof drinks up his spirit; temporal afflictions, and spirituall afflictions meet in him, like two clouds, and beat out a thunder upon him, like two currents, and swallow him like two milstones, and grinde him, and then he comes to his *Domine quid retribuam? Lord, what shall I give thee, to deliver* [Psal. 116.12] *me now? & non facit quæ dixerat,* he payes none of those vowes, performes no part of that which he promised then. Christ had his *Consummatum est,* and this sinner hath his: Christ ends his passion, [John 19.30] and he ends his action; Christ ends his affliction, and he ends his affection: *Distulit securim, attulit securitatem,* sayes S. *Augustine* of this case; as soon as the Danger is removed, his Devotion is removed too. The end of all is, that what punishment soever God reserves for them, who never heard of the Name of his Son Christ Jesus at all, or for them who have pretended to receive him, but have done it Idolatrously, superstitiously; we that have heard him, we that have had the Scriptures preached and applied to us sincerely, shall certainly have the heavier condemnation, for having had that which they wanted: Our multiplicity of Preachers, and their assiduity in preaching; our true interpretation of their labours, when we doe heare, and our diligent coming, that we may hear, shall leave us in worse state then they found us, *si non fecerimus,* If we doe not doe that which we heare. And to doe the Gospel, is to doe what we can for the preservation of the Gospel. I know what I can do, as a Minister of the Gospel, and of Gods Word; out of his Word I can preach against Linsey-woolsey garments; out of his Word I can preach against plowing with an Oxe, and with an Asse, against mingling of Religions. I know what I can do, as a Father, as a Master; I can preserve my Family from attempts of Jesuits. Those that are of higher place, Magistrates, know what they can do too: They know they can execute lawes; if not to the taking of Life, yet to the restraining of Liberty: And it is no seditious saying, it is no saucinesse, it is no bitternesse, it is no boldnesse, to say, that the spirituall death of those soules, who perish by the practise of those seducers, whom they might have stopp'd, lies upon them. And how knowes he, who lets a Jesuit scape, whether he let go but a Fox, that will deceive some simple soule in matter of Religion; or a Wolfe, who, but the protection of the Almighty, would adventure upon the person of the highest of all? *Non facient quæ dixeris,* is as far as the Text goes; they will not do that we say: but *Quæ dixerint,* is more; they will not do that which themselves have said: But, *Quæ juraverint,* is most of all; If they will not do that, which for the preservation of the Gospel, they have taken an Oath to do, The Increpation, the Malediction, intended by God, in this Text, that all our preaching, and all our hearing shall aggravate our condemnation, will fall upon us: And therefore, this being the season, in which, especially, God affords you the performance of that part of this Prophecy, assiduous, and laborious, and acceptable, and usefull preaching; where all you, of all sorts, are likely to hear the Duties of Administration towards others, and of Mortification in your selves, powerfully represented unto you, this may have been somewhat necessarily said by me now, for the removing of some [Psal. 22.14] stones out of their way, and the chafing of that wax, in which they may thereby make the deeper, and clearer impressions; that so, we may not onely be to you, *as a lovely song,* sung to an Instrument; nor you onely *heare our words,* but *doe them.* Amen.

Number 8.

Preached February 21. [*1618/19*]

[DEDICATORY LETTER]

To the right honourable the Countess of MONTGOMERY

MADAM,

Of my ability to doe your Ladiship service, any thing spoken may be an embleme good enough; for as a word vanisheth, so doth any power in me to serve you; things that are written are fitter testimonies, because they remain and are permanent: in writing this Sermon which your Ladiship was pleased to hear before, I confesse I satisfie an ambition of mine own, but it is the ambition of obeying your commandment, not onely an ambition of leaving my name in your memory, or in your Cabinet: and yet, since I am going out of the Kingdom, and perchance out of the world, (when God shall have given my soul a place in heaven) it shall the lesse diminish your Ladiship, if my poor name be found about you. I know what dead carkasses things written are, in respect of things spoken. But in things of this kinde, that soul that inanimates them, receives debts from them: The Spirit of God that dictates them in the speaker or writer, and is present in his tongue or hand, meets himself again (as we meet our selves in a glass) in the eies and eares and hearts of the hearers and readers: and that Spirit, which is ever the same to an equall devotion, makes a writing and a speaking equall means to edification. In one circumstance, my preaching and my writing this Sermon is too equall: that that your Ladiship heard in a hoarse voyce then, you read in a course hand now: but in thankfulnesse I shall lift up my hands as clean as my infirmities can keep them, and a voyce as clear as his spirit shall be pleased to tune in my prayers for your Ladiship in all places of the world, which shall either sustain or bury

Your Ladiships
humble servant in Christ Iesus
J. D.

MATTHEW 21.44. *WHOSOEVER SHALL FALL ON THIS STONE, SHALL BE BROKEN; BUT ON WHOMSOEVER IT SHALL FALL, IT WILL GRINDE HIM TO POWDER.*

ALMIGHTY GOD made us for his glory, and his glory is not the glory of a Tyrant, to destroy us, but his glory is in our happinesse. He put us in a faire way towards that happinesse in nature, in our creation, that way would have brought us to heaven, but then we fell, and (if we consider our selves onely) irrecoverably. He put us after into another way, over thorny hedges and ploughed Lands, through the difficulties and incumbrances of all the Ceremoniall Law; there was no way to heaven then, but that; after that, he brought us a crosse way, by the Crosse of Jesus Christ, and the application of his Gospell, and that is our way now. If we compare the way of nature, and our way, we went out of the way at the Townes end, as soone as we were in it, we were out of it. *Adam* dyed as soone as he lived, and fell as soone as he was set on foote; If we compare the way of the Law, and ours, the Jewes and the Christians, their Synagogue was but as Gods farme, our Church is as his dwelling
Verse 33 house; to them *locavit vineam,* he let out his Vine to husbandmen, and then *peregrè profectus,* he went into a farre Countrey, he promised a *Messias,* but deferred his coming a long time; but to us *Dabitur Regnum,* a Kingdome is given; the Vineyard is changed into a Kingdome, here is a good improvement, and the Lease into an absolute deed of gift, here is a good inlargement of the Terme. He gives, therefore he will not take away againe. He gives a Kingdome, therefore there is a fulnesse and all-sufficiency in the gift; and he does not go into any farre Countrey, but stayes with us, to governe us,
[Mat. 28.20] *usque ad consummationem,* till the end of the world; here therefore God takes all into his owne hands, and he comes to dwell upon us himself, to which purpose he ploughs up our hearts, and he builds
1 Cor. 3.9 upon us; *Vos Dei agricultura, & Dei ædificium, Ye are Gods husbandry, and Gods building:* Now of this husbandry God speaks

familiarly and parabolicaly many times in Scriptures: of this building particularly and principally in this place, where having intimated unto us the severall benefits we have received from Christ Jesus in that appellation, as he is *a stone,* he tells us also our dangers in misbehaving our selves towards it; *Whosoever shall fall on this stone, he shall be broken.*

Christ then is a stone, and we may run into two dangers: first, we may fall upon this stone, and then this stone may fall upon us; but yet we have a great deale of comfort presented to us, in that Christ is presented to us as a stone, for there we shall finde him, first, to be the *foundation stone,* nothing can stand which is not built upon Christ; Secondly, to be *Lapis Angularis,* a *corner stone,* that unites things most dis-united; and then to be *Lapis Jacob,* the stone that *Jacob* slept upon; fourthly, to be *Lapis Davidis,* the stone that *David* slew *Goliah* withall; And lastly, to be *Lapis Petra,* such a stone as is a Rock, and such a Rock as no Waters nor Stormes can remove or shake: these are benefits, Christ Jesus is a stone, no firmnesse but in him; a fundamentall stone, no building but on him; a corner stone, no piecing nor reconciliation, but in him; and *Jacobs stone,* no rest, no tranquillity, but in him; and *Davids* stone, no anger, no revenge, but in him; and a rocky stone, no defence against troubles and tribulations, but in him; And upon this stone we fall and are broken, and this stone may fall on us, and *grinde us to powder.*

First in the metaphor, that Christ is called a stone, the firmnesse is expressed: Forasmuch as he loved his owne which were in the world, *In finem dilexit eos,* sayes St. *John, He loved them to the end;* and not to any particular end, for any use of his owne, but to their end; *Qui erant in mundo,* sayes *Cyrill, ad distinctionem Angelorum,* he loved them in the world, and not Angels; he loved not onely them who were in a confirmed estate of mutuall loving him too, but even them who were themselves conceived in sinne, and then conceived all their purposes in sinne too, them who could have no cleansing but in his blood, and when they were cleansed in his blood, their *owne clothes would defile them* againe, them who by nature are not able to love him at all, and when by grace they are brought to love him, can expresse their love no other way, but to be glad that he was betrayed, and scourged, and scorned, and nayled, and crucified; and to be glad,

Lapis

Ioh. 13.1

Cyrill

Iob 9.31

that if all this were not already done, it might be done yet, to long, and wish, that if Christ were not crucified, he might be crucified now, (which is a strange manner of expressing love) those men he loved, and *loved unto the end;* Men and not Angels; and then men, *Ad distinctionem mortuorum,* sayes *Chrysostome,* not onely the Patriarchs, who were departed out of the world, who had loved him so well, as to take his word for their salvation, and had lived and dyed in the faithfull contemplation of a future promise, which they never saw performed; but those who were partakers of the performance of all those promises, those into the midst of whom he came in person, those upon whom he wrought with his piercing Doctrine, and his powerfull miracles, those who for all this loved not him, he loved: *Et in finem, he loved them to the end:* It is much that he should love them *in fine,* at their end, that he should looke graciously on them at last, that when their sunne sets, their eyes faint, his sunne of grace should arise, and his East be brought to their West, that then in the shadow of death, the Lord of life should quicken and inanimate their hearts: that when their last bell tolls, and calls them to their first Judgement, (and first and last Judgement to this purpose is all one) the passing bell, and Angels trump sound all but one note, *Surgite qui dormitis in pulvere, Arise ye that sleepe in the dust,* which is the voyce of the Angels, and *Surgite qui vigilatis in plumis,* Arise ye that cannot sleepe in feathers, for the pangs of death, which is the voyce of the bell, is but one voyce; for God at the generall Judgement, shall never reverse any particular Judgement, formerly given; that God should then come to the beds side, *ad sibilandum populum suum,* as the Prophet *Ezekiel* speaks, to hisse softly for his childe, to speake comfortably in his eare, to whisper gently to his departing soule, and to drowne and overcome with this soft Musick of his, all the clangor of the Angels Trumpets, all the horror of the ringing Bell, all the cryes, and vociferations of a distressed, and distracted, and scattering family, yea all the accusations of his owne conscience, and all the triumphant acclamations of the Devill himselfe; that God should love a man thus *in fine,* at his end, and returne to him then, though he had suffered him to go astray from him before, it is a great testimony of an unspeakable love: but his love is not onely *in fine,* at the end, but *in finem, to the end,* all the way to the end. He leaves them not un-

[Dan. 12.2]

called at first, he leaves them not unaccompanied in the way, he leaves them not unrecompensed at the last, that God who is Almighty, *Alpha* and *Omega,* first and last, that God is also love it selfe, and therefore this love is *Alpha* and *Omega,* first and last too; Consider Christs proceeding with *Peter* in the ship, in the storme; first he suffered him to be in some danger, but then he visites him with that strong assurance, *Noli timere, Be not afraid, it is I,* any testimony of his presence rectifies all. This puts *Peter* into that spirituall knowledge and confidence, *Jube me venire, Lord bid me come to thee;* he hath a desire to be with Christ, but yet stayes his bidding; he puts not himselfe into an unnecessary danger, without a commandment; Christ bids him, and *Peter* comes, but yet, though Christ were in his sight, and even in the actuall exercise of his love to him, yet as soone as he saw a gust, a storme, *timuit,* he was afraid, and Christ letteth him feare, and letteth him sinke, and letteth him crie; But he directeth his feare, and his crie to the right end, *Domine salvum me fac,* Lord save me, and thereupon he stretcheth out his hand and saved him: God doth not raise his children to honour, and great estates, and then leave them, and expose them to be subjects, and exercises of the malice of others, nor he doth not make them mightie, and then leave them, *ut glorietur in malo qui potens est,* that he should thinke it a glory to be able to do harm. He doth not impoverish and dishonour his children, and then leave them; leave them unsensible of that Doctrine, that patience is as great a blessing as aboundance: God giveth not his children health, and then leaveth them to a boldnesse in surfetting; nor beauty, and leave them to a confidence and opening themselves to all sollicitations; nor valour, and then leaveth them to a spirit of quarrelsomnesse: God maketh no patterns of his works, no modells of his houses, he maketh whole pieces, he maketh perfect houses, he putteth his children into good wayes, and he directeth and protecteth them in those wayes: For this is the constancy and the perseverance of the love of Christ Jesus, as he is called in this Text a stone. To come to the particular benefits; the first is that he is *lapis fundamentalis,* a foundation stone; for other foundation can no man lay then that which is laid, which is Christ Jesus. Now where Saint *Augustine* saith, (as he doth in two or three places) that this place of Saint *Pauls* to the *Corinthians,* is one of these places of which Saint *Peter* saith

[Apoc. 1.8]
Matth. 14.24–31
[Psal. 52.1]
Fundamentalis
1 Cor. 3.11

Quædam difficilia, There are some things in Saint *Paul* hard to be understood: Saint *Augustines* meaning is, that the difficulty is in the [1 Cor. 3.12] next words, how any man should build hay or stubble upon so good a foundation as Christ, how any man that pretendeth to live in Christ, should live ill, for in the other there can be no difficulty, how Christ Jesus to a Christian, should be the onely foundation; And therefore to place salvation or damnation in such an absolute Decree of God, as should have no relation to the fall of man, or reparation in a Redeemer; this is to remove this stone out of the foundation, for a Christian may be well content to beginne at Christ: If any man therefore have laid any other foundation to his Faith, or any other foundation to his Actions, possession of great places, alliance in great Families, strong practise in Courts, obligation upon dependants, acclamations of people; if he have laid any other foundations for pleasure, and contentment, care of health, and complexion, appliablenesse in conversation, delightfulnesse in discourses, cheerefulnesse in disportings, interchanging of secrets, and such other small wares of Courts and Cities as these are: whosoever hath laid such foundations as these, must proceed as that Generall did, who when he received a besieged Towne to mercy, upon condition that in signe of subjection they should suffer him to take off one row of stones from their walls, he tooke away the lowest row, the foundation, and so ruined and demolished the whole walls of the Citie: So must he that hath these false foundations, (that is, these habits) divest the habite, roote out the lowest stone, that is, the generall, and radicall inclination to these disorders: For he shall never be able to watch and resist every particular temptation, if he trust onely to his Morall Constancy; No, nor if he place Christ for the roofe to cover all his sinnes, when he hath done them; his mercy worketh by way of pardon after, not by way of *Non obstante,* and priviledge to doe a sinne before hand; but before hand we must have the foundation in our eye; when we undertake any particular Action, in the beginning, we must looke how that will suite with the foundation, with Christ; for there is his first place, to be *Lapis fundamentalis.*

Angularis And then, after we have considered him, first, in the foundation (as we are all Christians) he growes to be *Lapis Angularis,* the Corner stone, to unite those Christians, which seem to be of divers ways, divers aspects, divers professions together; as wee consider him in the foundation, there he is the root of faith, As we consider him in the Corner, there hee is the root of charity, In *Esay* hee is both together, *A sure foundation* and a *Corner stone,* as he was in the place Esay 28.16 of *Esay, Lapis probatus,* I will lay in *Sion* a tryed stone, and in the *Psalm, Lapis reprobatus,* a stone that the builders refused, In this 118.[22] consideration, he is *Lapis approbatus,* a stone approved by all sides, [Acts. 2.22] that unites all things together: Consider first, what divers things he unites in his own person; That he should be the sonne of a woman, and yet no sonne of man, That the sonne of a woman should be the sonne of God, that mans sinfull nature, and innocency should meet together, a man that should not sinne, that Gods nature and mortality should meet together, a God that must die; Briefly, that he should doe and suffer so many things impossible as man, impossible as God. Thus hee was a Corner stone, that brought together natures, naturally incompatible. Thus he was *Lapis Angularis,* a Corner stone in his Person. Consider him in his Offices, as a Redeemer, as a Mediatour, and so, hee hath united God to man; yea, rebellious man to jealous God: Hee is such a Corner stone, as hath united heaven, and earth, Jerusalem and Babylon together.

Thus in his Person, and thus in his Offices, Consider him in his power, and hee is such a Corner stone, as that hee is the God of Peace, and Love, and Union, and Concord. Such a Corner stone as is able to unite, and reconcile (as it did in *Abrahams* house) a Wife, and a [Gen. 16] Concubine in one bed, a covetous Father, and a wastfull Sonne in one family, a severe Magistrate, and a licentious people in one City, an absolute Prince, and a jealous People in one Kingdome, Law, and Conscience in one Government, Scripture, and tradition in one Church. If we would but make Christ Jesus and his peace, the life and soule of all our actions, and all our purposes; if we would mingle that sweetnesse and supplenesse which he loves, and which he is, in all our undertakings; if in all controversies, booke controversies, and sword controversies, we would fit them to him, and see how neere they would meet in him, that is, how neere we might come to be friends, and yet both sides be good Christians; then wee placed this stone in his second right place, who as hee is a Corner stone reconciling God and man in his owne Person, and a Corner stone in reconciling God and mankinde in his Office, so hee desires to bee a Corner stone in reconciling man and man, and setling peace among our selves, not for worldly ends, but for this respect, that wee might all meet in him to love one another, not because wee made a stronger party by that love, not because wee made a sweeter conversation by that love, but because wee met closer in the bosome of Christ Jesus; where wee must at last either rest altogether eternally, or bee altogether eternally throwne out, or bee eternally separated and divorced from one another.

Lapis Jacob

Having then received Christ for the foundation stone, (wee beleeve aright) and for the Corner stone (we interpret charitably the opinions, and actions of other men) The next is, that hee bee *Lapis Jacob,* a stone of rest and security to our selves. When *Jacob* was in his journey, hee tooke a stone, and that stone was his pillow, upon that hee slept all night, and resting upon that stone, hee saw the Ladder that reached from heaven to earth; it is much to have this egresse and regresse to God, to have a sense of being gone from him, and a desire and meanes of returning to him; when wee doe fall into particular sinnes, it is well if wee can take hold of the first step of this Ladder, with that hand of *David, Domine respice in Testamentum, O Lord, consider thy Covenant,* if wee can remember God of his Covenant, to his people, and to their seed, it is well; it is more, if wee can clamber a step higher on this ladder to a *Domine labia mea aperies,* if we come to open our lips in a true confession of our wretched condition and of those sinnes by which we have forfeited our interest in that Covenant, it is more; and more then that too, if we come to that *inebriabo me lacrymis,* if we overflow and make our selves drunke with teares, in a true sense, and sorrow for those sinnes, still it is more; And more then all this, if we can expostulate with God in an *Vsque quo Domine, How long, O Lord, shall I take counsell in my self, having wearinesse in my heart?* These steps, these gradations towards God, do well; warre is a degree of peace, as it is the way of peace; and these colluctations and wrestlings with God, bring a man to peace with him; But then is a man upon this *stone* of *Jacob,* when in a faire, and even, and constant religious course of life, he enters into his sheets every night, as though his neighbours next day were to shrowd and wind him in those sheets; he shuts up his

Gen. 28.[10–12]

Psal. 74.20

[Psal. 51.15]

Esay 16.9

Psal. 13.2

eyes every night, as though his Executors had closed them; and lies downe every night, not as though his man were to call him up next morning to hunt, or to the next dayes sport, or businesse, but as though the Angels were to call him to the resurrection; And this is our third benefit, as Christ is a *stone,* we have security and peace of conscience in him.

Lapis David

The next is, That he is *Lapis David,* the stone with which *David* slew *Goliah,* and with which we may overcome all our enemies; *Sicut baculus crucis, ita lapis Christi habuit typum;* (August.) *Davids* sling was a type of the Crosse, and the stone was a type of Christ: we will chuse to insist upon spirituall enemies, sinnes; And this is that stone that enables the weakest man to overthrow the strongest sinne, if he proceed as *David* did: *David* sayes to *Goliah, Thou comest to me with a sword with a speare and with a shield, but I come to thee in the name of the God of the hosts of Israel, whom thou hast railed upon,* (1 Sam. 17.45) if thou watch the approach of any sinne, any giant sinne that transports thee most; if thou apprehend it to rayle against the Lord of Hosts, (that is, that there is a loud and active blasphemy against God, in every sinne) if thou discerne it to come with a *sword,* or a *speare,* (that is, perswasions of advancement if thou do it, or threatnings of dishonour, if thou do it not,) if it come with a *shield,* (that is, with promises to cover and palliate it, though thou do it,) If then this *David,* (thy attempted soule) can put his hand into his bag (as *David* did) (for *quid cor hominis nisi sacculus Dei?* (Gregory) a mans heart is that bag in which God layes up all good directions) if he can but take into his consideration his Jesus, his Christ, and sling one of his works, his words, his commandments, his merits, This *Goliah,* this Giant sinne, will fall to the ground, and then, as it is said of *David,* that he slew him when he had no sword in his hand, and yet in the next verse, that he tooke his sword and slew him with that: [1 Sam. 17.50, 51] so even by the consideration of what my Lord hath done for me, I shall give that sinne the first deaths wound, and then I shall kill him with his owne sword, that is, his owne abomination, his owne foulenesse shall make me detest him. If I dare but looke my sinne in the face, if I dare tell him, *I come in the name of the Lord,* if I consider my sinne, I shall triumph over it, *Et dabit certanti victoriam qui dedit certandi audaciam,* (August.) That God that gave me courage to fight, will give me strength to overcome.

Lapis, Petra
Num. 20.11
Deut. 32.13
1 Cor. 10.4
Esay 42.11
[Song of the three Holy Children]
[Luke 11.11]
[Mat. 6.11; Luke 11.3]
[Mat. 4.3]

The last benefit which we consider in Christ, as he is a *stone,* is, That he is *Petra,* a Rock; The Rock gave water to the Israelites in the wildernesse; and he gave them honey out of the stone, and oyle out of the hard Rock: Now when Saint *Paul* sayes, That our Fathers dranke of the same Rock as we, he adds that the same Rock was Christ; So that all Temporall, and all Spirituall blessings to us, and to the Fathers, were all conferred upon us in Christ; but we consider not now any miraculous production from the Rock, but that which is naturall to the Rock; that it is a firme defence to us in all tempests, in all afflictions, in all tribulations; and therefore, *Laudate Dominum habitatores petræ,* sayes the Prophet, You that are inhabitants of this Rock, you that dwell in Christ, and Christ in you, you that dwell in this Rock, *Prayse ye the Lord, blesse him, and magnifie him for ever. If a sonne should aske bread of his father, will he give him a stone,* was Christs question? Yes, O blessed Father, we aske no other answer to our petition, no better satisfaction to our necessity, then when we say, *Da nobis hodie panem, Give us this day our daily bread,* that thou give us this Stone, this Rock, thy self in thy Church, for our direction, thy self in the Sacrament, for our refection; what hardnesse soever we finde there, what corrections soever we receive there, all shall be easie of digestion, and good nourishment to us; Thy holy spirit of patience shall command, *That these stones be made bread;* And we shall finde more juice, more marrow in these stones, in these afflictions, then worldly men shall do in the softnesse of their oyle, in the sweetnesse of their honey, in the cheerefulnesse of their wine; for as Christ is our foundation, we beleeve in him, and as he is our corner-stone, we are at peace with the world in him; as he is *Jacobs* stone, giving us peace in our selves, and *Davids* stone, giving us victory over our enemies, so he is a Rock of stone, (no affliction, no tribulation shal shake us.) And so we have passed through all the benefits proposed to be considered in this first part, As Christ is a stone.

2 Part

It is some degree of thankfulnesse, to stand long in the contemplation of the benefit which we have received, and therefore we have insisted thus long upon the first part. But it is a degree of spirituall wisdome too, to make haste to the consideration of our dangers, and therefore we come now to them, Wee may fall upon this stone, and be broken, this stone may fall upon us, and grinde us to powder.

And in the first of these, we may consider, *Quid cadere,* what the falling upon this stone is: and secondly, *Quid frangi,* what it is to be broken upon it: and then thirdly, the latitude of this *unusquisque,* that whosoever fals so, is so broken. First then, because Christ loves us to the end, therefore will we never put him to it, never trouble him till then; as the wise man sayd of *Manna,* that it had abundance of all (Wisd. 16.25) pleasure in it, and was meat for all tasts, that is, (as Expositors interpret it) that *Manna* tasted to every one, like that which every one liked best: so this stone Christ Jesus, hath abundance of all qualities of stone in it, and is all the way such a stone to every man, as he desires it should be. Unto you that beleeve, saith Saint *Peter,* it is a precious (1 Pet. 2.7) stone, but unto the disobedient, a stone to stumble at: for if a man walke in a gallery, where windowes, and tables, and statues, are all of marble, yet if he walke in the darke, or blindfold, or carelesly, he may breake his face as dangerously against that rich stone, as if it were but brick; So though a man walke in the true Church of God, in that Jerusalem which is described in the *Revelation,* the foundation, the gates, the walls, all precious stone, [Apoc. 21.10–21] yet if a man bring a misbelief, a mis-conceipt, that all this religion is but a part of civill government and order; if a man be scandalized, at that humility, that patience, that poverty, that lowlinesse of spirit which the Christian Religion inclines us unto; if he will say, *Si Rex Israel,* If Christ will [Mat. 27.42] be King, let him come downe from the Crosse, and then we will beleeve in him, let him deliver his Church from all crosses, first, of doctrine, and then of persecution, and then we will beleeve him to be King; if we will say, *Nolumus hunc regnare,* we will admit Christ, [Luke 19.14] but we will not admit him to reign over us, to be King; if he will be content with a Consulship, with a Collegueship, that he and the world may joyn in the government, that we may give the week to the world, and the Sabbath to him, that we may give the day of the Sabbath to him and the night to our licentiousnesse, that of the day we may give the forenoon to him, and the afternoon to our pleasures, if this will serve Christ, we are content to admit him, but *Nolumus regnare,* we will none of that absolute power, that whether we eat or drink, or whatsoever we doe, we must be troubled to thinke on him, and respect his glory in every thing. If he will say, *Præcepit Angelis,* God [Psal. 91.11] hath given us in charge to his Angels, and therefore we need not to look to our own ways, He hath locked us up safely, and lodged us softly under an eternall election, and therefore we are sure of salvation; if he will walke thus blindely, violently, wilfully, negligently in the true Church, though he walke amongst the Saphires, and Pearls, and Chrysolytes, which are mentioned there, that is, in the outward communion and fellowship of Gods Saints, yet he may bruise and break, and batter himselfe, as much against these stones, as against the stone Gods of the heathen, or the stone Idols of the Papists; for first, the place of this falling upon this *stone,* is the true Church; *Qui jacet in terra,* he that is already upon the ground, in no Church, can fall no lower, till he fall to hell; but he whom God hath brought into his true Church, if he come to a confident security, that he is safe enough in these outward acts of Religion, he falls, though it be upon this stone, he erreth, though in the true Church. This is the place, then, the true Church; the falling it selfe (as farre as will fall into our time of consideration now) is a falling into some particular sinne, but not such as quenches our faith; wee fall so, as we may rise againe. Saint *Hierome* expresseth it so, *Qui cadit, & tamen credit,* he that falls, but yet beleeves, that fals and hath a sense of his fall, *reservatur per pœnitentiam ad salutem,* that man is reserved by Gods purpose, to come by repentance, to salvation; for this man that fals there, fals not so desperately, as that he feeles nothing between hell and him, nothing to stop at, nothing to check him by the way, *Cadit super,* he falls upon some thing; nor he falls not upon flowers, to wallow and tumble in his sinne, nor upon feathers, to rest and sleep in his sinne, nor into a cooling river, to disport, and refresh, and strengthen himself in his sinne; but he falls upon a stone, where he may receive a bruise, a pain upon his fall, a remorse of that sinne that he is fallen into: And in this fall, our infirmitie appears three wayes: The first is *Impingere in lapidem,* To stumble, for though he be upon the right stone in the true Religion, and have light enough, yet *Impingimus meridie,* as the Prophet saith, even at noon we stumble; we have much more light, by Christ being come, then the Jews had, but we are sorry we have it: when Christ hath said to us for our better understanding of the Law, *He that looketh and lusteth hath committed Adultery, He that coveteth hath stollen, He that is angry hath murdered,* we stumble at this, and we are scandalized with it;

Hierome

Esa. 59.10

[Mat. 5.21–42]

and we thinke that other Religions are gentler, and that Christ hath dealt hardly with us, and we had rather Christ had not said so, we had rather he had left us to our libertie and discretion, to looke, and court, and to give a way to our passions, as we should finde it most conduce to our ease, and to our ends. And this is *Impingere,* to stumble, not to goe on in an equall and even pace, not to doe the will of God cheerefully. And a second degree is *calcitrare,* to kick, to spurne at this stone; that is, to bring some particular sinne, and some particular Law into comparison: To debate thus, if I doe not this now, I shall never have such a time; if I slip this, I shall never have the like opportunitie; if I will be a foole now, I shall be a begger all my life: and for the Law of God that is against it, there is but a little evill for a great deale of good; and there is a great deale of time to recover and repent that little evill. Now to remove a stone which was a landmarke, and to hide and cover that stone, was all one fault in the Law; to hide the will of God from our owne Consciences with excuses and extenuations, this is, *calcitrare,* as much as we can to spurn the stone, the landmarke out of the way; but the fulnesse and accomplishment of this is in the third word of the Text, *Cadere,* to fall; he falls as a piece of money falls into a river; we heare it fall, and we see it sink, and by and by we see it deeper, and at last we see it not at all: So no man falleth at first into any sinne, but he heares his own fall. There is a tendernesse in every Conscience at the beginning, at the entrance into a sinne, and he discerneth a while the degrees of sinking too: but at last he is out of his owne sight, till he meete this stone; (this stone is Christ) that is, till he meete some hard reprehension, some hard passage of a Sermon, some hard judgement in a Prophet, some crosse in the World, some thing from the mouth, or some thing from the hand of God, that breaks him: *He falls upon the stone and is broken.*

So that to be broken upon this stone, is to come to this sense, that though our integrity be lost, that we be no more whole and intire vessells, yet there are meanes of piecing us again: Though we be not vessells of Innocency, (for who is so?) (and for that enter not into judgement with any of thy servants O Lord) yet we may be vessells of repentance acceptable to God, and usefull to his service; for when any thing falls upon a stone, the harme that it suffereth, is not alwayes *Frangi* (or not onely) according to the proportion of the hardnesse of that which it fell upon, but according to the heighth that it falleth from, and according to that violence that it is throwne with: If their fall who fall by sinnes of infirmitie, should referre onely to the stone they fall upon, (the Majestie of God being wounded and violated in every sinne) every sinner would be broken to pieces, and ground to powder: But if they fall not from too far a distance, if they have lived within any nearnesse, any consideration of God, if they have not fallen with violence, taken heart and force in the way, grown perfect in the practise of their sinne, if they fall upon this stone, that is, sinne, and yet stoppe at Christ, after the sinne, this stone shall breake them; that is, breake their force, and confidence, breake their presumption, and security, but yet it shall leave enough in them, for the Holy Ghost to unite to his Service; yea, even the sinne it self, *cooperabitur in* Rom. 8.28 *bonum,* as the Apostle saith, the very fall it selfe shall be an occasion of his rising: And therefore though Saint *Augustine* seeme to venture farre, it is not too farre, when he saith, *Audeo dicere,* it is boldly said, and yet I must say it, *utile est ut caderem in aliquod manifestum peccatum;* A sinner falleth to his advantage, that falleth into some such sinne, as by being manifested to the World, manifesteth his owne sinnefull state, to his owne sinnefull Conscience too: It is well for that man that falleth so, as that he may thereby looke the better to his Bernard footing ever after; *Dicit Domino Susceptor meus es tu,* sayes St. *Bernard,* That man hath a new Title to God, a new name for God; all creatures (as St. *Bernard* inlarges this meditation) can say, *Creator meus es tu,* Lord thou art my Creator; all living creatures can say, *Pastor meus es tu,* Thou art my shepheard, Thou givest me meat in due season; all men can say, *Redemptor meus es tu,* thou art my Redeemer; but onely he which is fallen, and fallen upon this stone, can say, *Susceptor meus es tu,* only he which hath been overcome by a temptation, and is restored, can say, Lord thou hast supported me, thou hast recollected my shivers, and reunited me; onely to him hath this *stone* expressed, both abilities of stone; first to breake him with a sense of his sin, and then to give him peace and rest upon it.

Quicunque Now there is in this part this circumstance more, *Quicunque cadit,* whosoever falleth; where the *quicunque* is *unusquisque, whosoever* Esay 14.12 *falls,* that is, whosoever he be, he falls; *Quomodo de cœlo cecidisti*

Lucifer? says the Prophet, the Prophet wonders how *Lucifer* could fall, having nothing to tempt him (for so many of the Ancients interpret that place of the fall of the Angels, and when the Angels fell, there were no other creatures made,) but *Quid est homo aut filius hominis?* since the Father of man, *Adam,* could not, how shall the sonnes of him, that inherit his weaknesse, and contract more, and contribute their temptations to one another, hope to stand? *Adam* fell, and he fell *à longè,* farre off, for he could see no stone to fall upon, for when he fell, there was no such *Messias,* no such meanes of reparation proposed, nor promised when he fell, as now to us; The blessed Virgin, and the forerunner of Christ, *John Baptist,* fell too, but they fell *propè,* neerer hand, they fell but a little way, for they had this stone (Christ Jesus) in a personall presence, and their faith was alwaies awake in them; but yet he, and she, and they all fell into some sinne. *Quicunque cadit* is *unusquisque cadit, whosoever falls,* is, whosoever he be, he falls, and whosoever falls, (as we said before) is broken; If he fall upon something, and fall not to an infinite depth; If he fall not upon a soft place, to a delight in sinne; but upon a stone, and this *stone,* (no harder, sharper, ruggedder then this, not into a diffidence, or distrust in Gods mercy) he that falls so, and is broken so, that comes to a remorsefull, to a broken, and a contrite heart, he is broken to his advantage, left to a possibility, yea brought to a neerenesse of being pieced againe, by the Word, by the Sacraments, and other medicinall institutions of Christ in his Church.

[Psal. 8.4]

3 Part

We must end onely with touching upon the third part, *upon whom this stone falls, it will grinde him to powder;* where we shall onely tell you first, *Quid conteri,* what this grinding is; and then, *Quid cadere,* what the falling of this stone is; And briefly this grinding to powder, is to be brought to that desperate and irrecoverable estate in sinne, as that no medicinall correction from God, no breaking, no bowing, no melting, no moulding can bring him to any good fashion; when God can worke no cure, do no good upon us by breaking us; not by breaking us in our health, for we will attribute that to weaknesse of stomach, to surfeit, to indigestion; not by breaking us in our states, for we will impute that to falshood in servants, to oppression of great adversaries, to iniquity of Judges; not by breaking us in our honour, for we will accuse for that, factions, and practises, and supplantation in Court; when God cannot breake us with his corrections, but that we will attribute them to some naturall, to some accidentall causes, and never thinke of Gods judgements, which are the true cause of these afflictions; when God cannot breake us by breaking our backs, by laying on heavy loads of calamities upon us, nor by breaking our hearts, by putting us into a sad, and heavy, and fruitlesse sorrow and melancholy for these worldly losses, then he comes to breake us by breaking our necks, by casting us into the bottomlesse pit, and falling upon us there, in this wrath and indignation, *Comminuam* Psal. 18.42 *eos in pulverem,* sayth he, *I will beate them as small as dust before the winde,* and tread them as flat as clay in the streets, the breaking Esay 30.14 thereof shall be like the breaking of a Potters vessell, which is broken without any pity. (No pity from God, no mercy, neither shall any man pity them, no compassion, no sorrow:) And in the breaking thereof, saith the Prophet, there *is not found a sheard to take fire at the hearth,* nor to take water at the pit: that is, they shall be incapable of any beam of grace in themselves from heaven, or any spark of zeale in themselves, (not a sheard to fetch fire at the hearth) and incapable of any drop of Christs blood from heaven, or of any teare of Ierem. 19.11 contrition in themselves, not a sheard to fetch water at the pit, *I will breake them as a Potters vessell, quod non potest instaurari,* says God in *Jeremy,* There shall be no possible meanes (of those means which God hath ordained in his Church) to recompact them againe, no voice of Gods word to draw them, no threatnings of Gods judgements shall drive them, no censures of Gods Church shall fit them, no Sacrament shall cement and glue them to Christs body againe; In temporall blessings, he shall be unthankfull, in temporall afflictions, he shall be obdurate: And these two shall serve, as the upper and nether stone of a mill, to grinde this reprobate sinner to powder.

Cadere Lastly, this is to be done, by Christs falling upon him, and what is that? I know some Expositors take this to be but the falling of Gods judgements upon him in this world; But in this world there is no grinding to powder, all Gods judgements here, (for any thing that we can know) have the nature of Physick in them, and may, and are wont to cure; and no man is here so absolutely broken in pieces, but that he may be re-united: we chuse therfore to follow the Ancients in this, That the falling of this stone upon this Reprobate, is Christs last and irrecoverable falling upon him, in his last judgment; that when hee shall wish that the Hills might fall and cover him, this [Luke 23.30] stone shall fall, and *grinde him to powder; He shall be broken, and be no more found,* says the Prophet, *yea, he shall be broken and no more sought:* Dan. 11.19 No man shall consider him what he is now, nor remember him what he was before: For, that stone, which in *Daniel* was cut out without hands, Dan. 2.[31–35] (which was a figure of Christ, who came without ordinary generation) when that great Image was to be overthrown, broke not an arme or a leg, but brake the whole Image in peeces, and it wrought not onely upon the weak parts, but it brake all, the clay, the iron, the brasse, the silver, the gold; so when this stone fals thus, when Christ comes to judgement, he shall not onely condemn him for his clay, his earthly and covetous sinnes, nor for his iron, his revengefull oppressing, and rusty sinnes, nor for his brasse, his shining, and glittering sinnes, which he hath filed and polished, but he shall fall upon his silver and gold, his religious and precious sinnes, his hypocriticall hearing of Sermons, his singular observing of Sabbaths, his Pharisaicall giving of almes, and as well his subtill counterfeiting of Religion, as his Atheisticall opposing of religion, this stone, Christ himselfe, shall fall upon him, and a showre of other stones shall oppresse him too. *Sicut pluit laqueos,* says *David,* As God Psal. 11.6 rained springs and snares upon them in this world (abundance of temporall blessings to be occasions of sinne unto them:) So *pluet grandinem,* he shall raine such haile-stones upon them, as shall grinde [Psal. 105.32] them to powder; there shall fall upon him the naturall Law, which was written in his heart, and did rebuke him, then when he prepared for a sinne; there shall fall upon him the written Law, which cryed out from the mouthes of the Prophets in these places, to avert him from sinne; there shall fall upon him those sinnes which he hath done, and those sins which he hath not done, if nothing but want of means and opportunity hindred him from doing them; there shall fall upon him those sinnes which he hath done after anothers dehortation, and those, which others have done after his provocation; there the stones of Nineveh shall fall upon him, and of as many Cities as have repented with lesse proportions of mercy and grace, then God afforded him; there the rubbage of Sodom and Gomorrah shall fall upon him, and as many Cities as in their ruine might have been examples to him. All these stones shall fall upon him, and to add weight to all these, Christ Jesus himselfe shall fall upon his conscience, with unanswerable questions, and grinde his soule to powder. But Rev. 2.11 *hee that overcometh, shall not bee hurt by the second death,* he that feeles his own fall upon this stone, shall never feel this stone fall upon him, he that comes to a remorse, early, and earnestly after a sinne, and seeks by ordinary meanes, his reconcileation to God in his Church, is in the best state that man can be in now; for howsoever we cannot say that repentance is as happy an estate as Innocency, yet certainly every particular man feels more comfort and spirituall joy, after a true repentance for a sin, then he had in that degree of Innocence which he had before he committed that sinne; and therefore in this case also we may safely repeat those words of *Augustine, Audeo dicere,* I dare be bold to say, that many a man hath been the better for some sin.

Almighty God, who gives that civill wisdome, to make use of other mens infirmities, give us also this heavenly wisdome, to make use of our own particular sins, that thereby our own wretched conditions in our selves, and our meanes of reparation in Jesus Christ, may be the more manifested unto us; To whom with the blessed Spirit, &c.

Number 9.

Preached to the Lords upon Easter-day, at the Communion, The King being then dangerously sick at New-Market.

Psal. 89.48. *WHAT MAN IS HE THAT LIVETH, AND SHALL NOT SEE DEATH?*

At first, God gave the judgement of death upon man, when he should transgresse, absolutely, *Morte morieris,* Thou shalt surely dye: The woman in her Dialogue with the Serpent, she mollifies it, *Ne fortè moriamur,* perchance, if we eate, we may [Gen. 3.3, die; and then the Devill is as peremptory on the other side, *Nequaquam moriemini,* do what you will, surely you shall not die; And now God in this Text comes to his reply, *Quis est homo,* shall they not die? Give me but one instance, but one exception to this rule, *What man is hee that liveth, and shall not see death?* Let no man, no woman, no devill offer a *Ne fortè,* (perchance we may dye) much lesse a *Nequaquam,* (surely we shall not dye) except he be provided of an answer to this question, except he can give an instance against this generall, except he can produce that mans name, and history, that hath lived, and shall not see death. Wee are all conceived in close Prison; in our Mothers wombes, we are close Prisoners all; when we are borne, we are borne but to the liberty of the house; Prisoners still, though within larger walls; and then all our life is but a going out to the place of Execution, to death. Now was there ever any man seen to sleep in the Cart, between New-gate, and Tyborne? between the Prison, and the place of Execution, does any man sleep? And we sleep all the way; from the womb to the grave we are never throughly awake; but passe on with such dreames, and imaginations as these, I may live as well, as another, and why should I dye, rather then another? but awake, and tell me, sayes this Text, *Quis homo?* who is that other that thou talkest of? *What man is he that liveth, and shall not see death?*

In these words, we shall first, for our generall humiliation, consider the unanswerablenesse of this question, There is no man that lives, and shall not see death. Secondly, we shall see, how that modification of Eve may stand, *fortè moriemur,* how there may be a probable answer made to this question, that it is like enough, that there are some men that live, and shall not see death: And thirdly, we shall finde that truly spoken, which the Devill spake deceitfully then, we shall finde the *Nequaquam* verified, we shall finde a direct, and full answer to this question; we shall finde a man that lives, and shall not see death, our Lord, and Saviour Christ Jesus, of whom both S. *Augustine,* and S. *Hierome,* doe take this question to be principally asked, and this Text to be principally intended. Aske me this question then, of all the sons of men, generally guilty of originall sin, *Quis homo,* and I am speechlesse, I can make no answer; Aske me this question of those men, which shall be alive upon earth at the last day, when Christ comes to judgement, *Quis homo,* and I can make a probable answer; *fortè moriemur,* perchance they shall die; It is a problematicall matter, and we say nothing too peremptorily. Aske me this question without relation to originall sin, *Quis homo,* and then I will answer directly, fully, confidently, *Ecce homo,* there was a man that lived, and was not subject to death by the law, neither did he actually die so, but that he fulfilled the rest of this verse; *Eruit animam de inferno,* by his owne power, he delivered his soule from the hand of the grave. From the first, this lesson rises, Generall doctrines must be generally delivered, All men must die: From the second, this lesson, Collaterall and unrevealed doctrines must be soberly delivered, How we shall be changed at the last day, we know not so clearly: From the third, this lesson arises, Conditionall Doctrines must be conditionally delivered, If we be dead with him, we shall be raised with him.

1. Part
Quis homo?

First then, for the generality, Those other degrees of punishment, which God inflicted upon *Adam,* and *Eve,* and in them upon us, were as absolutely, and illimitedly pronounced, as this of death, and yet we see, they are many wayes extended, or contracted; To man it was said, *In sudore vultus, In the sweat of thy browes, thou shalt eate thy bread,* [Gen. 3.19] and how many men never sweat, till they sweat with eating? To the woman it was said, *Thy desire shall be to thy husband, and he shall rule over thee:* [Gen. 3.16] and how many women have no desire to their husbands, how many over-rule them? Hunger, and thirst, and wearinesse, and sicknesse are denounced upon all, and yet if you ask me *Quis homo?* What is that man that hungers and thirsts not, that labours not, that sickens not? I can tell you of many, that never felt any of these; but contract the question to that one of death, *Quis homo?* What man is he that shall not taste death? And I know none. Whether we consider the Summer Solstice, when the day is sixteen houres, and the night but eight, or the Winter Solstice, when the night is sixteen houres, and the day but eight, still all is but twenty foure houres, and still the evening and the morning make but a day: The Patriarchs in the old Testament had their Summer day, long lives; we are in the Winter, short lived; but *Quis homo?* Which of them, or us come not to our night in death? If we consider violent deaths, casuall deaths, it is almost a scornfull thing to see, with what wantonnesse, and sportfulnesse, death playes with us; We have seen a man Canon proofe in the time of War, and slain with his own Pistoll in the time of peace: We have seen a man recovered after his drowning, and live to hang himselfe. But for that one kinde of death, which is generall, (though nothing be in truth more against nature then dissolution, and corruption, which is death) we are come to call that death, naturall death, then which, indeed, nothing is more unnaturall; The generality makes it naturall; *Moses* sayes, that Mans age is seventy, and eighty is labour and pain; Psal. 90.10 and yet himselfe was more then eighty, and in a good state, and habitude when he said so. No length, no strength enables us to answer this *Quis homo? What man? &c.*

Take a flat Map, a Globe *in plano,* and here is East, and there is West, as far asunder as two points can be put: but reduce this flat Map to roundnesse, which is the true form, and then East and West touch one another, and are all one: So consider mans life aright, to be a Circle, *Pulvis es, & in pulverem reverteris, Dust thou art, and to dust thou must return;* [Gen. 3.19] *Nudus egressus, Nudus revertar, Naked I came, and naked I must go;* Job 1.[21] In this, the circle, the two points meet, the womb and the grave are but one point, they make but one station, there is but a step from that to this. This brought in that custome amongst the Greek Emperours, that ever at the day of their Coronation, they were presented with severall sorts of Marble, that they might then bespeak their Tombe. And this brought in that Custome into the Primitive Church, that they called the Martyrs dayes, wherein they suffered, *Natalitia Martyrum,* their birth dayes; birth, and death is all one.

Their death was a birth to them into another life, into the glory of God; It ended one Circle, and created another; for immortality, and eternity is a Circle too; not a Circle where two points meet, but a Circle made at once; This life is a Circle, made with a Compasse, that passes from point to point; That life is a Circle stamped with a print, an endlesse, and perfect Circle, as soone as it begins. Of this Circle, the Mathematician is our great and good God; The other Circle we make up our selves; we bring the Cradle, and Grave together by a course of nature. Every man does; *Mi Gheber,* sayes the Originall; It is not *Ishe,* which is the first name of man, in the Scriptures, and signifies nothing but a *sound,* a voyce, a word; a Musicall ayre dyes, and evaporates, what wonder if man, that is but *Ishe,* a *sound,* dye too? It is not *Adam,* which is another name of man, and signifies nothing but *red earth;* Let it be earth red with blood, (with that murder which we have done upon our selves) let it be earth red with blushing, (so the word is used in the Originall) with a conscience of our own infirmity, what wonder if man, that is but *Adam,* guilty of this self-murder in himself, guilty of this in-borne frailty in himself, dye too? It is not *Enos,* which is also a third name of man, and signifies nothing but a *wretched and miserable creature;* what wonder if man, that is but earth, that is a burden to his Neighbours, to his friends, to his kindred, to himselfe, to whom all others, and to whom himself desires death, what wonder if he dye? But this question is framed upon none of these names; Not *Ishe,* not *Adam,* not *Enos;* but it is *Mi Gheber, Quis vir;* which is the word alwayes signifying a man accomplished in all excellencies, a man accompanied with all advantages; fame, and good opinion justly conceived, keepes him from being *Ishe,* a meere sound, standing onely upon popular acclamation; Innocency and integrity keepes him from being *Adam,* red earth, from bleeding, or blushing at any thing hee hath done; That holy and Religious Art of Arts, which S. *Paul* professed, *That he knew how to want, and how to abound,* [Phil. 4.11, 12] keepes him from being *Enos,* miserable or wretched in any fortune; Hee is *Gheber,* a great Man, and a good Man, a happy Man, and a holy Man, and yet *Mi Gheber, Quis homo,* this man must see death.

And therefore we will carry this question a little higher, from *Quis homo,* to *Quis deorum,* Which of the gods have not seene death? Aske it of those, who are Gods by participation of Gods power, of those of whom God saies, *Ego dixi, dii estis,* and God answers for them, and of them, and to them, *You shall dye like men;* [Psal. 82.6, 7] Aske it of those gods, who are gods by imputation, whom Creatures have created, whom Men have made gods, the gods of the Heathen, and do we not know, where all these gods dyed? Sometimes divers places dispute, who hath their tombes; but do not they deny their godhead in confessing their tombes? doe they not all answer, that they cannot answer this text, *Mi Gheber, Quis homo,* What man, *Quis deorum,* What god of mans making hath not seen death? As *Iustin Martyr* asks that question, Why should I pray to *Apollo* or *Esculapius* for health, *Qui apud Chironem medicinam didicerunt,* when I know who taught them all that they knew? so why should I looke for Immortality from such or such a god, whose grave I finde for a witnesse, that he himselfe is dead? Nay, carry this question higher then so, from this *Quis homo,* to *quid homo,* what is there in the nature and essence of Man, free from death? The whole man is not, for the dissolution of body and soule is death. The body is not; I shall as soone finde an immortall Rose, an eternall Flower, as an immortall body. And for the Immortality of the Soule, It is safelier said to be immortall, by preservation, then immortall by nature; That God keepes it from dying, then, that it cannot dye. We magnifie God in an humble and faithfull acknowledgment of the immortality of our soules, but if we aske, *quid homo,* what is there in the nature of Man, that should keepe him from death, even in that point, the question is not easily answered.

Videbit

It is every mans case then; every man dyes; and though it may perchance be but a meere Hebraisme to say, that every man shall *see death,* perchance it amounts to no more, but to that phrase, *Gustare mortem, To taste death,* yet thus much may be implied in it too, That as every man must dye, so every man may see, that he must dye; as it cannot be avoided, so it may be understood. A beast dyes, but he does not see death; S. *Basil* sayes, he saw an Oxe weepe for the death of his yoke-fellow; but S. *Basil* might mistake the occasion of that Oxes teares. Many men dye too, and yet doe not see death; The approaches of death amaze them, and stupifie them; they feele no colluctation with Powers, and Principalities, upon their death bed; that is true; they feele no terrors in their consciences, no apprehensions of Judgement, upon their death bed; that is true; and this we call going away like a Lambe. But the Lambe of God had a sorrowfull sense of death; His soule was heavy unto death, and he had an apprehension, that his Father had forsaken him; And in this text, the Chalde Paraphrase expresses it thus, *Videbit Angelum mortis,* he shall see a Messenger, a forerunner, a power of Death, an executioner of Death, he shall see something with horror, though not such as shall shake his morall, or his Christian constancy.

Basil orat. de Morte

So that this *Videbunt, They shall see,* implies also a *Viderunt,* they have seene, that is, they have used to see death, to observe a death in the decay of themselves, and of every creature, and of the whole World. Almost fourteene hundred yeares agoe, S. *Cyprian* writing against *Demetrianus,* who imputed all the warres, and deaths, and unseasonablenesses of that time, to the contempt, and irreligion of the Christians, that they were the cause of all those ils, because they would not worship their Gods, *Cyprian* imputes all those distempers to the age of the whole World; *Canos videmus in pueris,* saies hee, Wee see Children borne gray-headed; *Capilli deficiunt, antequam crescant,* Their haire is changed, before it be growne. *Nec ætas in senectute desinit, sed incipit a senectute,* Wee doe not dye with age, but wee are borne old. Many of us have seene Death in our particular selves; in many of those steps, in which the morall Man expresses it; Wee have seene *Mortem infantiæ, pueritiam,* The death of infancy in youth; and *Pueritiæ, adolescentiam,* and the death of youth in our middle age; And at last we shall see *Mortem senectutis, mortem ipsam,* the death of age in death it selfe. But yet after that, a step farther then that Morall man went, *Mortem mortis in morte Iesu,* We shall see the death of Death it self in the death of Christ. As we

Cyprian ad Demetrianum

Seneca

could not be cloathed at first, in Paradise, till some Creatures were dead, (for we were cloathed in beasts skins) [Gen. 3.21] so we cannot be cloathed in Heaven, but in his garment who dyed for us.

This *Videbunt,* this future sight of Death implies a *viderunt,* they have seene, they have studied Death in every Booke, in every Creature; and it implies a *Vident,* they doe presently see death in every object, They see the houre-glasse running to the death of the houre; They see the death of some prophane thoughts in themselves, by the entrance of some Religious thought of compunction, and conversion to God; and then they see the death of that Religious thought, by an inundation of new prophane thoughts, that overflow those. As Christ [1 Cor. 11.24] sayes, that as often as wee eate the Sacramentall Bread, we should remember his Death, so as often, as we eate ordinary bread, we may Bern. remember our death; for even hunger and thirst, are diseases; they are *Mors quotidiana,* a daily death, and if they lasted long, would Aug. kill us. In every object and subject, we all have, and doe, and shall see death; not to our comfort as an end of misery, not onely as such a misery in it selfe, as the Philosopher takes it to be, *Mors omnium miseriarum,* That Death is the death of all miserie, because it destroyes and dissolves our beeing; but as it is *Stipendium peccati, The reward of sin;* That as *Solomon* sayes, *Indignatio Regis nuncius mor-* Prov. 16.14 *tis, The wrath of the King, is as a messenger of Death,* so *Mors nuncius indignationis Regis,* We see in Death a testimony, that our Heavenly King is angry; for, but for his indignation against our sinnes, we should not dye. And this death, as it is *Malum,* ill, (for if ye weigh it in the Philosophers balance, it is an annihilation of our present beeing, and if ye weigh it in the Divine Balance, it is a seale of Gods anger against sin) so this death is generall; of this, this question there is no answer, *Quis homo,* What man, &c.

2 Part

We passe then from the *Morte moriemini,* to the *fortè moriemini,* from the generality and the unescapablenesse of death, from this question, as it admits no answer, to the *Fortè moriemini,* perchance we shall dye; that is, to the question as it may admit a probable answer. Of which, we said at first, that in such questions, nothing becomes a Christian better then sobriety; to make a true difference betweene problematicall, and dogmaticall points, betweene upper buildings, and foundations, betweene collaterall doctrines, and Doc-

Aug. trines in the right line: for fundamentall things, *Sine hæsitatione credantur,* They must be beleeved without disputing; there is no more to be done for them, but beleeving; for things that are not so, we are to weigh them in two balances, in the balance of Analogy, and in the balance of scandall: we must hold them so, as may be analogall, proportionable, agreeable to the Articles of our Faith, and we must hold them so, as our brother be not justly offended, nor scandalized by them; wee must weigh them with faith, for our own strength, and we must weigh them with charity, for others weaknesse. Certainly nothing endangers a Church more, then to draw indifferent things to be necessary; I meane of a primary necessity, of a necessity to be beleeved *De fide,* not a secondary necessity, a necessity to be performed and practised for obedience: Without doubt, the Roman Church repents now, and sees now that she should better have preserved her selfe, if they had not denied so many particular things, which were indifferently and problematically disputed before, to bee had necessarily *De fide,* in the Councell of Trent.

Taking then this Text for a probleme, *Quis homo, What man lives, and shall not see Death?* we answer, It may be that those Men, whom Christ shal find upon the earth alive, at his returne to Judge the World, shall dye then, and it may be they shall but be changed, and not dye. That Christ shall judge quick and dead, is a funda-
Acts 10.42 mentall thing; we heare it in S. *Peters* Sermon, to *Cornelius* and his company, and we say it every day in the Creed, *Hee shall judge the quick and the dead.* But though we doe not take the quick and the
August. dead, as *Augustine* and *Chrysostome* doe, for the Righteous which
Chrys. lived in faith, and the unrighteous, which were dead in sinne, Though wee doe not take the quick and the dead, as *Ruffinus* and others doe, for the soule and the body, (He shall judge the soule, which was alwaies alive, and he shall the body, which was dead for a time) though we take the words (as becomes us best) literally, yet the letter does not conclude, but that they, whom Christ shall finde alive upon earth, shall have a present and sudden dissolution, and a present and
1 Cor. 15.51 sudden re-union of body and soul again. Saint *Paul* sayes, *Behold I shew you a mystery;* Therefore it is not a cleare case, and presently, and peremptorily determined; but what is it? *We shall not all sleep, but we shall all be changed.* But whether this sleeping be spoke of

death it self, and exclude that, that we shall not die, or whether this sleep be spoke of a rest in the grave, and exclude that, we shall not be buried, and remain in death, that may be a mystery still. S. *Paul* sayes too, *The dead in Christ shall rise first; Then we which are alive, and remain, shall be caught up together with them in the clouds, to meet the Lord in the ayre.* But whether that may not still be true, that S. *Augustine* sayes, that there shall be *Mors in raptu,* An instant and sudden dis-union, and re-union of body and soul, which is death, who can tell? So on the other side, when it is said to him, in whom all we were, to *Adam, Pulvis es, Dust thou art, and into dust thou shalt return,* when it is said, *In Adam all die,* when it is said, *Death passed upon all men, for all have sinned,* Why may not all those sentences of Scripture, which imply a necessity of dying, admit that restriction, *Nisi dies judicii naturæ cursum immutet,* We shall all die, except those, in whom the comming of Christ shall change the course of Nature.

1 Thes. 4.[16, 17]
August.
Gen. 3.19
1 Cor. 15.22
Rom. 5.12
Pet. Mar.

Consider the Scriptures then, and we shall be absolutely concluded neither way; Consider Authority, and we shall finde the Fathers for the most part one way, and the Schoole for the most part another; Take later men, and all those in the Romane Church; Then *Cajetan* thinks, that they shall not die, and *Catharin* is so peremptory, that they shall, as that he sayes of the other opinion, *Falsam esse confidenter asserimus, & contra Scripturas satis manifestas, & omnino sine ratione;* It is false, and against Scriptures, and reason, saith he; Take later men, and all those in the reformed Church; and *Calvin* sayes, *Quia aboletur prior natura, censetur species mortis, sed non migrabit anima à corpore:* S. *Paul* calls it death, because it is a destruction of the former Beeing; but it is not truly death, saith *Calvin;* and *Luther* saith, That S. *Pauls* purpose in that place is only to shew the suddennesse of Christs comming to Judgement, *Non autem inficiatur omnes morituros; nam dormire, est sepeliri:* But S. *Paul* doth not deny, but that all shall die; for that sleeping which he speaks of, is buriall; and all shall die, though all shall not be buried, saith *Luther.*

Cajetan
Catherinus
Calvin
Luther

Take then that which is certain; It is certain, a judgement thou must passe: If thy close and cautelous proceeding have saved thee from all informations in the Exchequer, thy clearnesse of thy title from all Courts at Common Law, thy moderation from the Chancery, and Star-Chamber, If heighth of thy place, and Authority, have saved thee, even from the tongues of men, so that ill men dare not slander thy actions, nor good men dare not discover thy actions, no not to thy self, All those judgements, and all the judgements of the world, are but interlocutory judgements; There is a finall judgement, *In judicantes & judicatos,* against Prisoners and Judges too, where all John 5.[22, 27] shalbe judged again; *Datum est omne judicium,* All judgement is given to the Son of man, and upon all the sons of men must his judgement passe. A judgement is certain, and the uncertainty of this judgement is certain too; perchance God will put off thy judgement; thou shalt not die yet; but who knows whether God in his mercy, do put off this judgement, till these good motions which his blessed Spirit inspires into thee now, may take roote, and receive growth, and bring forth fruit, or whether he put it off, for a heavier judgement, to let thee see, by thy departing from these good motions, and returning to thy former sins, after a remorse conceived against those sins, that thou art inexcusable even to thy self, and thy condemnation is just, even to thine own conscience. So perchance God will bring this judgement upon thee now; now thou maist die; but whether God will bring that judgement upon thee now, in mercy, whilest his Graces, in his Ordinance of preaching, work some tendernesse in thee, and give thee some preparation, some fitnesse, some courage to say, *Veni Domine Iesu, Come Lord Iesu,* come quickly, come now, or whether he will come now in judgement, because all this can work no tendernesse in thee, who can tell?

Thou hearest the word of God preached, as thou hearest an Oration, with some gladnesse in thy self, if thou canst heare him, and never be moved by his Oratory; thou thinkest it a degree of wisdome, to be above perswasion; and when thou art told, that he that feares God, feares nothing else, thou thinkest thy self more valiant then so, if thou feare not God neither; Whether or why God defers, or hastens the judgement, we know not; This is certain, this all S. *Pauls* places collineate to, this all the Fathers, and all the Schoole, all the *Cajetans,* [1 Cor. 15.52] and all the *Catharins,* all the *Luthers,* and all the *Calvins* agree in, *A judgement must be,* and it must be *In ictu oculi, In the twinkling* [1 Thess. 5.2] *of an eye,* and *Fur in nocte, A thiefe in the night.* Make the question, *Quis homo?* What man is he that liveth, and shall not passe this judgement? or, what man is he that liveth, and knowes when this judgement shall be? So it is a *Nemo scit,* A question without an answer; but ask it, as in the text, *Quis homo?* Who liveth, and shall not die? so it is a problematicall matter; and in such things as are problematicall, if thou love the peace of Sion, be not too inquisitive to know, nor too vehement, when thou thinkest thou doest know it.

3. Part

Come then to ask this question, not problematically, (as it is contracted to them that shall live in the last dayes) nor peremptorily of man, (as he is subject to originall sin) but at large, so, as the question may include Christ himself, and then to that *Quis homo? What man is he?* We answer directly, here is the man that shall not see death; And of him principally, and literally, S. *Augustine* (as we said before) takes this question to be framed; *Vt quæras, dictum, non ut desperes,* saith he, this question is moved, to move thee to seek out, and to have thy recourse to that man which is the Lord of Life, not to make thee despaire, that there is no such man, in whose self, and in whom, for all us, there is Redemption from death: For, sayes he, this question is an exception to that which was said before the text; which is, *Wherefore hast thou made all men in vain?* Consider it better, sayes the Holy Ghost, here, and it will not prove so; Man is not made in vain at first, though he do die now; for, *Perditio tua ex te,* This death proceeds from man himself; and *Quare moriemini domus Israel? Why will ye die, O house of Israel?* God made not death, neither hath he pleasure in the destruction of the living; The Wise man sayes it, and the true God sweares it, *As I live saith the Lord, I would not the death of a sinner.* God did not create man in vain then, though he die; not in vain, for since he will needs die, God receives glory even by his death, in the execution of his justice; not in vaine neither, because though he be dead, God hath provided him a Redeemer from death, in his mercy; Man is not created in vain at all; nor all men, so neare vanity as to die; for here is one man, God and Man Christ Jesus, which liveth, and shall not see death. And conformable to S. *Augustines* purpose, speakes S. *Hierome* too, *Scio quòd nullus homo carneus evadet, sed novi Deum sub velamento carnis latentem;* I know there is no man but shall die; but I know where there is a God clothed in mans flesh, and that person cannot die.

August.

[Psal. 89.47]

[Ezek. 18.31]

Sap. 1.13

[Ezek. 33.11]

Hieron.

But did not Christ die then? Shall we joyne with any of those Heretiques, which brought Christ upon the stage to play a part, and say he was born, or lived, or dyed, *In phantasmate,* In apparance only, and representation; God forbid; so all men were created in vain indeed, if we had not a regeneration in his true death. Where is the [Luke 24.26] contract between him, and his Father, that *Oportuit pati, All this Christ ought to suffer, and so enter into glory:* Is that contract void, and of none effect? Must he not die? Where is the ratification of that Esay, 53.4, 9 contract in all the Prophets? Where is *Esays Verè languores nostros tulit, Surely he hath born our sorrows; and, he made his grave with the wicked in his death;* Is the ratification of the Prophets cancelled? Shall he not, must he not die? Where is the consummation, and the [John 19.30] testification of all this? Where is the Gospell, *Consummatum est? And he bowed his head, and gave up the ghost?* Is that fabulous? Did he not die? How stands the validity of that contract, Christ must die; the dignity of those Prophecies, Christ will die; the truth of the Gospell, Christ did die, with this answer to this question, Here is a man that liveth and shall not see death? Very well; For though Christ Jesus did truly die, so as was contracted, so as was prophecied, so as was related, yet hee did not die so, as was intended in this question, so as other naturall men do die.

For first, Christ dyed because he would dye; other men admitted to the dignity of Martyrdome, are willing to dye; but they dye by the torments of the Executioners, they cannot bid their soules goe out, and say, now I will dye. And this was Christs case: It was not John 10.15 [also 18] only, *I lay down my life for my sheep,* but he sayes also, *No man can take away my soule;* And, *I have power to lay it down;* And *De facto,* he did lay it down, he did dye, before the torments could have extorted his soule from him; Many crucified men lived many dayes upon the Crosse; The thieves were alive, long after Christ was dead; Mar. 15.44 and therefore Pilate wondred, that he was already dead. His soule August. did not leave his body by force, but because he would, and when he would, and how he would; Thus far then first, this is an answer to this question, *Quis homo?* Christ did not die naturally, nor violently, as all others doe, but only voluntarily.

Again, the penalty of death appertaining only to them, who were derived from *Adam* by carnall, and sinfull generation, Christ Jesus being conceived miraculously of a Virgin, by the over-shadowing of the Holy Ghost, was not subject to the Law of death; and therefore in his person, it is a true answer to this *Quis homo?* Here is a man, that shall not see death, that is, he need not see death, he hath not incurred Gods displeasure, he is not involved in a general rebellion, and therfore is not involved in the generall mortality, not included in the generall penalty. He needed not have dyed by the rigour of any Law, all we must; he could not dye by the malice, or force of any Executioner, all we must; at least by natures generall Executioners, Age, and Sicknesse; And then, when out of his own pleasure, and to advance our salvation, he would dye, yet he dyed so, as that though there were a dis-union of body and soule, (which is truly death) yet there remained a Nobler, and faster union, then that of body and soule, the Hypostaticall Union of the God-head, not onely to his soule, but to his body too; so that even in his death, both parts were still, not onely inhabited by, but united to the Godhead it selfe; and in respect of that inseparable Union, we may answer to this question, *Quis homo?* Here is a man that shall not see death, that is, he shall see no separation of that, which is incomparably, and incomprehensibly, a better soul then his soule, the God-head shall not be separated from his body.

But, that which is indeed the most direct, and literall answer, to this question, is, That whereas the death in this Text, is intended of such a death, as hath Dominion over us, and from which we have no power to raise our selves, we may truly, and fully answer to his *Quis homo?* here is a man, that shall never see death so, but that he shall even in the jawes, and teeth of death, and in the bowels and wombe of the grave, and in the sink, and furnace of hell it selfe, retaine an Almighty power, and an effectuall purpose, to deliver his soule from death, by a glorious, a victorious, and a Triumphant Resurrection: So it is true, Christ Jesus dyed, else none of us could live; but yet hee dyed not so, as is intended in this question; Not by the necessity of any Law, not by the violence of any Executioner, not by the separation of his best soule, (if we may so call it) the God-head, nor by such a separation of his naturall, and humane soule, as that he would not, or could not, or did not resume it againe.

If then this question had beene asked of Angels at first, *Quis An-*

gelus? what Angel is that, that stands, and shall not fall? though as many of those Angels, as were disposed to that answer, *Erimus* [Isa. 14.14] *similes Altissimo,* We will be like God, and stand of our selves, without any dependance upon him, did fall, yet otherwise they might have answered the question fairly, All we may stand, if we will; If this question had been asked of *Adam* in Paradise, *Quis homo?* though when he harkned to her, who had harkned to that voyce, [Gen. 3.5] *Eritis sicut Dii, You shall be as Gods,* he fell too, yet otherwise, he might have answered the question fairly so, I may live, and not dye, if I will; so, if this question be asked of us now, as the question implies the generall penalty, as it considers us onely as the sons of *Adam,* we have no other answer, but that by *Adam* sin entred upon all, and death by sin upon all; as it implies the state of them onely, whom Christ at his second comming shall finde upon earth, wee have no other answer but a modest, *non liquet,* we are not sure, whether we shall dye then, or no; wee are onely sure, it shall be so, as most conduces to our good, and Gods glory; but as the question implies us to be members of our Head, Christ Jesus, as it was a true answer in him, it is true in every one of us, adopted in him, Here is a man that liveth, and shall not see death.

Prov. 18.21 *Death and life are in the power of the tongue,* sayes *Solomon,* in another sense; and in this sense too, If my tongue, suggested by my heart, and by my heart rooted in faith, can say, *Non moriar, non moriar;* If I can say, (and my conscience doe not tell me, that I belye mine owne state) if I can say, That the blood of my Saviour runs in my veines, That the breath of his Spirit quickens all my purposes, that all my deaths have their Resurrection, all my sins their remorses, all my rebellions their reconciliations, I will harken no more after this question, as it is intended *de morte naturali,* of a naturall death, I know I must die that death, what care I? nor *de morte spirituali,* the death of sin, I know I doe, and shall die so; why despaire I? but I will finde out another death, *mortem raptus,* a death of rapture, and of extasie, that death which S. *Paul* died more then once, The death which S. *Gregory* speaks of, *Divina contemplatio quoddam sepulchrum animæ,* The contemplation of God, and heaven, is a kinde of buriall, and Sepulchre, and rest of the soule; and in this death of rapture, and extasie, in this death of the Contemplation of

2 Cor. 12.[1–4]
Acts 9
Greg.

my interest in my Saviour, I shall finde my self, and all my sins enterred, and entombed in his wounds, and like a Lily in Paradise, out of red earth, I shall see my soule rise out of his blade, in a candor, and in an innocence, contracted there, acceptable in the sight of his Father.

Though I have been dead, in the delight of sin, so that that of S. *Paul, That a Widow that liveth in pleasure, is dead while she* 1 Tim. 5.6 *liveth,* be true of my soule, that so, *viduatur, gratiâ mortuâ,* when Christ is dead, not for the soule, but in the soule, that the soule hath no sense of Christ, *Viduatur anima,* the soul is a Widow, and no Dowager, she hath lost her husband, and hath nothing from him; yea though *I have made a Covenant with death, and have been at an* Esay 28.15 *agreement with hell,* and in a vain confidence have said to my self, *that when the overflowing scourge shall passe through, it shall not come to me,* yet God shall annull that covenant, he shall bring that scourge, that is, some medicinall correction upon me, and so give me a participation of all the stripes of his son; he shall give me a sweat, that is, some horrour, and religious feare, and so give me a participation of his Agony; he shall give me a diet, perchance want, and penury, and so a participation of his fasting; and if he draw blood, if he kill me, all this shall be but *Mors raptus,* a death of rapture towards him, into a heavenly, and assured Contemplation, that I have a part in all his passion, yea such an intire interest in his whole passion, as though all that he did, or suffered, had been done, and suffered for my soule alone; *Quasi moriens, & ecce vivo:* some shew 2 Cor. 6.9 of death I shall have, for I shall sin; and some shew of death again, for I shall have a dissolution of this Tabernacle; *Sed ecce vivo,* still the Lord of life will keep me alive, and that with an *Ecce,* Behold, I live; that is, he will declare, and manifest my blessed state to me; I shall not sit in the shadow of death; no nor I shall not sit in darknesse; his gracious purpose shall evermore be upon me, and I shall ever discerne that gracious purpose of his; I shall not die, nor I shall not doubt that I shall; If I be dead within doores, (If I have sinned in my heart) why, *Suscitavit in domo,* Christ gave a Resurrection to Mat. 9.23 the Rulers daughter within doores, in the house; If I be dead in the [also 24, 25] gate, (If I have sinned in the gates of my soule) in mine Eies, or Luke 7.11 Eares, or Hands, in actuall sins, why, *Suscitavit in porta,* Christ gave [also 12–15]

a Resurrection to the young man at the gate of *Naim*. If I be dead in the grave, (in customary, and habituall sins) why,
John 11 *Suscitavit in Sepulchro,* Christ gave a Resurrection to *Lazarus* in the grave too. If God give me *mortem raptus,* a death of rapture, of extasie, of fervent Contemplation of Christ Jesus, a Transfusion, a Transplantation, a Transmigration, a Transmutation into him, (for good digestion brings alwaies assimilation, certainly, if I come to a true meditation upon Christ, I come to a conformity with Christ) this is principally
Psal. 116.15 that *Pretiosa mors Sanctorum, Pretious in the sight of the Lord, is the death of his Saints,* by which they are dead and buryed, and risen again in Christ Jesus: pretious is that death, by which we apply that pretious blood to our selves, and grow strong enough by it, to meet *Davids* question, *Quis homo?* what man? with Christs answer, *Ego homo,* I am the man, in whom whosoever abideth, shall not see death.

Number 10.

Preached at Lincolns Inne, preparing them to build their Chappell.

GEN. 28.16 and 17. *THEN JACOB AWOKE OUT OF HIS SLEEP, AND SAID, SURELY THE LORD IS IN THIS PLACE, AND I WAS NOT AWARE. AND HE WAS AFRAID, AND SAID, HOW FEARFULL IS THIS PLACE! THIS IS NONE OTHER BUT THE HOUSE OF GOD, AND THIS IS THE GATE OF HEAVEN.*

IN THESE verses *Jacob* is a *Surveyor;* he considers a fit place for the house of *God;* and in the very next verse, he is a *Builder,* he erects *Bethel,* the house of *God* it selfe. All was but a drowsinesse, but a sleep, till he came to this Consideration; as soon as he *awoke,* he took knowledge of a fit place; as soon as he found the place, he went about the work. But to that we shall not come yet. But this Text, being a preparation for the building of a house to *God,* though such a house as *Jacob* built then, require no contribution, yet because such *Churches,* as we build now, doe, we shall first say a little, of that great vertue of *Charity;* and then somewhat of that vertue, as it is exercis'd by advancing the *house of God,* and his outward worship; And thirdly we shall consider *Jacob*'s steps, and proceedings, in this action of his.

1. Part *Charitas*

This vertue then, *Charity,* is it, that conducts us in this life, and accompanies us in the next. In heaven, where we shall *know God,* there may be no use of *faith;* In heaven, where we shall *see God,* there may be no use of *hope;* but in heaven, where *God* the Father, and the Son, love one another in the Holy Ghost, the bond of charity shall everlastingly unite us together. But *Charitas in patria,* and *Charitas in via,* differ in this, That there we shall love one another because we shall not need one another, for we shall all be full; Here the exercise of our charity is, because we doe stand in need of one another. August. *Dives & pauper duo sunt sibi contraria; sed iterum duo sunt sibi necessaria;* Rich, and poor are *contrary* to one another, but yet both *necessary* to one another; They are both necessary to one another; but the poor man is the more necessary; because though one man might be rich, though no man were poor, yet he could have no exercise of his charity, he could send none of his riches to heaven, to help him there, except there were some poor here.

He that is too fat, would fain devest some of that, though he could give that to no other man, that lack'd it; And shall not he that is wantonly pampered, nay, who is heavily laden, and encombred with temporall abundances, be content to discharge himselfe of some of that, wherewith he is over-fraighted, upon those poor souls, whom God hath not made poor for any sin of theirs, or of their fathers, but onely to present rich men exercise of their charity, and occasions of testifying their love to Christ; who having given himselfe, to convey salvation upon thee, if that conveyance may be sealed to thee, by giving a little of thine own, is it not an easie purchase? When a poore wretch beggs *of* thee, and thou givest, thou dost but justice, it is his. But when he begs of *God for* thee, and God gives thee, this is mercy; this was none of thine.

[Luke 16.2] When we shall come to our *Redde rationem villicationis,* to give an accompt of our Stewardship, when we shall not measure our inheritance by Acres, [Apoc. 14.4] but all heaven shall be ours, and we shall follow the Lamb, wheresoever he goes, when our estate, and term shall not be limited by years, and lives, but, as we shall be in the presence of [Dan. 7.9, 13, 32] the *Ancient of dayes,* so our dayes shall be so far equall to his, as that they shall be without end; Then will our great Merchants, great practisers, great purchasers, great Contracters, find another language, another style, then they have been accustom'd to, here. There no man shall be call'd a *prodigall,* but onely the Covetous man; Onely he that hath been too diligent a keeper, shall appear to have been an unthrift, and to have wasted his best treasure, the price of the bloud of *Christ Jesus,* his own soule. There no man shall be call'd *good security,* but he that hath made sure his salvation. No man shall be call'd a *Subsidy man,* but he that hath relieved Christ Jesus, in his sick, and hungry Members. No man shall be call'd a *wise Steward,* [Luke 16.8, 9] but he that hath made friends of the wicked *Mammon;* Nor provident *Merchant,* but he that sold all to buy the *pearle;* [Mat. 13.45, 46] Nor a great officer, but he that desires to be a *dore-keeper* in the kingdome of Heaven. [Psal. 84.10]

Now, every man hath a *key* to this dore of heaven: Every man hath some means to open it; every man hath an oyle to anoint this key, and make it turn easily; he may goe with more ease to Heaven, then he doth to Hell. Every man hath some means to pour this oile of gladnesse and comfort into anothers heart; No man can say, *Quid retribuam tibi Domine;* [Psal. 116.12] Lord what have I to give thee? for every man hath something to give *God:* Money, or labor, or counsail, or prayers: Every man can give; and he gives to God, who gives to them that need it, for his sake. Come not to that expostulation, *When did we see thee* hungry, or sick, or imprisoned, and did not minister? [Mat. 25.44] Nor to that, *Quid retribuam,* What can I give, that lack my selfe? lest *God* come also to that silence, and wearinesse of asking at thy hands, to say, as he sayes in the Psalme, *If I be hungry, I will not tell thee;* [Psal. 50.12] That though he have given thee abundance, though he lack himselfe in his children, yet he will not tell thee, he will not ask at thy hands, he will not enlighten thine understanding, he will not awaken thy charity, he will not give thee any occasion of doing good, with that which he hath given thee.

But God hath given thee a key: yea as he sayes to the Church of Philadelphia, Revel. 3.8 *Behold I set before thee an open dore, and no man can shut it.* Thou hast a gate into Heaven in thy selfe; If thou beest not sensible of other mens poverties, and distresses, yet *Miserere animæ tuæ,* [Ecclus. 30.23] have mercy on thine own soule; thou hast a poor guest, an Inmate, a sojourner, within these mudwals, this corrupt body of thine; be mercifull and compassionate to that Soule; cloath that Soul, which is stripp'd and left naked, of all her originall righteousnesse; feed that Soule, which thou hast starv'd; purge that Soule, which thou hast infected; warm, and thaw that Soul, which thou hast frozen with indevotion; coole, and quench that Soul, which thou hast inflamed with licentiousness; *Miserere animæ tuæ,* begin with thine own Soule;

be charitable to thy self first, and thou wilt remember, that God hath made of one bloud, all Mankind, and thou wilt find out thy selfe, in every other poor Man, and thou wilt find Christ Jesus himselfe in them all.

2. Part

Now of those divers gates, which *God* opens in this life, those divers exercises of charity, the particular which we are occasion'd to speak of here, is not the cloathing, nor feeding of Christ, but the *housing* of him, The providing Christ a house, a dwelling; whether this were the very place, where *Solomons Temple* was after built, is perplexedly, and perchance, impertinently controverted by many; but howsoever, here was the house of *God,* and here was the gate of Heaven. It is true, God may be devoutly worshipped any where; *Ubique* *In omni loco dominationis ejus benedic anima mea Domino;* In all [Psal. places of his dominion, my Soule shall praise the Lord, sayes *David.* 103.22] It is not only a concurring of men, a meeting of so many bodies that makes a *church;* If thy soule, and body be met together, an humble preparation of the mind, and a reverent disposition of the body, if thy knees be bent to the earth, thy hands and eyes lifted up to heaven, if thy tongue pray, and praise, and thine ears hearken to his answer, if all thy senses, and powers, and faculties, be met with one unanime purpose to worship thy *God,* thou art, to this intendment, a Church, [Mat. 18.20] thou art a Congregation, here are *two or three met together in his name,* and he is in the midst of them, though thou be alone in thy chamber. The Church of God should be built upon a Rock, and yet [Job. 2.8] *Job* had his Church upon a Dunghill; The bed is a scene, and an [2 Kings embleme of wantonnesse, and yet *Hezekiah* had his Church in his 20.1–3] Bed; The Church is to be placed upon the top of a Hill, and yet the [Jer. 38.6] Prophet *Jeremy* had his Church *in Luto,* in a miry Dungeon; Con- [Jonah 2] stancy, and setlednesse belongs to the Church, and yet *Jonah* had his Church in the Whales belly; The Lyon that roares, and seeks whom he may devour, is an enemy to this Church, and yet *Daniel* [Psal. 23.2] had his Church in the Lions den; *Aquæ quietudinum,* the waters of rest in the Psalme, were a figure of the Church, and yet the three [Acts 12 children had their Church in the fiery furnace; Liberty and life ap- and 16] pertaine to the Church, and yet *Peter,* and *Paul* had their Church in [1 Cor. prison, and the thiefe had his Church upon the Crosse. Every par- 6.19] ticular man is himselfe *Templum Spiritus sancti,* a Temple of the holy Ghost; yea, *Solvite templum hoc,* destroy this body by death, and corruption in the grave, yet there shall be *Festum encæniorum,* a renuing, a reedifying of all those Temples, in the generall Resurrection: when we shall rise againe, not onely as so many Christians, but as so many *Christian Churches,* to glorifie the Apostle, and High-priest of our profession, Christ Jesus, in that eternall Sabbath. *In omni loco dominationis ejus,* Every person, every place is fit to glorifie God in.

Iohn 2.19

Heb. 3.1

In templo Augustin.

God is not tyed to any *place;* not by essence; *Implet & continendo implet,* God fills every place, and fills it by containing that place in himselfe; but he is tyed *by his promise* to a manifestation of himselfe, by working in some certain places. Though *God* were long before he required, or admitted a sumptuous Temple, (for *Solomons* Temple was not built, in almost *five hundred years* after their returne out of Egypt) though God were content to accept their worship, and their sacrifices, at the *Tabernacle,* (which was a transitory, and moveable Temple) yet at last he was so carefull of his house, as that himselfe gave the modell, and platforme of it; and when it was built, and after repaired again, he was so jealous of appropriating, and confining all his solemne worship to that particular place, as that he permitted that long schisme, and dissention, between the *Samaritans,* and the *Jews,* onely about the place of the worship of God; They differed not in other things: but whether in *Mount Sion,* or in *Mount Garizim.* And the feast of the dedication of this Temple, which was yearly celebrated, received so much honor, as that Christ himselfe vouchsafed to be personally present at that solemnity; though it were a feast of the institution of the Church, and not of *God* immediately, as their other festivalls were, yet Christ forbore not to observe it, upon that pretence, that it was *but* the Church that had appointed it to be observed. So that, as in all times, God had manifested, and exhibited himselfe in some particular *places,* more then other, (in the *Pillar* in the *wildernesse,* and in the *Tabernacle,* and in the *poole,* which the Angell troubled) so did Christ himselfe, by his owne presence, ceremoniously, justifie, and authorise this *dedication* of places consecrated to Gods outward worship, not onely once, but *anniversarily* by a yearly celebration thereof.

[1 Kings 6.1]

[John 10.22, 23]

[Exod. 13.21]

[John 5.4]

Synagogue

To descend from this great Temple at Jerusalem, to which God had annexed his solemne, and publique worship, the lesser *Synagogues*, and Chappells of the *Jews*, in other places, were ever esteemed great testimonies of the sanctity and piety of the founders, for Christ accepts of that reason which was presented to him, in the behalfe of the

Luke 7.4 [and 5]

Centurion, He is worthy that thou shouldst do this for him, for *he loveth our Nation;* And how hath he testified it? *He hath built us a Synagogue.* He was but a stranger to them, and yet he furthered, and advanced the service of God amongst them, of whose body he was

Ambros.

no member. This was that Centurions commendation; *Et quanto commendatior qui ædificat Ecclesiam,* How much more commendation deserve they, that build a Church for Christian service? And therefore the *first Christians* made so much haste to the expressing of their devotion, that even in the *Apostles* time, for all their poverty, and persecution, they were come to have *Churches:* as most of the Fathers, and some of our later Expositors, understand these words,

1 Cor. [11.22]

(Have ye not houses to eate and drinke, or doe ye despise the *Church* of God?) to be spoken, not of the Church as it is a *Congregation,* but

Abdias Anaclet. Durant. d.rit.l.1.c.2

of the Church as it is a *Materiall building.* Yea, if we may beleeve some authors, that are pretended to be very ancient, there was one Church dedicated to the memory of *Saint John,* and another by *Saint Marke,* to the memory of *Saint Peter,* whilest yet both *Saint Iohn,* and *Saint Peter* were alive. Howsoever, it is certaine, that the purest and most *innocent* times, even the *infancy* of the Primitive Church, found this double way of expressing their devotion, in this particular of building Churches, first that they built them onely to the honour, and glory of God, without giving him any partner, and then they built them for the conserving of the memory of those blessed servants of God, who had sealed their profession with their bloud, and at whose Tombs, God had done such Miracles, as these times needed, for the propagation of his Church. They built their Churches principally for the glory of God, but yet they added the names of some of his blessed servants and Martyrs; for so says he, (who as he was

Leo

Peters successor, so he is the most sensible feeler, and most earnest, and powerfull promover and expresser, of the dignities of Saint *Peter,* of all the Fathers) speaking of Saint *Peters* Church, *Beati Petri Basilica, quæ uni Deo vero & vivo dicata est,* Saint *Peters* Church is dedicated to the onely living God; They are things compatible enough to beare the name of a Saint, and yet to be dedicated to God. There the *bodies* of the blessed *Martyrs,* did peacefully attend their glorification; There the *Histories* of the Martyrs were recited and proposed to the Congregation, for their example, and imitation; There the *names* of the Martyrs were inserted into the publique prayers, and liturgies, by way of presenting the thanks of the Congregation to *God,* for having raised so profitable men in the Church; and there the Church did present their prayers to God, for those Martyrs, that God would hasten their glory, and finall consummation, in reuniting their bodies, and soules, in a joyfull resurrection. But yet though this divers mention were made of the Saints of God, in the house of God, *Non* Augustin *Martyres ipsi, sed Deus eorum, nobis est Deus,* onely God, and not those Martyrs, is our God; we and they serve all one Master; we dwell all in one house; in which God hath appointed us severall services; Those who have done their days work, God hath given them their wages, and hath given them leave to goe to bed; they have laid down their bodies in peace to sleep there, till the Sunne rise againe; till the Sunne of grace and glory, *Christ Jesus,* appeare in judgment; we that are yet left to work, and to watch, we must goe forward in the services of God in his house, with that moderation, and that equality, as that we worship onely our Master, but yet despise not our fellow servants, that are gone before us: That we give to no person, the glory of God, but that we give God the more glory, for having raised such servants: That we acknowledge the Church to be the house *onely* of God, and that we admit no Saint, no Martyr, to be a *Iointenant* with him; but yet that their memory may be an encouragement, yea and a seale to us, that that peace, and glory, which they possesse, belongs also unto us in reversion, and that therefore we may cheerfully gratulate their present happinesse, by a devout commemoration of them, with such a temper, and evennesse, as that we neither dishonor God, by attributing to them, that which is inseparably his, nor dishonor them in taking away that which is theirs, in removing their Names out of the Collects, and prayers of the Church, or their Monuments, and memorialls out of the body of the Church: for, those respects to them, the first Christian founders of Churches did admit in those pure times, when *Illa obsequia, ornamenta memoriarum, non sacrificia* Damasc. *mortuorum,* when those devotions in their names, were onely commemorations of the dead, not sacrifices to the dead, as they are made now in the Romane Church: when *Bellarmine* will needs falsifie *Chrysotome,* to read *Adoramus monumenta,* in stead of *Adornamus;* and to make that which was but an *Adorning,* an *adoring* of the Tombes of the Martyrs.

This then was in all times, a religious work, an acceptable testimony of devotion, to build God a house; to contribute something to his outward glory. The goodnesse, and greatnesse of which work, appears evidently, and shines gloriously, even in those severall *names,* by which the Church was called, and styled, in the writings, and monuments of the Ancient Fathers, and the Ecclesiastique story. It may serve to our edification (at least) and to the exalting of our devotion, to consider some few of them: First then the Church was

Ecclesia

[Mat. 11.12]

called *Ecclesia,* that is, a company, a Congregation; That whereas from the time of *John Baptist,* the *kingdome of heaven suffers violence,* and every *violent* Man, that is, every earnest, and zealous, and spiritually valiant Man, may take hold of it, we may be much more

Tertul.

sure of doing so, in the Congregation, *Quando agmine facto Deum obsidemus,* when in the whole body, we Muster our forces, and *besiege* God. For, here in the congregation, not onely the kingdome

[Luke 17.21]

[Mat. 18.20]

of heaven, is fallen into our hands, *The kingdome of heaven is amongst you,* (as *Christ* says) but the *King* of heaven is fallen into our hands; *When two, or three are gathered together in my Name, I will be in the midst of you;* not onely in the midst of us, to encourage us, but in the midst of us, to be taken by us, to be bound by us, by those bands, those covenants, those contracts, those rich, and sweet promises, which he hath made, and ratified unto us in his Gospell.

Dominicum

A second name of the Church then in use, was *Dominicum:* The Lords possession; It is absolutely, it is intirely his; And therefore, as to shorten, and contract the possession and inheritance of God, the Church, so much, as to confine the Church onely within the obedience of *Rome,* (as the *Donatists* imprisoned it in *Afrique*) or to change the *Landmarks* of Gods possession, and inheritance, which is the Church; either to set up new works, of outward *prosperity,* or of personall, and *Locall succession* of Bishops, or to remove the old, and true marks, which are the Word, and Sacraments, as this is *Injuria Dominico mystico,* a wrong to the mysticall body of Christ, the Church, so is it *Injuria Dominico materiali,* an injury to the Materiall body of Christ sacrilegiously to dilapidate, to despoile, or to demolish the possession of the Church, and so farre to remove the marks of *Gods* inheritance, as to mingle that amongst your temporall revenues, that *God* may never have, nor ever distinguish his owne part againe.

Domus

And then (to passe faster over these names) It is called *Domus Dei,* Gods dwelling house. Now, his most glorious *Creatures* are but *vehicula Dei;* they are but chariots, which convey God, and bring him to our sight; The *Tabernacle* it selfe was but *Mobilis domus,* and *Ecclesia portatilis,* a house without a foundation; a running, a progresse house: but the Church is his standing house; there are his offices fixed: there are his provisions, which fat the Soule of Man, as with [Psal. 63.5] marrow and with fatnesse, his precious bloud, and body: there work his seales; there beats his Mint; there is absolution, and pardon for past sinnes, there is grace for prevention of future in his Sacraments. But the Church is not onely *Domus Dei,* but *Basilica;* not onely his *Basilica* house, but his Court: he doth not onely dwell there, but reigne there: which multiplies the joy of his houshold servants: *The Lord reigneth, let all the earth rejoyce, yea let the multitude of the Islands be glad thereof.* That the Church was usually called *Martyrium,* that is, a *Martyrium* place of *Confession,* where we open our wounds and receive our remedy, That it was called *Oratorium,* where we might come, and aske *Oratorium* necessary things at Gods hands, all these teach us our severall duties in that place, and they adde to their spirituall comfort, who have been Gods instruments, for providing such places, as God may be glorified in, and the godly benefited in all these ways.

But of all Names, which were then usually given to the Church, the name of *Temple* seems to be most large, and significant, as they derive it *à Tuendo;* for *Tueri* signifies both our beholding, and contemplating *God* in the Church: and it signifies Gods protecting, and defending those that are his, in his Church: *Tueri* embraces both; And therefore, though in the very beginning of the Primitive Church, to depart from the custome, and language, and phrase of the *Jews,* and *Gentiles,* as farre as they could, they did much abstain from this name of *Temple,* and of *Priest,* so that till *Ireneus* time, some *hundred eighty years after Christ,* we shall not so often find those words,

Temple, or *Priest,* yet when that danger was overcome, when the Christian Church, and doctrine was established, from that time downward, all the *Fathers* did freely, and safely call the Church the *Temple,* and the *Ministers* in the Church, *Priests,* as names of a religious, and pious signification; where before out of a loathnesse to doe, or say any thing like the *Jews,* or *Gentiles,* where a concurrence with them, might have been misinterpretable, and of ill consequence, they had called the Church by all those other names, which we passed through before; and they called their *Priests,* by the name of *Elders, Presbyteros:* but after they resumed the use of the word Temple againe, as the Apostle had given a good patterne, who to expresse the principall holinesse of the Saints of God, he chooses to 2 Cor. 6.16 doe it, in that word, *ye are the Temples of the holy Ghost:* which should encline us to that moderation, that when the danger of these ceremonies which corrupt times had corrupted, is taken away, we should returne to a love of that Antiquity, which did purely, and harmelesly induce them: when there is no danger of abuse, there should be no difference for the use of things, (in themselves indifferent) made necessary by the just commandement of lawfull authority.

Thus then you see (as farre as the narrownesse of the time will give us leave to expresse it) the generall manner of the best times, to declare devotion towards God, to have been in appropriating certaine places to his worship; And since it is so in this particular history of *Jacobs* proceeding in my text, I may be bold to invert these words of [Psal. 127.1] *David, Nisi Deus ædificaverit domum,* unlesse the Lord doe build the house, in vaine doe the labourers work, thus much, as to say, *Nisi Domino ædificaveritis domum,* except thou build a house for the Lord, in vaine dost thou goe about any other buildings, or any other businesse in this world. I speake not meerly literally of building *Materiall Chappells;* (yet I would speake also to further that;) but I speake principally of building such a Church, as every man may build in himselfe: for whensoever we present our prayers, and devotions deliberately, and advisedly to God, there we *consecrate* that place, there we build a Church. And therefore, beloved, since every master of a family, who is a *Bishop in his house,* should call his family together, to humble, and powre out their soules to God, let him consider, that when he comes to kneele at the *side of his table,* to pray, he comes to build a Church there; and therefore should sanctifie that place, with a due, and penitent consideration how voluptuously he hath formerly abused Gods blessings at that place, how superstitiously, and idolatrously he hath flatter'd and humour'd some great and usefull ghests invited by him to that place, how expensively, he hath served his owne ostentation and vain-glory, by excessive feasts at that place, whilest *Lazarus* hath lien panting, and gasping at the gate; and [Luke let him consider what a dangerous Mockery this is to Christ *Jesus,* 16.19, 20] if he pretend by kneeling at that table, fashionally to build Christ a Church by that solemnity at the table side, and then crucifie Christ again, by these sinnes, when he is sat at the table. When thou kneelest down at thy *bed side,* to shut up the day at night, or to beginne it in the morning, thy servants, thy children, thy little flock about thee, there thou buildest a Church too: And therefore sanctifie that place; wash it with thy tears, and with a repentant consideration; That in that bed thy children were conceived in sinne, that in that bed thou hast turned mariage which God afforded thee for remedy, and physique to voluptuosnesse, and licenciousnesse; That thou hast made that bed which God gave thee for rest, and for reparation of thy weary body, to be as thy dwelling, and delight, and the bed of idlenesse, and stupidity. Briefly, you that are Masters, continue in this building of Churches, that is, in drawing your families to pray, and praise God, and sanctifie those severall places of bed, and board, with a right use of them; And for you that are servants, you have also foundations of Churches in you, if you dedicate all your actions, consecrate all your services principally to God, and respectively to them, whom God hath placed over you. But principally, let all of all sorts, who present themselves at *this table,* consider, that in that receiving his body, and his bloud, every one doth as it were conceive Christ Jesus anew; Christ Jesus hath in every one of them, as it were a *new incarnation,* by uniting himselfe to them in these visible signes. And therefore let no Man come hither, without a search, and a privy search, without a consideration, and re-consideration of his conscience. Let him that beganne to think of it, but this morning, stay till the next. When *Moses* pulled his hand first out of his bosome, it was Exod. 4.6 *white* as snow, but it was *leprous;* when he pulled it the second time, it was of the color of flesh, but it was sound. When thou examinest thy conscience but once, but slightly, it may appear, white as snow, innocent; but examine it againe, and it will confesse many fleshly infirmities, and then it is the sounder for that; though not for the infirmity, yet for the confession of the infirmity. Neither let that hand, that reaches out to this body, in a guiltinesse of pollution, and uncleannesse, or in a guiltinesse of extortion, or undeserved fees, ever hope to signe a conveyance, that shall fasten his inheritance upon his children, to the third generation, ever hope to assigne a will that shall be observed after his death; ever hope to lift up it selfe for mercy to God, at his death; but his case shall be like the case of *Judas,* if the devill have put in his heart, to betray *Christ,* to make the body and bloud of Christ Jesus false witnesses to the congregation of his hypocriticall sanctity, Satan shall enter into him, with this sop, and seale his condemnation. [John 13.27] Beloved, in the bowels of that Jesus, who is coming into you, even in spirituall riches, it is an unthrifty thing, to anticipate your monies, to receive your rents, before they are due: and this treasure of the soule, the body, and bloud of your Saviour, is not due to you yet, if you have not yet passed a mature, and a severe examination, of your conscience. It were better that your particular friends, or that the congregation, should observe in you, an abstinence and forbearing to day, and make what interpretation they would, of that forbearing, then that the *holy Ghost* should deprehend you, in an unworthy receiving; lest, as the Master of the feast said to him that came without his wedding garment, then when he was set, *Amice quomodo intrâsti,* friend how came you in? [Mat. 22.11, 12] so Christ should say to thee, then when thou art upon thy knees, and hast taken him into thy hands, *Amice quomodo intrabo,* friend how can I enter into thee, who hast not swept thy house, who hast made no preparation for me? But to those that have, he knocks and he enters, and he sups with them, and he is a supper to them. [Apoc. 3.20] And so this consideration of making Churches of our houses, and of our hearts, leads us to a third part, the particular circumstances, in *Jacobs* action.

3. Part

In which there is such a change, such a dependence, whether we consider the Metall, or the fashion, the severall doctrines, or the sweetnesse, and easinesse, of raising them, as scarce in any other place, a fuller harmony.

Divisio

The first linke is the *Tunc Jacob,* then *Jacob;* which is a *Tunc consequentiæ,* rather then a *Tunc temporis;* It is not so much, at what time *Jacob* did, or said this, as upon what *occasion*. The second linke is, *Quid operatum,* what this wrought upon *Jacob;* It *awaked* him out *of his sleep;* A third is *Quid ille,* what he did, and that was, *Et dixit,* he came to an open profession of that, which he conceived, he said; and a fourth is, *Quid dixit,* what this profession was; And in that, which is a branch with much fruit, a pregnant part, a part containing many parts, thus much is considerable, that he presently acknowledged, and assented to that light which was given him, *the Lord is in this place;* And he acknowledged his owne darknesse, till that light came upon him, *Et ego nesciebam,* I knew it not; And then upon this light received, he admitted no scruple, no hesitation, but came presently to a confident assurance, *Verè Dominus,* surely, of a certainty, the Lord is in this place; And then another doctrine is, *Et timuit,* he was afraid; for all his confidence he had a reverentiall feare; not a distrust, but a reverent respect to that great Majesty; and upon this feare, there is a second *Et dixit,* he spoke againe; this feare did not stupifie him, he recovered againe and discerned the manifestation of God, in that particular place, *Quàm terribilis,* how fearfull is this place; And then the last linke of this chaine is, *Quid inde,* what was the effect of all this; and that is, that he might erect a Monument, and marke for the worship of God in this place, *Quia non nisi domus,* because this is none other then the house of God, and the gate of heaven. Now I have no purpose to make you afraid of enlarging all these points: I shall onely passe through some of them, *paraphrastically,* and trust them with the rest, (for they insinuate one another) and trust your christianly meditation with them all.

Tunc

The first linke then is, the *Tunc Jacob,* the *occasion,* (then *Jacob* did this) which was, that God had revealed to *Jacob,* that vision of the ladder, whose foot stood upon earth, and whose top reached to heaven, upon which ladder God stood, and Angels went up and down. Now this ladder is for the most part, understood to be *Christ* himselfe; whose foot, that touched the earth, is his *humanity,* and his top that reached to heaven, his *Divinity;* The ladder is Christ, and upon him the Angels, (his Ministers) labour for the edifying of the Church; And in this labour, upon this ladder, God stands above it, governing, and ordering all things, according to his providence in his

Church. Now when this was revealed to *Jacob,* now when this is revealed to you, that God hath let fall a ladder, a bridge between heaven, and earth, that Christ, whose divinity departed not from heaven, came downe to us into this world, that God the father stands upon this ladder, as the *Originall* hath it, *Nitzab,* that he leanes upon this ladder, as the *vulgar* hath it, *Innixus scalæ,* that he rests upon it, as the holy Ghost did, upon the same ladder, that is, upon Christ, in his baptisme, that upon this ladder, which stretches so farre, and is provided so well, the Angels labour, the Ministers of God doe their offices, when this was, when this is manifested, then it became *Jacob,* and now it becomes every Christian, to doe something for the advancing of the outward glory, and worship of God in his Church: when Christ is content to be this ladder, when God is content to govern this ladder, when the Angels are content to labour upon this ladder, which ladder is Christ, and the Christian Church, shall any Christian Man forbeare his help to the necessary building, and to the sober and modest adorning of the materiall Church of God? God studies the good of the Church, Angels labour for it; and shall Man, who is to receive all the profit of this, doe nothing? This is the *Tunc Jacob;* when there is *a free preaching* of the Gospell, there should be a free, and liberall disposition, to advance his house.

Quid operatum

Well; to make haste, the second linke is *Quid operatum,* what this wrought upon *Jacob:* and it is, *Jacob awoke out of his sleep.* Now in this place, the holy Ghost imputes no sinfull sleep to *Jacob;* but it is a naturall sleep of lassitude and wearinesse after his travell; there is an ill sleep, an indifferent, and a good sleep, which is that heavenly sleep, that tranquillity, which that soul, which is at peace with God, and divided from the storms, and distractions of this world, enjoys in it selfe. That peace, which made the blessed Martyrs of Christ Jesus sleep upon the rack, upon the burning coales, upon the points of swords, when the persecutors were more troubled to invent torments, then the Christians to suffer. That sleep, from which, ambition, nor danger, no nor when their own house is on fire, (that is, their own concupiscences) cannot awaken them; not so awaken them, that it can put them out of their own constancy, and peacefull confidence in God. That sleep, which is the sleep of the spouse, *Ego dormio, sed cor meum vigilat, I sleep, but my heart is awake;* It was no dead sleep

Cant. 5.[2]

when shee was able to speak advisedly in it, and say she was asleep, and what sleep it was: It was no stupid sleep, when her heart was awake. This is the sleep of the Saints of God, which Saint *Gregory* describes, *Sancti non torpore, sed virtute sopiuntur;* It is not sluggishnesse, but innocence, and a good conscience, that casts them asleep. *Laboriosiùs dormiunt,* they are busier in their sleep; nay, *Vigilantiùs dormiunt,* they are more awake in their sleep, then the watchfull men of this world; for when they close their eyes in meditation of God, even their dreames are services to him, *Somniant se dicere Psalmos,* says Saint *Ambrose;* they dream that they sing psalmes; and they doe more then dream it, they do sing.

Gregory

Ambros.

But yet even from this holy, and religious sleep (which is a departing from the allurements of the world, and a retiring to the onely contemplation of heaven, and heavenly things) *Jacob* may be conceived to have awaked, and we must awake; It is not enough to shut our selves in a cloister, in a Monastery, to sleep out the tentations of the world, but since the ladder is placed, the Church established, since God, and the Angels are awake in this businesse, in advancing the Church, we also must labour, in our severall vocations, and not content our selves with our own spirituall sleep; the peace of conscience in our selves; for we cannot have that long, if we doe not some good to others. When the storm had almost drown'd the ship, Christ was at his ease, in that storm, asleep upon a pillow. Now Christ was in no danger himself; All the water of *Noahs* flood, multiplyed over again by every drop, could not have drown'd him. All the swords of an Army could not have killed him, till the houre was come, when hee was pleased to lay down his soul. But though he were safe, yet they awaked him, and said, *Master car'st thou not though we perish?* So though a man may be in a good state, in a good peace of conscience, and sleep confidently in it, yet other mens necessities must awaken him, and though perchance he might passe more safely, if he might live a retired life, yet upon this ladder some Angels ascended, some descended, but none stood still but God himself. Till we come to him, to sleep an eternall Sabbath in heaven, though this religious sleep of enjoying or retiring and contemplation of God, be a heavenly thing, yet we must awake even out of this sleep, and contribute our paines, to the building, or furnishing, or serving of God in his Church.

Mar. 4.37 [also 38]

Quid ille dixit

Out of a sleep (conceive it what sleep soever) *Jacob* awaked; and then, *Quid ille?* what did he? *Dixit,* he spoke, he entred presently into an *open profession* of his thoughts, he smother'd nothing, he disguised nothing. God is light, and loves cleernesse; thunder, and wind, and tempests, and chariots, and roaring of Lyons, and falling of waters are the ordinary emblems of his messages, and his messengers in the Scriptures. Christ who is *Sapientia Dei,* the wisdome of God, is *Verbum, Sermo Dei,* the word of God, he is the wisdome, and the uttering of the wisdome of God, as Christ is express'd to be the word, so a Christians duty is to speak clearly, and professe his religion. [Luke 11.49] [Apoc. 19.13] With how much scorn and reproach Saint *Cyprian* fastens the name of *Libellaticos* upon them, who in time of persecution durst not say they were Christians, but under-hand compounded with the State, that they might live unquestioned, undiscovered, for though they kept their religion in their heart, yet Christ was defrauded of his honour. And such a reproach, and scorn belongs to them, who for fear of losing worldly preferments, and titles, and dignities, and rooms at great Tables, dare not say, of what religion they are. Beloved, it is not enough to awake out of an ill sleep of sinne, or of ignorance, or out of a good sleep, out of a retirednesse, and take some profession, if you winke, or hide your selves, when you are awake, you shall not see the Ladder, not discern Christ, nor the working of his Angels, that is, the Ministery of the Church, and the comforts therein, you shall not hear that Harmony of the quire of heaven, if you will bear no part in it; an inward acknowledgment of Christ is not enough, if you forbear to professe him, where your testimony might glorify him. Chrys. *Si sufficeret fides cordis, non creasset tibi Deus os,* If the heart were enough, God would never have made a mouth; And to that, we may adde, *Si sufficeret os, non creasset manus,* if the mouth were enough, God would never have made hands; for as the same Father says, *Omni tuba clarior est per opera demonstratio,* no voice more audible, none more credible, then when thy *hands* speak as well as thy heart or thy tongue; Thou are then perfectly awaked out of thy sleep, when thy words and works declare, and manifest it.

Quid

The next is, *Quid dixit;* he spake, but what said he? first, he assented to that light which was given him, *The Lord is in this place.* He resisted not this light, he went not about to blow it out, by admitting reason, or disputation against it. He imputed it not to witchcraft, to illusion of the Devill; but *Dominus est in loco isto,* The Lord is in this place; O how many heavy sinnes, how many condemnations might we avoid, if wee would but take knowledge of this, *Dominus in loco isto,* That the Lord is present, and sees us now, and shall judge hereafter, all that we doe, or think. It keeps a man sometimes from corrupting, or soliciting a woman, to say, *Pater, Maritus in loco,* the Father, or the Husband is present; it keeps a man from an usurious contract to say, *Lex in loco,* the Law will take knowledge of it; it keeps a man from slandering or calumniating another, to say, *Testis in loco,* here is a witnesse by; but this is *Catholica Medicina,* and *Omnimorbia,* an universall medicine for all, to say, *Dominus in loco,* The Lord is in this place, and sees, and heares, and therefore I will say, and think, and do, as if I were now summon'd by the last Trumpet, to give an account of my thoughts, and words, and deeds to him.

But the Lord was there and *Jacob knew it not.* As he takes knowledge by the first light of Gods presence, so he acknowledges that he had none of this light, of himself, *Ego nesciebam, Jacob* a Patriarch and dearly beloved of God, knew not that God was so near him. How much lesse shall a sinfull man, that multiplies sinnes, like clouds between God and him, know, that God is near him? As Saint *Augustine* said, when hee came out of curiosity to hear Saint *Ambrose* preach at *Milan,* without any desire of profiting thereby, *Appropinquavi, & nesciebam,* I came neer God, but knew it not; So the customary and habituall sinners, may say, *Elongavi, & nesciebam,* I have eloyn'd my selfe, I have gone farther, and farther from my God, and was never sensible of it; It is a desperate ignorance, not to bee sensible of Gods absence; but to acknowledge with *Jacob,* that we cannot see light, but by that light, that we cannot know Gods presence but by his revealing of himself, is a religious, and a Christian humility. To know it by *Reason,* by *Philosophy,* is a dimme and a faint knowledge, but onely by the testimony of his own spirit, and his own revealing, we come to that confidence, *Verè Domine,* Surely the Lord is in this place.

Nesciebam

Verè

Est apud malos, sed dissimulans, God is with the wicked, but he dissembles his beeing there, that is, conceals it; he will not be known

Bern.

of it; *Et ibi, malorum dissimulatio quodammodo Veritas non est,* when God winks at mens sinnes, when he dissembles, or disguises his knowledge we may almost say, says Saint *Bernard, Veritas non est,* Here is not direct dealing, here is not intire truth, his presence is scarce a true presence. And therefore as the same Father proceeds, *Si dicere licet,* if we may be bold to expresse it so, *Apud impios est, sed in dissimulatione,* he is with the wicked, but yet he dissembles, he disguises his presence, he is there to no purpose, to no profit of theirs; but *Est apud justos in veritate,* with the righteous he is in truth, and in clearnesse. *Est apud Angelos in fœlicitate,* with the Angels and Saints in heaven, he is in an established happinesse; *Est apud inferos in feritate,* he is in Hell in his fury, in an irrevocable, and undeterminable execution of his severity: God was surely, and truly with *Jacob,* and with all them, who are sensible of his approaches, and of his gracious manifestation of himself. Idem *Verè non erat apud eos quibus dixit, quid vocatis me Dominum, & non facitis quæ dixi vobis?* God is not truly with them, whom he rebukes, saying; *Why call ye me Lord, and do not my commandements?* but Idem *ubi in ejus nomine Angeli simul & homines congregantur,* When Angels and men, Priests and people, the Preacher and the congregation labour together upon this Ladder, study the advancing of his Church (as by the working of Gods gratious Spirit we doe at this time) *Ibi verè est & ibi verè Dominus est, surely* he is in this place, and *surely* he is Lord in this place, he possesses, he fills us all, he governs us all: and as, though we say to him, *Our Father which art in heaven,* yet we beleeve that he is within these walls, so though we say *Adveniat regnum tuum,* thy kingdome come, we beleeve that his kingdome is come, and is amongst us in *grace* now, as it shall be in *glory* hereafter.

Timuit When he was now throughly awake, when he was come to an open profession, when he acknowledged himselfe to stand in the sight of God, when he confessed his owne ignorance of Gods presence, and when after all he was come to a setled confidence, *Verè Dominus,* surely the Lord is here, yet it is added, *Et timuit,* and he was afraid. No man may thinke himselfe to bee come to that familiar acquaintance with God, as that it should take away that reverentiall feare which belongs to so high and supreme a Majesty. Iudg. 13.[6] When the Angell appeared to the wife of *Manoah,* foretelling *Samsons* birth, she says to her husband, the fashion of him was like the fashion of the Angell of God; what's that? *Exceeding fearfull.* When God appears to thy soule, even in mercy, in the forgivenes of thy sins, yet there belongs a fear even to this apprehension of mercy: Not a fearfull *diffidence,* not a distrust, but a fearfull *consideration,* of that height, and depth; what a high Majesty thou hast offended, what a desperate depth thou wast falling into, what a fearfull thing it had been, to have fallen into the hands of the living God, [Heb. 10.31] and what an irrecoverable wretch thou hadst been, if God had not manifested himselfe, to have been in that place, with thee. And therefore though he have appeared unto thee in mercy, yet be afraid, lest he goe away againe; As *Manoah* prayed, and said, [Judges 13.8] I beseech thee my Lord, *let the Man of God, whom thou sentest, come againe unto us, and teach us, what we shall doe with the child, when he is born,* so when God hath once appeared to thy soul in mercy, pray him to come again, and tell thee what thou shouldest doe with that mercy, how thou shouldest husband those first degrees of grace and of comfort, to the farther benefit of thy soule, and the farther glory of his name, and be afraid that thy dead flyes may putrefie his ointment; those reliques of sinne, (though the body of sinne, be crucified in thee) which are left in thee, may overcome his graces: for upon those words, Iob 4.14 *Pavor tenuit me & tremor, & omnia ossa mea perterrita sunt,* feare came upon me, and trembling, which made all my bones to shake, Saint *Gregory* says well, Gregory *Quid per ossa nisi fortia acta designantur,* our good deeds, our strongest works and those which were done in the best strength of grace, are meant by our bones, and yet *ossa perterrita* our strongest works tremble at the presence and examination of God. And therefore to the like purpose (upon those words of the *Psalme*) Psalm. 35.10 the same Father says, *Omnia ossa mea dicent, Domine quis similis tibi,* all my bones say, Lord who is like unto thee? *Carnes meæ, verba non habent,* (my fleshly parts, my *carnall affections*) *Infirma mea funditus silent,* my sinnes, or my infirmities dare not speak at all, not appear at all, *Sed ossa mea, quæ fortia credidi, sua consideratione tremiscunt,* my very bones shake, there is no degree, no state neither of innocence, nor of repentance, nor of faith, nor of sanctification, above that fear of God: and he is least acquainted with God, who thinks that he is so familiar, that he need not stand in feare of him.

[*Et dixit*] But this fear hath no ill effect. It brings him to a second profession, *Et dixit;* and he spoke againe. He waked, and then he spoke, as soon as he came out of ignorance; He was afraid, and then he spoke againe that he might have an increase of grace. The earth stands still: and [Bern.] earthly Men may be content to doe so: but he whose conversation is in heaven, is as the heavens are in continuall progresse. For *Inter profectum, & defectum, medium in hac vita non datur.* A Christian is always in a proficiency, or deficiency: If he goe not forward, he goes backward. *Nemo dicat, satis est, sic manere volo;* Let no man say, I have done enough, I have made my profession already, I have been catechiz'd, I have been thought fit to receive the Communion, *sufficit mihi esse sicut heri & nudiustertius;* though he be in the way, in the Church, yet he sleeps in the way, he is got no farther in the way, then [Idem] his godfathers carried him in their armes, to engraffe him in the Church by Baptisme: for this man, says he, *In via residet, in scala subsistit, quod nemo angelorum fecit,* he *stands still* upon the ladder, [Luke 2.52] and so did none of the Angels. Christ himself, *increased* in wisdome, and in stature, and in favour with God, and Man; so must a Christian also labour to grow and to encrease, by speaking and speaking again, by asking more, and more questions, and by farther, and farther informing his understanding, and enlightening his faith; *pertransiit* [Acts 10.38] *benefaciendo, & sanavit omnes,* says Saint *Peter* of Christ; *He went about doing good, and healing all that were oppressed of the Devill;* [Psal. 19.[5]] and it was prophesied of him, *Exultavit ut Gigas ad currendam viam,* He went forth as a Gyant, to run a race; If it be Christs pace, it must be a Christians pace too. *Currentem non apprehendit, nisi qui &* [Bern.] *pariter currit;* There is no overtaking of him that runnes, without running too. *Quid prodest Christum sequi, si non consequamur?* and to what purpose do we follow Christ, if not to overtake him, and lay [[1 Cor. 9.24]] hold upon him? *Sic currite, ut comprehendatis, fige Christiane cursus & profectus metam ubi Christus suum;* runne so as ye may obtain; and if thou beest a Christian, propose the same end of thy [[Phil. 2.8]] course, as Christ did; *factus est obediens usque ad mortem;* and the end of his course was, to be obedient unto death.

Speak then, and talke continually of the name, and the goodnesse of God; speak again, and again; It is no tautology, no babling, to speak, and iterate his prayses: Who accuses Saint *Paul* for repeating the sweet name of Jesus so very many times in his Epistles? Who accuses *David* for repeating the same phrase, the same sentence [*for his mercy endureth for ever*] so many times, as he doth in his *Psalms?* nay, the one hundred and nineteenth Psalm is scarce any thing else, then an often repetition of the same thing. *Thou spokest assoon as thou wast awake, assoon as thou wast born, thou spokest in Baptism.* So proceed to the farther knowledge of Religion, and the mysteries of Gods service in his house; and conceive a fearfull reverence of them in their institution, and speak again, enquire what they mean, what they signify, what they exhibit to thee. Conceive a reverence of them, first, out of the authority that hath instituted them, and then speak, and inform thy self of them. God spent a whole week in speaking for thy good; *Dixit Deus, God spake that there might be light, Dixit Deus, God spake that there might be a firmament;* [Gen. 1.3, 6] for immediately upon Gods speaking, the work follow'd: *Dixit & factum,* he spake the word, *and the world was created.* As God did, a godly man shall do; If he delight to talk of God, to mention often upon all occasions, the greatnesse, and goodnesse of God, to prefer that discourse, before obscene, and scurrile, and licentious, and profane, and defamatory, and ridiculous, and frivolous talke; If he delight in professing God with his tongue, out of the abundance of his heart, his works shall follow his words, he will do as he says. If God had given over, when he had spake of Light, and a Firmament, and Earth, and Sea, and had not continued speaking till the last day, when he made thee, what hadst thou got by all that? what hadst thou been at all for all that? If thou canst speak when thou awakest, when thou beginnest to have an apprehension of Gods presence, in a remorse, if then, that presence, and Majesty of God, make thee afraid, with the horrour and greatnesse of thy sinnes, if thou canst not speak again then, not goe forward with thy repentance, thy former speech is forgotten by God, and unprofitable to thee. *Jacob* at first speaking confessed God to be in that place; but so he might be every where; but he conceived a reverentiall fear at his presence; and then he came to speak the second time, to professe, that that was none other *but the house of God, and the gate of heaven;* that there was an entrance for him in particular, a fit place for him to testifie and exercise his Devotion; he came to see, what it was fit for him to doe, towards the advancing of Gods house.

Domus

Now whensoever a man is proceeded so far with *Jacob,* first to sleep, to be at peace with God, and then to wake, to doe something for the good of others, and then to speak, to make profession, to publish his sense of Gods presence, and then to attribute all this onely to the Light of God himself, by which light he grows from faith to faith, and from grace to grace, whosoever is in this disposition, he may say in all places, and in all his actions, *This is none other but the house of God, and this is the gate of heaven.* He shall see heaven open, and dwell with him, in all his undertakings: and particularly, and principally in his expressing of a care, and respect, both to Christs Mysticall, and to his materiall body; both to the sustentation of the poor, and to the building up of Gods house. In both which kinds of Piety, and Devotion, [Psal. 115.1] (*non nobis Domine, non nobis, sed nomini tuo da gloriam; Not unto us O Lord, not unto us, but unto thy Name be given the glory;*) As to the confusion of those shamelesse slanderers, who place their salvation in works, and accuse us to avert men from good works, there have been in this Kingdome, since the blessed reformation of Religion, more publick charitable works perform'd, more *Hospitals* and *Colleges* erected, and endowed in threescore, then in some hundreds of years, of superstition before, so may God be pleased to adde one example more amongst us, that here in this place, we may have some occasion to say, of a house erected, and dedicated to his service, *This is none other but the house of God,* and *this is the gate of heaven:* and may he vouchsafe to accept at our hands, in our intention, and in our endevour to consummate that purpose of ours, that thanksgiving, that acclamation which he received from his Royall servant *Salomon,* at the Consecration of his great Temple, when he said, 1 Reg. 8.27 Is it *true indeed, that God will dwell on the earth? Behold, the heavens, and the heaven of heavens are not able to contain thee, how much more unable shall this house bee, that we intend to build? But have thou respect unto the prayer of thy servant, and to his supplication, O Lord, my God, to hear the cry and the prayer that thy servant shall make before thee that day; That thine eye may bee open towards that house night and day, that thou mayst heare the supplications of thy servants, and of thy people, which shall pray in that place, and that thou mayst hear them in the place of thy habitation even in heaven, and when thou hearest, mayst have mercy.* Amen.

Number 11.

A Sermon of Valediction at my going into Germany, at Lincolns-Inne, April 18. 1619.

ECCLESIAST. 12.1. *REMEMBER NOW THY CREATOR IN THE DAYES OF THY YOUTH.*

WEE may consider two great virtues, one for the society of this life, Thankfulness, and the other for attaining the next life, Repentance; as the two pretious Mettles, Silver and Gold: Of Silver (of the virtue of thankfulness) there are whole Mines, books written by Philosophers, and a man may grow rich in that mettle, in that virtue, by digging in that Mine, in the Precepts of moral men; of this Gold (this virtue of Repentance) there is no Mine in the Earth; in the books of Philosophers, no doctrine of Repentance; this Gold is for the most part in the washes; this Repentance in matters of tribulation; but God directs thee to it in this Text, before thou come to those waters of Tribulation, remember now thy Creator before those evill dayes come, and then thou wilt repent the not remembring him till now. Here then the holy-Ghost takes the neerest way to bring a man to God, by awaking his memory; for, for the understanding, that requires long and cleer instruction; and the will requires an instructed understanding before, and is in it self the blindest and boldest faculty; but if the memory doe but fasten upon any of those things which God hath done for us, it is the neerest way to him. Remember therefore, and remember now, though the Memory be placed in the hindermost part of the brain, defer not thou thy remembring to the hindermost part of thy life, but doe that now *in die,* in the day, whil'st thou hast light, now *in diebus,* in the days, whilst God presents thee many lights, many means; and *in diebus juventutis,* in the days of thy youth, of strength, whilst thou art able

Divisio

to doe that which thou purposest to thy self; And as the word imports, *Bechurotheica, in diebus Electionum tuarum,* in the dayes of thy choice, whilst thou art able to make thy choyce, whilst the Grace of God shines so brightly upon thee, as that thou maist choose the way, and so powerfully upon thee, as that thou maist walke in that way. Now, *in this day,* and *in these dayes* Remember first the Creator, That all these things which thou laborest for, and delightest in, were created, made of nothing; and therfore thy memory looks not far enough back, if it stick only upon the Creature, and reach not to the Creator, Remember the Creator, and remember thy Creator; and in that, first that he made thee, and then what he made thee; He made thee of nothing, but of that nothing he hath made thee such a thing as cannot return to nothing, but must remain for ever; whether happy or miserable, that depends upon thy *Remembring thy Creator now in the dayes of thy youth.*

Memento

Gen. 8.1

say 49.15

First *remember;* which word is often used in the Scripture for considering and taking care: for, God remembred *Noah* and every beast with him in the Ark; as the word which is contrary to that, forgetting, is also for the affection contrary to it, it is neglecting, *Can a woman forget her child, and not have compassion on the son of her womb?* But here we take not remembring so largly, but restrain it to the exercise of that one faculty, the memory; for it is *Stomachus animæ.* The memory, sayes St. *Bernard,* is the stomach of the soul, it receives and digests, and turns into good blood, all the benefits formerly exhibited to us in particular, and exhibited to the whole Church of God: present that which belongs to the understanding, to that faculty, and the understanding is not presently setled in it; present any of the prophecies made in the captivity, and a Jews understanding takes them for deliverances from *Babylon,* and a Christians understanding takes them for deliverances from sin and death, by the Messias Christ Jesus; present any of the prophecies of the Revelation concerning Antichrist, and a Papist will understand it of a single, and momentane, and transitory man, that must last but three yeer and a half; and a Protestant may understand it of a succession of men, that have lasted so 1000. yeers already: present but the name of Bishop or of elder, out of the Acts of the Apostle[s], or their Epistles, and other men will take it for a name of equality, and parity, and we for a name and office of distinction in the Hierarchy of Gods Church. Thus it is in the understanding that's often perplexed; consider the other faculty, the will of man, by those bitternesses which have passed between the Jesuits and the Dominicans, (amongst other things belonging to the will) whether the same proportion of grace, offered to men alike disposed, must necessarily work alike upon both their wills? And amongst persons neerer to us, whether that proportion of grace, which doth convert a man, might not have been resisted by perversness of his will? By all these difficulties we may see, how untractable, and untameable a faculty the wil of man is. But come not with matter of law, but matter of fact, *Let God make his wonderful works to be* Psal. 111.4 *had in remembrance:* present the history of Gods protection of his children, from the beginning, in the ark, in both captivities, in infinite dangers; present this to the memory, and howsoever the understanding be beclouded, or the will perverted, yet both Jew and Christian, Papist and Protestant, Puritan and Protestant, are affected with a thankfull acknowledgment of his former mercies and benefits, this issue of that faculty of their memory is alike in them all: And therefore God in giving the law, works upon no other faculty but this, *I am the Lord thy God which brought thee out of the land of* Exod. 20.[2] *Egypt;* He only presents to their memory what he had done for them. And so in delivering the Gospel in one principal seal thereof, the sacrament of his body, he recommended it only to their memory, *Do* [1 Cor. *this in remembrance of me.* 11.24] This is the faculty that God desires to work upon; And therefore if thine understanding cannot reconcile differences in all Churches, if thy will cannot submit it self to the ordinances of thine own Church, go to thine own memory; for as St. *Bernard* calls that the stomach of the soul, we may be bold to call it the Gallery of the soul, hang'd with so many, and so lively pictures of the goodness and mercies of thy God to thee, as that every one of them shall be a catachism to thee, to instruct thee in all thy duties to him for those mercies: And as a well made, and well plac'd picture, looks alwayes upon him that looks upon it; so shall thy God look upon thee, whose memory is thus contemplating him, and shine upon thine understanding, and rectifie thy will too. If thy memory cannot comprehend his mercy at large shewed to his whole Church, (as it is almost an incomprehensible thing, that in so few yeers he made us of the Reformation, equall even in number to our adversaries of the Roman Church,) If thy memory have not held that picture of our general deliverance from the Navy; (if that mercy be written in the water and in the sands, where it was perform'd, and not in thy heart) if thou remember not our deliverance from that artificiall Hell, the Vault, (in which, though his instruments failed of their plot, they did not blow us up; yet the Devil goes forward with his plot, if ever he can blow out; if he can get that deliverance to be forgotten.) If these be too large pictures for thy gallery, for thy memory, yet every man hath a pocket picture about him, a manuall, a bosome book, and if he will turn over but one leaf, and remember what God hath done for him even since yesterday, he shall find even by that little branch a navigable river, to sail into that great and endless Sea of Gods mercies towards him, from the beginning of his being.

Nunc

Jam. 1.18

Do but remember, but remember now: Of his own wil begat he us with the word of truth, that we should be as the first fruits of his creatures: That as we consecrate all his creatures to him, in a sober, and religious use of them, so as the first fruits of all, we should principally consecrate our selves to his service betimes. Now there were three payments of first fruits appointed by God to the Jews: The first was, *Primitiæ Spicarum,* of their Ears of Corn, and this was early about *Easter;* The second was *Primitiæ panum,* of Loaves of Bread, after their corn was converted to that use; and this, though it were not so soon, yet it was early too, about *Whitsontide;* The third was *Primitiæ frugum,* of all their Fruits and Revenues; but this was very late in *Autumn,* at the fall of the leaf, in the end of the yeer. The two first of these, which were offered early, were offered partly to God, and partly to Man, to the Priest; but in the last, which came late, God had no part: He had his part in the corn, and in the loaves, but none in the latter fruits. Offer thy self to God; first, as *Primitias spicarum,* (whether thou glean in the world, or bind up whole sheaves, whether thy increase be by little and little, or apace;) And offer thy self, as *primitias panum,* (when thou hast kneaded up riches, and honor, and favour in a setled and established fortune) offer at thy *Easter,* whensoever thou hast any resurrection, any sense of raising thy soul from the shadow of death; offer at thy Pentecost, when the holy Ghost visits thee, and descends upon thee in a fiery tongue, and melts thy bowels by the power of his word; for if thou defer thy offering til thy fal, til thy winter, til thy death, howsoever they may be thy first fruits, because they be the first that ever thou gavest, yet they are such, as are not acceptable to God; God hath no portion in them, if they be not offered til then; offer thy self now; for that's an easie request; yea offer to thy self now, that's more easie; *Viximus mundo; vivamus reliquum nobis ipsis;* Thus long we have Basil served the world; let us serve our selves the rest of our time, that is, the best part of our selves, our souls. *Expectas ut febris te vocet ad* Idem *pœnitentiam?* Hadst thou rather a sickness should bring thee to God, than a sermon? hadst thou rather be beholden to a Physitian for thy salvation, than to a Preacher? thy business is to remember; stay not for thy last sickness, which may be a Lethargy in which thou mayest forget thine own name, and his that gave thee the name of a Christian, Christ Jesus himself: thy business is to remember, and thy time is now; stay not till that Angel come which shall say and swear, that Apo. 10.6 time shall be no more.

In Die

Remember then, and remember now; *In Die,* in the day; The Lord will hear us *In die qua invocaverimus,* in the day that we shall call Ps. 19.10 [Vulg. numbering] upon him; and *in quacunque die,* in what day soever we call, and *in quacunque die velociter exaudiet,* as soon as we call in any day. But all this is *Opus diei,* a work for the day; for in the night, in our last Ps. 138.3 night, those thoughts that fall upon us, they are rather dreams, then Ps. 102.2 true remembrings; we do rather dream that we repent, then repent indeed, upon our death-bed. To him that travails by night a bush seems a tree, and a tree seems a man, and a man a spirit; nothing hath the true shape to him; to him that repents by night, on his death-bed, neither his own sins, nor the mercies of God have their true proportion. Fool, saies Christ, this night they will fetch away thy soul; but he neither tels him, who they be that shall fetch it, nor whether they shall carry it; he hath no light but lightnings; a sodain flash of horror first, and then he goes into fire without light. *Numquid Deus* Chrysosto. *nobis ignem paravit? non, sed Diabolo, et Angelis:* did God ordain hell fire for us? no, but for the Devil, and his Angels. And yet we that are vessels so broken, as that there is not a sheard left, to fetch water Esa. 30.[14] at the pit, that is, no means in our selves, to derive one drop of Christs blood upon us, nor to wring out one tear of true repentance from us, have plung'd our selves into this everlasting, and this dark fire, which was not prepared for us: A wretched covetousness, to be intruders upon the Devil; a wretched ambition, to be usurpers upon damnation. God did not make the fire for us; but much less did he make us for that fire; that is, make us to damn us. But now the Judgment is [Mat. 25.41] given, *Ite maledicti*, go ye accursed; but yet this is the way of Gods justice, and his proceeding, that his Judgments are not alwaies executed, though they be given. The Judgments and Sentences of Medes and Persians are irrevocable, but the Judgments and Sentences of God, if they be given, if they be published, they are not executed. The Ninevites had perished, if the sentence of their destruction had not been given; and the sentence preserv'd them; so even in this cloud of *Ite maledicti,* go ye accursed, we may see the day break, and discern beams of saving light, even in this Judgment of eternal darkness; if the contemplation of his Judgment brings us to remember him in that day, in the light and apprehension of his anger and correction.

In Diebus For this circumstance is enlarged; it is not *in die,* but *in diebus,* not in one, but in many dayes; for God affords us many dayes, many lights to see and remember him by. This remembrance of God is our regeneration, by which we are new creatures; and therefore we may consider as many dayes in it, as in the first creation. The first day was the making of light; and our first day is the knowledg of him, who [John 8.12; 9.5] saies of himself, *ego sum lux mundi,* I am the light of the world, and of whom St. *John* testifies, *Erat lux vera,* he was the true light, that Joh. 1.[9] lighteth every man into the world. This is then our first day the true profession of Christ Jesus. God made light first, that the other creatures Ambro. might be seen; *Frustra essent si non viderentur,* It had been to no purpose to have made creatures, if there had been no light to manifest them. Our first day is the light and love of the Gospel; for the noblest creatures of Princes, (that is, the noblest actions of Princes, war, and peace, and treaties) *frustra sunt,* they are good for nothing, they are nothing, if they be not shew'd and tried by this light, by the love and preservation of the Gospel of Christ Jesus: God made light first, that his other works might appear, and he made light first, that himself (for our example) might do all his other works in the light: that we also, as we had that light shed upon us in our baptism, so we might make all our future actions justifiable by that light, and not *Erubes-*

cere Evangelium, not be ashamed of being too jealous in this profession of his truth. Then God saw that the light was good: the seeing implies a consideration; that so a religion be not accepted blindly, nor implicitly; and the seeing it to be good implies an election of that religion, which is simply good in it self, and not good by reason of advantage, or conveniency, or other collateral and by-respects. And when God had seen the light, and seen that it was good, then he severed light from darkness; and he severed them, *non tanquam duo positiva,* not as two essential, and positive, and equal things; not so, as that a brighter and a darker religion, (a good and a bad) should both have a beeing together, but *tanquam positivum et primitivum,* light and darkness are primitive, and positive, and figure this rather, that a true religion should be established, and continue, and darkness utterly removed; and then, and not till then, (till this was done, light severed from darkness) there was a day; And since God hath given us this day, the brightness of his Gospel, that this light is first presented, that is, all great actions begun with this consideration of the Gospel; since all other things are made by this light, that is, all have relation to the continuance of the Gospel, since God hath given us such a head, as is sharp-sighted in seeing the several lights, wise in discerning the true light, powerful in resisting forraign darkness; since God hath given us this day, *qui non humiliabit animam suam in die hac,* as *Moses* speaks of the dayes of Gods institution, he that will not remember God now in this day, is impious to him, and unthankful to that great instrument of his, by whom this day spring from on high hath visited us.

Levit. 23.[29]

To make shorter dayes of the rest, (for we must pass through all the six dayes in a few minuts) God in the second day made the firmament to divide between the waters above, and the waters below; and this firmament in us, is *terminus cognoscibilium,* the limits of those things which God hath given man means and faculties to conceive, and understand: he hath limited our eyes with a firmament beset with stars, our eyes can see no farther: he hath limited our understanding in matters of religion with a starry firmament too; that is, with the knowledg of those things, *quæ ubique, quæ semper,* which those stars which he hath kindled in his Church, the Fathers and Doctors, have ever from the beginning proposed as things necessary to be explicitely believ'd, for the salvation of our souls; for the eternal decrees of God, and his unreveal'd mysteries, and the inextricable perplexities of the School, they are waters above the firmament: here [1 Cor. 3.6] *Paul* plants, and here *Apollo* waters; here God raises up men to convey to us the dew of his grace, by waters under the firmament; by visible sacraments, and by the word so preach'd, and so interpreted, as it hath been constantly, and unanimously from the beginning of the Church. And therefore this second day is perfited in the third, in the *congregentur aquæ,* let the waters be gathered together; God hath gathered all the waters, all the waters of life in one place; that is, all the doctrine necessary for the life to come, into his Church: And then *producet terra,* here in this world are produced to us all herbs and fruits, all that is necessary for the soul to feed upon. And in this third daies work God repeats here that testimony, *vidit quod bonum,* he saw that it was good; good, that here should be a gathering of waters in one place, that is, no doctrine receiv'd that had not been taught in the Church; and *vidit quod bonum,* he saw it was good, that all herbs and trees should be produced that bore seed; all doctrines that were to be proseminated and propagated, and to be continued to the end, should be taught in the Church: but for doctrines which were but to vent the passion of vehement men, or to serve the turns of great men for a time, which were not seminal doctrines, doctrines that bore seed, and were to last from the beginning to the end; for these interlineary doctrines, and marginal, which were no part of the first text, here's no testimony that God sees that they are good. And, *In diebus istis,* if in these two daies, the day when God makes thee a firmament, shewes thee what thou art, to limit thine understanding and thy faith upon, and the day where God makes thee a sea, a collection of the waters, (showes thee where these necessary things must be taught in the Church) if in those daies thou wilt not remember thy Creator, it is an irrecoverable Lethargy.

In the fourth daies work, let the making of the Sun to rule the day be the testimony of Gods love to thee, in the sunshine of temporal prosperity, and the making of the Moon to shine by night, be the refreshing of his comfortable promises in the darkness of adversity; Amos [8.9] and then remember that he can make thy sun to set at noon, he can blow out thy taper of prosperity when it burns brightest, and he can turn the Moon into blood, he can make all the promises of the Gospel, [Act. 2.20] which should comfort thee in adversity, turn into despair and obduration. Let the fift daies work, which was the creation *Omnium reptibilium,* and *omnium volatilium,* of all creeping things, and of all flying things, produc'd out of water, signifie and denote to thee, either thy humble devotion, in which thou saist of thy self to God, *vermis* [Psal. 22.6] *ego et non homo,* I am a worm and no man; or let it be the raising of thy soul in that, *pennas columbæ dedisti,* [Psal. 55.6] that God hath given thee the wings of a dove to fly to the wilderness, in a retiring from, or a resisting of tentations of this world; remember still that God can suffer even thy humility to stray, and degenerate into an uncomly dejection and stupidity, and senselesness of the true dignity and true liberty of a Christian: and he can suffer this retiring thy self from the world, to degenerate into a contempt and despising of others, and an overvaluing of thine own perfections. Let the last day in which both man and beasts were made out of the earth, but yet a living soul breath'd into man, remember thee that this earth which treads upon thee, must return to that earth which thou treadst upon; thy body, that loads thee, and oppresses thee to the grave, and thy spirit to him that gave it. And when the Sabbath day hath also remembered thee, that God hath given thee a temporal Sabbath, plac'd thee in a land of peace, and an ecclesiastical Sabbath, plac'd in a Church of peace, perfect all in a spirituall Sabbath, a conscience of peace, by remembring now thy Creator, at least in one of these daies of the week of thy regeneration, either as thou hast light created in thee, in the first day, that is, thy knowledg of Christ; or as thou hast a firmament created in thee the second day, that is, thy knowledg what to seek concerning Christ, things appertaining to faith and salvation; or as thou hast a sea created in thee the third day, that is, a Church where all the knowledg is reserv'd and presented to thee; or as thou hast a sun and moon in the fourth day, thankfulness in prosperity, comfort in adversity, or as thou hast *reptilem humilitatem,* or *volatilem fiduciam,* a humiliation in thy self, or an exaltation in Christ in thy fift day, or as thou hast a contemplation of thy mortality and immortality in the sixth day, or a desire of a spiritual Sabbath in the seaventh, In those daies remember thou thy Creator.

Now all these daies are contracted into less room in this text, *In*

Juventutis *diebus Bechurotheica,* is either, *in the daies of thy youth,* or *electionum tuarum,* in the daies of thy hearts desire, when thou enjoyest all that thou couldest wish. First, therefore if thou wouldest be heard Ps. 25.7 in *Davids* prayer; *Delicta juventutis;* O Lord remember not the sins of my youth; remember to come to this prayer, *In diebus juventutis,* [Job] 29.4 in the dayes of thy youth. *Job* remembers with much sorrow, how he was in the dayes of his youth, when Gods providence was upon his Tabernacle: and it is a late, but a sad consideration, to remember with what tenderness of conscience, what scruples, what remorces we entred into sins in our youth, how much we were afraid of all degrees and circumstances of sin for a little while, and how indifferent things they are grown to us, and how obdurate we are grown in them now. [Tobit] 1.4 This was *Jobs* sorrow, and this was *Tobias* comfort, when I was but young, all my Tribes fell away; but I alone went after to *Jerusalem*. Though he lacked the counsail, and the example of his Elders, yet he Thren. 3.27 served God; for it is good for a man, that he bear his yoke in his youth: For even when God had delivered over his people purposely Esa. 47.6 to be afflicted, yet himself complains in their behalf, *That the persecutor laid the very heaviest yoke upon the ancient:* It is a lamentable Basil thing to fall under a necessity of suffering in our age. *Labore fracta instrumenta, ad Deum ducis, quorum nullus usus?* wouldest thou consecrate a Chalice to God that is broken? no man would present a Aug. lame horse, a disordered clock, a torn book to the King. *Caro jumentum,* thy body is thy beast; and wilt thou present that to God, when it is lam'd and tir'd with excesse of wantonness? when thy clock, (the whole course of thy time) is disordered with passions, and perturbations; when thy book (the history of thy life,) is torn, 1000. sins of thine own torn out of thy memory, wilt thou then present Basil thy self thus defac'd and mangled to almighty God? *Temperantia non est temperantia in senectute, sed impotentia incontinentiæ,* chastity is not chastity in an old man, but a disability to be unchast; and therefore thou dost not give God that which thou pretendest to give, for thou hast no chastity to give him. *Senex bis puer,* but it is not *bis juvenis;* an old man comes to the infirmities of childhood again; but he comes not to the strength of youth again.

Electionum Do this then *In diebus juventutis,* in thy best strength, and when thy natural faculties are best able to concur with grace; but do it

In diebus electionum, in the dayes when thou hast thy hearts desire; for if thou have worn out this word, in one sense, that it be too late now, *to remember him in the dayes of youth,* (that's spent forgetfully) yet as long as thou art able to make a new choise, to chuse a new sin, that when thy heats of youth are not overcome, but burnt out, then thy middle age chooses ambition, and thy old age chooses covetousness; as long as thou art able to make thy choice thou art able to make a better than this; God testifies that power, that he hath given thee; *I call heaven and earth to record this day, that I have set* Deut. 30.19 *before you life and death; choose life:* If this choice like you not, *If* Jos. 24.15 *it seem evil unto you to serve the Lord,* saith *Josuah* then, *choose ye this day whom ye will serve.* Here's the election day; bring that which ye would have, into comparison with that which ye should have; that is, all that this world keeps from you, with that which God offers to you; and what will ye choose to prefer before him? for honor, and favor, and health, and riches, perchance you cannot have them though you choose them; but can you have more of them than they have had, to whom those very things have been occasions of ruin? The Market is open till the bell ring; till thy last bell ring the Church is open, grace is to be had there: but trust not upon that rule, that men buy cheapest at the end of the market, that heaven may be had for a breath at last, when they that hear it cannot tel whether it be a sigh or a gasp, a religious breathing and anhelation after the next life, or natural breathing out, and exhalation of this; but find a spiritual good husbandry in that other rule, that the prime of the market is to be had at first: for howsoever, in thine age, there may be by Gods strong working, *Dies juventutis,* A day of youth, in making thee then a new creature; (for as God is *antiquissimus dierum,* so in his school no man [Dan. 7.9, is super-annated,) yet when age hath made a man impotent to sin, 13, 22] this is not *Dies electionum,* it is not a day of choice; but remember God now, when thou hast a choice, that is, a power to advance thy self, or to oppress others by evil means; now *in die electionum,* in those thy happy and sun-shine dayes, *remember him.*

This is then the faculty that is excited, the memory; and this is the *Creatorem* time, now, now whilest ye have power of election: The object is, the Creator, *Remember the Creator:* First, because the memory can go no farther then the creation; and therefore we have no means to conceive, or apprehend any thing of God before that. When men therefore speak of decrees of reprobation, decrees of condemnation, before decrees of creation; this is beyond the counsail of the holy Ghost here, *Memento creatoris,* Remember the Creator, for this is to remember God a condemner before he was a creator: This is to put a preface to *Moses* his *Genesis,* not to be content with his *in principio,* to know that *in the beginning God created heaven and earth,* but we must remember what he did *ante principium,* before any such beginning was. *Moses* his *in principio,* that beginning, the creation we can remember; but St. *Johns in principio,* that beginning, eternity, we cannot; we can remember Gods *fiat* in *Moses,* but not Gods *erat* in St. *John:* what God hath done for us, is the object of our memory, not what he did before we were: and thou hast a good and perfect memory, if it remember all that the holy Ghost proposes in the Bible; and it determines in the *memento Creatoris:* There begins the Bible, and there begins the Creed, *I believe in God the Father, maker of* [Jo. 7.39] *Heaven and Earth;* for when it is said, *The holy Ghost was not given, because Jesus was not glorified,* it is not truly *Non erat datus,* but *non erat;* for, *non erat nobis antequam operaretur;* It is not said there, the holy Ghost was not given, but it is the holy Ghost was not: for he is not, that is, he hath no being to us ward, till he works in us, which was first in the creation: *Remember the Creator then,* because thou canst remember nothing backward beyond him, and remember him so too, that thou maist stick upon nothing on this side of him, [Ro. 8 ult.] That so neither *height, nor depth, nor any other creature may separate thee from God;* not only not separate thee finally, but not separate so, as to stop upon the creature, but to make the best of them, thy way to the Creator; We see ships in the river; but all their use is gone, if they go not to sea; we see men fraighted with honor, and riches, but all their use is gone, if their respect be not upon the honor and glory [1 Pet. 4 ult.] of the Creator; and therefore sayes the Apostle, *Let them that suffer, commit their souls to God, as to a faithful Creator;* that is, He made them, and therefore will have care of them. This is the true contracting, and the true extending of the memory, to *Remember the Creator,* and stay there, because there is no prospect farther, and to *Remember the Creator,* and get thither, because there is no safe footing upon the creature, til we come so far.

Remember then the Creator, and *remember thy Creator,* for, *Quis magis fidelis Deo?* who is so faithful a Counsailor as God? *Quis prudentior Sapiente?* who can be wiser than wisdome? *Quis utilior bono?* or better than goodness? *Quis conjunctior Creatore?* or neerer then our Maker? and therefore remember him. What purposes soever thy parents or thy Prince have to make thee great, how had all those purposes been frustrated, and evacuated if God had not made thee before? this very being is thy greatest degree; as in Arithmatick how great a number soever a man expresse in many figures, yet when we come to number all, the very first figure is the greatest and most of all; so what degrees or titles soever a man have in this world, the greatest and the foundation of all, is, that he had a being by creation: For the distance from nothing to a little, is ten thousand times more, than from it to the highest degree in this life: and therefore *remember thy Creator,* as by being so, he hath done more for thee than all the world besides; and remember him also, with this consideration, that whatsoever thou art now, yet once thou wast nothing. *Tuum* Basil

He created thee, *ex nihilo,* he gave thee a being, there's matter of exaltation, and yet all this from nothing; thou wast worse then a worm, there's matter of humiliation; but he did not create thee *ad nihilum,* to return to nothing again, and there's matter for thy consideration, and study, how to make thine immortality profitable unto thee; for it is a deadly immortality, if thy immortality must serve thee for nothing but to hold thee in immortal torment. To end all, that being which we have from God shall not return to nothing, nor the being which we have from men neither. As St. *Bernard* sayes of the Image of God in mans soul, *uri potest in gehenna, non exuri,* That soul that descends to hell, carries the Image [of] God in the faculties of that soul thither, but there that Image can never be burnt out, so those Images and those impressions, which we have received from men, from nature, from the world, the image of a Lord, the image of a Counsailor, the image of a Bishop, shall all burn in Hell, and never burn out; not only these men, but these offices are not to return to nothing; but as their being from God, so their being from man, shal have an everlasting being, to the aggravating of their condemnation. And therefore *remember thy Creator,* who, as he is so, by making thee of nothing, so he will ever be so, by holding thee to his glory, though *Ex nihilo* Bern.

to thy confusion, from returning to nothing; for the Court of Heaven is not like other Courts, that after a surfet of pleasure or greatness, a man may retire; after a surfet of sin there's no such retiring, as a dissolving of the soul into nothing; but God is from the beginning the Creator, he gave all things their being, and he is still thy Creator, thou shalt evermore have that being, to be capable of his Judgments.

Now to make up a circle, by returning to our first word, remember: As we remember God, so for his sake, let us remember one another. In my long absence, and far distance from hence, remember me, as I shall do you in the ears of that God, to whom the farthest East, and the farthest West are but as the right and left ear in one of us; we hear with both at once, and he hears in both at once; remember me, not my abilities; for when I consider my Apostleship that I was sent to you, I am in St. *Pauls quorum, quorum ego sum minimus,* the least of them that have been sent; and when I consider my infirmities, I am in his *quorum,* in another commission, another way, *Quorum ego maximus;* the greatest of them; but remember my labors, and endeavors, at least my desire, to make sure your salvation. And I shall remember your religious cheerfulness in hearing the word, and your christianly respect towards all them that bring that word unto you, and towards myself in particular far [a]bove my merit. And so as your eyes that stay here, and mine that must be far of, for all that distance shall meet every morning, in looking upon that same Sun, and meet every night, in looking upon that same Moon; so our hearts may meet morning and evening in that God, which sees and hears every where; that you may come thither to him with your prayers, that I, (if I may be of use for his glory, and your edification in this place) may be restored to you again; and may come to him with my prayer that what *Paul* soever plant amongst you, or what *Apollos* soever water, God himself will give the increase: That if I never meet you again till we have all passed the gate of death, yet in the gates of heaven, I may meet you all, and there say to my Saviour and your Saviour, that which he said to his Father and our Father, *Of those whom thou hast given me, have I not lost one.* Remember me thus, you that stay in this Kingdome of peace, where no sword is drawn, but the sword of Justice, as I shal remember you in those Kingdomes, where ambition on one side, and a necessary defence from unjust

Cor. 15.9

Tim. 1.15

[John 18.9]

persecution on the other side hath drawn many swords; and Christ Jesus remember us all in his Kingdome, to which, though we must sail through a sea, it is the sea of his blood, where no soul suffers shipwrack; though we must be blown with strange winds, with sighs and groans for our sins, yet it is the Spirit of God that blows all this wind, and shall blow away all contrary winds of diffidence or distrust in Gods mercy; where we shall be all Souldiers of one Army, the Lord of Hostes, and Children of one Quire, the God of Harmony and consent: where all Clients shall retain but one Counsellor, our Advocate Christ Jesus, nor present him any other fee but his own blood, and yet every Client have a Judgment on his side, not only in a not guilty, in the remission of his sins, but in a *Venite benedicti,* in being called to the participation of an immortal Crown of glory: where there shall be no difference in affection, nor in mind, but we shall agree as fully and perfectly in our *Allelujah,* and *gloria in excelsis,* as God the Father, Son, and Holy Ghost agreed in the *faciamus hominem* at first; [Gen. 1.26] where we shall end, and yet begin but then; where we shall have continuall rest, and yet never grow lazie; where we shall be stronger to resist, and yet have no enemy; where we shall live and never die, where we shall meet and never part.

Number 12.

Two Sermons, to the Prince and Princess Palatine, the Lady Elizabeth at Heydelberg, when I was commanded by the King to wait upon my L. of Doncaster in his Embassage to Germany.

First Sermon as we went out, June 16. 1619.

Rom. 13.11. *FOR NOW IS OUR SALVATION NEARER THEN WHEN WE BELIEVED.*

There is not a more comprehensive, a more embracing word in all Religion, then the first word of this Text, *Now;* for the word before that, *For,* is but a word of connexion, and rather appertains to that which was said before the Text, then to the Text it self: The Text begins with that important and considerable particle, *Now, Now is salvation nearer, &c.* This present word, *Now,* denotes an Advent, a new coming, or a new operation, otherwise then it was before: And therefore doth the Church appropriate this Scripture to the celebration of the *Advent,* before the Feast of the Birth of our Saviour. It is an extensive word, *Now;* for though we dispute whether this *Now,* that is, whether an instant be any part of time or no, yet in truth it is all time; for whatsoever is past, was, and whatsoever is future, shall be an instant; and did and shall fall within this *Now.* We consider in the Church four *Advents* or Comings of Christ, of every one of which we may say *Now,* now it is otherwise then before: For first there is *verbum in carne,* the word came in the flesh, in the

[John 1.14]

Incarnation; and then there is *caro in verbo,* he that is made flesh comes in the word, that is, Christ comes in the preaching thereof; and he comes again *in carne saluta,* when at our dissolution and transmigration, at our death he comes by his spirit, and testifies to our spirit that we die the Children of God: And lastly he comes *in carne reddita,* when he shall come at the Resurrection, to redeliver our bodies to our souls, and to deliver everlasting glory to both. The Ancients for the most part understand the word of our Text, of Christs first coming in the flesh to us in this world; the latter Exposition understand them rather of his coming in glory: But the Apostle could not properly use this present word *Now,* with relation to that which is not now, that is, to future glory, otherwise then as that future glory hath a preparation and an inchoation in present grace; for so even the future glory of heaven hath a *Now,* now the elect Children of God have by his powerful grace a present possession of glory. So then it will not be impertinent to suffer this flowing and extensive word *Now* to spread it self into all three: for the whole duty of Christianity consists in these three things; first *in pietate erga Deum,* in religion towards God; in which the Apostle had enlarged himself from the beginning to the twelfth chapter of his Epistle: And secondly, *in charitate erga proximum,* in our mutual duties of society towards our Equals and Inferiors, and of Subjection towards our Superiours, in which that twelfth chapter, and this to the eighth verse is especially conversant: And then thirdly, *in sanctimonia propria,* in the works of sanctification and holiness in our selves: And this Text the Apostle presents as a forcible reason to induce us to that, to those works of sanctification, because *Now our salvation is nearer us then when we believed.* Take then this *now,* the first way of the coming of Christ in person, in the flesh into this world; and then the Apostle directs himself principally to the Jews converted to the faith of Christ, and he tels them, That their salvation is nearer them now, now they had seen him come, then when they did only believe that he would come: Take the words the second way, of his coming in grace into our hearts; and so the Apostle directs himself to all Christians; now, now that you have bin bred in the Christian Church, now that you are grown from Grace to grace, from faith to faith, now that God by his spirit strengthens and confirms you; *now is your salvation nearer then when ye believed,* that is, when you began to believe, either by the faith of your Parents, or the faith of the Church, or the faith of your Sureties at your Baptism; or when you began to have some notions, and impressions, and apprehensions of faith in your self, when you came to some degrees of understanding and discretion: Take the word of Christs coming to us at the hour of death, or of his coming to us at the day of Judgment (for those two are all one to our present purpose, because God never reverses any particular judgement given at a mans death at the day of the general Judgment:) take the word so, and this is the Apostles argument, you have believed, and you have lived accordingly, and that faith, and that good life hath brought salvation nearer you, that is, given you a fair and modest infallibility of salvation, in the nature of reversion; but now, now that you are come to the approches of death, which shall make your reversion a possession; *Now is salvation nearer you then when you believed.* Summarily, the Text is a reason why we ought to proceed in good and holy wayes; and it works in all the three acceptations of the word; for whether salvation be said to be near us, because we are Christians, and so have advantage of the Jews, or near us, because we have made some proficiency in holiness and sanctimony; or near us, because we are near our end, and thereby near a possession of our endless joy and glory: Still from all these acceptations of the word arise religious provocations to perseverance in holiness of life; and therefore we shall pursue the words in all three acceptations.

Part 1 In all three acceptations we must consider three termes in the Text; First, *Quid salus,* what this Salvation is that is intended here; and then, *Quid prope,* what this Distance, this nearness is; and lastly, *Quid credere,* what Belief this is. So then, taking the words first the first way, as spoken by the Apostles, to the Jews newly converted to the Christian Faith, salvation is the outward means of salvation, which are more and more manifest to the Christians, then they were to the Jews. And then the second Term, Nearness (salvation is nearer) is in this, That salvation to the Christian is in things present or past, in things already done, and of which we are experimentally sure; but to the Jews it was of future things, of which, howsoever they might assure themselves that they would be, yet they had no assurance when: And therefore (in the third place) their Believing was but a confident expectation, and faithfull assenting to their Prophets; *quando credidistis,* when you believed, that is, when you did only believe, and saw nothing.

Salus

First then, the first Terme in the first acceptation, Salvation, is the outward means of salvation. Outward and visible means of knowing God, God hath given to all Nations in the book of Creatures, from the first leaf of that book, the firmament above, to the last leaf, the Mines under our feet; there is enough of that. There they have a book which they read; and they have a sentence of condemnation if they doe not, *porro inexcusabilis, Therefore art thou inexcusable O man.*

Rom. 2.1

The visible God was presented in visible things, and thou mightst, and wouldst not see him: but this is only such a knowledge of God as Philosophers, moral and natural men may have, and yet be very farre from making this knowledge any means of salvation. A man that hath often travelled by that way where there stands a fair house will say, and say truly, that he knows that house; but yet he knows not the wayes that lead nearest and fairest to it, nor he knows not the lodgings and conveniencies of that house as he doth that hath been an often and welcome guest to it, or a continuall dweller in it. Natural men by passing often through the contemplation of nature have such a knowledge of God; but the knowledge which is to salvation, is by being in Gods house, in the Houshold of the Faithfull, in the Communion of Saints, and by having such a conversation in heaven in this life. That which our Saviour Christ says, *In domo Patris, In my Fathers house there are many Mansions,* as it is intended principally

[John 14.2]

of our state of glory, and diversity of degrees of that in heaven; so is it true also of Gods house at large, *Multæ mansiones.* In Gods house, which is All (all this world, and the next too, is Gods house) there are out-houses, rooms without the house; so considered in this world are the Gentils, and the Heathen, which are without the Church, and yet amongst them God hath some Servants: so in his house there are women below stairs, that is, in his visible Church here upon Earth; and women above stairs, that is, degrees of Glory in the triumphant Church. To them that are lodged in these out-houses, out of the Covenant out of the Church, salvation comes sometimes, God doth save some of them: but yet is not near them, that is, they have no ordinary nor established way of attaining to it, because Christ is not manifested to them in an ordinary preaching of the Word, and an ordinary administration of the Sacraments. And then to them who are above stairs, that is in possession of salvation in heaven, we cannot say salvation is nearer and nearer to them, because they are already in an actuall possession thereof. But to them who are in Gods House, and yet below stairs; to them who have salvation presented unto them by sensible and visible means; to them their salvation is properly said to be near. And such a people God had from the beginning, and shall have to the end; and that people the Jewes were; and therefore their glory was just and true glory, when they glorified themselves in that, *Deut. 4.7, 8* *What nation is so great?* wherein consisted their greatness? that followes; *Unto whom is the Lord so nigh as he is to us?* and in what consisted this nearness? in this; *What Nation hath ordinances and lawes so righteous as we have?* Here then was their salvation; first God withdrew them from the nations; he naturaliz'd them, he denizend *[Rom. 4.11]* them into his own kingdom, *sub sigillo circumcisionis,* in the seal of their blood in circumcision, he gave them an interest in his blood to be shed in his passion: and then, this was their farther salvation, that when he had thus taken them into his service, and put them into his livery, a livery of his own color, of blood in their circumcision, then he gave them a particular law for all their actions, how they should live in his favour; and he gave them a particular form of outward religious worship, which should be acceptable to him; the law, which was a sensible rule of their life, and their sacrifices, which were the *Psa. 147.20* sensible rule of their religion, was salvation: *non taliter,* saies *David,* God hath not dealt so with other nations; for though God from other nations do here and there pick out a servant, yet he hath not given other nations salvation, that is, setled an ordinary means of salvation amongst them. That was true of the Jews, and will alwaies be true of the whole Church of God, which *Calvin* saies, *quia nec oculis perspicitur, nec manibus palpatur spiritualis gratia,* because the grace of God it self cannot be discerned by the eye, nor distinguished by the touch, *non possumus nisi externis signis adjuti, statuere Deum nobis esse propitium,* we could not assure our selves of the mercies of God, if we had not outward and sensible signs and seals of those mercies; and therefore God never left his Church without such external and visible means and seals of grace. And though all those means were not properly seals, (for that is proper to sacraments, as a sacrament is strictly taken to be a seal of grace) yet the Fathers did often call many of these things by that name sacraments, because they had so much of the nature of a true sacrament, as that they advanc'd and furthered the working of grace. How a visible sign, water, or wine, (even in a true and proper sacrament) should confer grace, *fateor me non posse capere,* saies a learned Bishop in the Roman Church; as easie a matter as they make it, he professes that he cannot understand it: he argues it subtilly, but he concludes it modestly; *omnia brevi sententia dicenda sunt, consistere in pactis;* this must saies he be the end of all, that these things are not to be considered in the reason of man, but in the Covenant of God: God hath covenanted with his people, to be present with them in certain places, in the Church at certain times, when they make their congregation, in certain actions, when they meet to pray; and though he be not bound in the nature of the action, yet he is bound in his covenant to exhibit grace, and to strengthen grace, in certain sacrifices, and certain sacraments; and so other sacramental, and ritual and ceremonial things ordained by God in the voice of his Church, because they further salvation, are called salvation in this sense, and acceptation of the word, the first way.

Catarin. Eph. 5

Prope

This was the first branch, in the first sense of these words; *salus adminicula salutis,* salvation is means of salvation; and the next is the *propè,* wherein these means and helps were nearer to the Jews, after they were converted to the Christian religion, then before: and we consider them justly, to have been nearer, that is, more discernable; first, *quia plura,* because the helps of the Christians are more; and then, *quia potiora,* because in their nature they are better; and lastly, *quia manifestiora,* because they have a better evidence towards us; for so as the more bodies are together, the greater the object is, and so made the more visible; so they are nearer, *quia plura,* because they are more; and so, as the more beautiful, and better proportioned a body is, the more it draws the eye to look upon it; so they are nearer, *quia potiora,* because they are better; and so as the more evidence, and light and lustre they have in themselves, the easier things are discerned, so they are nearer, *quia manifestiora,* because they are more visible. First, how there should be more helps in the Christian re-

Plura

ligion, then in the Jewish, is not so evident at first: for first, if we consider the law to be salvation, they had a vast multiplicity of laws, scarce less than 600 several laws; whereas the honor of the Christian religion is, that it is *verbum abbreviatum,* an abridgment of all into ten words, as *Moses* calls the Commandements; and then a re-abridgment of that abridgment into two, love God, and love thy Neighbour, that is, faith and works. [Mat. 22.37–39] If we consider their laws to be their salvation, they had more; and if we consider their sacrifices to be their salvation, they had more too; for their Rabbins observe at least 50 several kinds of contracting uncleanness, to which there were appropriated several expiations and sacrifices; whereas we have only the sacrifices of prayer, and of praise, and of Christ in the sacrament; for so it is the ordinary phrase and manner of speech in the Fathers, to call that a sacrifice; not only as it is a commemorative sacrifice, (for that is amongst our selves, and so every person in the congregation may sacrifice, that is, do that in remembrance of Christ,) but as it is a real sacrifice, in which the Priest doth that, which none but he does; that is, really to offer up Christ Jesus crucified to Almighty God for the sins of the people, so, as that that very body of Christ, which offered himself for a propitiatory sacrifice upon the cross, once for all, that body, and all that that body suffered, is offered again, and presented to the Father, and the Father is intreated, that for the merits of that person, so presented and offered unto him, and in contemplation thereof, he will be merciful to that congregation, and applie those merits of his, to their particular souls. These are our sacrifices, prayer and praise, and Christ thus offered; and how are these more then the Jews had? they had more laws, and more sacrifices, and as many sacraments as we; and if nearness of salvation consist in the plurality of these, how is salvation nearer to us then to them? *quatenus plura,* in that first respects as the means are more, as it is truly and properly said, that there are more ingredients, more simples, more means of restoring in one dram of triacle or mithridate, then in an ounce of any particular syrup, in which there may be 3 or 4, in the other perchance so many hundred; so in that receit of our Saviour Christ, *quicquid ligaveris,* [Mat. 16.19] in the absolution of the Minister, that whatsoever he shall bind or loose upon earth, shall be bound or loose in heaven; there is more physick, then in all the expiations and sacrifices of the old law. There an expiation would serve to day, which would not serve to morrow; if it were omitted till the sun were set upon it, it required a more severe expiation: and so also an expiation would serve for one transgression, which would not serve for another; but here, in the absolution of the Minister, there is a concurrence, a confluence of medecines of all qualities; purgative in confession, and restorative in absolution; corasive in the preaching of Judgments, and cordial in the balm of the sacrament: here is no limitation of time, at what time soever a sinner repenteth, nor limitation of sins, whatsoever is forgiven in earth is forgiven in heaven: salvation is nearer us in this respect, that we have *plura adminicula,* more outward and visible means then the Jews had, because we may receive more in one action, then they could in all theirs.

Potiora

It is so also, not only *quia plura,* because we have more means, but *quia potiora,* because those means which we have are in their nature better, more attractive, and more winning. The means, (as we have said before) were their laws, and their sacrifices, and their sacraments, and for their law, it was *lex interficiens, non perficiens;* it was a law, that punished unrighteousness, but it did not confer righteousness: and their sacrifices, being in blood, (if we remove from them their typical signification, and what they prefigured, which was the shedding of the blood of the lamb which takes away the sins of the world) must necessarily create and excite a natural horror in man, and an aversness from them. Take their sacraments into comparison, and then one of their sacraments, Circumcision, was limited to one sex, it reached not to women; and their other sacrament, the passover, was in the primary signification and institution thereof, only a gratulatory commemoration of a temporal benefit of their deliverance from *Egypt.* And therefore to constitute a judgment proportionably by the effects, we see the law, and the sacrifice, and the sacraments of the Jews, did not much work upon foraign Nations; it was salvation, but salvation shut up amongst themselves; whereas we see that the law of the Christians, which is, to conforme our selves to our great example and pattern, Christ Jesus, who, (if we would consider him meerly as man) was the most exemplar man, for all Theological vertues, and moral too, that ever any history presented; and the sacrifices of Christians, which are all spiritual, and therein more pro-

August.

[John 1.2

portional to God who is all spirit; and the sacraments of Christians, in which, though not *ex opere operator,* not because that action is performed, not because that sacrament is administred, yet *ex pacto,* and *quando opus operamur:* by Gods covenant, when soever that action is performed, whensoever that sacrament is administred, the grace of God is exhibited and offered; *nec fallaciter,* as *Calvin* saies well, it is offered with a purpose on Gods part, that that grace should be accepted; we see, I say, that these laws, and these sacrifices, and these sacraments have gain'd upon the whole world; for in their nature, and in their attractiveness, and in their applyableness, and so in their effect, they are *potiora,* better, and in that respect, salvation is nearer us then it was to the Jews.

Manifestiora

And so it is, lastly, *quia manifestiora,* because they have an evidence and manifestation of themselves, in themselves. Now, this is especially true in the sacraments, because the sacraments exhibit and convey grace; and grace is such a light, such a torch, such a beacon, as where it is, it is easily seen. As there is a lustre in a precious stone, which no mans eye or finger can limit to a certain place or point in that stone, so though we do not assign in the sacrament, where, that is, in what circumstance or part of that holy action grace is; or when, or how it enters, (for though the word of consecration alter the bread, not to another thing, but to another use, and though they leave it bread, yet they make it other bread; yet the enunciation of those words doth not infuse nor imprint this grace, which we speak of, into that bread) yet whosoever receives this sacrament worthily, sees evidently an entrance, and a growth of grace in himself. But this evidence which we speak of, this manifestation, is not only, (though especially) in the sacraments, but in other sacramental and ceremonial things, which God (as he speaks by his Church) hath ordained, as the cross in baptism, and adoration at the sacrament (I do not say, I am far from saying, adoration of the sacrament; there is a fair distance and a spacious latitude between those two, an adoring of God in a devout humiliation of the body in that holy action, and an adoring the bread, out of a false imagination that that bread is God: A rectified man may be very humble and devout in that action, and yet a great way on this side the superstition and Idolatry in the practise of the Roman Church) in these sacramental and ritual, and ceremonial things, which are the bellows of devotion, and the subsidies of religion, and which were alwaies in all Churches, there is a more evident manifestation and clearness in these things in the Christian Church, then was amongst the Jews in the ceremonial parts of their religion, because almost all ours have reference to that which is already done and accomplished, and not to things of a future expectation, as those of the Jews were: So you know the passover of the Jews, had a relation to their comming out of *Egypt;* that was past, and thereby obvious to every man apprehension; every man that eat the passover, remembered their deliverance out of *Egypt;* but then the passover had also relation to that lamb which was to redeem that world; and this was a future thing; and this certainly very few amongst them understood, or considered upon that occasion, that as thy lamb is killed here, so there shall be a lamb killed for all the world hereafter. Now, our actions in the Church, do most respect things formerly done, and so they awaken, and work upon our memory, which is an easier faculty to work upon, then the understanding or the will. Salvation is nearer us, in these outward helps, because their signification is clearer to us, and more apprehensible by us, being of things past, and accomplished already. So then the Apostle might *Credidistis* well say that salvation, that is, outward means of salvation, was nearer, that is, more in number, better in use, clearer in evidence then it was before; *quando crediderunt,* when they believed, which is the third and last term, in this first acceptation of the word. Salvation was brought into the world, in the first promise of a Messias in the semen contract, *That the seed of the woman shall bruise the serpents* [Gen. 3.15] *head;* and it was brought nearer, when this Messias was fixed in *Abrahams* race, *in semine tuo In thy seed shall all nations be blessed;* [Gen. 22.18] it was brought nearer then that, when it was brought from *Abrahams* race to *Davids* family, *in solio tuo, The scepter shall not depart from* [Gen. 49.10] *thee, till he come;* and still nearer in *Esaias virgo concipiet,* when so [Isa. 7.14] particular mark was set upon the Messias as that he should be the son of a virgin; and yet nearer in *Micheas, & tu Bethlem,* that *Bethlem* [Micah 5.2] was design'd for the place of his birth; and nearer in *Daniels* 70 [Dan. 9.24] weeks, when the time was manifested. And though it were nearer then all this, when *John Baptist* came to say *Repent for the Kingdome* Mat. 3.2 *of God is at hand,* yet it was truly very near, nearest of all, when

Luc. 17.21 Christ came to say, *Behold the Kingdom of God is amongst you;* for all the rest were in the *crediderunt,* he was nearer them because they believed he would come; but then it was brought to the *viderunt,* Joh. 20.29 they saw he was come. *Beati* says Christ: *Blessed are they that have believed, and have not seen:* they had salvation brought nearer unto them by their believing; but yet Christ speaks of another manner of Mat. 13.16 [and 17] blessedness conferred upon his Disciples, *Blessed are your eyes for they see, and your ears for they hear; for, verily I say unto you, that many Prophets and Righteous men, have desired to see the things which ye see, and have not seen them.* To end this, the belief of the Patriarks was blessedness; and it was a kind of seeing too; for so Joh. 8.56 Christ saies, *your Father Abraham rejoyced to see my day, and he saw it;* but this was a seeing with the eye of faith which discovers future things; but Christ prefers the blessedness of the Disciples, because they saw things present and already done. All our life is a [Luke, 2.29, 30] passing bell, but then was *Simeon* content his bell should ring out, when his eyes had seen his salvation. In that especially doth St. *John* 1 Joh. 1.1 [also 3] exalt the force of his argument; *quæ vidimus: That which we have seen with our eyes, which we have looked upon, and our hands have handled of the word of life, that declare we unto you.* Here is then the inestimable prerogative of the Christian religion, it is grounded so far upon things which were seen to be done; it is brought so far from matter of faith, to matter of fact; from prophecy to history; from what the Messias should do, to what he hath done; and that was their case to whom this Apostle spake these words, as we take them in the first acceptation; salvation, that is, outward means of salvation in the Church is nearer, that is, more and better and clearer to you now, that is, when you have seen Christ in the flesh, then when you prefigured him in your law, or sacrifices, or sacraments, or believed him in your Prophets.

Second part In a second sence we took these words, of Christs second *Advent,* or comming, his comming to our heart, in the working of his grace; And so the Apostles words are directed to all Christians, and not only to the new convertits of that nation; and so these three terms, salvation, nearness, and believing, (which we proposed to be considered in all the three acceptations of the words) will have this signification. Salvation is the inward means of salvation, the working of the spirit, that sets a seal to the eternal means: the *prope,* the nearness lies in this, that this grace which is this salvation in this sense, grows out of that which is in you already; not out of any thing which is in you naturally, but Gods first graces that are in you, grows into more and more grace. Grace does not grow out of nature; for nature in the highest exaltation and rectifying thereof cannot produce grace. Corn does not grow out of the earth, it must be sowd; but corn grows only in the earth; nature, and naturall reason do not produce grace, but yet grace can take root in no other thing but in the nature and reason of man; whether we consider Gods subsequent graces, which grow out of his first grace, formerly given to us, and well employed by us, or his first grace, which works upon our natural faculties, and grows there; still this salvation, that is, this grace is near us, for it is within us; and then the third term believing, is either, *quando credidistis primum,* when you began to believe, either in an imputative belief of others in your baptism, or a faint belief, upon your first Catechisings and Instructions; or *quando credidistis tantum,* when you only professed a belief, or faith, and did nothing in declaration of that faith, to the edification of others.

Salus

First then, salvation in this second sense is the internal operation of the holy Ghost, in infusing grace: for therefore doth St. *Basil* call the holy Ghost *verbum Dei,* the word of God, (which is the name properly peculiar to the Son) *quia interpres filii, sicut filius patris;* that as the Father had revealed his will in the Prophets, and then the Son comes and interprets all that actually, this prophecy is meant of my coming, this of my dying; and so makes a real comment, and an actual interpretation of all the prophecies, for he does come, and he does die accordingly; so the holy Ghost comes, and comments upon this comment, interprets this interpretation, and tels thy soul that all this that the Father had promised, and the Son had performed, was intended by them, and by the working of their spirit, is now appropriated to thy particular soul. In the constitution and making of a natural man, the body is not the man, nor the soul is not the man, but the union of these two makes up the man; the spirits in a man which are the thin and active part of the blood, and so are of a kind of middle nature, between soul and body, those spirits are able to doe, and they doe the office, to unite and apply the faculties of the soul to the organs of the body, and so there is a man: so in a regenerate man, a Christian man, his being born of Christian Parents, that gives him a body, that makes him of the body of the Covenant, it gives him a title, an interest in the Covenant, which is *jus ad rem;* thereby he may make his claim to the seal of the Covenant, to baptism, and it cannot be denied him: and then in his baptism, that Sacrament gives him a soul, a spiritual seal, *jus in re,* an actual possession of Grace; but yet, as there are spirits in us, which unite body and soul, so there must be subsequent acts, and works of the blessed spirit, that must unite and confirm all, and make up this spiritual man in the wayes of sanctification; for without that his body, that is, his being born within the Covenant, and his soul, that is, his having received Grace in baptism, do not make him up. This Grace is this Salvation; and when this Grace works powerfully in thee, in the ways of sanctification, then is this Salvation neer thee; which is our second term in this second acceptation, *propè,* near.

Prope
Heb. 4.12

This neerness, which is the effectuall working of Grace, the Apostle expresses fully, That it *pierceth to the dividing asunder of soul and spirit;* for, though properly the soul and spirit of a man be all one, yet divers faculties and operations give them somtimes divers names in the Scriptures; *Anima quia animat,* sayes St. *Ambrose,* and *spiritus quia spirat:* The quickning of the body, is the soul; but the quickning of the soul, is the spirit. If this Salvation be brought to this neerness, that is, this grace to this powerfulness, thou shalt find it *in anima,* in thy soul, in those organs wherein thy soul uses thy body, in thy senses, and in the sensible things ordain'd by God in his Church, Sacraments and Ceremonies; and thou shalt find it neerer, *in spiritu,* as the spirit of God hath seal'd it to thy spirit invisibly, inexpressibly: It shall be neer to thee, so as that thy reason shall apprehend it; and neerer then that, thy faith shall establish it; and neerer then all this, it shall create in thee a modest and sober, but yet an infallible assurance, that thy salvation shall never depart from [Luke 1.46] thee: *Magnificabit anima tua Dominum,* as the B. Virgin speaks, *Thy soul shall magnifie the Lord;* all thy natural faculties shall be employed upon an assent to the Gospel, thou shalt be able to prove it to thy self, and to prove it to others, to be the Gospel of Salvation: [Luke 1.47] And then *Exultabit spiritus,* Thy spirit shall rejoyce in God thy

Saviour, because by the farther seal of sanctification, thy spirit shall receive testimony from the spirit; that as Christ is *Idem homo cum te,* the same man that thou art, so thou art *Idem spiritus cum Domino,* the same spirit that he is; so far, as that as a spirit cannot be separated in it self, so neither canst thou be separated from God in Christ; And this, this exaltation of Grace, when it thus growes up to this height of sanctification, is that neerness, which brings Salvation farther than our believing does: and that's the last term in this part; Believing.

Credidistis

Now, neerer then Believing, neerer than Faith, a man might well think nothing can bring Salvation; for Faith is the hand that reaches it, and takes hold of it. But yet, as though our bodily hand reach to our temporal food, yet the mouth and the stomach must do their office too; and so that meat must be distributed into all parts of the body, and assimilated to them; so though our faith draw this salvation neer us, yet when our mouth is imployed, that we have a delight to glorifie God in our discourses, and to declare his wonderfull works to the sons of men, in our thankfulness: And when this faith of ours is distributed over all the body, that the body of Christs Church is edified, and alienated by our good life and sanctification, then is this Salvation neerer us, that is, safelier seal'd to us, then when we believed only.

Either then, this *quando credidistis,* when you believed, may be refer'd to Infants, or to the first faith, and the first degrees thereof in men. In Infants, when that seminall faith, or potentiall faith, which is by some conceived to be in the Infants of Christian parents at their baptism; or that actuall faith, which from their parents, or from the Church, is thought to be applyed to them, accepted in their behalf, in that Sacrament, when this faith growes up after, by this new comming of Christ in the power of his Grace and his Spirit, to be a lively faith, expressed in charity; then *Salus propior,* then is Salvation neerer than when they believed; whether this belief were their own, or their parents, or the Churches, we have no ground to deny, that Salvation is neer, and present to all children rightly baptized; but, for those who have made sure their Salvation by a good use of Gods graces after, we have another fair peece of evidence, that Salvation is neerer them. It is so too, if this believing be refer'd to our first elements and beginnings of faith: A man believes the history of Christ, because it is matter of fact, and a story probable, and well testified: A man may believe the Christian Religion, or the Reformed Religion for his ease, either because he cannot or will not debate controversies, and reconcile differences, or because he sees it best for order and quiet, and civil ends, which he hath in that state where he lives. These be kinds of faith and morall assents: and somtimes when a man is come thus far, to a historical and a moral faith, God super-infuses true faith; for howsoever he wrought by reason, and natural faculties, and moral, and civil wayes, yet it was God that wrought from the beginning, and produced this faith, though but historical or moral. And then, if God do exalt this moral or historical faith farther then so, to believe not only the History, but the Gospel; not only that such a Christ lived, and did those miracles, and dyed, but that he was the Son of God, and dyed for the redemption of the world; this brings Salvation neerer him, than when he believed; but then, when this grace comes to appropriate Christ to him, and more than that, to annunciate Christ by him, when it makes him (as *John Baptist* was) [John 5.35] *a burning and a shining lamp;* That Christ is shewed to him, and by him to others in a holy life, *Then is Salvation neerer him than when he believed,* either as it is *credidit primum,* when he began to believe, but had some scruples, or *credidit tantum,* that he laid all upon faith, but had no care of works. To end this, this neerness of Salvation, is that union with God, which may be had in this life: It is the peace of conscience, the undoubting trust and assurance of Salvation. This assurance (so far as they will confess it may be had) the Roman Church places in faith, and so far, well; but then, *In fide formata;* and so far well enough too; In those works which declare and testifie that faith; for, though this good work do nothing toward my Salvation, it does much towards this neerness, that is, towards my assurance of this Salvation; but herein they lead us out of the way, that they call these works the soul, the form of faith: for, though a good tree cannot be without good fruits, yet it were a strange manner of speech to call that good fruit, the life or the soul, or the form of that tree; so is it, to call works which are the fruits of faith, the life or soul, or form of faith; for that is proper to grace only which infuses faith. They would acknowledge this neerness of salvation, this assurance in good works; but say they, men cannot be sure, that their works is good, and therefore they can have no such assurance. They who undertook the reformation of Religion in our Fathers dayes, observing that there was no peace without this assurance, expressed this assurance thus, That when a man is sure that he believes aright, that he hath no scruples of God, no diffidence in God, and uses all endeavors to continue it, and to express it in his life, as long as he continues so, he is sure of Salvation; and farther they went not: And then there arose men, which would reform the Reformers, and refine Salvation and bring it into a lesse room; They would take away the condition, if you hold fast, if you express it; and so came up roundly and presently to that, If ever you did believe, if ever you had faith, you are safe for ever, and upon that assurance you may rest. Now I make no doubt, but that both these sought the truth, that truth which concerns us, peace and assurance; and I dispute not their resolutions now; only I say, for these words which we have in hand now there is a conditional assurance implyed in them; for when it is said now, now that you are in this state, Salvation is neer you: thus much is pugnantly intimated, that if you were not in this state, Salvation were farther removed from you howsoever you pretend to believe.

3 Part

Now this hath brought us to our third and last sense and acceptation of these words, as they are spoken of Christs last comming, his comming in glory; which is to us at our deaths, and that judgment which we receive then. And in this acceptation of the word, these three terms, Salvation, Neerness and Believing, are thus to be understood: Salvation is Salvation perfected, consummated; Salvation which was brought neer [in] baptism, and neerer in outward holyness, must be brought neerer than that: And this *prope,* this neerness is, that now being neer death, you are neer the last seal of your perseverance; and so the *credidistis,* the believing amounts to this: though you have believed and liv'd accordingly, believed with the belief of a Jew, believed all the Prophets, and with the beliefe of a Christian, believed all the Gospel, believed with a seminal belief of your own, or an actuall belief of others at your baptism, with a historical belief, and with an Evangelical belief too, with a belief in your root, in the heart, and a belief in the fruits, expressed in a good life too, yet there is a continuance and a perseverance that must crown all this; and because that cannot be discern'd till thine end, then only is it safely pronounced, *Now is Salvation neerer you than when you believed.*

Salus Here then Salvation is eternall Salvation; not the outward seals of the Church upon the person, not visible Sacraments, nor the outward seal of the person, to the Church, visible works, nor the inward seal of the Spirit, assurance here, but fruition, possession of glory, in the Kingdome of Heaven; where we shall be infinitely rich, and that without labor in getting, or care in keeping, or fear in loosing; and fully wise, and that without ignorance of necessary, or study of unnecessary knowledge, where we shal not measure our portion by acres, for all heaven shall be all ours; nor our term by yeers, for it is life and everlasting life; nor our assurance by precedent, for we shal be safer then the Angels themselves were in the creation; where [2 Tim. 4.8] our exaltation shal be to have a crown of righteousness, and our pos- [Apoc. 4.10] session of that crown shal be, even the throwing it down at the feet of the Lamb; where we shal leave off all those petitions of *Adveniat regnum,* thy Kingdom come, for it shal be come in abundant power; and the *da nobis hodiè,* give us this day our dayly bread, for we shal have all that which we can desire now, and shall have a power to desire more, and then have that desire so enlarged, satisfied; And the *Libera nos,* we shall not pray to be delivered from evil, for no evil, *culpæ* or *pœnæ,* either of sin to deserve punishment, or of punishmen for our former sins shal offer at us; where we shall see God face [1 Cor. 13.12] to face, for we shall have such notions and apprehensions, as shall enable us to see him, and he shall afford such an imparting, such a manifestation of himself, as he shall be seen by us; and where we shall be as inseparably united to our Saviour, as his humanity and divinity are united together: This unspeakable, this unimaginable happiness is this Salvation, and therefore let us be glad when this is brought neer us.

Prope And this is brought neerer and neerer unto us, as we come neerer and neerer to our end. As he that travails weary, and late towards a great City, is glad when he comes to a place of execution, becaus he knows that is neer the town; so when thou comest to the gate of death, be glad of that, for it is but one step from that to thy *Jerusalem.* Jo. 4.42 Christ hath brought us in some neerness to Salvation, as he is *vere Salvator mundi,* in that we *know, that this is indeed the Christ, the Saviour of the world:* and he hath brought it neerer than that, as he is *Salvator corporis sui,* in that we know, *That Christ is the head of the Church, and the Saviour of that body:* (Eph. 5.23) And neerer than that, as he is *Salvator tuus sanctus,* In that we know, *He is the Lord our God, the holy One of Israel, our Saviour:* (Esay 43.3) But neerest of all, in the *Ecce Salvator tuus venit,* (Esa. 62.11) Behold thy Salvation commeth. It is not only promised in the Prophets, nor only writ in the Gospel, nor only seal'd in the Sacraments, nor only prepared in the visitations of the holy Ghost, but *Ecce,* behold it, now, when thou canst behold nothing else: The sun is setting to thee, and that for ever; thy houses and furnitures, thy gardens and orchards, thy titles and offices, thy wife and children are departing from thee, and that for ever; a cloud of faintnesse is come over thine eyes, and a cloud of sorrow over all theirs; when his hand that loves thee best hangs tremblingly over thee to close thine eyes, *Ecce Salvator tuus venit,* behold then a new light, thy Saviours hand shall open thine eyes, and in his light thou shalt see light; and thus shalt see, that though in the eyes of men thou lye upon that bed, as a Statue on a Tomb, yet in the eyes of God, thou standest as a *Colossus,* one foot in one, another in another land; one foot in the grave, but the other in heaven; one hand in the womb of the earth, and the other in *Abrahams* bosome: [Luke 16.22, 23] And then *vere prope,* Salvation is truly neer thee, and neerer than when thou believedst, which is our last word.

Credidistis

Take this Belief in the largest extent; a patient assent to all foretold of Christ and of Salvation by the Prophets; a historical assent to all that is written of Christ in the Gospel; an humble and supple, and applyable assent to the Ordinances of the Church; a faithful application of all this to thine own soul, a fruitful declaration of all that to the whole world in thy life, yet all this (though this be inestimable riches) is but the earnest of the holy Ghost, it is not the full payment; it is but the first fruits, it is not the harvest; it is but a truce, it is not an inviolable peace; *There remaineth a rest to the people of God,* (Heb. 4.9) sayes the Apostle; they were the people of God before, and yet there remained a rest, which they had not yet; not that there is not a blessed degree of rest, in the *Credidi,* a happy assurance in the strength of faith here, but yet there remaineth a rest better than that; And therefore sayes that Apostle there, *Let us labor to enter into that rest;* as though we have rest in our consciences all the six dayes of the week, if we do the works of our callings sincerely, yet all that while we

labor; and there remains a Sabbath, which we have not all the week;
so though we have peace and rest in the testimony of our faith and
obedience in this life, yet there remains a rest, a Sabbath, for which
v. 11 we must labor; for the Apostle in that place adds the danger; *Labor
to enter into that rest,* sayes he, *lest any man fall after the same
example of unbelief:* He speaks of the people of God, and yet they
might fall; He speaks of such as had believed, and yet they might
fall, after the example of unbelief, as far as they that never believed,
if they labored not to the last and set the seal of final perseverance to
their former faith. To conclude all with the force of the Apostles
argument, in urging the words of this text, since God hath brought
salvation nearer to you, then to them that believed; nearer to you in
the Gospel, when you have seen Christ come there to the Jews in the
Prophets, where they only read that he should come, and nearer to
you, then when you believed, either seminally and potentially, and
imputatively at our baptism, or actually, and declaratorily in some
parts of your life, by having persisted therein thus far; and since he
is now bringing it nearer to you, then when you believed at best,
Eccles. because your end grows nearer, now, *whilst the evill daies come not,*
12.[1–5] *nor the years approach, wherein thou shalt say, I have no pleasure in
them;* before the grinders cease, because they are few, and they wax
dark, that look out at the windows, before thou go to the house of
thine age, and the mourners go about in the streets, prepare thy self
by casting off thy sins, and all that is gotten by thy sins: for, as the
plague is got as soon in linings, as in the outside of a garment, salva-
tion is lost, as far, by retaining ill gotten goods, as by ill getting;
forget not thy past sins so far, as not to repent them, but remember
not thy repented sins so far, as to delight in remembring them, or to
doubt that God hath not fully forgiven them; and whether God have
brought this salvation near thee, by sickness, or by age, or by general
dangers, put off the consideration of the incomodities of that age, or
that sickness, and that danger, and fill thy self with the consideration
of the nearness of thy salvation, which that age, and sickness, and
danger, minister to thee: that so, when the best Instrument, and the
best song shall meet together, thy bell shall towl, and thy soul shall
hear that voice, *Ecce salvator,* behold thy Saviour cometh, thou maist
[Apoc. bear a part, and chearfully make up that musick, with a *veni Domine*
22.20] *Jesu,* Come Lord Jesu, come quickly, come now.

Number 13.

At the Haghe Decemb. 19. 1619. I Preached upon this Text. Since in my sicknesse at Abrey-hatche in Essex, 1630, revising my short notes of that Sermon, I digested them into these two.

MAT. 4.18, 19, 20. *AND IESUS WALKING BY THE SEA OF GALILE SAW TWO BRETHREN, SIMON CALLED PETER, AND ANDREW HIS BROTHER, CASTING A NET INTO THE SEA, (FOR THEY WERE FISHERS,) AND HE SAITH UNTO THEM, FOLLOW ME, AND I WILL MAKE YOU FISHERS OF MEN; AND THEY STRAIGHTWAY LEFT THEIR NETS, AND FOLLOWED HIM.*

SOLOMON presenting our Saviour Christ, in the name and person of Wisdome, in the booke of Proverbs, puts, by instinct of the Holy Ghost, these words into his mouth, *Deliciæ meæ esse* Prov. 8.31 *cum filiis hominum, Christs delight is to be with the children of men;* And in satisfaction of that delight, he sayes in the same verse, in the person of Christ, *That he rejoyced to be in the habitable parts of the Earth,* (that is, where he might converse with men) *Ludens in orbe terrarum,* (so the Vulgat reads it) and so our former Translation had it, *I tooke my solace in the compasse of the Earth.* But since Christs adversary Satan does so too, (Satan came *from compassing* Job 1.7 *the Earth to and fro, and from walking in it;*) since the Scribes and

[Mat. 23.15] Pharisees doe more then so, *They compasse Land and Sea, to make one of their own profession,* the mercy of Christ is not lesse active, not lesse industrious then the malice of his adversaries, He preaches in populous Cities, he preaches in the desart wildernesse, he preaches in the tempestuous Sea: and as his Power shall collect the severall dusts, and atomes, and Elements of our scattered bodies at the Resurrection, as materialls, members of his Triumphant Church; so he collects the materialls, the living stone, and timber, for his Militant Church, from all places, from Cities, from Desarts, and here in this Text, from the Sea, (*Iesus walking by the Sea, &c.*)

Divisio In these words we shall onely pursue a twofold consideration of the persons whom Christ called here to his Apostleship, *Peter* and *Andrew;* What their present, what their future function was, what they were, what they were to be; They were *fishermen,* they were to be *fishers of men.* But from these two considerations of these persons, arise many Circumstances, in and about their calling; and their preferment for their chearfull following. For first, in the first, we shall survay the place, *The Sea of Galile;* And their education and conversation upon that Sea, by which they were naturally lesse fit for this Church-service. At this Sea he found them *casting their Nets;* of which act of theirs, there is an emphaticall reason expressed in the text, *For they were fishers,* which intimates both these notes, That they did it because they were fishers; It became them, it behoved them, it concerned them to follow their trade; And then they did it as they were fishers, If they had not been fishers they would not have done it, they might not have usurped upon anothers Calling; (*They cast their Nets into the Sea, for they were fishers*) And then, in a nearer consideration of these persons, we finde that they were *two* that were called; Christ provided at first against singularity, He called not one alone; And then they were *two Brethren,* persons likely to agree; He provided at first against schisme; And then, they were two such as were nothing of kinne to him, (whereas the second payre of brethren, whom he called, *Iames* and *Iohn,* were his kinsmen) He provided at first, against partiality, and that kinde of Simony, which prefers for affection. These men, thus conditioned naturally, thus disposed at this place, and at this time, our blessed Saviour calls; And then we note their readinesse, they obeyed the call, they did all they were bid, They were bid *follow,* and they *followed,* and *followed presently;* And they did somewhat more then seemes expresly to have been required, for, *They left their Nets, and followed him.* And all these substantiall circumstances invest our first part, these persons in their first estate. For those that belong to the second part, Their preferment upon this obedience, (*Follow me, and I will make you fishers of men*) it would be an impertinent thing, to open them now, because I doe easily foresee, that this day we shall not come to that part.

Andreas

In our first part, The consideration of these persons then, though in this Text *Peter* be first named, yet we are to note, that this was not the first time of their meeting; when Christ and they met first, which was, when *Iohn Baptist* made that declaration upon Christs walking by him, *Behold the Lamb of God, Peter* was not the first that applied himselfe to Christ, nor that was invited by Christs presenting himselfe to him, to doe it; *Peter* was not there; *Peter* was not the second; for, *Andrew,* and another, who were then *Iohn Baptists* Disciples, and saw Christ declared by him, were presently affected with a desire to follow Christ, and to converse with him, and to that purpose presse him with that question, *Magister, ubi habitas?* They professe that they had chosen him for their Master, and they desire to know where he dwelt, that they might waite upon him, and receive their instructions from him. And in *Andrews* thus early applying himselfe to Christ, we are also to note, both the fecundity of true Religion; for, as soone as he had found Christ, he sought his brother *Peter, Et duxit ad Iesum,* he made his brother as happy as himselfe, he led him to Jesus; (And that other Disciple, which came to Christ as soone as *Andrew* did, yet because he is not noted to have brought any others but himselfe, is not named in the Gospel) And we are to observe also, the unsearchable wisdome of God in his proceedings, that he would have *Peter,* whom he had purposed to be his principall Apostle, to be led to him by another, of inferior dignity, in his determination. And therefore *Conversus converte,* Thinke not thy selfe well enough preached unto, except thou finde a desire, that thy life and conversation may preach to others, And *Edoctus disce,* thinke not that thou knowest any thing, except thou desire to learne more; neither grudge to learne of him, whom thou thinkest lesse learned then thy

[Joh. 1.40–42]
Joh. 1.36
[Joh. 1.37, 38]

selfe; The blessing is in Gods Calling, and Ordinance, not in the good parts of the man; *Andrew* drew *Peter,* The lesser in Gods purpose for the building of the Church, brought in the greater. Therefore doth the Church celebrate the memory of S. *Andrew,* first of any Saint in the yeare; and after they have been altogether united in that one festivall of *All-Saints,* S. *Andrew* is the first that hath a particular

Bernar.

day. He was *Primogenitus Testamenti novi,* The first Christian, the first begotten of the new Testament; for, *Iohn Baptist,* who may seeme to have the birthright before him, had his conception in the

Mal. 3.1
Esa. 40.3

old Testament, in the wombe of those prophecies of *Malachy,* and of *Esay,* of his comming, and of his office, and so cannot be so intirely referred to the new Testament, as S. *Andrew* is. Because therefore, our adversaries of the Romane heresie distill, and racke every passage of Scripture, that may drop any thing for the advantage of S. *Peter,* and the allmightines of his Successor, I refuse not the occasion offered from this text, compared with that other, *Ioh.* 1. to say, That if that first comming to Christ were but (as they use to say) *Ad notitiam & familiaritatem,* and this in our Text, *Ad Apostolatum,* That they that came there, came but to an acquaintance, and conversation with Christ, but here, in this text, to the Apostleship, yet, to that conversation, (which was no small happinesse) *Andrew* came clearly before *Peter,* and to this Apostleship here, *Peter* did not come before *Andrew;* they came together.

Mare Galilæum

These two then our Saviour found, *as he walked by the Sea of Galile.* No solitude, no tempest, no bleaknesse, no inconvenience averts Christ, and his Spirit, from his sweet, and gracious, and comfortable visitations. But yet, this that is called here, *The Sea of Galile,* was not properly a Sea; but according to the phrase of the Hebrews, who call all great meetings of waters, by that one name, A Sea, this, which was indeed a lake of fresh water, is called a Sea. From the roote of Mount Libanus, spring two Rivers, Jor, and Dan; and those two, meeting together, joyning their waters, joyne their names too, and make that famous river Jordan; a name so composed, as perchance our River is, Thamesis, of Thame, and Isis. And this River Jordan falling into this flat, makes this Lake, of sixteene miles long, and some sixe in breadth. Which Lake being famous for fish, though of ordinary kinds, yet of an extraordinary taste and relish, and then of extraordinary kinds too, not found in other waters, and famous, because divers famous Cities did engirt it, and become as a garland to it, *Capernaum,* and *Chorazim,* and *Bethsaida,* and *Tiberias,* and *Magdalo,* (all celebrated in the Scriptures) was yet much more famous for the often recourse, which our Saviour (who was of that Countrey) made to it; For this was the Sea, where he amazed *Peter,* with that great draught of fishes, that brought him to say, *Exi à me Domine, Depart from me, O Lord, for I am a sinfull man;* This was the Sea, where himselfe *walked upon the waters;* And where he *rebuked the tempest;* And where he manifested his Almighty power many times. And by this Lake, this Sea, dwelt *Andrew* and *Peter,* and using the commodity of the place, lived upon fishing in this Lake; and in that act our Saviour found them, and called them to his service. Why them? Why *fishers?*

Luk. 5.8
Matt. 14.25
[Matt.] 8.26

Cur Piscatores

First, Christ having a greater, a fairer Jerusalem to build then *Davids* was, a greater Kingdome to establish then Juda's was, a greater Temple to build then *Solomons* was, having a greater work to raise, yet he begun upon a lesse ground; Hee is come from his twelve Tribes, that afforded armies in swarmes, to twelve persons, twelve Apostles; from his *Iuda* and *Levi,* the foundations of State and Church, to an *Andrew* and a *Peter* fisher-men, sea-men; and these men accustomed to that various, and tempestuous Element, to the Sea, lesse capable of Offices of civility, and sociablenesse, then other men, yet must be employed in religious offices, to gather all Nations to one houshold of the faithfull, and to constitute a Communion of Saints; They were Sea-men, fisher-men, unlearned, and indocil; Why did Christ take them? Not that thereby there was any scandall given, or just occasion of that calumny of *Iulian* the Apostat, That Christ found it easie to seduce, and draw to his Sect, such poore ignorant men as they were; for Christ did receive persons eminent in learning, (*Saul* was so) and of authority in the State, (*Nicodemus* was so) and of wealth, and ability, (*Zacheus* was so, and so was *Ioseph* of Arimathea) But first he chose such men, that when the world had considered their beginning, their insufficiency then, and how unproper they were for such an employment, and yet seene that great work so farre, and so fast advanced, by so weake instruments, they might ascribe all power to him, and ever after, come to him cheerfully upon any invitation, how weake men soever he should send to them, because hee had done so much by so weak instruments before: To make his work in all ages after prosper the better, he proceeded thus at first. And then, hee chose such men for another reason too; To shew that how insufficient soever he received them, yet he received them into such a Schoole, such an University, as should deliver them back into his Church, made fit by him, for the service thereof. Christ needed not mans sufficiency, he took insufficient men; Christ excuses no mans insufficiency, he made them sufficient.

Nequid Instrumentis August.

His purpose then was, that the worke should be ascribed to the Workman, not to the Instrument; To himselfe, not to them; *Nec quæsivit per Oratorem piscatorem,* He sent not out Orators, Rhetoricians, strong or faire-spoken men to work upon these fisher-men, *Sed de piscatore lucratus est Imperatorem,* By these fisher-men, hee hath reduced all those Kings, and Emperours, and States which have embraced the Christian Religion, these thousand and six hundred yeares.

1 Sam. 16.6

When *Samuel* was sent with that generall Commission, to anoint a sonne of *Ishai King,* without any more particular instructions, when hee came, and *Eliab* was presented unto him, *Surely,* sayes *Samuel,* (noting the goodlinesse of his personage) *this is the Lords Anointed.*

1 Sam. 16.7

But the Lord said unto *Samuel, Looke not on his countenance, nor the height of his stature, for I have refused him; for,* (as it followeth there, from Gods mouth) *God seeth not as man seeth; Man looketh on the outward appearance, but the Lord beholdeth the heart.* And so *David,* in apparance lesse likely, was chosen. But, if the Lords arme be not shortned, let no man impute weaknesse to the Instrument. For so, when *David* himselfe was appointed by God, to pursue the Amalekites, the Amalekites that had burnt Ziklag, and done such

[1 Sam. 30] Ver 6

spoile upon Gods people, as that the people began to speak of stoning *David,* from whom they looked for defence, when *David* had no kind of intelligence, no ground to settle a conjecture upon, which way he must pursue the Amalekites, and yet pursue them he must,

[1 Sam. 30.11–20]

in the way he findes a poore young fellow, a famished, sicke young man, derelicted of his Master, and left for dead in the march, and by the meanes and conduct of this wretch, *David* recovers the enemy, recovers the spoile, recovers his honour, and the love of his people.

If the Lords arme bee not shortned, let no man impute weaknesse to his Instrument. But yet God will alwayes have so much weaknesse appeare in the Instrument, as that their strength shall not be thought to be their owne. When *Peter* and *Iohn* preached in the streets, *The people marvelled,* (sayes the Text) why? *for they had understood that they were unlearned.* But *beholding also the man that was healed standing by, they had nothing to say,* sayes that story. The insufficiency of the Instrument makes a man wonder naturally; but the accomplishing of some great worke brings them to a necessary acknowledgement of a greater power, working in that weake Instrument. For, if those Apostles that preached, had beene as learned men, as *Simon Magus,* as they did in him, (*This man is the great power of God,* not that he had, but that he was the power of God) the people would have rested in the admiration of those persons, and proceeded no farther. It was their working of supernaturall things, that convinced the world. For all *Pauls* learning, (though hee were very learned) never brought any of the Conjurers to burne his bookes, or to renounce his Art; But when God wrought extraordinary works by him, That sicknesses were cured by his napkins, and his handkerchiefs, (in which cures, *Pauls* learning had no more concurrence, no more cooperation, then the ignorance of any of the fisher-men Apostles) And when the world saw that those Exorcists, which went about to doe Miracles in the Name of Jesus, because *Paul* did so, could not doe it, because that Jesus had not promised to worke in them, as in *Paul,* Then the Conjurers came, and burnt their bookes, in the sight of all the world, to the value of fifty thousand pieces of silver. It was not learning, (that may have been got, though they that heare them, know it not; and it were not hard to assigne many examples of men that have stolne a great measure of learning, and yet lived open and conversable lives, and never beene observed, (except by them, that knew their Lucubrations, and night-watchings) to have spent many houres in study) but it was the calling of the world to an apprehension of a greater power, by seeing great things done by weake Instruments, that reduced them, that convinced them. *Peter* and *Iohns* preaching did not halfe the good then, as the presenting of one man, which had been recovered by them, did. Twenty of our Sermons edifie not so much, as if the Congregation might see one man converted by us. Any one of you might out-preach us. That one

Acts 4.13

[Acts 4.14]

Acts 8.10

Acts 19.11 [and 12]

[Acts 19] Verse 13

[Acts 19] Verse 19

[Acts 3.1–11]

man that would leave his beloved sinne, that one man that would restore ill-gotten goods, had made a better Sermon then ever I shall, and should gaine more soules by his act, then all our words (as they are ours) can doe.

Non in-idoneos

Such men he took then, as might be no occasion to their hearers, to ascribe the work to their sufficiency; but yet such men too, as should be no examples to insufficient men to adventure upon that great service; but men, though ignorant before, yet docil, and glad to learne. In a rough stone, a cunning Lapidary will easily foresee, what his cutting, and his polishing, and his art will bring that stone to. A cunning Statuary discerns in a Marble-stone under his feet, where there will arise an Eye, and an Eare, and a Hand, and other lineaments to make it a perfect Statue. Much more did our Saviour Christ, who was himselfe the Author of that disposition in them, (for no man hath any such disposition but from God) foresee in these fishermen, an inclinablenesse to become usefull in that great service of his Church. Therefore hee tooke them from their owne ship, but he sent them from his Crosse; Hee tooke them weatherbeaten with North and South winds, and rough-cast with foame, and mud; but he sent them back soupled, and smoothed, and levigated, quickned, and inanimated with that Spirit, which he had breathed into them from his owne bowels, his owne eternall bowels, from which the Holy Ghost proceeded; Hee tooke fisher-men, and he sent fishers of men. Hee sent them not out to preach, as soone as he called them to him; He called them *ad Discipulatum,* before hee called them *ad Apostolatum;* He taught them, before they taught others. As S. *Paul* sayes of himselfe, and the rest, *God hath made us able Ministers of the New Testament; Idoneos,* fit Ministers, that is, fit for that service. There is a fitnesse founded in Discretion; a Discretion to make our present service acceptable to our present Auditory; for if it be not acceptable, agreeable to them, it is never profitable.

2 Cor. 3.6

Wisd. 16.20

As God gave his children such Manna as was agreeable to every mans taste, and tasted to every man like that, that that man liked best: so are wee to deliver the bread of life agreeable to every taste, to fit our Doctrine to the apprehension, and capacity, and digestion of the hearers. For as S. *Augustine* sayes, That no man profits by a Sermon that he heares with paine, if he doe not stand easily; so if he doe not understand easily, or if he doe not assent easily to that that he heares, if he be put to study one sentence, till the Preacher have passed three or foure more, or if the doctrine be new and doubtfull, and suspitious to him, this fitnesse which is grounded in discretion is not shewed. But the generall fitnesse is grounded in learning, S. *Paul* hath joyned them safely together, *Rebuke and exhort with all long suffering, and learning.* Shew thy discretion in seasonable Rebuking; shew thy learning in Exhorting. Let the Congregation see that thou studiest the good of their soules, and they will digest any wholesome increpation, any medicinall reprehension at thy hands, *Dilige & dic quod voles.* We say so first to God, Lord let thy spirit beare witnesse with my spirit, that thou lovest me, and I can endure all thy Prophets, and all the *væ's,* and the woes that they thunder against me and my sin. So also the Congregation sayes to the Minister, *Dilige & dic quod voles,* shew thy love to me, in studying my case, and applying thy knowledge to my conscience, speake so, as God and I may know thou meanest me, but not the Congregation, lest that bring me to a confusion of face, and that to a hardnesse of heart; deale thus with me, love me thus, and say what thou wilt; nothing shall offend me. And this is the Idoneity, the fitnesse which we consider in the Minister, fitnesse in learning, fitnesse in discretion, to use and apply that learning. So Christ fits his.

2 Tim. 4.2

August.

Mittebant rete in Mare

Such men then Christ takes for the service of his Church; such as bring no confidence in their owne fitnesse, such as embrace the meanes to make them fit in his Schoole, and learne before they teach. And to that purpose he tooke *Andrew* and *Peter;* and he tooke them, when he found them *casting their net into the Sea.* This was a Symbolicall, a Propheticall action of their future life; This fishing was a type, a figure, a prophesie of their other fishing. But here (in this first part) we are bound to the consideration of their reall and direct action, and exercise of their present calling; *They cast their Net, for they were Fishers,* sayes the Text. In which, *for,* (as wee told you at first) there is a double reason involved.

1 *Quia piscatores*

First, in this *For* is intimated, how acceptable to God that labour is, that is taken in a calling. They did not forbeare to cast their nets because it was a tempestuous Sea; we must make account to meet stormes in our profession, yea and tentations too. A man must not leave his calling, because it is hard for him to be an honest man in that calling; but he must labour to overcome those difficulties, and as much as he can, vindicate and redeeme that calling from those aspersions and calumnies, which ill men have cast upon a good calling. They did not forbeare because it was a tempestuous Sea, nor because they had cast their nets often and caught nothing, nor because it was uncertaine how the Market would goe when they had catched. A man must not be an ill Prophet upon his own labours, nor bewitch them with a suspition that they will not prosper. It is the slothfull

Prov. 26.13

man that sayes, *A Lion in the way, A Lion in the street.* Cast thou thy net into the Sea, and God shall drive fish into thy net; undertake a lawfull Calling, and clogge not thy calling with murmuring, nor with an ill conscience, and God shall give thee increase, and worship in it, *They cast their nets into the Sea, for they were fishers;* it was their Calling, and they were bound to labour in that.

2
Quia piscatores

And then this *For* hath another aspect, lookes another way too, and implies another Instruction, *They cast their nets into the Sea, for they were fishers,* that is, if they had not beene fishers, they would not have done it; Intrusion into other mens callings is an unjust usurpation; and, if it take away their profit, it is a theft. If it be but a censuring of them in their calling, yet it is a calumny, because it is not in the right way, if it be extrajudiciall. To lay an aspersion upon any man (who is not under our charge) though that which we say of him be true, yet it is a calumny, and a degree of libelling, if it be not done judiciarily, and where it may receive redresse and remedy. And yet how forward are men that are not fishers in that Sea, to censure State Councels, and Judiciary proceedings? Every man is an

2 Sam. 15.3

Absolom, to say to every man, *Your cause is good, but the King hath appointed none to heare it;* Money brings them in, favour brings them in, it is not the King; or, if it must be said to be the King, yet it is the affection of the King and not his judgement, the King misled, not rightly informed, say our seditious *Absoloms,* and, *Oh that I were*

[2 Sam. 15]
Ver. 4

made Iudge in the land, that every man might come unto me, and I would doe him justice, is the charme that *Absolom* hath taught every man. They cast their nets into a deeper Sea then this, and where they are much lesse fishers, into the secret Councels of God. It is well provided by your Lawes, that Divines and Ecclesiasticall persons may not take farmes, nor buy nor sell, for returne, in Markets. I would it were as well provided, that buyers and sellers, and farmers might not be Divines, nor censure them. I speake not of censuring our lives; please your selves with that, till God bee pleased to mend us by that, (though that way of whispering calumny be not the right way to that amendment) But I speak of censuring our Doctrines, and of appointing our doctrines; when men are weary of hearing any other thing, then Election and Reprobation, and whom, and when, and how, and why God hath chosen, or cast away. We have liberty enough by your Law, to hold enough for the maintenance of our bodies, and states; you have liberty enough by our Law, to know enough for the salvation of your soules; If you will search farther into Gods eternall Decrees, and unrevealed Councels, you should not cast your nets into that Sea, for you are not fishers there. *Andrew and Peter cast their nets, for they were fishers,* (therefore they were bound to do it) And againe, *for they were fishers,* (if they had not been so, they would not have done so.)

Duo simul

These persons then thus disposed, unfit of themselves, made fit by him, and found by him at their labour, labour in a lawfull Calling, and in their owne Calling, our Saviour Christ cals to him; And he called them by couples, by paires; two together. So he called his Creatures into the world at the first Creation, by paires. [Gen. 1.27] So he called them into the Arke, for the reparation of the world, by paires, two and two. [Gen. 6.19, 20] God loves not singularity; The very name of Church implies company; It is *Concio, Congregatio, Cœtus;* It is a Congregation, a Meeting, an assembly; It is not any one man; neither can the Church be preserved in one man. And therefore it hath beene dangerously said, (though they confesse it to have beene said by many of their greatest Divines in the Roman Church) that during the time that our blessed Saviour lay dead in the grave, there was no faith left upon the earth, but onely in the Virgin *Mary;* for then there was no Church. God hath manifested his will in two Testaments; and though he have abridged and contracted the doctrine of both in a narrow roome, yet he hath digested it into two Commandements, *Love God, love thy neighbour*. [Mat. 22.37–39; Mark 12:30–31; Luke 10.27] There is but one Church; that is true, but one; but that one Church cannot be in any one man; There is but one Baptisme; that is also true, but one; But no man can Baptize himselfe; there must be *Sacerdos & competens,* (as our old Canons speake) a person to receive, and a Priest to give Baptisme. There is but one faith in the remission of sins; that is true too, but one; But no man can absolve himselfe; There must be a Priest and a penitent. God cals no man so, but that he cals him to the knowledge, that he hath called more then him to that Church, or else it is an illusory, and imaginary calling, and a dreame.

Take heed therefore of being seduced to that Church that is in one man; *In scrinio pectoris,* where all infallibility, and assured resolution is in the breast of one man; who (as their owne Authors say) is not bound to aske the counsell of others before, nor to follow their counsell after. And since the Church cannot be in one, in an unity, take heed of bringing it too neare that unity, to a paucity, to a few, to a separation, to a Conventicle. The Church loves the name of Catholique; and it is a glorious, and an harmonious name; Love thou those things wherein she is Catholique, and wherein she is harmonious, that is, *Quod ubique, quod semper,* Those universall, and fundamentall doctrines, which in all Christian ages, and in all Christian Churches, have beene agreed by all to be necessary to salvation; and then thou art a true Catholique. Otherwise, that is, without relation to this Catholique and universall doctrine, to call a particular Church Catholique, (that she should be Catholique, that is, universall in dominion, but not in doctrine) is such a solecisme, as to speak of a white blacknesse, or a great littlenesse; A particular Church to be universall, implies such a contradiction.

Lyri-nen[sis]

Duo fratres

Christ loves not singularity; he called not one alone; He loves not schisme neither between them whom he cals; and therefore he cals persons likely to agree, two brethren, (*He saw two brethren, Peter and Andrew, &c.*) So he began to build the Synagogues, to establish that first government, in *Moses* and *Aaron,* brethren; So he begins to build the Church, in *Peter* and *Andrew,* brethren. The principall fraternity and brotherhood that God respects, is spirituall; Brethren in the profession of the same true Religion. But *Peter* and *Andrew* whom he called here to the true Religion, and so gave them that second fraternity and brotherhood, which is spirituall, were naturall brethren before; And that God loves; that a naturall, a secular, a civill fraternity, and a spirituall fraternity should be joyned together;

when those that professe the same Religion, should desire to contract their alliances, in marrying their Children, and to have their other dealings in the world (as much as they can) with men that professe the same true Religion that they do. That so (not medling nor disputing the proceedings of States, who, in some cases, go by other rules then private men do) we doe not make it an equall, an indifferent thing, whether we marry our selves, or our children, or make our bargaines, or our conversation, with persons of a different Religion, when as our Adversaries amongst us will not goe to a Lawyer, nor call a Physitian, no, nor scarce a Taylor, or other Tradesman of another Religion then their owne, if they can possibly avoid it. God saw a better likelihood of avoyding Schisme and dissention, when those whom hee called to a new spirituall brotherhood in one Religion, were naturall brothers too, and tied in civill bands, as well as spirituall.

And as Christ began, so he proceeded; for the persons whom he *Non cognati* called were Catechisticall, instructive persons; persons, from whose very persons we receive instruction. The next whom he called, (which is in the next verse) were two too; and brethren too; *Iohn* and *Iames;* but yet his owne kinsmen in the flesh. But, as he chose two together to avoid singularity, and two brethren to avoid Schisme, so he preferred two strangers before his own kindred, to avoid partiality, and respect of persons. Certainly every man is bound to do good to those that are neare him by nature; The obligation of doing good to others lies (for the most part) thus; *Let us do good to all men, but* Gal. 6.10 *especially unto them which are of the houshold of the faithfull;* (They of our owne Religion are of the *Quorum*) Now, when all are so, (of the houshold of the faithfull, of our owne Religion) the obligation looks home, and lies thus, *He that provideth not for his own, denieth* 1 Tim. 5.8 *the faith, and is worse then an Infidel.* Christ would therefore leave no example, nor justification of that perverse distemper, to leave his kindred out, nor of their disposition, who had rather buy new friends at any rate, then relieve or cherish the old. But yet when Christ knew how far his stock would reach, that no liberality, howsoever placed, could exhaust that, but that he was able to provide for all, he would leave no example nor justification of that perverse distemper, to heape up preferments upon our owne kindred, without any consideration how Gods glory might be more advanced by doing good to others too; But finding in these men a fit disposition to be good labourers in his harvest, and to agree in the service of the Church, as they did in the band of nature, he calls *Peter* and *Andrew,* otherwise strangers, before he called his Cosins, *Iames* and *Iohn.*

Continuò sequuti

These Circumstances we proposed to be considered in these persons before, and at their being called. The first, after their calling, is their chearfull readinesse in obeying, *Continuò sequuti,* They were bid *follow,* and *forthwith they followed.* Which present obedience of theirs is exalted in this, that this was freshly upon the imprisonment of *Iohn Baptist,* whose Disciple *Andrew* had been; And it might easily have deterred, and averted a man in his case, to consider, that it was well for him that he was got out of *Iohn Baptists* schoole, and company, before that storme, the displeasure of the state fell upon him; and that it behoved him to be wary to apply himselfe to any such new Master, as might draw him into as much trouble; which Christs service was very like to doe. But the contemplation of future persecutions, that may fall, the example of persecutions past, that have falne, the apprehension of imminent persecutions, that are now falling, the sense of present persecutions, that are now upon us, retard not those, upon whom the love of Christ Jesus works effectually; They followed for all that. And they followed, when there was no more perswasion used to them, no more words said to them, but *Sequere me, Follow me.*

[Mat. 4.12]

And therefore how easie soever *Iulian* the Apostate might make it, for Christ to work upon so weake men, as these were, yet to worke upon any men by so weake means, onely by one *Sequere me, Follow me,* and no more, cannot be thought easie. The way of Rhetorique in working upon weake men, is first to trouble the understanding, to displace, and to discompose, and disorder the judgement, to smother and bury in it, or to empty it of former apprehensions and opinions, and to shake that beliefe, with which it had possessed it self before, and then when it is thus melted, to powre it into new molds, when it is thus mollified, to stamp and imprint new formes, new images, new opinions in it. But here in our case, there was none of this fire, none of this practise, none of this battery of eloquence, none of this verball violence, onely a bare *Sequere me, Follow me,* and *they followed.* No eloquence enclined them, no terrors declined them: No dangers withdrew them, no preferment drew them; they knew Christ, and his kindred, and his means; they loved him, himselfe, and not any thing they expected from him. *Minùs te amat, qui aliquid tuum amat, quod non propter te amat,* That man loves thee but a little, that begins his love at that which thou hast, and not at thy selfe. It is a weake love that is divided between Christ and the world; especially, if God come after the world, as many times he does, even in them, who thinke they love him well; that first they love the riches of this world, and then they love God that gave them. But that is a false Method in this art of love; The true is, radically to love God for himselfe, and other things for his sake, so far, as he may receive glory in our having, and using them.

August.

Relictis retibus

This *Peter* and *Andrew* declared abundantly; they did as much as they were bid; they were bid *follow, and they followed;* but it seemes they did more, they were not bid *leave their nets,* and yet *they left their nets, and followed him:* But, for this, they did not; no man can doe more in the service of God, then is enjoyned him, commanded him. There is no supererogation, no making of God beholden to us, no bringing of God into our debt. Every man is commanded *to love God with all his heart, and all his power,* and a heart above a whole heart, and a power above a whole power, is a strange extension. That therefore which was declared explicitely, plainly, directly by Christ, to the young man in the Gospel, *Vade, & vende, & sequere, Goe and sell all, and follow me,* was implicitely implied to these men in our text, Leave your nets, and follow me. And, though to doe so, (to leave all) be not alwayes a precept, a commandment to all men, yet it was a precept, a commandment to both these, at that time; to the young man in the Gospel, (for he was as expressly bid to sell away all, as he was to follow Christ) and to these men in the text, because they could not performe that that was directly commanded, except they performed that which was implied too; except they left their nets, they could not follow Christ. When God commands us to follow him, he gives us light, how, and in which way he will be followed; And then when we understand which is his way, that way is as much a commandment, as the very end it selfe, and not to follow him that way, is as much a transgression, as not to follow him at all.

[Mat. 22.37; Mark 12:30; Luke 10.27]

Mat. 19.21

If that young man in the Gospel, who was bid sell all, and give to the poore, and then follow, had followed, but kept his interest in his land; If he had devested himselfe of the land, but let it fall, or conveyed it to the next heire, or other kinsmen; If he had employed it to pious uses, but not so, as Christ commanded, to the poore, still he had been in a transgression: The way when it is declared, is as much a command, as the end.

But then, in this command, which was implicitely, and by necessary consequence laid upon *Peter* and *Andrew,* to leave their nets, (because without doing so, they could not forthwith follow Christ) there is no example of forsaking a calling, upon pretence of following Christ; no example here, of devesting ones selfe of all means of defending us from those manifold necessities, which this life lays upon us, upon pretence of following Christ; It is not an absolute leaving of all worldly cares, but a leaving them out of the first consideration; [Mat. 6.33] *Primùm quærite regnum Dei,* so, as our first businesse be to seeke the kingdome of God. For, after this leaving of his nets, for this time, Mat. 8.14 [and 15] *Peter* continued owner of his house, and Christ came to that house of his, and found his mother in law sicke in that house, and recovered her there. Mat. 9.[9 and] 10 Upon a like commandment, upon such a *Sequere, Follow me, Matthew* followed Christ too; but after that following, Christ went with *Matthew* to his house, and sate at meat with him at home. And for this very exercise of fishing, though at that time when Christ said, Follow me, they left their nets, yet they returned to that trade, sometimes, upon occasions, in all likelihood, in Christs life; Joh. 21.1 [also 2–4] and after Christs death, clearly they did returne to it; for Christ, after his Resurrection, found them fishing.

They did not therefore abandon and leave all care, and all government of their own estate, and dispose themselves to live after upon the sweat of others; but transported with a holy alacrity, in this present and chearfull following of Christ, in respect of that then, they neglected their nets, and all things else. August. *Perfecta obedientia est sua imperfecta relinquere,* Not to be too diligent towards the world, is the diligence that God requires. S. *Augustine* does not say, *sua relinquere,* but *sua imperfecta relinquere,* That God requires we should leave the world, but that we should leave it to second considerations; That thou do not forbeare, nor defer thy conversion to God, and thy restitution to man, till thou have purchased such a state, bought such an office, married, and provided such and such children, but *imperfecta relinquere,* to leave these worldly things unperfected, till thy repentance have restored thee to God, and established thy reconciliation in him, and then the world lyes open to thy honest endeavours. Others take up all with their net, and *they sacrifice to their nets, be-* [Hab. 1.16] *cause by them their portion is fat, and their meat plenteous.* They are confident in their own learning, their own wisedome, their own practise, and (which is a strange Idolatry) they sacrifice to themselves, they attribute all to their own industry. These men in our text were far from that; they left their nets.

But still consider, that they did but leave their nets, they did not burne them. And consider too, that they left but nets; those things, which might entangle them, and retard them in their following of Christ. And such nets, (some such things as might hinder them in the service of God) even these men, so well disposed to follow Christ, had about them. And therefore let no man say, *Imitari vellem, sed* [Gregor.] *quod relinquam, non habeo,* I would gladly doe as the Apostles did, leave all to follow Christ, but I have nothing to leave; alas, all things have left me, and I have nothing to leave. Even that murmuring at poverty, is a net; leave that. Leave thy superfluous desire of having the riches of this world; though thou mayest flatter thy selfe, that thou desirest to have onely that thou mightest leave it, that thou mightest employ it charitably, yet it might prove a net, and stick too close about thee to part with it. *Multa relinquitis, si desideriis renunciatis,* You [Idem] leave your nets, if you leave your over-earnest greedinesse of catching; for, when you doe so, you doe not onely fish with a net, (that is, lay hold upon all you can compasse) but, (which is strange) you fish for a net, even that which you get proves a net to you, and hinders you in the following of Christ, and you are lesse disposed to follow him, when you have got your ends, then before. He that hath least, hath enough to waigh him down from heaven, by an inordinate love of that little which he hath, or in an inordinate and murmuring desire of more. And he that hath most, hath not too much to give for heaven; *Tantum valet regnum Dei, quantum tu vales,* Heaven is [Idem] alwayes so much worth, as thou art worth. A poore man may have heaven for a penny, that hath no greater store; and, God lookes, that he to whom he hath given thousands, should lay out thousands upon the purchase of heaven. The market changes, as the plenty of money changes; Heaven costs a rich man more then a poore, because he hath more to give. But in this, rich and poore are both equall, that both must leave themselves without nets, that is, without those things, which, in their own Consciences they know, retard the following of Christ. Whatsoever hinders my present following, that I cannot follow to day, whatsoever may hinder my constant following, that I cannot follow to morrow, and all my life, is a net, and I am bound to leave that.

And these are the pieces that constitute our first part, the circumstances that invest these persons, *Peter,* and *Andrew,* in their former condition, before, and when Christ called them.

Number 14.

MAT. 4.18, 19, 20. *AND IESUS WALKING BY THE SEA OF GALILE SAW TWO BRETHREN, SIMON CALLED PETER, AND ANDREW HIS BROTHER, CASTING A NET INTO THE SEA, (FOR THEY WERE FISHERS.) AND HE SAITH UNTO THEM, FOLLOW ME, AND I WILL MAKE YOU FISHERS OF MEN; AND THEY STRAIGHTWAY LEFT THEIR NETS, AND FOLLOWED HIM.*

WE ARE now in our Order proposed at first, come to our second part, from the consideration of these persons, *Peter* and *Andrew,* in their former state and condition, before, and at their calling, to their future estate in promise, but an infallible promise, Christs promise, if they followed him, (*Follow me, and I will make you fishers of men.*) In which part we shall best come to our end, (which is your edification) by these steps. First, that there is an Humility enjoyned them, in the *Sequere, follow,* come after. That though they bee brought to a high Calling, that doe not make them proud, nor tyrannous over mens consciences; And then, even this Humility is limited, *Sequere me, follow me;* for there may be a pride even in Humility, and a man may follow a dangerous guide; Our guide here is Christ, *Sequere me, follow me.* And then we shall see the promise it selfe, the employment, the function, the preferment; In which there is no new state promised them, no Innovation, (They were *fishers,* and they shall be *fishers* still) but there is an improvement, a bettering, a reformation, (They were *fisher-men* before, and now they shall be *fishers of men;*) To which purpose, wee shall finde the world to be the Sea, and the Gospel their Net. And lastly, all this is presented to them, not as it was expressed in the former part, with a *For,* (it is not, Follow me, for I will prefer you) he will not have that the reason of their following; But yet it is, Follow me, and I will prefer you; It is a subsequent addition of his owne goodnesse, but so infallible a one, as we may rely upon; Whosoever doth follow Christ, speeds well. And into these considerations will fall all that belongs to this last part, *Follow me, and I will make you fishers of men.*

Sequere Humilitas

First then, here is an impression of Humility, in following, in comming after, *Sequere, follow,* presse not to come before; And it had need be first, if we consider how early, how primarie a sinne Pride is, and how soone it possesses us. Scarce any man, but if he looke back seriously into himselfe, and into his former life, and revolve his owne history, but that the first act which he can remember in himselfe, or can be remembred of by others, will bee some act of Pride. Before Ambition, or Covetousnesse, or Licentiousnesse is awake in us, Pride is working; Though but a childish pride, yet pride; and this Parents rejoyce at in their children, and call it spirit, and so it is, but not the best. Wee enlarge not therefore the consideration of this word *sequere, follow,* come after, so farre, as to put our meditations upon the whole body, and the severall members of this sinne of pride; Nor upon the extent and diffusivenesse of this sinne, as it spreads it selfe over every other sinne; (for every sinne is complicated with pride, so as every sinne is a rebellious opposing of the law and will of God) Nor to consider the waighty hainousnes of pride, how it aggravates every other sin, how it makes a musket a Canon bullet, and a peble a Milstone; but after we have stopped a little upon that usefull consideration, That there is not so direct, and Diametrall a contrariety between the nature of any sinne and God, as between him and pride, wee shall passe to that which is our principall observation in this branch, How early and primary a sin pride is, occasioned by this, that the commandement of Humility is first given, first enjoyned in our first word, *Sequere, follow.*

Nihil tam contrarium Deo

But first, wee exalt that consideration, That nothing is so contrary to God, as Pride, with this observation, That God in the Scriptures is often by the Holy Ghost invested, and represented in the qualities and affections of man; and to constitute a commerce and familiarity

between God and man, God is not onely said to have bodily linea-
ments, eyes and eares, and hands, and feet, and to have some of the
naturall affections of man, as Joy, in particular, (*The Lord will re-* Deut. 30.9
joyce over thee for good, as he rejoyced over thy Fathers) And so,
pity too, (*The Lord was with Ioseph, and extended kindnesse unto* Gen. 39.21
him) But some of those inordinate and irregular passions and per-
turbations, excesses and defects of man, are imputed to God, by the
holy Ghost in the Scriptures. For so, lazinesse, drowsinesse is imputed
to God; (*Awake Lord, why sleepest thou?*) So corruptiblenesse, and Psal. 44.23
deterioration, and growing worse by ill company, is imputed to God;
(*Cum perverso perverteris,* God is said to grow froward with the [Psal.] 18.26
froward, and that hee learnes to go crookedly with them that go
crookedly) And prodigality and wastfulnesse is imputed to God;
(*Thou sellest thy people for naught, and doest not increase thy wealth* [Psal.] 44.12
by their price) So sudden and hasty choler; (*Kisse the Son lest he* [Psal.] 2.12
be angry, and ye perish In ira brevi, though his wrath be kindled but
a little) And then, illimited and boundlesse anger, a vindicative irrec-
onciliablenesse is imputed to God; (*I was but a little displeased,* Zech. 1.15
(but it is otherwise now) *I am very sore displeased*) So there is *Ira*
devorans; (*Wrath that consumes like stubble*) So there is *Ira mul-* Exod. 15.7
tiplicata, (*Plagues renewed, and indignation increased*) So God him- Iob 10.17
selfe expresses it, (*I will fight against you in anger and in fury*) And Ier. 21.5
so for his inexorablenesse, his irreconciliablenesse, (*O Lord God of* Psal. 80.4
Hosts, Quousque, how long wilt thou be angry against the prayer of
thy people?) Gods owne people, Gods own people praying to their
owne God, and yet their God irreconciliable to them. Scorne and
contempt is imputed to God; which is one of the most enormious,
and disproportioned weakenesses in man; that a worme that crawles
in the dust, that a graine of dust, that is hurried with every blast of
winde, should find any thing so much inferiour to it selfe as to scorne
it, to deride it, to contemne it; yet scorne, and derision, and contempt
is imputed to God, (*He that sitteth in the Heavens shall laugh, the* Psal. 2.4
Lord shall have them in derision) and againe, (*I will laugh at your* Prov. 1.26
calamity, I will mock you when your feare commeth.) Nay beloved,
even inebriation, excesse in that kinde, Drunkennesse, is a Metaphor
which the Holy Ghost hath mingled in the expressing of Gods pro-
ceedings with man; for God does not onely threaten to make his

enemies drunke, (and to make others drunke is a circumstance of drunkennesse) (so Jerusalem being in his displeasure complaines, [Lam 3.15] *Inebriavit absynthio, (He hath made me drunke with wormewood)* [Esay 49.26] and againe, (*They shall be drunke with their owne blood, as with new Wine*) Nor onely to expresse his plentifull mercies to his friends [Ier. 31.14] and servants, does God take that Metaphore, (*Inebriabo animam Sacerdotis, I will make the soule of the Priest drunke;* fill it, satiate [[Ier. 31] Ver. 25] it) and againe, (*I will make the weary soule, and the sorrowfull soule drunke*) But not onely all this, (though in all this God have a hand) not onely towards others, but God in his owne behalfe complaines of the scant and penurious Sacrificer, [Esay 43.24] *Non inebriasti me, Thou hast not made me drunke with thy Sacrifices.* And yet, though for the better applying of God to the understanding of man, the Holy Ghost impute to God these excesses, and defects of man (lazinesse and drowsiness, deterioration, corruptiblenesse by ill conversation, prodigality and wastfulnesse, sudden choler, long irreconciliablenesse, scorne, inebriation, and many others) in the Scriptures, yet in no place of the Scripture is God, for any respect said to be proud; God in the Scriptures is never made so like man, as to be made capable of Pride; for this had not beene to have God like man, but like the devill.

God is said in the Scriptures to apparell himself gloriously; [Psal. 104.2] (*God covers him with light as with a garment*) And so of his Spouse the Church it is said, [[Psal.] 45.13 [and 14]] (*Her cloathing is of wrought gold, and her raiment of needle worke*) and, as though nothing in this world were good enough for her wearing, she is said [Rev. 12.1] *to be cloathed with the Sun.* But glorious apparell is not pride in them, whose conditions require it, and whose revenews will beare it. God is said in the Scriptures to appeare with greatnesse and majesty, [Dan. 7.10] (*A streame of fire came forth before him; thousand thousands ministred unto him, and ten thousand times ten thousand stood before him.*) And so Christ shall come at Judgement, with his Hosts of Angels, in majesty, and in glory. But these outward appearances and acts of greatnesse are not pride in those persons, to whom there is a reverence due, which reverence is preserved by this outward splendor, and not otherwise. God is said in the Scriptures to triumph over his enemies, and to be jealous of his glory; [Exod. 34.14] (*The Lord, whose name is Iealous, is a jealous God*) But, for Princes to be jealous of their glory, studious of their honour, for any private man to be jealous of his good name, carefull to preserve an honest reputation, is not pride. For, Pride is *Appetitus celsitudinis perversus,* It is an inordinate desire of being better then we are.

Now there is a lawfull, nay a necessary desire of being better and better; And that, not onely in spirituall things, (for so every man is bound to be better and better, better today then yesterday, and to morrow then to day, and he that growes not in Religion, withers, There is no standing at a stay, He that goes not forward in godlinesse, goes backward, and he that is not better, is worse) but even in temporall things too there is a liberty given us, nay there is a law, an obligation laid upon us, to endeavour by industry in a lawfull calling, to mend and improve, to enlarge our selves, and spread, even in worldly things. The first Commandement that God gave man, was not prohibitive; God, in that, forbad man nothing, but enlarged him with that *Crescite, & multiplicamini, Increase and multiply,* Gen. 1.28 which is not onely in the multiplication of children, but in the enlargement of possessions too; for so it followes in the same place, not onely *Replete,* but *Dominamini,* not onely replenish the world, but subdue it, and take dominion over it, that is, make it your owne. For, *Terram dedit filiis hominum,* As God hath given sons to men, so God gives the possession of this world to the sons of men. For so when God delivers that commandement, the second time, to *Noah,* for the reparation of the world, *Crescite & multiplicamini, Increase and multiply,* he accompanies it with that reason, *The feare of you, and* Gen. 9.1 *the dread of you shall be upon all, and all are delivered into your* [and 2] *hands;* which reason can have no relation to the multiplying of Children, but to the enlarging of possessions. God planted trees in Paradise in a good state at first; at first with ripe fruits upon them; but Gods purpose was, that even those trees, though well then, should grow greater. God gives many men good estates from their parents at first; yet Gods purpose is that they should increase those estates. He that leaves no more, then his father left him, (if the fault be in himselfe) shall hardly make a good account of his stewardship to God; for, he hath but kept his talent in a handkercheif. And *the sloth-* Mat. 18.25 *full man is even brother to the waster.* The holy Ghost in *Solomon,* Prov. 18.9 scarce prefers him that does not get more, before him that wasts all.

Ier. 48.10 He makes them brethren; almost all one. *Cursed be he that does the worke of God negligently;* that does any Commandement of God by halves; And this negligent and lazy man, this in-industrious and illaborious man that takes no paines, he does one part of Gods Commandement, He does multiply, but he does not the other, he does not increase; He leaves Children enow, but he leaves them nothing; not in possssions and maintenance, nor in vocation and calling.

1 Tim. 6.10 And truly, howsoever *the love of money be the roote of all evill,* [1 Tim. 6.]9 (He cannot mistake that told us so) Howsoever *they that will be rich* (that resolve to be rich by any meanes) *shall fall into many tentations,* Howsoever a hasty desire of being suddenly and prematurely rich, be a dangerous and an obnoxious thing, a pestilent and contagious disease, (for what a perverse and inordinate anticipation and prevention of God and nature is it, to looke for our harvest in May, or to looke for all grains at once? and such a perversnesse is the hasty desire of being suddenly and prematurely rich) yet, to go on industriously in an honest calling, and giving God his leasure, and giving God his portion all the way, in Tithes, and in Almes, and then, still to lay up something for posterity, is that, which God does not onely permit and accept from us, but command to us, and reward in us. And certainly, that man shall not stand so right in Gods eye at the last day, that leaves his Children to the Parish, as he that leaves the Parish to his Children, if he have made his purchases out of honest gaine, in a lawfull Calling, and not out of oppression.

In all which, I would be rightly understood; that is, that I speake of such poverty as is contracted by our owne lazinesse, or wastfulnesse. For otherwise, poverty that comes from the hand of God, is as rich a blessing as comes from his hand. He that is poore with a good conscience, that hath laboured and yet not prospered, knows to whom Psal. 4.7 to go, and what to say, *Lord, thou hast put gladnesse into my heart,* [and 8] *more then in the time when corne and wine increased;* (more now, then when I had more) *I will lay me downe and sleepe, for thou Lord onely makest me to dwell in safety.* Does every rich man dwell in safety? Can every rich man lye downe in peace and sleepe? no, nor every poore man neither; but he that is poore with a good conscience, can. And, though he that is rich with a good conscience may, in a good measure, do so too, (sleepe in peace) yet not so out of the spheare and latitude of envy, and free from the machinations, and supplantations, and underminings of malicious men, that feed upon the confiscations, and build upon the ruines of others, as the poore man is.

Though then S. *Chrysostome* call riches *Absurditatis parentes,* the parents of absurdities, That they make us doe, not onely ungodly, but inhumane things, not onely irreligious, but unreasonable things, uncomely and absurd things, things which we our selves did not suspect that we could be drawne to, yet there is a growing rich, which is not covetousnesse, and there is a desire of honor and preferment, which is not Pride. For, Pride is, (as we said before) *Appetitus perversus,* A perverse and inordinate desire, but there is a desire of honor and preferment, regulated by rectified Reason; and rectified Reason is Religion. And therefore, (as we said) how ever other affections of man, may, and are, by the Holy Ghost, in Scriptures, in some respects ascribed to God, yet never Pride. Nay, the Holy Ghost himselfe seemes to be straitned, and in a difficulty, when he comes to expresse Gods proceedings with a proud man, and his detestation of him, and aversion from him. There is a considerable, a remarkable, indeed a singular manner of expressing it, (perchance you finde not the like in all the Bible) where God sayes, *Him that hath a high looke, and* Psal. 101.5 *a proud heart, I will not,* (in our last) *I cannot,* (in our former translation) Not what? Not as it is in those translations, *I cannot suffer him, I will not suffer him;* for that word of *Suffering,* is but a voluntary word, supplied by the Translators; In the Originall, it is as it were an abrupt breaking off on Gods part, from the proud man, and, (if we may so speake) a kinde of froward departing from him. God does not say of the proud man, I cannot worke upon him, I cannot mend him, I cannot pardon him, I cannot suffer him, I cannot stay with him, but meerly *I cannot,* and no more, I cannot tell what to say of him, what to doe for him; (*Him that hath a proud heart, I cannot*) Pride is so contrary to God, as that the proud man, and he can meet in nothing. And this consideration hath kept us thus long, from that which we made our first and principall collection, That this commandment of Humility, was imprinted in our very first word, *Sequere, follow,* be content to come after, to denote how early and primary a sin Pride is, and how soone it entred into the world, and how soone into us; and that consideration we shall pursue now.

Superbia in Angelis [Gen. 1.3]

We know that light is Gods eldest childe, his first borne of all Creatures; and it is ordinarily received, that the Angels are twins with the light, made then when light was made. And then the first act, that these Angels that fell, did, was an act of Pride. They [did] not thanke nor praise God, for their Creation; (which should have been their first act) They did not solicite, nor pray to God for their Sustentation, their Melioration, their Confirmation; (so they should have proceeded) But the first act that those first Creatures did, was an act of pride, a proud reflecting upon themselves, a proud over-valuing of their own condition, and an acquiescence in that, in an imaginary possibility of standing by themselves, without any farther relation, or beholdingnesse to God. So early, so primary a sin is Pride, as that it was the first act of the first of Creatures.

Superbia positiva Luk. 18.11

Psal. 52.1

So early, so primary a sin, as that whereas all Pride now is but a comparative pride, this first pride in the Angels was a positive, a radicall pride. The Pharisee is but proud, *that he is not as other men are;* that is but a comparative pride. No King thinks himselfe great enough, yet he is proud that he is independant, soveraigne, subject to none. No subject thinks himselfe rich enough, yet he is proud that he is able to oppresse others that are poorer, *Et gloriatur in malo, quia potens est,* He boasteth himselfe in mischiefe, because he is a mighty man. But all these are but comparative prides; and there must be some subjects to compare with, before a King can be proud, and some inferiors, before the Magistrate, and some poore, before the rich man can be proud. But this pride in those Angels in heaven, was a positive pride; There were no other Creatures yet made, with whom these Angels could compare themselves, and before whom these Angels could prefer themselves, and yet before there was any other creature but themselves, any other creature, to undervalue, or insult over, these Angels were proud of themselves. So early, so primary a sin is Pride.

Superbia in Paradiso [Gen. 2.19, 20]

So early, so primary, as that in that ground, which was for goodnesse next to heaven, that is, Paradise, Pride grew very early too. *Adams* first act was not an act of Pride, but an act of lawfull power and jurisdiction, in naming the Creatures; *Adam* was above them all, and he might have called them what he would; There had lyen no action, no appeale, if *Adam* had called a Lyon a Dog, or an Eagle an Owle. And yet we dispute with God, why he should not make all us vessels of honor, and we complaine of God, that he hath not given us all, all the abundances of this world. Comparatively *Adam* was better then all the world beside, and yet we finde no act of pride in *Adam,* when he was alone. Solitude is not the scene of Pride; The danger of pride is in company, when we meet to looke upon another. But in *Adams* wife, *Eve,* her first act (that is noted) was an act of Pride, a hearkning to that voyce of the Serpent, *Ye shall be as* [Gen. 3.5] *Gods.* As soone as there were two, there was pride. How many may we have knowne, (if we have had any conversation in the world) that have been content all the weeke, at home alone, with their worky day faces, as well as with their worky day clothes, and yet on Sundayes, when they come to Church, and appeare in company, will mend both, their faces as well as their clothes. Not solitude, but company is the scene of pride; And therefore I know not what to call that practise of the Nunnes in Spaine, who though they never see man, yet will paint. So early, so primary a sin is Pride, as that it grew instantly from her, whom God intended for a *Helper,* because he saw *that it was not good for man to be alone.* [Gen. 2.18] God sees that it is not good for man to be without health, without wealth, without power, and jurisdiction, and magistracy, and we grow proud of our helpers, proud of our health and strength, proud of our wealth and riches, proud of our office and authority over others.

So early, so primary a sin is pride, as that, out of every mercy, and blessing, which God affords us, (and, *His mercies are new every* [Lam. 3.22, 23] *morning*) we gather Pride; wee are not the more thankfull for them, and yet we are the prouder of them. Nay, we gather Pride, not onely out of those things, which mend and improve us, (Gods blessings and mercies) but out of those actions of our own, that destroy and ruine us, we gather pride; sins overthrow us, demolish us, destroy and ruine us, and yet we are proud of our sinnes. How many men have we heard boast of their sinnes; and, (as S. *Augustine* confesses of himselfe) belie themselves, and boast of more sinnes then ever they committed? Out of every thing, out of nothing sin grows. Therefore was this commandment in our text, *Sequere, Follow,* come after, well placed first, for we are come to see even children strive for place and precedency, and mothers are ready to goe to the Heralds to know how Cradles shall be ranked, which Cradle shall have the highest place; Gen. 25.26 Nay, even in the wombe, there was contention for precedency; *Iacob* tooke hold of his brother *Esaus* heele, and would have been borne before him.

Superbia in monumentis

And as our pride begins in our Cradle, it continues in our graves and Monuments. It was a good while in the primitive Church, before any were buried in the Church; The best contented themselves with the Churchyards. After, a holy ambition, (may we call it so) a holy Pride brought them *ad Limina,* to the Church-threshold, to the Church-doore, because some great Martyrs were buried in the Porches, and devout men desired to lie neare them, as one Prophet did to lie neare another, (*Lay my bones besides his bones.*) 1 King. 13.31 But now, persons whom the Devill kept from Church all their lives, Separatists, Libertines, that never came to any Church, And persons, whom the Devill brought to Church all their lives, (for, such as come meerly out of the obligation of the Law, and to redeem that vexation, or out of custome, or company, or curiosity, or a perverse and sinister affection to the particular Preacher, though they come to Gods house, come upon the Devils invitation) Such as one Devill, that is, worldly respect, brought to Church in their lives, another Devill, that is, Pride and vain-glory, brings to Church after their deaths, in an affectation of high places, and sumptuous Monuments in the Church. And such as have given nothing at all to any pious uses, or have determined their almes and their dole which they have given, in that one day of their funerall, and no farther, have given large annuities, perpetuities, for new painting their tombes, and for new flags, and scutcheons, every certaine number of yeares.

O the earlinesse! O the latenesse! how early a Spring, and no Autumne! how fast a growth, and no declination, of this branch of this sin Pride, against which, this first word of ours, *Sequere, Follow,* come after, is opposed! this love of place, and precedency, it rocks us in our Cradles, it lies down with us in our graves. There are diseases proper to certaine things, Rots to sheepe, Murrain to cattell. There are diseases proper to certaine places, as the Sweat was to us. There are diseases proper to certaine times, as the plague is in divers parts of the Eastern Countryes, where they know assuredly, when it will begin and end. But for this infectious disease of precedency, and love of place, it is run over all places, as well Cloysters as Courts, And over all men, as well spirituall as temporall, And over all times, as well the Apostles as ours. The Apostles disputed often, *who should be greatest,* [Mark 9.34] and it was not enough to them, that Christ assured them, *that they should sit upon the twelve thrones, and judge the twelve Tribes;* Matt. 19.28 it was not enough for the sonnes of *Zebedee,* to be put into that Commission, but their friends must solicite the office, to place them high in that Commission; their Mother must move, that one may sit at Christs right hand, and the other at his left, in the execution of that Commission. [Mat. 20.20, 21] Because this sin of pride is so early and primary a sin, is this Commandment of Humility first enjoyned, and because this sin appeares most generally in this love of place, and precedency, the Commandment is expressed in that word, *Sequere, Follow,* Come after. But then, even this Humility is limited, for it is *Sequere me,* follow me, which was proposed for our second Consideration, *Sequere me.*

Sequere me

There may be a pride in Humility, and an over-weaning of our selves, in attributing too much to our owne judgement, in following some leaders; for so, we may be so humble as to goe after some man, and yet so proud, as to goe before the Church, because that man may be a Schismatike. Therefore Christ proposes a safe guide, himself, *Sequere me, follow me.* It is a dangerous thing, when Christ sayes, *Vade post me, Get thee behind me;* for that is accompanied with a shrewd name of increpation, Satan, *Get thee behind me Satan;* Christ speaks it but twice in the Gospell; once to *Peter,* Matt. 16.23 who because he then did the part of an Adversary, Christ calls Satan, and once to Satan himselfe, [Mat.] 4.10 because he pursued his tentations upon him; for there is a going behind Christ, which is a casting out of his presence, without any future following, and that is a fearefull station, a fearefull retrogradation; But when Christ sayes, not *Vade retro, Get thee behind me,* see my face no more, but *Sequere me, follow me,* he meanes to look back upon us; so *the Lord turned and looked upon Peter, and Peter wept bitterly,* Luk. 22.61, 62 and all was well; when hee bids us follow him, he directs us in a good way, and by a good guide.

The Carthusian Friers thought they descended into as low pastures as they could goe, when they renounced all flesh, and bound themselves to feed on fish onely; and yet another Order followes them in their superstitious singularity, and goes beyond them, *Foliantes,* the Fueillans, they eat neither flesh, nor fish, nothing but leafes, and rootes; and as the Carthusians in a proud humility, despise all other Orders that eat flesh, so doe the Fueillans the Carthusians that eat fish. There is a pride in such humility. That Order of Friers that called themselves *Ignorantes,* Ignorant men, that pretended to know nothing, sunk as low as they thought it possible, into an humble name and appellation; And yet the Minorits, (Minorits that are lesse then any) think they are gone lower, and then the Minimes, (Minimes that are lesse then all) lower then they. And when one would have thought, that there had not been a lower step then that, another Sect went beyond all, beyond the Ignorants, and the Minorits, and the Minimes, and all, and called themselves, *Nullanos,* Nothings. But yet, even these Diminutives, the Minorits, and Minimes, and Nullans, as little, as lesse, as least, as very nothing as they professe themselves, lie under this disease, which is opposed in the *Sequere me,* follow, come after, in our Text; For no sort nor condition of men in the world are more contentious, more quarrelsome, more vehement for place, and precedency, then these Orders of Friers are, there, where it may appeare, that is, in their publique Processions, as we finde by those often troubles, which the Superiours of the severall Orders, and Bishops in their severall Dioceses, and some of those Councels, which they call Generall, have been put to, for the ranking, and marshalling of these contentious, and wrangling men. Which makes me remember the words, in which the eighteenth of Queene *Elizabeths* Injunctions is conceived, That to take away fond Curtesie, (that is, needlesse Complement) and to take away challenging of places, (which it seemes were frequent and troublesome then) To take away fond curtesie, and challenging of places, Processions themselves were taken away, because in those Processions, these Orders of Friers, that pretended to follow, and come after all the world, did thus passionately, and with so much scandalous animosity pursue the love of place, and precedency. Therefore is our humility here limited, *Sequere me, follow me,* follow Christ. How is that done?

Sequendus in Doctrina

Consider it in Doctrinall things first, and then in Morall; First how we are to follow Christ in beleeving, and then how in doing, in practising. First in Doctrinall things, There must have gone some body before, else it is no following; Take heed therefore of going on with thine owne inventions, thine owne imaginations, for this is no following; Take heed of accompanying the beginners of Heresies and Schismes; for these are no followings where none have gone before: Nay, there have not gone enow before, to make it a path to follow in, except it have had a long continuance, and beene much trodden in. And therfore to follow Christ doctrinally, is to embrace those Doctrins, in which his Church hath walked from the beginning, and not to vexe thy selfe with new points, not necessary to salvation. That is the right way, and then thou art well entred; but that is not all; thou must walke in the right way to the end, that is, to the end of thy life. So that to professe the whole Gospel, and nothing but Gospel for Gospel, and professe this to thy death, for no respect, no dependance upon any great person, to slacken in any fundamentall point of thy Religion, nor to bee shaken with hopes or fears in thine age, when thou wouldst faine live at ease, and therefore thinkest it necessary to do, as thy supporters doe; To persevere to the end in the whole Gospel, this is to follow Christ in Doctrinall things.

Sequendu in vitæ

Iam. 5.11

In practicall things, things that belong to action, wee must also follow Christ, in the right way, and to the end. They are both (way and end) laid together, *Sufferentiam Iob audiistis, & finem Domini vidistis; You have heard of the patience of Iob, and you have seen the end of the Lord;* and you must goe *Iobs* way to Christs end. *Iob* hath beaten a path for us, to shew us all the way; A path that affliction walked in, and seemed to delight in it, in bringing the Sabæan upon his Oxen, the Chaldean upon his Camels, the fire upon his Sheep, destruction upon his Servants, and at last, ruine upon his Children. One affliction makes not a path; iterated, continued calamities doe; and such a path Iob hath shewed us, not onely patience, but cheerfulnesse; more, thankfulnesse for our afflictions, because they were multiplied. And then, wee must set before our eyes, as the way of *Iob,* so the end of the Lord; Now the end of the Lord was the crosse: So that to follow him to the end, is not onely to beare afflictions, though to death, but it is to bring our crosses to the Crosse of Christ. How is that progresse made? (for it is a royall progresse, not a pilgrimage to follow Christ to his Crosse) Our Saviour saith, *Hee that*

[Job 1.14-19]

Matt. 16.2

will follow me, let him take up his crosse, and follow me. You see foure stages, foure resting, baiting places in this progresse. It must bee a *crosse,* And it must be *my crosse,* And then it must be *taken up by me,* And with this crosse of mine, thus taken up by me, I must *follow Christ,* that is, carry my crosse to his.

Crux

First it must bee a *Crosse, Tollat crucem;* for every man hath afflictions, but every man hath not crosses. Onely those afflictions are Gal. 6.14 crosses, *whereby the world is crucified to us, and we to the world.* The afflictions of the wicked exasperate them, enrage them, stone and pave them, obdurate and petrifie them, but they doe not crucifie them. The afflictions of the godly crucifie them. And when I am Col. 1.24 come to that conformity with my Saviour, as to *fulfill his sufferings in my flesh,* (as I am, when I glorifie him in a Christian constancy and cheerfulnesse in my afflictions) then I am crucified with him, car- 2 King. 4.34 ried up to his Crosse: And as *Elisha* in raysing the *Shunamits* dead child, put his mouth upon the childs mouth, his eyes, and his hands, upon the hands, and eyes of the child; so when my crosses have carried mee up to my Saviours Crosse, I put my hands into his hands, and hang upon his nailes, I put mine eyes upon his, and wash off all my former unchast looks, and receive a soveraigne tincture, and a lively verdure, and a new life into my dead teares, from his teares. [Mat. 27.46; Mark 15.34] I put my mouth upon his mouth, and it is I that say, *My God, my God, why hast thou forsaken me?* and it is I that recover againe, and [Luke 23.46] say, *Into thy hands, O Lord, I commend my spirit.* Thus my afflictions are truly a crosse, when those afflictions doe truely crucifie me, and souple me, and mellow me, and knead me, and roll me out, to a conformity with Christ. It must be this *Crosse,* and then it must be *my crosse* that I must take up, *Tollat suam.*

Crux mea

Other mens crosses are not my crosses; no man hath suffered more then himselfe needed. That is a poore treasure which they boast of in the Romane Church, that they have in their Exchequer, all the works of supererogation, of the Martyrs in the Primitive Church, that suffered so much more then was necessary for their owne salvation, and those superabundant crosses and merits they can apply to me. If the treasure of the blood of Christ Jesus be not sufficient, Lord what addition can I find, to match them, to piece out them! And if it be sufficient of it selfe, what addition need I seek? Other mens crosses are not mine, other mens merits cannot save me. Nor is any crosse mine owne, which is not mine by a good title; If I be not Possessor *bonæ fidei,* If I came not well by that crosse. And *Quid habeo quod non accepi?* is a question that reaches even to my crosses; what have I that I have not received? not a crosse; And from whose hands can I receive any good thing, but from the hands of God? So that that onely is my crosse, which the hand of God hath laid upon me. Alas, that crosse of present bodily weaknesse, which the former wantonnesses of my youth have brought upon me, is not my crosse; That crosse of poverty which the wastfulnesse of youth hath brought upon me, is not my crosse; for these, weaknesse upon wantonnesse, want upon wastfulnesse, are Natures crosses, not Gods, and they would fall naturally, though there were (which is an impossible supposition) no God. Except God therefore take these crosses in the way, as they fall into his hands, and sanctifie them so, and then lay them upon me, they are not my crosses; but if God doe this, they are. And then this crosse thus prepared, I must *take up; Tollat.*

1 Cor. 4.7

Tollat

Forraine crosses, other mens merits are not mine; spontaneous and voluntary crosses, contracted by mine owne sins, are not mine; neither are devious, and remote, and unnecessary crosses, my crosses. Since I am bound to take up my crosse, there must be a crosse that is mine to take up; that is, a crosse prepared for me by God, and laid in my way, which is tentations or tribulations in my calling; and I must not go out of my way to seeke a crosse; for, so it is not mine, nor laid for my taking up. I am not bound to hunt after a persecution, nor to stand it, and not flye, nor to affront a plague, and not remove, nor to open my selfe to an injury, and not defend. I am not bound to starve my selfe by inordinate fasting, nor to teare my flesh by inhumane whippings, and flagellations. I am bound to take up my Crosse; and that is onely mine which the hand of God hath laid for me, that is, in the way of my Calling, tentations and tribulations incident to that.

Sequatur me

If it be mine, that is, laid for me by the hand of God, and taken up by me, that is, voluntarily embraced, then *Sequatur,* sayes Christ, I am bound to *follow him,* with that crosse, that is, to carry my crosse to his crosse. And if at any time I faint under this crosse in the way, let this comfort me, that even Christ himselfe was eased by *Simon*

Mat. 27.32

of Cyrene, in the carrying of his Crosse; and in all such cases, I must flye to the assistance of the prayers of the Church, and of good men, that God, since it is his burden, will make it lighter, since it is his yoake, easier, and since it is his Crosse, more supportable, and give me the issue with the tentation. When all is done, with this crosse thus laid for me, and taken up by me, I must follow Christ; Christ to his end; his end is his Crosse; that is, I must bring my crosse to his; lay downe my crosse at the foote of his; Confesse that there is no dignity, no merit in mine, but as it receives an impression, a sanctification from his. For, if I could dye a thousand times for Christ, this were nothing, if Christ had not dyed for me before. And this is truly to follow Christ, both in the way, and to the end, as well in doctrinall things as in practicall. And this is all that lay upon these two, *Peter* and *Andrew, Follow me*. Remaines yet to be considered, what they shall get by this; which is our last Consideration.

Piscatores hominum

They shall be *fishers;* and what shall they catch? *men*. They shall be fishers of men. And then, for that the world must be their Sea, and their net must be the Gospel. And here in so vast a sea, and with so small a net, there was no great appearance of much gaine. And in this function, whatsoever they should catch, they should catch little for themselves. The Apostleship, as it was the fruitfullest, so it was the barrennest vocation; They were to catch all the world; there is their fecundity; but the Apostles were to have no Successors, as Apostles; there is their barrennesse. The Apostleship was not intended for a function to raise houses and families; The function ended in their persons; after the first, there were no more Apostles.

And therefore it is an usurpation, an imposture, an illusion, it is a forgery, when the Bishop of Rome will proceed by Apostolicall authority, and with Apostolicall dignity, and Apostolicall jurisdiction; If he be S. *Peters* Successor in the Bishopricke of Rome, he may proceed with Episcopall authority in his Dioces. If he be; for, though we doe not deny that S. *Peter* was at Rome, and Bishop of Rome; though we receive it with an historicall faith, induced by the consent of Ancient writers, yet when they will constitute matter of faith out of matter of fact, and, because S. *Peter* was (*de facto*) Bishop of Rome, therefore we must beleeve, as an Article of faith, such an infallibility in that Church, as that no Successor of S. *Peters* can ever erre, when they stretch it to matter of faith, then for matter of faith, we require Scriptures; and then we are confident, and justly confident, that though historically we do beleeve it, yet out of Scriptures (which is a necessary proofe in Articles of faith) they can never prove that S. *Peter* was Bishop of Rome, or ever at Rome. So then, if the present Bishop of Rome be S. *Peters* Successor, as Bishop of Rome, he hath Episcopall jurisdiction there; but he is not S. *Peters* Successor in his Apostleship; and onely that Apostleship was a jurisdiction over all the world. But the Apostleship was an extraordinary office instituted by Christ, for a certaine time, and to certaine purposes, and not to continue in ordinary use. As also the office of the Prophet was in the Old Testament an extraordinary Office, and was not transferred then, nor does not remaine now in the ordinary office of the Minister.

And therefore they argue impertinently, and collect and infer sometimes seditiously that say, The Prophet proceeded thus and thus, therefore the Minister may and must proceed so too; The Prophets would chide the Kings openly, and threaten the Kings publiquely, and proclaime the fault of the Kings in the eares of the people confidently, authoritatively, therefore the Minister may and must do so. God sent that particular Prophet *Ieremy* with that extraordinary Commission, *Behold I have this day set thee over the Nations, and* Ier. 1.10
over the Kingdomes, to roote out, and to pull downe, to destroy and throw downe, and then to build, and to plant againe; But God hath given none of us his Ministers, in our ordinary function, any such Commission over nations, and over Kingdomes. Even in *Ieremies* Commission there seemes to be a limitation of time; *Behold this day I have set thee over them,* where that addition (*this day*) is not onely the date of the Commission, that it passed Gods hand that day, but (*this day*) is the terme, the duration of the Commission, that it was to last but that day, that is, (as the phrase of that language is) that time for which it was limited. And therefore, as they argue perversely, frowardly, dangerously that say, The Minister does not his duty that speakes not as boldly, and as publiquely too, and of Kings, and great persons, as the Prophets did, because theirs was an Extraordinary, ours an Ordinary office, (and no man will thinke that the Justices in their Sessions, or the Judges in their Circuits may proceed

to executions, without due tryall by a course of Law, because Marshals, in time of rebellion and other necessities, may doe so, because the one hath but an ordinary, the other an extraordinary Commission) So doe they deceive themselves and others, that pretend in the Bishop of Rome an Apostolicall jurisdiction, a jurisdiction over all the world, whereas howsoever he may be S. *Peters* Successor, as Bishop of Rome, yet he is no Successor to S. *Peter* as an Apostle; upon which onely the universall power can be grounded, and without which that universall power fals to the ground: The Apostolicall faith remaines spread over all the world, but Apostolicall jurisdiction is expired with their persons.

Piscatores, quia nomen humile

These twelve Christ cals *Fishers;* why fishers? because it is a name of labour, of service, and of humiliation; and names that tast of humiliation, and labour, and service, are most properly ours; (fishers we may be) names of dignity, and authority, and command are not so properly ours, (Apostles wee are not in any such sense as they were) Nothing inflames, nor swels, nor puffes us up, more then that leaven of the soule, that empty, aery, frothy love of Names and Titles. We have knowne men part with ancient lands for new Titles, and with old Mannors for new Honours; and as a man that should bestow all his money upon a faire purse, and then have nothing to put into it; so whole Estates have melted away for Titles and Honours, and nothing left to support them. And how long last they? How many winds blast them? That name of God, in which, *Moses* was sent to *Pharaoh,* is by our Translators and Expositors ordinarily said to be *I Am that I Am,* (*Go and say, I Am hath sent me,* sayes God there) But in truth, in the Originall, the name is conceived in the future, it is, *I shall be.* Every man is that he is; but onely God is sure that he shall be so still. Therefore Christ cals them by a name of labour and humiliation. But why by that name of labour and humiliation, *Fishers?*

Exod. 3.14

Piscatores, quia nomen primitivum

Because it was *Nomen primitivum,* their owne, their former name. The Holy Ghost pursues his owne way, and does here in Christ, as hee does often in other places, he speakes in such formes, and such phrases, as may most worke upon them to whom he speaks. Of *David,* that was a shepheard before, God sayes, he tooke him to feed his people. To those *Magi* of the East, who were given to the study of the Stars, God gave a Star to be their guide to Christ at Bethlem.

Psal. 78.70 [and 71]

Mat. 2.2

Iohn 6.24

[John] 4.11 [also 6, 7, 13, 14]

[Mat. 13.44, 45]

To those which followed him to Capernaum for meat, Christ tooke occasion by that, to preach to them of the spirituall food of their souls. To the Samaritan woman, whom he found at the Well, he preached of the water of Life. To these men in our Text accustomed to a joy and gladnesse, when they tooke great, or great store of fish, he presents his comforts agreeably to their tast, They should be fishers still. Beloved, Christ puts no man out of his way, (for sinfull courses are no wayes, but continuall deviations) to goe to heaven. Christ makes heaven all things to all men, that he might gaine all: To the mirthfull man he presents heaven, as all joy, and to the ambitious man, as all glory; To the Merchant it is a Pearle, and to the husbandman it is a rich field. Christ hath made heaven all things to all men, that he might gaine all, and he puts no man out of his way to come thither. These men he calls Fishers.

Non Innovatio, sed Renovatio

He does not call them from their calling, but he mends them in it. It is not an Innovation; God loves not innovations; Old doctrines, old disciplines, old words and formes of speech in his service, God loves best. But it is a Renovation, though not an Innovation, and Renovations are alwayes acceptable to God; that is, the renewing of a mans selfe, in a consideration of his first estate, what he was made for, and wherein he might be most serviceable to God. Such a renewing it is, as could not be done without God; no man can renew himselfe, regenerate himselfe; no man can prepare that worke, no man can begin it, no man can proceed in it of himselfe. The desire and the actuall beginning is from the preventing grace of God, and the constant proceeding is from the concomitant, and subsequent, and continuall succeeding grace of God; for there is no conclusive, no consummative grace in this life; no such measure of grace given to any man, as that that man needs no more, or can lose or frustrate none of that. The renewing of these men in our text, Christ takes to himselfe; *Faciam vos, I will make yee fishers of men;* no worldly respects must make us such fishers; it must be a calling from God; And yet, (as the other Euangelist in the same history expresses it) it is *Faciam fieri vos, I will cause yee to be made fishers of men,* that is, I will provide an outward calling for you too. Our calling to this Man-fishing is not good, *Nisi Dominus faciat, & fieri faciat,* except God make us fishers by an internall, and make his Church to make us so

Mar. 1.17

too, by an externall calling. Then we are fishers of men, and then we are successors to the Apostles, though not in their Apostleship, yet in this fishing. And then, for this fishing, the world is the Sea, and our net is the Gospel.

Mundus Mare

The world is a Sea in many respects and assimilations. It is a Sea, as it is subject to stormes, and tempests; Every man (and every man is a world) feels that. And then, it is never the shallower for the calmnesse, The Sea is as deepe, there is as much water in the Sea, in a calme, as in a storme; we may be drowned in a calme and flattering fortune, in prosperity, as irrecoverably, as in a wrought Sea, in adversity; So the world is a Sea. It is a Sea, as it is bottomlesse to any line, which we can sound it with, and endlesse to any discovery that we can make of it. The purposes of the world, the wayes of the world, exceed our consideration; But yet we are sure the Sea hath a bottome, and sure that it hath limits, that it cannot overpasse; The power of the greatest in the world, the life of the happiest in the world, cannot exceed those bounds, which God hath placed for them; So the world is a Sea. It is a Sea, as it hath ebbs and floods, and no man knowes the true reason of those floods and those ebbs. All men have changes and vicissitudes in their bodies, (they fall sick) And in their estates, (they grow poore) And in their minds, (they become sad) at which changes, (sicknesse, poverty, sadnesse) themselves wonder, and the cause is wrapped up in the purpose and judgement of God onely, and hid even from them that have them; and so the world is a Sea. It is a Sea, as the Sea affords water enough for all the world to drinke, but such water as will not quench the thirst. The world affords conveniences enow to satisfie Nature, but these encrease our thirst with drinking, and our desire growes and enlarges it selfe with our abundance, and though we sayle in a full Sea, yet we lacke water; So the world is a Sea. It is a Sea, if we consider the Inhabitants. In the Sea, the greater fish devoure the lesse; and so doe the men of this world too. And as fish, when they mud themselves, have no hands to make themselves cleane, but the current of the waters must worke that; So have the men of this world no means to cleanse themselves from those sinnes which they have contracted in the world, of themselves, till a new flood, waters of repentance, drawne up, and sanctified by the Holy Ghost, worke that blessed effect in them.

All these wayes the world is a Sea, but especially it is a Sea in this respect, that the Sea is no place of habitation, but a passage to our habitations. So the Apostle expresses the world, *Here we have no* (Heb. 13.14) *continuing City, but we seeke one to come;* we seeke it not here, but we seeke it whilest we are here, els we shall never finde it. Those are the two great works which we are to doe in this world; first to know, that this world is not our home, and then to provide us another home, whilest we are in this world. Therefore the Prophet sayes, *Arise, and depart, for this is not your rest.* (Mic. 2.10) Worldly men, that have no farther prospect, promise themselves some rest in this world, (*Soule, thou hast much goods laid up for many yeares, take thine* (Luk. 12.19) *ease, eate, drinke, and be merry,* sayes the rich man) but this is not your rest; indeed no rest; at least not yours. You must depart, depart by death, before yee come to that rest; but then you must arise, before you depart; for except yee have a resurrection to grace here, before you depart, you shall have no resurrection to glory in the life to come, when you are departed.

Status navigantium

Now, in this Sea, every ship that sayles must necessarily have some part of the ship under water; Every man that lives in this world, must necessarily have some of his life, some of his thoughts, some of his labours spent upon this world; but that part of the ship, by which he sayls, is above water; Those meditations, and those endevours which must bring us to heaven, are removed from this world, and fixed entirely upon God. And in this Sea, are we made fishers of men; Of men in generall; not of rich men, to profit by them, nor of poore men, to pierce them the more sharply, because affliction hath opened a way into them; Not of learned men, to be over-glad of their approbation of our labours, Nor of ignorant men, to affect them with an astonishment, or admiration of our gifts: But we are fishers of men, of all men, of that which makes them men, their soules. And for this fishing in this Sea, this Gospel is our net.

Rete Euangelium

Eloquence is not our net; Traditions of men are not our nets; onely the Gospel is. The Devill angles with hooks and bayts; he deceives, and he wounds in the catching; for every sin hath his sting. The

Gospel of Christ Jesus is a net; It hath leads and corks; It hath leads, that is, the denouncing of Gods judgements, and a power to sink down, and lay flat any stubborne and rebellious heart, And it hath corks, that is, the power of absolution, and application of the mercies of God, that swimme above all his works, means to erect an humble and contrite spirit, above all the waters of tribulation, and affliction.

Rete nodosum

A net is *Res nodosa,* a knotty thing; and so is the Scripture, full of knots, of scruple, and perplexity, and anxiety, and vexation, if thou wilt goe about to entangle thy selfe in those things, which appertaine not to thy salvation; but knots of a fast union, and inseparable alliance of thy soule to God, and to the fellowship of his Saints, if thou take the Scriptures, as they were intended for thee, that is, if thou beest content to rest in those places, which are cleare, and evident in things necessary.

Rete diffusivum

A net is a large thing, past thy fadoming, if thou cast it from thee, but if thou draw it to thee, it will lie upon thine arme. The Scriptures will be out of thy reach, and out of thy use, if thou cast and scatter them upon Reason, upon Philosophy, upon Morality, to try how the Scriptures will fit all them, and beleeve them but so far as they agree with thy reason; But draw the Scripture to thine own heart, and to thine own actions, and thou shalt finde it made for that; all the promises of the old Testament made, and all accomplished in the new Testament, for the salvation of thy soule hereafter, and for thy consolation in the present application of them.

Non quia tanquam causa

Rom. 6.23

[Mat. 7.7]

Now this that Christ promises here, is not here promised in the nature of wages due to our labour, and our fishing. There is no merit in all that we can doe. *The wages of sin is Death;* Death is due to sin, the proper reward of sin; but the Apostle does not say there, That eternall life is the wages of any good worke of ours. (*The wages of sinne is death, but eternall life is the gift of God, through Iesus Christ our Lord*) Through Jesus Christ, that is, as we are considered in him; and in him, who is a Saviour, a Redeemer, we are not considered but as sinners. So that Gods purpose works no otherwise upon us, but as we are sinners; neither did God meane ill to any man, till that man was, in his sight, a sinner. God shuts no man out of heaven, by a lock on the inside, except that man have clapped the doore after him, and never knocked to have it opened againe, that is, except he have sinned, and never repented. Christ does not say in our text,

Follow me, for I will prefer you; he will not have that the reason, the cause. If I would not serve God, except I might be saved for serving him, I shall not be saved though I serve him; My first end in serving God, must not be my selfe, but he and his glory. It is but an addition from his own goodnesse, *Et faciam,* Follow me, and I will doe this; but yet it is as certaine, and infallible as a debt, or as an effect upon a naturall cause. Those propositions in nature are not so certaine; The Earth is at such a time just between the Sunne, and the Moone, therefore the Moone must be Eclipsed, The Moone is at such time just betweene the Earth and the Sunne, therefore the Sunne must be Eclipsed; for upon the Sunne, and those other bodies, God can, and hath sometimes wrought miraculously, and changed the naturall courses of them; (The Sunne stood still in *Ioshua,* And there was an [Joshua 10.13] unnaturall Eclipse at the death of Christ) But God cannot by any Miracle so worke upon himselfe, as to make himselfe not himselfe, [Luke 23.44, 45] unmercifull, or unjust; And out of his mercy he makes this promise, (Doe this, and thus it shall be with you) and then, of his justice he performes that promise, which was made meerely, and onely out of mercy, If we doe it, (though not because we doe it) we shall have eternall life.

Therefore did *Andrew,* and *Peter* faithfully beleeve, such a net should be put into their hands. Christ had vouchsafed to fish for them, and caught them with that net, and they beleeved that he that made them fishers of men, would also enable them to catch others with that net. And that is truly the comfort that refreshes us in all our Lucubrations, and night-studies, through the course of our lives, that that God that sets us to Sea, will prosper our voyage, that whether he fix us upon our owne, or send us to other Congregations, he will open the hearts of those Congregations to us, and blesse our labours to them. For as S. *Pauls Væ si non,* lies upon us wheresoever we are, [1 Cor. 9.16] (Wo be unto us if wee doe not preach) so, (as S. *Paul* sayes too) we were of all men the most miserable, if wee preached without hope of [1 Cor. 15.19] doing good. With this net S. *Peter* caught three thousand soules in one day, at one Sermon, and five thousand in another. With this net Acts 2.41 [Acts] 4.4 S. *Paul* fished all the Mediterranean Sea, and caused the Gospel of Christ Jesus to abound from Jerusalem round about to Illyricum. This Rom. 15.19 is the net, with which if yee be willing to bee caught, that is, to lay downe all your hopes and affiances in the gracious promises of his Gospel, then you are fishes reserved for that great Mariage-feast, which is the Kingdome of heaven; where, whosoever is a dish, is a ghest too; whosoever is served in at the table, sits at the table; whosoever is caught by this net, is called to this feast; and there your [Psal. 63.5] soules shall be satisfied as with marrow, and with fatnesse, in an infallible assurance, of an everlasting and undeterminable terme, in inexpressible joy and glory. Amen.

Number 15.

Preached at Lincolns Inne
[January 30, 1619/20]

JOHN 5.22. *THE FATHER JUDGETH NO MAN, BUT HATH COMMITTED ALL JUDGEMENT TO THE SONNE.*

WHEN OUR Saviour forbids us to cast pearl before swine, we understand ordinarily in that place, that by pearl, are understood the Scriptures; and when we consider the naturall generation and production of Pearl, that they grow bigger and bigger, by a continuall succession, and devolution of dew, and other glutinous moysture that fals upon them, and there condenses and hardens, so that a pearl is but a body of many shels, many crusts, many films, many coats enwrapped upon one another, To this Scripture which we have in hand, doth that Metaphor of pearl very properly appertain; because our Saviour Christ in this Chapter undertaking to prove his own Divinity and God-head to the Jews, who acknowledged, and confessed the Father to be God, but denyed it of him, he folds and wraps up reason upon reason, argument upon argument, that all things are common between the Father and him, that whatsoever the Father does, he does, whatsoever the Father is, he is; for first, he says, he is a partner, a cooperator with the Father, in the present administration and government of the world, *My Father worketh hitherto, and I work;* well, if the Father do ease himself upon instruments now, yet was it so from the beginning? had he a part in the Creation? Yes; *What things soever the Father doth, those also doth the Son likewise.* But doe those extend to the work properly, and naturally belonging to God, to the remission of sinnes, to the infusion of grace, to the spirituall resurrection of them that are

Mat. 7.6

[John 5] Verse 17

Verse 19

Verse 21 dead in their iniquities? Yes, even to that too, *For as the Father raiseth up the dead, and quickneth them, even so the Son quickneth whom he will.* But hath not this power of his a determination, or expiration? shall it not end, at least when the world ends? No, not then, for Verse 27 *God hath given him authority to execute judgment, because he is the Son of man.* Is there then no *Supersedeas* upon this commission? Is the Sonne *equall* with the Father in our eternall election, in our creation, in the meanes of our salvation, in the last judgement, in all? In all, *Omne judicium,* God hath committed all judgement to the Son; And here is a pearl made up; the dew of Gods grace sprinkled upon your souls, the beams of Gods Spirit shed upon your soules, that effectuall and working knowledge, That he who dyed for your salvation is perfect God, as well as perfect man, fit, as willing to accomplish that salvation.

Divisio In handling then this *Iudgement,* which is a word that embraces and comprehends all, All from our Election, where no merit or future actions of ours were considered by God, to our fruition and possession of that election, where all our actions shall be considered and recompensed by him, we shall see first that Judgment belongs properly to God; And secondly, that God the Father whom we consider to be the root and foundation of the Deity, can no more devest his Judgment then he can his Godhead, and therefore in the third place we consider, what that committing of Judgment, which is mentioned here imports, and then to whom it is committed, To the Sonne: and lastly the largnesse of that which is committed, *Omne,* all Judgment, so that we cannot carry our thoughts so high, or so farre backwards, as to think of any Judgment given upon us in Gods purpose or decree without relation to Christ; Nor so far forward, as to think that there shall be a Judgment given upon us, according to our good morall dispositions or actions, but according to our apprehension and imitation of Christ. Judgment is a proper and inseparable Character of God; that's first: the Father cannot devest himself of that; that's next. The third is that he hath committed it to another; And then the person that is his delegate, is his onely Sonne; and lastly his power is everlasting, And that Judgment day that belongs to him, hath, and shall last from our first Election, through the participation of the meanes prepared by him in his Church, to our association and union with him in glory, and so the whole circle of time, and before time was, and when time shall be no more, makes up but one Judgment day to him, to whom the Father who judgeth no man hath committed all Judgment.

First then Judgment appertaines to God, It is his in Criminall causes, *Vindicta mihi, Vengeance is mine, I will repay, saith the Lord;* It is so in civill things too; for God himself is proprietary of all, *Domini est terra et plenitudo ejus, The earth is the Lords,* and all that is in, and on the earth; *Your silver is mine, and your gold is mine,* says the Prophet, *and the beasts on a Thousand hills are mine,* says *David,* you are usufructuaries of them, but I am proprietary; No attribute of God is so often iterated in the Scriptures, no state of God so often inculcated, as this of Judge, and Judgment, no word concerning God so often repeated: but it is brought to the height, where in that place of the Psalm, where we read, *God judgeth among the Gods,* the Latine Church ever read it, *Deus dijudicat Deos, God judgeth the Gods themselves;* for though God say of Judges and Magistrats, *Ego dixi dii estis, I have said ye are Gods,* (and if God say it, who shall gainsay it?) yet he says too, *Moriemini, sicut homines, The greatest Gods upon earth shall die like men;* And if that be not humiliation enough, there is more threatned in that which follows, *yee shall fall like one of the Princes,* for the fall of a Prince involves the ruine of many others too, and it fills the world with horror for the present, and ominous discourse for the future; but the farthest of all is *Deus dijudicat Deos,* even these Judges must come to Judgment, and therefore that Psalme which begins so, is concluded thus, *Surge Domine, arise O God, and judge the earth:* If he have power to judge the earth, he is God, and even in God himselfe it is expressed as a kind of rising, as some exaltation of his power, that he is to Judge; And that place in the beginning of that Psalme many of the antients read in the future *Dijudicabit,* God shall judge the Gods, because the frame of the Psalme seems to referre it to the last Judgment; *Tertullian* reads it *Dijudicavit,* as a thing past, God hath judged in all times; and the letter of the text requires it to be in the present, *Dijudicat.* Collect all, and Judgment is so essentiall to God, as that it is coeternall with him, he hath, he doth, and he will judge the world, and the Judges of the world; other Judges die

1. Part *Iudicium Dei*
Rom. 12.19
[Psal. 24.1]
[Haggai 2.8]
[Psal. 50.10]
Psal. 82.1
[Psal. 82.6, 7]

like men, weakely, and they fall, that's worse, ignominiously, and they fall like Princes, that's worst, fearfully, and yet scornfully, and when they are dead and faln, they rise no more to execute Judgement, but have Judgment executed upon them. The Lord dyes not, nor he falls not, and if he seem to slumber, the Martyrs under the Altar [Apoc. 6.10] awake him with their *Vsque quo Domine, how long O Lord before thou execute Iudgment?* And he will arise and Judge the world, for Psal. 75.7 Judgment is his; *God putteth downe one, and setteth up another,* says *David;* where hath he that power? Why, God is the Judge, not a Judge, but the Judge, and in that right he putteth downe one, and setteth up another.

Iudicium detestationis

Now for this Judgment, which we place in God, we must consider in God three notions, three apprehensions, three kinds of Judgment. First, God hath *Judicium detestationis,* God doth naturally know, and therefore naturally detest evill; for no man in the extreamest corruption of nature is yet fallen so far, as to love or approve evill at the same time that he knows, and acknowledges it to be evill. But we are so blind in the knowledge of evill, that we needed that great supplement, and assistance of the law it self to make us know what [Deut. 4.7] was evill; *Moses* magnifies (and justly) the law, *Non appropinquavit,* says *Moses,* God came not so neare to any nation as to the *Jews;* [Psal. 147.20] *Non taliter fecit,* God dealt not so well with any nation, as with the *Jews;* and wherein? because he had given them a law: and yet we Rom. 3.20 see the greatest dignity of this law, to be, That by the law is the knowledge of sinne; for though by the law of nature written in our hearts, there be some condemnation of some sinnes, yet to know that every sinne was Treason against God, to know that every sinne hath the reward of death, and eternall death annexed to it; this knowledge we have onely by the law. Now if man will pretend to be a Judge, what an exact knowledge of the law is required at his hand? for some things are sinne to one nation, which are not to another, as where the just authority of the lawfull Magistrate, changes the nature of the thing, and makes a thing naturally indifferent, necessary to them, who are under his obedience; some things are sinnes at one time, which are not at another, as all the ceremoniall law, created new sinnes which were not sinnes before the law was given, nor since it expir'd; some things are sinnes in a man now, which will not be sinnes in the same man to morrow, as when a man hath contracted a just scruple, against any particular action, it is a sinne to doe it during the scruple, and it may be sinne in him to omit it, when he hath devested the scruple; onely God hath *Judicium detestationis,* he knows, and therefore detests evill, and therefore flatter not thy self with a Tush, God sees it not, or, Tush, God cares not, Doth it disquiet him or trouble his rest in heaven that I breake his Sabbath here? Doth it wound his body, or draw his bloud there, that I swear by his body and bloud here? Doth it corrupt any of his virgins there, that I sollicit the chastity of a woman here? Are his Martyrs withdrawn from their Allegeance, or retarded in their service to him there, because I dare not defend his cause, nor speake for him, nor fight for him here? Beloved, as it is a degree of superstition, and an effect of an undiscreet zeale, perchance, to be too forward in making indifferent things necessary, and so to imprint the nature, and sting of sin where naturally it is not so: certainly it is a more slippery and irreligious thing to be too apt to call things meerely indifferent, and to forget that even in eating and drinking, waking and sleeping, the glory of God is intermingled; as if we knew exactly the prescience and foreknowledge of God, there could be nothing contingent or casuall, (for though there be a contingency in the nature of the thing, yet it is certain to God) so if we considered duly, wherein the glory of God might be promov'd in every action of ours, there could scarce be any action so indifferent, but that the glory of God would turne the scale and make it necessary to me, at that time; but then private interests, and private respects create a new indifferency to my apprehension, and calls me to consider that thing as it is in nature, and not as it is considered with that circumstance of the glory of God, and so I lose that *Judicium detestationis,* which onely God hath absolutely and perfectly to know, and therefore to detest evill, and so he is a Judge.

Iudicium discretionis

And as he is a Judge, so *Judicat rem,* he judges the nature of the thing, he is so too, as he hath *Judicium discretionis,* and so *Judicat personam,* he knows what is evill, and he discernes when thou committest that evill. Here you are fain to supply defects of laws, that things done in one County may be tryed in another; And that in offences of high nature, transmarine offences may be inquir'd and tryed here; But as the Prophet says, *Who measured the waters in the* Esay 40.12

hollow of his hand, or meted out the heavens with a span, who comprehended the dust of the earth in a measure, or weighed the mountains in a scale? So I say, who hath divided heaven into shires or parishes, or limited the territories and Jurisdictions there, that God should not have and exercise *Judicium discretionis,* the power of discerning all actions, in all places? When there was no more to be seen, or considered upon the whole earth but the garden of Paradise, for [Prov. 8.31] from the beginning *Deliciæ ejus esse cum filiis hominum,* Gods delight was to be with the sons of men, and man was only there, shal we not diminish God nor speak too vulgarly of him to say, that he hovered like a Falcon over Paradise, and that from that height of heaven, the piercing eye of God, saw so little a thing, as the forbidden fruit, and what became of that, and the reaching eare of God heard the hissing of the Serpent, and the whispering of the woman, and what was concluded upon that? Shall we think it little to have seen things done in Paradise when there was nothing else to divert his eye, nothing else to distract his counsels, nothing else done upon the face of the earth? Take the earth now as it is replenished, and take it either as it is torn and crumbled into raggs, and shivers, not a kingdome, not a family, not a man agreeing with himselfe; Or take it in Psalm 2.2 that concord which is in it, as *All the Kings of the earth set themselves, and all the Rulers of the earth take counsell together against the Lord;* take it in this union, or this division, in this concord, or [Psal. 2.4] this discord, still the Lord that sitteth in the heavens discernes all, looks at all, laughs at all, and hath them all in derision. Earthly Judges have their distinctions, and so their restrictions; some things they cannot know, what mortall man can know all? Some things they cannot take knowledge of, for they are bound to evidence: But God hath *Iudicium discretionis,* no mist, no cloud, no darknesse, no disguise keeps him from discerning, and judging all our actions, and so he is a Judge too.

Iudicium retributionis

And he is so lastly, as he hath *Iudicium retributionis,* God knows what is evill, he knows when that evill is done, and he knows how to punish and recompense that evill: for the office of a Judge who judges according to a law, being not to contract, or extend that law, but to declare what was the true meaning of that Law-maker when hee made that law, God hath this judgement in perfection, because hee himself made that law by which he judges, and therefore when he hath said, *Morte morieris, If thou do this, thou shalt die a double* [Gen. 2.17] *death;* where he hath said, *Stipendium peccati mors est,* every sin [Rom. 6.23] shall be rewarded with *death; If I sinne against the Lord, who shall* 1 Sam. 2.25 *entreat for me?* Who shall give any other interpretation, any modification, any *Non obstante* upon his law in my behalf, when he comes to judge me according to that law which himself hath made? Who shall think to delude the Judge, and say, Surely this was not the meaning of the Law-giver, when he who is the Judge was the Law-maker too?

And then as God is Judge in all these three respects, so is he a Judge in them all, *Sine Appellatione,* and *Sine judiciis,* man cannot *Sine Appellatione* appeal from God, God needs no evidence from man; for, for the Appeal first, to whom should we appeal from the Soveraign? Wrangle as long as ye will who is Chief Justice, and which Court hath Jurisdiction over another; I know the Chief Justice, and I know the Soveraign Court; the King of heaven and earth shall send his ministring Spirits, his Angels to the womb, and bowels of the Earth, and to the bosome, and bottome of the Sea, and Earth and Sea must deliver, *Corpus cum causâ,* all the bodies of the dead, and all their actions, to receive a judgement in this Court: when it will be but an erroneous, and frivolous Appeal, to call to the Hils to fall down upon us, [Luke 23.30] and the Mountains to cover, and hide us from the wrathfull judgment of God. He is a Judge then *Sine appellatione,* without any Appeal, from him, he is so too *Sine judiciis,* without needing any evidence *Sine Judiciis* from us. Now if I be wary in my actions here, incarnate Devils, detractors, and informers cannot accuse me; If my sinne come not to action, but lye onely in my heart, the Devill himself who is the accuser of the brethren, hath no evidence against me; but God knows my heart; doth not he that *pondereth the heart, understand it?* where Prov. 24.12 it is not in that faint word, which the vulgar Edition hath expressed it in, *inspector cordium,* That God sees the heart; but the word is *Tochen,* which signifies every where to weigh, to number, to search, to examine; as the word is used by *Salomon* again, *The Lord weigheth the spirits,* Prov. 16.2 and it must be a steady hand, and exact scales that shall weigh spirits. So that though neither man, nor Devill, nay nor my self give evidence against me, yea, though I know nothing by

my selfe, I am not thereby justified; why? where is the farther dan-
1 Cor. 4.4 ger? In this which follows there in Saint *Paul, He that judges me is the Lord,* and the Lord hath meanes to know my heart better then
my self: And therefore, as Saint *Augustine* makes use of those words,
Psal. 42.7 *Abyssus Abyssum invocat,* one depth cals upon another, The infinite
depth of my sins must call upon the more infinite depth of Gods
mercy; for if God, who is Judge in all these respects, *judicio detestationis,* he knows, and abhors evill, and *judicio discretionis,* he discerns
every evill person, and every evill action, and *judicio retributionis,*
he can, and will recompense evill with evill; And all these *Sine Appellatione,* we cannot appeal from him, and *Sine judiciis,* he needs
no evidence from us; If this Judge enter into judgement with me, not
onely not I, but not the most righteous man, no, nor the Church
[Eph. whom he hath washed in his blood, that she might be without spot
5.25–27] or wrinckle, shall appear righteous in his sight.

2. Part This being then thus, that *Judgement* is an unseparable character
of God the Father, being *Fons Deitatis,* the root and spring of the
whole Deity, how is it said, that the Father judgeth no man? Not
that we should conceive a wearinesse, or retiring in the Father, or a
discharging of himself upon the shoulders, and labours of another, in
the administration, and judging of this world; for as it is truly said,
that God rested the seventh day, that is, he rested from working in
[John 5.17] that kind, from creating, so it is true that Christ says here, *My Father worketh yet, and I work;* and so as it is truly said here, *The Father*
Joh. 8.50 *judgeth no man,* it is truly sayd by Christ too, of the Father, *I seek not mine own glory, there is one that seeketh, and judgeth;* still it is
[Habakkuk true, that God hath *Judicium detestationis, Thy eyes are pure eyes*
1.13] *O Lord, and cannot behold iniquity,* says the Prophet; still it is true,
Ier. 29.23 that hee hath *Judicium discretionis* (because *they committed villany in Israel, even I know it,* saith the Lord;) still it is true, that he hath
1 Sam. 2.6 *Judicium retributionis, The Lord killeth and maketh alive, he bringeth down to the grave, and bringeth up;* still it is true, that he hath
[Psal. all these *sine appellatione;* for go to the Sea, or Earth, or Hell, as
139.8–10] *David* makes the distribution, and God is there; and he hath them
Iob 16.19 *sine judiciis,* for *our witnesse is in heaven, and our record is on high:*
All this is undeniably true, and besides this, that great name of God,
by which he is first called in the Scriptures *Elohim,* is not incon-

veniently deriv'd from *Elah,* which is *Jurare* to swear, God is able as a Judge to minister an oath unto us, and to draw evidence from our own consciences against our selves, so that then, the Father he judges still, but he judges as God, and not as the Father. In the three great judgements of God, the whole Trinity judges; In the first judgement, before all times, which was Gods Judiciary separating of vessels of honour, from vessels of dishonour, in our Election, and Reprobation; In his second judgement, which is in execution now, which is Gods judiciary separating of servants from enemies, in the seales, and in the administration of the Christian Church; and in the last judgement, which shall be Gods Judiciary separating of sheep from goats, to everlasting glory, or condemnation; in all these three judgements, all the three Persons of the Trinity are Judges. Consider God altogether, and so in all outward works, all the Trinity concurres, because all are but *one* God; but consider God in relation, in distinct Persons, and so the severall Persons do something in which the other Persons are not interessed; The Sonne hath not a generation from himself, so, as he had from the Father, and from the holy Ghost, as a distinct person, he had none at all; the holy Ghost had a proceeding from the Father and Son, but from the Sonne as a person, who had his generation from another, but not so from the Father. Not to stray into clouds, or perplexities in this contemplation, God, that is, the whole Trinity, judges still, but so as the Sonne judgeth, the Father judgeth not, for that Judgment he hath committed.

Commisit

That we may husband our hour well, and reserve as much as we can for our two last considerations, the *Cui, & Quid,* to whom, and that's *to the Sonne,* and what he hath committed, and that's *all Iudgement,* we will not stand much upon this, more needs not then this; That God in his wisdome foreseeing, that man for his weaknesse would not be able to settle himself upon the consideration of God and his judgments, as they are meerly heavenly, and spirituall, out of his abundant goodnesse hath established a judgement, and ordained a Judge upon earth like himself, and like our selves too, That as no man hath seen God, so no man should goe about to see his unsearchable decrees, and judgements, but rest in those sensible, and visible meanes which he hath afforded, that is, Christ Jesus speaking in his Church, and applying his blood unto us in the Sacraments to the worlds end: God might have suffered *Abraham* to rest in the first [Gen. 3.15] generall promise, *Semen mulieris, the Seed of the woman shall bruise the Serpents head,* but he would bring it neerer to a visible, to a [Gen. 22.18] personall Covenant, *In semine tuo, In thy Seed shall all nations be blessed;* he might well have let him rest in that appropriation of the promise to his race, but he would proceed farther, and seal it with a sensible seal in his flesh with Circumcision; he might have let him rest in that ratification, that a Messias should come by that way, but he would continue it by a continuall succession of Prophets, till that Messias should come; and now that he is come and gone, still God [Rom. 10.14] pursues the same way; *How should they believe, except they hear?* and therefore God evermore supplies his Church with visible and sensible meanes, and knowing the naturall inclination of man, when he cannot have, or cannot comprehend the originall, and prototype, to satisfie, and refresh himself with a picture, or representation; So, though God hath forbidden us that slippery, and frivolous, and dan- Col. 1.15 gerous use of graven Images, yet hee hath afforded us his Sonne, who is the image of the invisible God, and so more proportionall unto us, more apprehensible by us; And so this committing is no more but that God, in another form then that of God, hath manifested his power of judging, and this committing, this manifestation is *in Filio,* in his Son.

Filio

But in the entrance into the handling of this, we aske onely this question, *Cui filio,* to which Sonne of God is this commission given? Not that God hath more Sons then one; but because that Sonne is his Sonne by a two-fold filiation, by an eternall, and inexpressible generation, and by a temporary, but miraculous incarnation, in which of these rights is this commission derived upon him? doth he judge as he is the Son of God? or as he is the Son of man? I am not ordinarily bold in determining points (especially if they were fundamentall) wherein I find the Fathers among themselves, and the School in it selfe, and the reverend Divines of the Reformation amongst themselves to differ; But yet neither am I willing to raise doubts, and leave the auditory unsatisfyed, and unsetled; we are not upon a Lecture, but upon a Sermon, and therefore we will not multiply variety of opinions; summe up the Fathers upon one side in Saint *Ambrose* mouth, and they will say with him, *Huic dedit ubique generando, non largiendo,* God gave his Sonne this commission then must have it by his eternall generation, as the Son of God: sum up the Fathers on the other side, in *Saint Augustines* mouth, and there they will say with him, that it is so clear, and so certain, that whatsoever is said in the Scripture to be committed, and given to Christ, belongs to Christ as the Son of man, and not as the Son of God, as that th'other opinion cannot be maintained; and at this distance we shall never bring them to meet: but take in this rule, *Iudicium convenit ei ut homo, causa ut Deus,* God hath given Christ this commission as man, but *Christ* had not been capable of this commission if he had not been God too, and so it is easily reconcil'd: If we shall hold simply to the letter of the text, *Pater dedit,* then it will seem to have been committed to him in his eternall generation, because that was a work of the Fathers onely, and in that generation the holy Ghost had no part; But since in this judgement, which is now committed to him, the holy Ghost hath a part, (for as we said before, the Judgement is an act of the whole Trinity) we must look for a commission from the whole Trinity, and that is as he is man, for, *tota* August. *Trinitas univit humanitatem,* The hypostaticall union of God and man in the person of Christ, was a work of the whole Trinity.

Taking it then so setled, that the capacity of this Judgment, and (if we may say so) the future title to it, was given to him, as God by his essence, in his eternall generation, by which *non vitæ particeps, sed* Cyrill *vita naturaliter est,* we cannot say that Christ hath life, but that he is life, and the Life, for whatsoever the Father is, he is, excepting onely the name and relation of Father, the capacity, the ability is in him, eternally before any imaginable, any possible consideration of time; But the power of the actuall execution of this Judgement, which is given, and is committed, is in him as man: because as the same Father says, *Ad hominem dicitur, Quid habes quod non accepisti?* When *Saint Paul* says, *What hast thou that thou has not received?* [1 Cor. 4.7] he asks that question of a man, that which is received, is received as man; For as *Bellarmine,* in a place where he disposes himself to De Christo quarrell at some few words of *Calvins,* though he confesse the matter l. 2. c. 19 to be true, and (as he cals it there) Catholique, says, *Essentiam genitam negamus,* we confesse that Christ hath not his essence from his Father by generation, the relation, the filiation, he hath from his Father, he hath the name of Son, but he hath not this execution of this judgement by that relation, by that filiation; still as the Son of

God, he hath the capacity, as the Sonne of man, he hath the execution; And therefore *Prosper* that follows *S. Augustine* limits it perchance too narrowly to the very flesh, to the humanity, *Ipsa* (not *Ipsæ*) *erit Judex, quæ sub Judice stetit,* and *ipsa judicabit, quæ judicata est,* where he places not this Judgement upon the mixt person (which is the safest way) of God and man, but upon man alone.

Act. 17.31

God hath appointed a day, in which he will judge the world in righteousnesse; But by whom? By that man whom he hath ordained. God will judge still; but still in Christ; and therefore says S. *Augustine* upon those

Psal. 82.8

words, *Arise O God, and judge the earth: Cui Deo dicitur surge, nisi ei qui dormivit?* What God doth *David* call upon to arise, but that God who lay down to sleep in the grave? as though he should say (says *Augustine*) *Dormivisti judicatus à terra, surge & judica terram.* So that to collect all, though judgement be such a character of God as he cannot devest, yet the Father hath committed such a Judgement to the Sonne, as none but he can execute.

Omne judicium

And what is that? *Omne judicium,* all judgement, that is, *omne imperium, omnem potestatem;* It is presented in the name of Judgement, but it involves all. It is literally, and particularly Judgement in S. *Iohn, The Father hath given him authority to execute judgement;* It is extended unto power in *Saint Matthew, All power is given unto me in heaven and in earth;* And it is enlarg'd as far farther, as can be expressed or conceived in another place of *Saint Matthew, All things are deliver'd to me of my Father.*

[John] 5.27

[Mat.] 28.18

[Mat.] 11.27

Now all things our Saviour Christ Jesus exercises, either *per carnem,* or at least *in carne,* whatsoever the Father does, the Sonne does too, *In carne,* because now there is an unseparable union betwixt God and the humane nature: The Father creates new souls every day in the inanimation of Children, and the Sonne creates them with him; The Father concurs with all second causes as the first moving cause of all, in naturall things, and all this the Sonne does too; but all this *in carne;* Though he be in our humane flesh, he is not the lesse able to doe the acts belonging to the Godhead, but *per carnem,* by the flesh instrumentally, visibly, he executes judgement, because he is the Son of man, God hath been so indulgent to man, as that there should be no judgement given upon man, but man should give it.

Iudicium Electionis

Christ then having all Judgment, we refresh to your memory those three Judgements which we toucht upon before; first, the Judgement of our Election, severing of vessels of honour and dishonor; next, the Judgement of our Justification here, severing of friends from enemies; and then the Judgment of our Glorification, severing sheep from goats; and for the first, of our Election, As if I were under the condemnation of the Law, for some capitall offence, and going to execution, and the Kings mercy expressed in a sealed pardon were presented me, I should not stand to enquire what mov'd the King to doe it, what hee said to any body else, what any body else said to him, what hee saw in mee, or what hee look't for at my hands, but embrace that mercy cheerfully, and thankfully, and attribute it onely to his abundant goodnesse: So, when I consider my selfe to have been let fall into this world, *in massa Damnata,* under the generall condemnation of mankind, and yet by the working of Gods Spirit, I find at first a desire, and after a modest assurance, that I am delivered from that condemnation, I enquire not what God did in his bed-chamber, in his cabinet counsell, in his eternall decree, I know that hee hath made *Judicium electionis* in Christ Jesus: And therefore that I may know, whether I doe not deceive my selfe, in presuming my self to be of that number, I come down, and examine my selfe whether I can truly tell my conscience, that Christ Jesus dyed for mee, which I cannot doe, if I have not a desire and an endevour to conform my self to him; And if I do that, there I finde my Predestination, I am a Christian, and I will not offer to goe before my Master Christ Jesus, I cannot be sav'd before there was a Saviour, In Christ Jesus is *Omne judicium,* all judgement, and therefore the judgment of Election, the first separation of vessels of honour and dishonour in Election and Reprobation was in Christ Jesus.

Judicium iustificationis

Much more evidently is the second judgement of our Justification by means ordain'd in the Christian Church, the Judgement of Christ, it is the Gospel of Christ which is preacht to you there, it is the bloud of Christ which is presented to you there; There is no name given under heaven whereby you should be saved, there are no other means wherby salvation should be applyed in his name given, but those which he hath instituted in his Church; So that when I come to the second judgement, to try whether I stand justifyed in the sight of Christ, or no, I come for that Judgement to Christ in his Church; Doe I remember what I contracted with Christ Jesus, when I took the name of a Christian at my entrance into his Church by Baptism? Doe I find I have endevoured to perform those Conditions? Doe I find a remorse when I have not performed them? Doe I feele the remission of those sinnes applyed to me when I hear the gracious promises of the Gospel shed upon repentant sinners by the mouth of his Minister? Have I a true and solid consolation, (without shift, or disguise, or flattering of my conscience) when I receive the seal of his pardon in the Sacrament? Beloved, not in any morall integrity, not in keeping the conscience of an honest man, in generall, but in using well the meanes ordain'd by Christ in the Christian Church, am I justified. And therefore this Judgement of Justification is his too.

Judicium Glorificationis

Apoc. 1.7

And then the third and last judgement, which is the judgment of Glorification, that's easily agreed by all to appertain unto Christ, *Idem Iesus, The same Iesus that ascended, shall come to judgement, Videbunt quem pupugerunt, Every eye shall see him, and they also which pierc't him;* Then the Son of man shall come in glory, and he, as man, shall give the judgement, for things done, or omitted towards him as man, for not feeding, for not clothing, for not harbouring, for not visiting. The sum of all is, that this is the overflowing goodnesse of God, that he deales with man by the sonne of man; and that hee hath so given all judgement to the Sonne, as that if you would be tryed by the first judgement, are you elected or no? The issue is, doe you believe in Christ Jesus, or no? If you would be tryed by the second judgement, are you justified or no? The issue is, doe you find comfort in the application of the Word, and Sacraments of Christ Jesus, or no? If you would be tryed by the third Judgement, do you expect a Glorification, or no? The issue is, Are you so reconcil'd to Christ Jesus now, by hearty repentance for sinnes past, and by detestation of occasion of future sin, that you durst welcome that Angel which should come at this time, and sweare that time should be no more, that your transmigration out of this world should be this minute, and that this minute you might say unfeignedly and effectually, *Veni Domine Iesu,* Come Lord Jesus, come quickly, come now; if this be your state, then are you partakers of all that blessednesse, which the Father intended to you, when for your sake, he committed all Judgment to the Son.

[Mat. 25.34–40]

[Apoc. 22.20]

Number 16.

Preached at Lincolns Inne
[January 30, 1619/20]

JOHN 8.15. *I JUDGE NO MAN.*

THE RIVERS of Paradise did not all run one way, and yet they flow'd from one head; the sentences of the Scripture flow all from one head, from the holy Ghost, and yet they seem to present divers senses, and to admit divers interpretations; In such an appearance doth this Text differ from that which I handled in the forenoon, and as heretofore I found it a usefull and acceptable labour, to employ our Evening exercises, upon the vindicating of some such places of Scripture, as our adversaries of the Roman Church had detorted in some point of controversie between them and us, and restoring those places to their true sense, (which course I held constantly for one whole year) so I think it a usefull and acceptable labour, now to employ for a time those Evening exercises to reconcile some such places of Scripture, as may at first sight seem to differ from one another; In the morning we saw how Christ judged all; now we are to see how he judges none; *I judge no man.*

To come then to these present words, here we have the same person Christ Jesus, and hath not he the same Office? Is not he Judge? certainly though he retain'd all his other Offices, though he be the Redeemer, and have shed his blood in value satisfactory for all our sins, though he be our Advocate and plead for us in heaven, and present our evidence to that Kingdome, written in his blood, seal'd in his wounds, yet if hee bee not our Judge, wee cannot stand in judgement; shall hee bee our Judge, and is hee not our Judge yet? Long before wee were hee was our Judge at the separation of the Elect and Reprobate, in Gods eternall Decree. Was he our Judge then, and is hee not so still? still he is present in his Church, and cleares us in all scruples, rectifies us in all errors, erects us in all dejections of spirit, pronounces peace and reconciliation in all apprehensions of his Judgements, by his Word and by his Sacraments, was hee, and is hee, and shall he not be our Judge still? *I am sure my Redeemer liveth, and he shall stand the last on earth.* So that Christ Jesus is the same to day, and yesterday, and for ever, before the world begun, and world without end, *Sicut erat in principio,* as he was in the beginning, he is, and shall be ever our Judge.

Iob 19.25
Heb. 13.8

Divisio

So that then these words are not *De tempore,* but *De modo,* there was never any time when Christ was not Judge, but there were some manner of Judgements which Christ did never exercise, and Christ had no commission which he did not execute; for hee did all his Fathers will. 1. *In secularibus,* in civill, or criminall businesses, which belong meerly to the Judicatures, and cognisance of this world, *Judicat neminem,* Christ judges no man. 2. *Secundum carnem,* so as they to whom Christ spake this, who judged, as himself says here, according to fleshly affections, *Judicat neminem,* he judges no man: and 3. *Ad internecionem,* so as that upon that Judgement, a man should despair of any reconciliation, any redintegration with God again, and be without hope of pardon, and remission of sins in this world, *Iudicat neminem,* he judges no man; 1. Christ usurps upon no mans Jurisdiction, that were against justice. 2. Christ imputes no false things to any man, that were against charity. 3. Christ induces no man to desperation, that were against faith; and against Justice, against charity, against faith, *Judicat neminem.*

1. Part
Non secularia
Luke 12.[13 and] 14

First then, Christ judgeth not in secular judgements, and we note his abstinence therein; first, in civill matters, when one of the company said to him, *Master, bid my brother divide the inheritance with me,* as *Saint Augustine* says, the Plaintiffe thought his cause to be just, and hee thought Christ to bee a competent Judge in the cause, and yet Christ declines the judgement, disavows the authority, and he answers, *Homo, quis me constituit Judicem,* Man, who made me a Judge between you? To that Generall, which we had in the morning, *Omne judicium,* the Son hath all judgement, here is an exception of the same Judges own making; for in secular judgements, *Nemo constituit,* he had no commission, and therefore *Judicat neminem,* he judges no man; he forbore in criminall matters too, for when the woman taken in adultery, was brought before him, he condemned [John 8.3–11] her not; It is true, he absolv'd her not, the evidence was pregnant against her, but he condemned her not, he undertook no office of a Judge, but of a sweet and spirituall Counsellor, *Go, and sinne no more,* for this was his Element, his Tribunall.

When then Christ says of himself, with such a pregnant negative, *Quis me constituit Judicem,* may not we say so too, to his pretended Vicar, the Bishop of *Rome, Quis te?* Who made you Judge of Kings, that you should depose them, in criminall causes? Or who made you proprietary of Kingdomes, that you should dispose of them, as of civill inheritances? when to countenance such a pretence, they detort places of Scripture, not onely perversly, but senselessly, blasphemously, ridiculously, (as ridiculously as in their pasquils, when in an undiscreet shamlesnes, to make their power greater then it is, they make their fault greater then it is too, and fil their histories with examples of Kings deposed by Popes, which in truth were not depos'd by them, for in that they are more innocent then they will confesse themselves to be) when some of their Authors say, that the Primitive Church abstain'd from deposing Emperors, onely because she was not strong enough to do it, when some of them say, That all Christian Kingdomes of the earth, may fall into the Church of Rome, by faults in those Princes, when some of them say, that *De facto,* the Pope hath already a good title to every Christian Kingdome, when some of them say, that the world will never be well governed, till the Pope put himself into possession of all, (all which severall propositions are in severall Authors of good credit amongst them) will he not endure Christs own question, *Quis te constituit?* Who made you Judge of all this? If they say Christ did; did he it in his Doctrine? It [Mat. 21.12; Mark 11.15; John 2.14–15] is hard to pretend that, for such an institution as that must have very cleer, very pregnant words to carry it; did he doe it by his example and practice? Wee see hee abstain'd in civill, he abstain'd in criminall causes. When they come to their last shift, that is, that Christ did [Mat. 21.19; Mark 11.13–14] exercise Judiciary Authority, when he whipped Merchants out of the Temple, when he curs'd the fig-tree, and damnified the owner thereof, and when he destroyed the Heard of Swine, [Mat. 8.32; Mark 5.13; Luke 8.33] (for there, say they, the Devill was but the Executioner, Christ was the Judge) to all these, and such as these, it is enough to say, All these were miraculous, and not ordinary; and though it might seem half a miracle how that Bishop should exercise so much authority as he hath done over the world, yet when we look neerer, and see his means, that he hath done all this by Massacres of millions, by withdrawing Subjects from their Allegiance, by assasinating and murthering of Princes, when we know that miracles are without meanes, and we see the means of his proceedings, the miracle ceases: howsoever that Bishop as Christs Vicar can claim no other power, then was ordinary in Christ, and so exercis'd by Christ, and so *Judicavit neminem;* In secular judgement, Christ judges no man, and therefore that Bishop as his Vicar should not.

2. Part *Detractio*

Secondly, Christ judges no man by calumny, by imputing, or laying false aspersions upon him, nor truths extrajudicially, for that's a degree of calumny; We enter into a large field, when we go about to speak against calumny, and slander, and detraction, so large a field, as that we may fight out the last drop of our bloud, preach out the last gaspe of our breath, before we overcome it. Those to whom Christ spake here, were such as gave perverse judgments, calumniating censures upon him, and so he judges no man, we need not insist upon that, for it is *manifestè verum;* but that we may see our danger, and our duty, what calumny is, and so how to avoid it actively, and how to beare it passively, I must by your leave stop a little upon it.

When then we would present unto you that monster Slander, and Calumny, though it be hard to bring it within any compasse of a division, yet to take the largenesse of the schoole, and say, that every calumny is either direct, or indirect, that will comprehend all, and then a direct calumny, will have three branches, either to lay a false and unjust imputation, or else to aggravate a just imputation, with unnecessary, but heavy circumstances, or thirdly to reveale a fault which in it selfe was secret and I by no duty bound to discover it, and then the indirect calumny will have three branches too, either to deny expressly some good that is in another, or to smother it in silence, when my testimony were due to him, and might advantage him, or lastly to diminish his good parts, and say they are well, but yet not such as you would esteeme them to be; collect then again, for that's all that we shall be able to doe, that he is a calumniator directly, that imputes a false crime, that aggravates a true crime, that discovers any crime extrajudicially; That he is an indirect calumniator, that denies another mans sufficiencies, that conceales them, that diminishes them; Take in some of Saint *Bernards* examples of these rules, that it is a calumny to say, *Doleo vehementer,* I am sorry at the heart for such a man because I love him, but I could never draw him from such and such a vice, or to say, *per me nunquam innotuisset,* I would never have spoken of it, yet since all the world talkes of it, the truth must not be disguised, and so take occasion to discover a fault which no body knew before, and thereby (as the same Father says) *cum gravitate et tarditate aggredi maledictionem,* to cut a mans throat gravely, and soberly, and so much the more perswasively, because he seems, and pretends to do it all against his will; This being the rule, and this the example, who amongst us is free from the passive calumny? Who amongst us hath not some other man calumniated? Nay who is free from the active part? Which of us in some of these degrees hath not calumniated some other? But those to whom Christ makes his exception here, that he judges no man as they judge, were such calumniators, as *David* speaks of, *Sedens adversus fratrem tuum loquebaris, Thou sittest and speakest against thy neighbour,* as Saint *Augustin* notes upon that place, *Non transitoriè, non surreptionis passione, sed quasi ad hoc vacans,* not by chance, and unawares, not in passion because he had offended thee, not for company, because thou wouldest be of their minds, but as though thy profession would beare thee out in it, to leave the cause and lay aspersion upon the person, so thou art a calumniator. *They eate up my people as bread,* as *David* says in Gods person: And upon those words of the same Prophet, says the same Father, *De cæteris,* when we eate of any thing else, we taste of this dish, and we tast of that, *non semper hoc olus,* says he, we doe not always eate one sallet, one meate, one kinde of fruit, *sed semper panem,* whatsoever we eate else wee always eate bread: howsoever they imploied their thoughts, or their wits otherways, it was always one exercise of them to calumniate Christ Jesus, and in that kinde of calumny, which is the bitterest of all, they abounded most, which is in scorne and derision. *David,* and *Iob,* who were slander proofe, in a good measure, yet every where complaine passionately that they were made a scorne, that the wits made libells, that drunkards sung songs, that fooles, and the children of fooles

Serm. 24 in Can.

Psal. 50.20

Psal. 53.4

1 Chro. 10.4 derided them; And when *Saul* was in his last, and worst agony, and had abandoned himselfe to a present death, and prayed his armour-bearer to kill him, it was not because the uncircumcised should not kill him, (for he desired death, and he had their deadly arrowes already in his bosome) but it was (as it is expressed there) lest the uncircumcised should come and abuse him, he was afraid of scorne when he had but a few minutes of life. Since then Christ judges no man (as they did) *secundum carnem ejus,* according to the outward appearance, for they thought no better of Christ then he seemed to be, (as some Fathers take that phrase) nor *secundum carnem suam,* according to his owne fleshly passions, (as some others take it) judge Mat. 7.1 not you so neither, first *judge not that ye be not judged,* that is, as Saint *Ambrose* interprets it well enough, *Nolite judicare de judiciis* [Luke 13.4] *Dei,* when you see Gods judgments fall upon a man, when you see the tower of *Silo* fall upon a man, doe not you judge that that man had sinned more then you, when you see another borne blind, doe not you thinke that he or his Father had sinned, and that you onely are Lev. 19.14 derived from a pure generation; especially *non maledicas surdo,* speake not evill of the deafe that heares not; That is, (as *Gregory* interprets it if not literally, yet appliably, and usefully) calumniate not him who is absent, and cannot defend himselfe, it is the devills [Apoc. 12.10] office to be *Accusator fratrum:* and though God doe not say in the law, *Non erit,* yet he says, *Non eris criminator,* it is not plainely, Lev. 19.16 there shall be no Informer: (for as we dispute, and for the most part affirme in the Schoole, that though we could, we might destroy no intire species of those creatures, which God made at first, though it be a Tyger, or a viper, because this were to take away one link of Gods chaine out of the world, so such vermine as Informers may not, for some good use that there is of them, be taken away) though it be not *non erit,* there shall be none, yet it is at least by way of good counsaile to thee, *non eris,* thou shalt not be the man, thou shalt not be the Informer, and for resisting those that are, we are bound, not onely not to harme our neighbours house, but to help him, if casually his house fall on fire, wee are bound where wee have authority to stoppe the mouthes of other calumniators; where wee have no au- Prov. 25.23 thority, yet since as the North wind driveth away raine, an angry countenance driveth away a back-biting tongue, at least deale so with

a libeller, with a calumniator, for he that lookes pleasantly, and hearkens willingly to one libell, makes another, occasions a second; always remember *Davids* case, when he thought that he had been giving judgment against another he was more severe, more heavy, then the law admitted; The law was, that he that had stoln the sheep should returne fourefold, and *Davids* anger was kindled says the text, and he said, and he swore, As the Lord liveth, that man shall restore fourfold, *Et filius mortis,* and he shall surely dye: *O judicis superfluentem justitiam,* O superabundant and overflowing Justice, when we judge another in passion; But this is *judicium secundum carnem,* according to which Christ judges no man, for Christ is love, and that *non cogitat malum,* love thinks no evill any way; The charitable man neither meditates evill against another, nor beleeves not easily any evill to be in another, though it be told him.

2 Sam. 12.5, 6

Chrysost.

1 Cor 13.5

Non ad internecionem

Lastly, Christ judges no man *Ad internecionem,* he judges no man so in this world, as to give a finall condemnation upon him here; There is no error in any of his Judgments, but there is an appeal from all his Judgments in this world; There is a verdict against every man, every man may find his case recorded, and his sinne condemned in the law, and in the Prophets, there is a verdict, but before Judgment God would have every man sav'd by his book, by the apprehension and application of the gratious promises of the Gospell, to his case, and his conscience. Christ judges no man so, as that he should see no remedy, but to curse God, and die, not so, as that he should say, his sinne is greater then God could forgive, for God sent not his Sonne into the world to condemne the world, but that the world through him might be saved.

Iohn 3.17

Doe not thou then give malitious evidence against thy selfe, doe not weaken the merit, nor lessen the value of the bloud of thy Saviour, as though thy sinne were greater then it: Doth God desire thy bloud now, when he hath abundantly satisfied his justice with the bloud of his Sonne for thee? what hast thou done? hast thou come hypocritically to this place upon collaterall reasons, and not upon the direct service of God? not for love of Information, of Reformation of thy selfe? If that be thy case, yet if a man hear my words, says Christ, and beleeve not, *I judge him not, he hath one that judgeth him,* says Christ, and who is that? *The word that I have spoken,* the same shall

Ioh. 12.47 [and 48]

judge him; It shall, but when? It shall judge him, says Christ, *at the last day,* for till the last day, the day of his death, no man is past recovery, no man's salvation is impossible. Hast thou gone farther then this? hast thou admitted scruples of diffidence, and distrust in Gods mercy, and so tasted of the lees of desperation? It is true, *perpetrare flagitium est mors animæ, sed desperare est descensus ad inferos,* In every sinne the soule dies, but in desperation it descends into hell; but yet *portæ inferi non prævalebunt,* even the gates of this hell shall not prevaile against thee; Assist thy selfe, argue thine own case, desperation it selfe may be without infidelity; desperation aswell as hope is rooted in the desire of happinesse; desperation proceeds out of a feare of God and a horror of sinne; desperation may consist with faith thus farre, that a man may have a true and faithfull opinion in the generall, that there is a remission of sinne to be had in the Church, and yet have a corrupt imagination in the particular, that to him in this sinfull state that he is in, this remission of sinnes shall not be applied; so that the resolution of the Schoole is good, *Desperatio potest esse ex solo excessu boni,* desperation may proceed from an excesse of that which is good in it selfe, from an excessive over fearing of Gods Justice, from an excessive over hating thine own sinnes; *Et virtute quis malè utitur?* Can any man make so ill use of so great virtues, as the feare of God and the hate of sinne? Yes they may, so froward a weed is sinne, as that it can spring out of any roote, and therefore if it have done so in thee, and thou thereby have made thy case the harder, yet know stil, that *Objectum spei est arduum, et possibile,* the true object of hope is hard to come by, but yet possible to come by, and therefore as *David* said, *By my God have I leaped over a wall,* so by thy God maist thou breake through a wall, through this wall of obduration, which thou thy selfe hast begunne to build about thy selfe. Feather thy wings againe, which even the flames of hell have touched in these beginnings of desperation, feather them againe with this text *Neminem judicat, Christ judges no man,* so as a desperate man judges himselfe: doe not make thy selfe beleeve, that thou hast sinned against the holy Ghost; for this is the nearest step thou hast made to it, to think that thou hast done it; walke in that large field of the Scriptures of God, and from the first flower at thy entrance, the flower of Paradise, *Semen mulieris,* the generall promise

Isidor

Mat. 16.18

Thom. 1.2[d] q. 40 ar. 4

2 Sam. 22.30

[Gen. 3.15]

of the seed of the woman should bruise the Serpents head, to the last word of that Messias upon the Crosse, *Consummatum est,* that all [John 19.30] that was promised for us is now performed, and from the first to the last thou shalt find the savour of life unto life in all those flowers; walke over the same alley againe and consider the first man *Adam* in the beginning who involv'd thee in originall sinne; and the thiefe [Luke upon the Crosse who had continued in actuall sinnes all his life, and 23.39–43] sealed all with the sinne of reviling Christ himselfe a little before his expiration, and yet he recovered Paradise, and Paradise that day, and see if thou canst make any shift to exclude thy selfe; receive the fragrancy of all these Cordialls, *Vivit Dominus,* as the Lord liveth I [Ezek. would not the death of a sinner, *Quandocunque,* At what time soever 33.11] a sinner repenteth, and of this text *Neminem judicat, Christ judgeth no man* to destruction here, and if thou find after all these Antidotes a suspitious ayre, a suspicious working in that *Impossibile est,* that it Heb. 6.4 is impossible for them, who were once inlightened if they fall away, [also 5, 6] to renew them againe by repentance, sprinkle upon that worme-wood of *Impossibile est,* that Manna of *Quorum remiseritis, whose sinnes* [John *yee remit, are remitted,* and then it will have another tast to thee, and 20.23] thou wilt see that that impossibility lies upon them onely, who are utterly fallen away into an absolute Apostasie, and infidelity, that make a mocke of Christ, and crucifie him againe, as it is expressed there, who undervalue, and despise the Church of God, and those means which Christ Jesus hath instituted in his Church for renewing such as are fallen. To such it is impossible, because there are no other ordinary meanes possible; but that's not thy case, thy case is onely a doubt that those meanes that are shall not be applied to thee; and even that is a slippery state, to doubt of the mercy of God to thee in particular, this goes so neare making thy sinne greater then Gods mercy, as that it makes thy sinne greater then daily adulteries, daily murthers, daily blasphemies, daily prophanings of the Sabbath could have done, and though thou canst never make that true in this life that thy sinnes are greater then God can forgive, yet this is a way to make them greater, then God will forgive.

Now to collect both our Exercises, and to connexe both Texts, *Christ judgeth all men* and *Christ judgeth no man,* he claimes all judgment, and he disavows all judgement, and they consist well together. He was at our creation, but that was not his first scene; the Arians who say, *Erat quando non erat,* there was a time when Christ was not, intimating that he had a beginning, and therefore was a creature, yet they will allow that he was created before the generall creation, and so assisted at ours, but he was infinite generations before that, in the bosome of his Father, at our election, and there in him was executed the first judgment of separating those who were his, the elect from the reprobate: And then he knows who are his by that first Judgment, and so comes to his second Judgment, to seale all those in the visible Church with the outward mark of his baptisme, and the inward marke of his Spirit, and those whom he calls so, he justifies, and sanctifies, and brings them to his third Judgment, to an established and perpetuall glory. And so all Judgment is his. But then to judge out of humane affections and passions, by detraction and calumny, as they did to whom he spoke at this time, so he judges no man, so he denies judgment: To usurpe upon the jurisdiction of others, or to exercise any other judgment, then was his commission, as his pretended Vicar doth, soe he judges no man, so he disavows all judgment: To judge so as that our condemnation should be irremediable in this life, so he judges no man, so he forswears all judgment. As I live, saith the Lord of hosts, and as I have died, saith the Lord Jesus, so I judge none. Acknowledge his first Judgment, thy election in him, cherish his second Judgment, thy justification by him, breath and pant after his third Judgement, thy Crown of glory for him; intrude not upon the right of other men, which is the first, defame not, calumniate not other men, which is the second, lay not the name of reprobate in this life upon any man, which is the third Judgement, that Christ disavows here, and then thou shalt have well understood, and well practised both these texts, *The Father hath committed all Judgment to the Sonne,* and yet *The Sonne judges no man.*

Number 17.

Preached at Sir Francis Nethersole's Marriage.

GEN. 2.18. *AND THE LORD GOD SAID, IT IS NOT GOOD, THAT THE MAN SHOULD BE ALONE; I WILL MAKE HIM A HELPE, MEET FOR HIM.*

IN THE Creation of the world, when God stocked the Earth, and the Sea, with those creatures, which were to be the seminary, and foundation, and roote of all that should ever be propagated in either of those elements, and when he had made man, to rule over them, he spoke to man, and to other creatures, in one and the same phrase, and forme of speech, *Crescite, & multiplicamini,* Be fruitfull and multiply; and thereby imprinted in man, and in other creatures, a *naturall* desire to conserve, and propagate their kinde by way of *Generation.* But after God had thus imprinted in man, the same naturall desire of propagation, which he had infused into other creatures too, after he had communicated to him that blessing, (for so it is said, *God blessed them, and said, Be fruitfull, and multiply*) till an ability and a desire of propagating their kinde, was infused into the creature, there is no mention of any blessing in the creation; after God had made men partakers of that blessing, that naturall desire of propagation, he takes a farther care of man, in giving him a proper and peculiar blessing, in contracting, and limiting that naturall desire of his: He leaves all other creatures to their *generall use* and execution of that Commission, *Crescite et multiplicamini,* the *Male* was to take the *Female* when and where their naturall desire provoked them; but, for man, *Adduxit Deus ad Adam;* God left not them to goe to one another, but *God brought the woman to the man:* and so this

Gen. 1.22, 28

Gen. 2.22

conjunction, this desire of propagation, though it be naturall in man, as in other creatures, by his creation, yet it is limited by God himselfe, to be exercised onely between such persons, as God hath brought together in mariage, according to his Institution, and Ordinance. Though then societies of men doe grow up, and spread themselves into Townes, and into Cities, and into Kingdomes, yet the root of all societies is in families, in the relation between man and wife, parents and children, masters and servants: so though the state of the children of God, in this world be dignified by the name of a *kingdome,* (for, so we pray by Christs owne institution, *Thy kingdome* Luk. 17.21 *come,* and so Christ saies, *Ecce Regnum, The kingdome of God is amongst you*) and though the state of Gods children here, be called Apoc. 21.2 *a City, a new Jerusalem, comming downe from heaven,* and in *David,* Psal. 87.3 *Glorious things are spoken of thee, O City of God,* yet for all these glorious titles of *City* and *Kingdome,* we must remember, that it is [Gal. 6.10] called *a family* too; *The Houshold of the faithfull:* And so the Heb. 3.6 Apostle says, in preferring Christ before *Moses, That Christ as the sonne was over Gods house, whose house we are.* So that, both of *Civill* and of *Spirituall* societies, the first roote is a *family;* and of families, the first roote is *Mariage;* and of mariage, the first roote, that growes out into words, is in this Text; *And the Lord God said, It is not good &c.*

If we should employ this exercise onely upon these two generall considerations, first, that God puts even his care and his study to finde out *what is good for man,* and secondly, that God doth provide and furnish whatsoever he findes to be necessary, *faciam, I will make him a Helper,* though they be *common places* we are bound to thanke God that they are so; that it is a *common place* to God, that he ever does it towards us, that it is a *common place to us,* that we ever acknowledge it in him. But you may be pleased to admit a more particular distribution. For, upon the first, will be grounded this consideration, that in regard of the *publique* good, God pretermits *private,* and particular respects; for, God doth not say, *Non bonum homini,* it is not good for man to be alone, man might have done well enough so; nor God does not say, *non bonum hunc hominem,* it is not good for *this,* or that *particular* man to be alone; but *non bonum, Hominem,* it is not good in the *generall,* for the *whole frame of the world,* that *man should be alone,* because then both Gods purposes had been frustrated, of being glorified by man here, in this world, and of glorifying man, in the world to come; for neither of these could have been done, without a succession, and propagation of man; and therefore, *non bonum hominem,* it was *not good, that man should be alone.* And then upon the second consideration, will arise these branches; first, that whatsoever the defect be, there is no remedy, but from God; for it is, *faciam,* I will doe it. Secondly, that even the workes of God, are not equally excellent; this is but *faciam,* it is not *faciamus;* in the creation of man, there is intimated a Consultation, a Deliberation of the whole *Trinity;* in the making of *women,* it is not expressed so; it is but *faciam.* And then, that that is made here, is but *Adjutorium,* but an accessory, not a principall; but a *Helper.* First the wife must be so *much,* she must *Helpe;* and then she must be *no more,* she must *not Governe.* But she cannot be that, except she have that quality, which God intended in the first woman, *Adjutorium simile sibi,* a helper *fit for him:* for otherwise he will ever returne, to the *bonum esse solum,* it had been better for him, to have been alone, then in the likenesse of a Helper, to have had a wife unfit for him.

First then, that in regard of the *publique good,* God pretermits private respects, if we take examples upon that stage, upon that scene, the face of Nature, we see that for the conservation of the whole, God hath imprinted in the particulars, a disposition to depart from their owne nature: water will clamber up hills, and ayre will sinke down into vaults, rather then admit Vacuity. But take the example nearer, in Gods bosome, and there we see, that for the publique, for the *redemption* of the whole world, God hath (shall we say, pretermitted?) derelicted, forsaken, abandoned, his own, and onely Sonne. Do you so too? *Regnum Dei intra nos;* the kingdome of God is within you; *planted* in your *election; watred* in your *Baptisme; fatned* with the *blood* of Christ Jesus, *ploughed* up with many *calamities,* and tribulations; *weeded* with often *repentances* of particular sins; *The kingdome of God is within you;* and will ye not depart from private affections, from *Ambition* and *Covetousnesse,* from *Excesse,* and *voluptuousnesse,* from *chambring* and *wantonnesse,* in which the kingdome of God doth not consist, for the conservation of this kingdome?

I Part

will ye not *pray* for this kingdome, in your private, and publique devotions? will ye not *fast* for this kingdome, in cutting off superfluities? will ye not *fight* for this kingdome, in resisting suggestions? will ye not *take Counsaile* for this kingdome, in consulting with religious friends? will ye not give *subsidies* for this kingdome, in relieving their necessities, for whom God hath made you his stewards? weigh and measure your selves, and spend that, be negligent of that, which is least, and worst in you. Is your soule lesse then your body, because it is in it? How easily lies a letter in a Boxe, which if it were unfolded, would cover that Boxe? unfold your soule, and you shall see, that it reaches to heaven; from thence it came, and thither it should pretend; whereas the body is but *from* that earth, and *for* that earth, upon which it is now; which is but a short, and an inglorious progresse. To contract this, the soule is larger then the body, and the glory, and the joyes of heaven, larger then the honours, and the pleasures of this world: what are seventy yeares, to that latitude, of continuing as long as the Ancient of dayes? what is it, to have spent our time, with the great ones of this time; when, when the [Apoc. 10.6] Angels shall come and say, that *Time shall be no more,* we shall have [Heb. 13.8] no beeing with him, who is *yesterday, and to day, and the same for ever?* We see how ordinarily ships goe many leagues out of their [John 3.8] direct way, to fetch the winde. *Spiritus spirat ubi vult,* sayes Christ; [Bel and the Dragon, ver. 34–37] the spirit blowes where he will; and, as the Angel took *Habakkuk by the haire,* and placed him where he would, this winde, the spirit of God, can take thee at last, *by thy gray haires,* and place thee in a good station then. *Spirat ubi vult,* he blowes where he will, and *spirat ubi vis,* he blowes where thou wilt too, if thou beest appliable to his inspirations. They are but hollow places that returne *Ecchoes;* last syllables: It is but a hollownesse of heart, to answer God *at last.* Be but as liberall of thy body in thy mortifications as in thy excesse, and licentiousnesse, and thou shalt in some measure, have followed Gods example, for the publique to pretermit the private, for the larger, and better, to leave the narrower, and worser respects.

Non homini

To proceed, when we made that observation, *that* God *pretermitted the private for the publique,* we noted, that God did not say, *non bonum Homini, It was not good for man to be alone;* man might have done well enough in that state, so, as his *solitarinesse* might have been supplied with a farther creation of more men. In making the inventaries of those goods which man possesseth in the world, we see a great Author says, *In possessionibus sunt amici, & inimici,* not Xenoph. onely our friends, but even our enemies, are part of our goods, and we may raise as much profit from these, as from those, It may be as good a lesson to a mans sonne, *Study that enemy,* as *Observe that friend.* As *David* says, *propitius fuisti, & ulciscens, Thou heardst them* Psal. 99.8 *O Lord our God, and wast favourable unto them, and didst punish all their inventions:* it was part of his mercy, part of his favour, that he did correct them. So we may say to our enemy, I owe you my watchfulnesse upon my selfe, and you have given me all the goodnesse that I have; for you have calumniated all my indifferent actions, and that kept me, from committing enormous ill ones. And if then our enemies be *in possessionibus,* to be inventaried amongst our goods, might not man have been abundantly rich in friends, without this addition of a woman? *Quanto congruentius,* says S. *Augustine;* how much more conveniently might two friends live together, then a man and a woman?

God doth not then say, *non bonum homini,* man got not so much by the bargaine, (especially if we consider how that wife carried her selfe towards him) but that for his particular, he had been better alone: nor he does not say now, *non bonum hunc hominem esse solum,* It is not good for *any man* to be alone; for, *Qui potest capere capiat,* says Christ: *he that is able to receive it, let him receive it.* What? *That some make themselves Eunuchs for the kingdome of* Mat. 19.12 *heaven:* that is, the better to un-entangle themselves from those impediments, which hinder them in the way to heaven, they abstaine from mariage; and *let them that can receive it, receive it.* Now certainly few try *whether they can* receive this, or no. Few strive, few *fast,* few *pray* for the gift of continency; few are content with that incontinency which they have, but are sorry they can expresse no more incontinency. There is a use of mariage now, which God never thought of in the first institution of mariage; that it is a *remedy* against burning. The two maine uses of mariage, which are propagation of *Children,* and mutuall *assistance,* were intended by God, at the present, at first; but the third, is a remedy against that, which was not then; for then there was no inordinatenesse, no irregularity in the affections of man. And experience hath taught us now, that those climates which are in reputation, hottest, are not uninhabitable; they may be dwelt in for all their heat. Even now, in the corruption of our nature, the clime is not so hot, as that *every one* must of necessity, mary. There may be fire in the house, and yet the house not on fire: there may be a distemper of heate, and yet no necessity to let blood. The Roman Church injures us, when they say, that we prefer mariage before virginity: and they injure the whole state of Christianity, when they oppose *mariage* and *chastity,* as though they were incompatible, and might not consist together. They may; for *mariage is honourable, and the bed undefiled;* and therefore it may be so. S. *Augustine* observes in mariage, *Bonum fidei,* a triall of one anothers truth; and that's good; And *bonum prolis,* a lawfull meanes of propagation; and that's good; and *bonum Sacramenti,* a mysticall representation of that union of two natures in Christ, and of him to us, and to his Church; and that's good too. So that there are divers degrees of good in mariage. But yet for all these goodnesses, God does not say, *non bonum,* it is not good *for any man* to be alone, but *Qui capere potest capiat;* according to Christs comment, upon his Fathers text, *He that can containe* and continue alone, *let him* doe so.

Heb. 13.4

But though God do not say, *non homini,* It is not good for *the man,* that he be alone, nor *quemvis hominem,* it is not good *for every man,* to be alone, yet, considering his generall purpose upon all the world, by man, he sayes *non bonum;* for that end, it is not good, that man should be alone, because those purposes of God could not consist with that solitude of man. In that production, and in that survay, which God made of all that he had made, still he gives the testimony, that he saw all was good, excepting onely in his *Second dayes worke,* and in his making of Man. He forbore it in the making of the firmament, because the firmament was *to divide* between waters and waters; it was an embleme of division, of disunion. He forbore it also in the making of man, because though man was to be an embleme of Gods union to his Church, yet because this embleme, and this representation, could not be in man alone, till the woman were made too, God does not pronounce upon the making of man, that the work was good: but upon Gods contemplation, that it was not good, that man should be alone, there arose a goodnesse, in having a companion. And from that time, if we seeke *bonum, quia licitum,* if we will call that good, which is lawfull, mariage is that, *If thou takest a wife thou* I Cor. 7.28 *sinnest not,* sayes God by the Apostle. If we seeke *bonum, quia bonus autor,* if we call that good whose author is good, mariage is that; *Adduxit ad Adam,* God brought her to man. If we seek such a good- Gen. 2.22 nesse, as hath *good witness,* good testimony, mariage is that; Christ Iohn 2 was present at a mariage, and honoured it with his first miracle. If we seek such a goodnesse, as is a *constant,* and not a temporary, an occasionall goodnesse, Christ hath put such a cement upon mariage, *What God hath joined, let no man put asunder.* Mat. 19.6 If we seek such a goodnesse, as no man, (that is, no sort nor degree of men) is the worse for having accepted, we see the holiest of all, the *High Priest,* [Levit. in the old Testament is onely limited, *what woman he shall not mary,* 21.13, 14] but not that he shall not mary; and the *Bishop* in the new Testament [1 Tim. what kinde of husband he must have been, but not that he must 3.1–5] have been no husband. To contract this, as mariage is good, in having the best author, *God,* the best witnesse, *Christ,* the longest terme, *Life,* the largest extent, even to the *highest persons, Priests,* and *Bishops;* as it is, all these wayes, *Positively* good, so it is good in *Comparison* of that, which justly seemes the best state, that is, *Virginity,* in S. *Augustines* opinion, *Non impar meritum Johannis & Abrahæ:* If we could consider merit in man, the merit of *Abraham,* the father of nations, and the merit of *John,* who was no father at all, is equall. But that wherein we consider the goodnesse of it here, is, that God proposed this way, to receive glory from the sonnes of men here upon earth, and to give glory to the sonnes of men in heaven.

But what glory can God receive from man, that he should be so carefull of his propagation? what glory more from man, then from the Sunne, and Moon, and Stars, which have no propagation? Why this, that S. *Augustine* observes; *Musca Soli præferenda, quia vivit,* A Fly is a nobler creature then the Sunne, because a fly hath life, and the Sunne hath not; for the degrees of dignity in the creature, are *esse, vivere,* and *intelligere:* to have a *beeing,* to have *life,* and to have *understanding:* and therefore man, who hath all three, is much more able to glorify God, then any other creature is, because he onely can chuse whether he will glorify God or no; the glory that the others give, they must give, but man is able to offer to God a *reasonable* Rom. 12.1

I Cor 12.2

sacrifice. When ye were Gentiles, saies the Apostle, *ye were caryed away unto dumb Idols, even as ye were led.* This is reasonable service, out of *Reason* to understand, and out of our willingnesse to doe God service. Now, when God had spent infinite millions of millions of generations, from all un-imaginable eternity, in contemplating one another in the Trinity, and then (to speake *humanly* of God, which God in his Scriptures abhors not) out of a satiety in that contemplation would create a world for his glory, and when he had wrought the first day, and created all the matter, and substance of the future creatures, and wrought foure dayes after, and a great part of the sixth, and yet nothing produced, which could give him any glory, (for glory is *rationabile obsequium,* reasonable service; and nothing could give that but a creature that understood it, and would give it) at last, as the knot of all, created man; then, to perpetuate his glory, he must perpetuate man: and to that purpose, *non bonum,* it was not good for man to be alone; as without man God could not have been glorified, so without woman man could not have been propagated.

Psal. 68.18

Eph. 4.8

But, as there is a place cited by S. *Paul* out of *David,* which hath some perplexity in it, we cannot tell, whether Christ be said to have received gifts *from men,* or *for men,* or to have given gifts *to men,* (for so S. *Paul* hath it) so it is not easie for us to discern, whether God had a care to propagate man, that he might receive glory *from* man, or that he might give glory *to* man. When God had taken it into his purpose to people heaven again, depopulated in the fall of Angels, by the substitution of man in their places, when God had a purpose to spend as much time with man in heaven after, as he had done with himself before, (for our perpetuity after the Resurrection, shall no more have an end, then his Eternity before the Creation had a beginning) And when God to prevent that time of the Resurrection, as it were to make sure of man before, would send down his *own Son* to assume our nature here; and, as not sure enough so, would take us up to him, and set us, in his Son, at his own right hand, whereas he never did, nor shall say to any of the Angels, *Sit thou there:* That God might not be frustrated of this great, and gracious, and glorious purpose of his, *non bonum,* it was not good that man should be alone; for without man God could not give this glory, and without woman there could be no propagation of man. And so,

[Psal. 110.1]

though it might have been *Bonum homini,* man might have done well enough alone; and *Bonum hunc hominem, some* men may doe better alone, yet God, who ever, for our example, prefers the publique before the private, because it conduced not to his *generall* end, of Having, and of Giving glory, saw, and said, *Non bonum hominem,* it was not good that man should be alone. And so we have done with the branches of our first part.

2d Part

We are come now to our second generall part: In which, as we saw in the former, that God studies man, and all things necessary for man, we shall also see, that wherein soever man is defective, his onely supply, and reparation is from God; *Faciam,* I will doe it. *Saul* wanted *counsell,* he was in a perplexity, and he sought to the Witch of *Endor,* and not to God; [1 Sam. 28.3–25] and what is the issue? he hears of his own, and of his son *Jonathans* death the next day. *Asa* wants *health,* and he seeks to the Physician, and not to God, [2 Chron. 16.12] and what is the issue? He dies. Doe not say, says S. *Chrysost. Quæro necessaria,* I desire nothing but that which is necessary for my birth, necessary for my place: *Quod non dat Deus, non est necessarium:* God hath made himself thy Steward, thy Bayliffe; and whatsoever God provides not for thee, is not necessary to thee. It was the poor way that *Mahomet* found out in his Alchoran, that in the next life all women should have eies of one bignesse, and a stature of one size; he could finde no means to avoid contention, but to make them all alike: But that is thy complexion, that is thy proportion which God hath given thee. It may be true that S. *Hierome* notes, who had so much conversation amongst women, that it did him harm, *Multas insignis pudicitiæ, quamvis nulli virorum, sibi scimus ornari;* I know, says he, as honest women as are in the world, that take a delight in making themselves handsomely ready, though for no other bodies sake but for their own. That may be; but, *manus Deo inferunt,* they take the pencill out of Gods hand, who goe about to mend any thing of his making. (Cyprian) *Quod nascitur Dei est, quod mutatur Diaboli,* says the same Father; God made us according to his image, and shall he be put to say to any of us, *Non imago mea,* this picture was not taken by the life, not by me, but is a Copy of the present distemper of the time? All good remedies are of God; none but he would ever have conceived such an invention as the Ark, without that modell, for the reparation of the world;

and he hath provided that means for the conservation of the world, Tertul. *mariage,* the association of one to one: *Plures costæ Adæ, nec fatigatæ manus Dei:* Adam had more ribs then one, neither were Gods hands wearied with making one; and yet he made no more. For him who Gen. 4.19 first exceeded that, *Lamech,* who had two wives, the first was *Adah,* and *Adah* signifies *Cœtum, congregationem;* there is company enough, society enough in a wife: His other wife was but *Zillah,* and *Zillah* is but *umbra,* but a shadow, but a *ghost,* that will *terrifie* at last.

Faciam

To proceed; Though God always provide remedies, and supplies of defects, it is not always in the greatest measure, nor in the presentest manner, that we conceive to our selves. So much may be intimated even in this, that in this remedy of Gods provision, the woman, God proceeded not, as he did in the making of man; it is not *Faciamus,* with such a counsell, such a deliberation as was used in that case. When the Creation of all the substance of the whole world is expressed, it is *Creavit Dii,* Gods created, as though more Gods were employed; and in the making of him, who was the abridgement of all, of man, it is *faciamus,* let us make him, as though more persons were employed: it is not so in the woman, for though the first Translation of the Bible that ever were and the Translation of the Roman Church have it in the plurall, yet it is not so in the Originall; it is but *faciam.* I presse no more upon this, but one lesson to our selves, That if God exercise us with temporall afflictions, narrownesse in our fortunes, infirmities in our constitutions, or with spirituall afflictions, ignorance in our understandings, scruples in our conscience, if God come not altogether in his *faciamus,* to powre down with both hands abundance of his worldly treasures, or of his spirituall light and clearnesse, let us content our selves with one hand from him, with that manner and that measure that he gives, and that time and that leasure which he takes. And then one lesson also to the other sexe, That they will be content, even by this form and change of phrase, [1 Pet. 3.7] to be remembred, that *they are the weaker vessell,* and *that Adam was* [1 Tim. 2.14 *not deceived* but *the woman was.* For whether you will ease that with *Theodorets* exposition, *Adam* was not deceived *first,* but the woman was *first* deceived; Or with *Chrysostoms* exposition, *Adam* was not deceived *by a Serpent,* a creature loathsom, and unacceptable, but by a lovely person, with whom he was transported: Or with *Oecumenius* his exposition; *Adam* was not deceived, because there is no charge laid upon him in the Scriptures, no mention that he was deceived in them, as it is said, that *Melchisedek* had no Father nor Mother, because there is no record of his pedegree in the Scriptures: [Heb. 7.1–3] Or in *Ambrose* his exposition; That *Adam* was not deceived *in prævaricationem,* not so deceived as that he deceived any body else: Take it any way, and it implies a weaknesse in the woman, and an occasion of soupling her to that just estimation of her self, *That she will be content to learn in silence with all subjection;* [I Tim. 2.11] That as she is not a servant, but a Mother in the house, so she is but a Daughter, and not a Mother of the Church.

Adjutorium

This is presented more fully in the next, that she is but *Adjutorium,* but a Help: and no body values his staffe, as he does his legges. It is not an ordinary disease now, to be *too uxorious;* that needs no great disswasion. But if any one man in a congregation be obnoxious to any one infirmity, one note is not ill spent: And let S. *Hierome* give this note, *Sapiens judicio amat, non affectu,* Discretion is the weight of love in a wise mans hand, and not affection. S. *Hierome* cannot stay there; he addes thus much more, *Nihil fœdius, quam uxorem amare tanquam adulteram,* There is not a more uncomely, a poorer thing, then to love a Wife like a Mistresse. S. *Augustine* makes that comparison, That whensoever the Apostles preached, they were glad when their auditory liked their preaching, *Non aviditate consequendæ laudis, sed charitate seminandæ virtutis;* not that they affected the praise of the people, but that thereby they saw, that they had done more good upon the people. And in another place he makes that comparison, That a righteous man desires *to be dissolved and to be with Christ,* [Phil. 1.23] and yet this righteous man dines, and sups, takes ordinary refections and ordinary recreations: So, for mariage, says he, in temperate men, *officiosum, non libidinosum,* it is to pay a debt, not to satisfie appetite; lest otherwise she prove *in Ruinam,* who was given *in Adjutorium,* and he be put to the first mans plea, *Mulier quam dedisti, The woman whom thou gavest me, gave me my death.* [Gen. 3.12]

So much then she should be, A Helper; for, for that she was made. She is not so, if she remember not those duties which are intimated in the stipulation and contract which she hath made. Call it *Con-*

jugium, and that is derived *à Jugo,* it is an equall patience in bearing the incommodities of this life. Call it *Nuptias,* and that is derived *à Nube,* a vaile, a covering; and that is an estranging, a withdrawing her self from all such conversation as may violate his peace, or her honour. Call it *Matrimonium,* and that is derived from a Mother, and that implies a religious education of her children. *De latere sumpta, non discedat à latere,* says *Augustine.* Since she was taken out of his side, let her not depart from his side, but shew her self so much as she was made for, *Adjutorium,* a Helper.

But she must be no more; If she think her self more then a Helper, she is not so much. He is a miserable creature, whose Creator is his Wife. God did not stay to joyn her in Commission with *Adam,* so far as to give names to the creatures; much lesse to give essence; essence to the man, essence to her husband. When the wife thinks her husband owes her all his fortune, all his discretion, all his reputation, *God help that man* himself, for he hath given him no helper yet. I know there are some glasses stronger then some earthen vessels, and some earthen vessels stronger then some wooden dishes, some of the weaker sexe, stronger in fortune, and in counsell too, then they to whom God hath given them; but yet let them not impute that in the eye nor eare of the world, nor repeat it to their own hearts, with such a dignifying of themselves, as exceeds the quality of a Helper. S. *Hierome* shall be her Remembrancer, She was not taken out of the *foot,* to be troden upon, nor out of the *head,* to be an overseer of him; but out of *his side,* where she weakens him enough, and therefore should do all she can, to be a Helper.

To be so, so much, and no more, she must be as God made *Eve, similis ei, meet* and *fit* for her husband. She is fit for any if she have those vertues, which always make the person that hath them *good;* as *chastity, sobriety, taciturnity, verity,* and such: for, for such vertues as may be had, and yet the possessor not the better for them, as *wit, learning, eloquence, musick, memory, cunning,* and such, these make her never the fitter. There is a Harmony of dispositions, and that requires particular consideration upon emergent occasions; but the fitnesse that goes through all, is a *sober continency;* for without that, *Matrimonium jurata fornicatio,* Mariage is but a continuall fornication, sealed with an oath: And mariage was not instituted to prostitute the chastity of the woman to one man, but to preserve her chastity from the tentations of more men. *Bathsheba* was a little too fit for [2 Sam. 11] *David,* when he had tried her so far before; for there is no fitnesse where there is not *continency*. To end all, there is a *Morall fitnesse,* consisting in those morall vertues, of which we have spoke enough; And there is a *Civill fitnesse,* consisting in Discretion, and accommodating her self to him; And there is a *Spirituall fitnesse,* in the unanimity of Religion, that they be not of repugnant professions that way. Of which, since we are well assured in both these, who are to be joyned now, I am not sorry, if either the houre, or the present occasion call me from speaking any thing at all, because it is a subject too mis-interpretable, and unseasonable to admit an enlarging in at this time. At this time, therefore, this be enough, for the explication and application of these words.

Number 18.

Preached at White-hall, March 3. 1619. [*1619/20*]

AMOS 5.18. *WOE UNTO YOU, THAT DESIRE THE DAY OF THE LORD: WHAT HAVE YEE TO DOE WITH IT? THE DAY OF THE LORD IS DARKNESSE AND NOT LIGHT.*

FOR THE presenting of the woes and judgements of God, denounced by the Prophets against Judah and Israel, and the extending and applying them to others, involved in the same sins as Judah and Israel were, *Solomon* seemes to have given us somewhat a cleare direction; Prov. 9.8 *Reprove not a scorner lest he hate thee, Rebuke a wise man and he will love thee.* But how if the wiseman and this scorner bee all in one man, all one person? If the wiseman of this world bee come to take S. *Paul* so literally at his word, as to thinke [1 Cor. 1.21] scornefully that *preaching* is indeed but *the foolishnesse of preaching,* and that as the Church is within the State, so preaching is a part of State government, flexible to the present occasions of time, appliable to the present dispositions of men? This fell upon this Prophet in this Amos 7.10 prophecie, *Amasias the Priest of Bethel informed the King that Amos medled with matters of State, and that the Land was not able to beare his words,* and to *Amos* himselfe he saies, *Eate thy bread in some other place, but prophecy here no more, for this is the Kings* Amos 7.14, 15 *Chappell, and the Kings Court; Amos* replies, *I was no Prophet nor the son of a Prophet, but in an other course, and the Lord tooke me and said unto me, Goe and Prophecie to my People.* Though we finde no *Amasiah* no mis-interpreting Priest here, (wee are farre from that, because we are far from having a *Ieroboam* to our King as he had, easie to give eare, easie to give credit to false informations) yet every man that comes with Gods Message hither, brings a little *Amasiah* of his owne, in his owne bosome, a little wisperer in his owne heart, that tels him, *This is the Kings Chappell, and it is the Kings Court,* and these woes and judgements, and the denouncers and proclaimers of them are not so acceptable here. But we must have our owne *Amos,* aswell as our *Amasias,* this answer to this suggestion, *I was no Prophet, and the Lord tooke me and bad me prophecy.* What shall I doe?

And besides, since the woe in this Text is not S. *Iohns wo?* his iterated, his multiplied *wo, Væ, væ, væ habitantibus terram,* a woe of Apoc. 8.13 desolation upon the whole world (for God loves this world, as the worke of his owne hands, as the subject of his providence, as the Scene of his glory, as the Garden-plot that is watered by the Blood of his Son:) Since the *Woe* in this Text is not *Esaies wo, Væ genti* Esay 1.4 *peccatrici,* an increpation and commination upon our whole Nation (for God hath not come so neare to any Nation, and dealt so well with any Nation as with ours:) Since the *Woe* in this Text is not Ezek. 24.6 *Ezekiels Woe, Væ Civitati sanguinum,* an imputation of injustice or oppression, and consequently of a malediction laid upon the whole City (for God hath carried his woes upon other Cities, *Væ Chorasin,* [Mat. *væ Bethsaida;* 11.21] God hath laid his heavy hand of warre and other calamities upon other Cities, that this City might see her selfe and her calamities long before in that glasse, and so avoid them:) Since the *Woe* in this Text, is not the Prophets other *woe, Væ domui,* not a Ezek. 44.6 woe upon any family (for when any man in his family comes to *Ioshua's* protestation, *Ego & domus mea, As for me and my house* Ios. 24.15 *we will serve the Lord,* the Lord comes to his protestation, *In mille generationes, I will shew mercy to thee and thy house for a thousand* [Deut. 7.9] *generations:*) Since the Woe in this Text, is not *Esaies* woe againe, Esay 28.1 *Væ Coronæ,* (for, the same Prophet tels us of what affection they are, that they are Idolaters, persons inclin'd to an idolatrous and super- Esay 8.21 stitious Religion, and fret themselves, and curse the King and their God; we know that the Prophets *Væ Coronæ* in that place is *Væ Coronæ superbiæ,* and the crowne and heighth of Pride is in him, who hath set himselfe above all that is called God. Christian Princes know that if their Crownes were but so as they seeme (all gold) they should bee but so much the heavier for being all gold; but they are but

Crownes of thornes gilded, specious cares, glorious troubles, and therefore no subject of pride:) To contract this, since the *Woe* in this Text, is no State woe, nor Church woe, for it is not *Ezechiels Væ* [Ezek. 13.3] *Pastoribus insipientibus,* which cannot feed their flock, nor *Ieremies Væ Pastoribus disperdentibus,* Woe unto those lazie Shepheards, [Ier. 23.1] which doe not feed their flock but suffer them to scatter: Since the *Woe* in this Text is not a woe upon the whole World, nor upon the whole Nation, nor upon the whole City, nor upon any whole Family, nor upon any whole ranke or calling of men, when I have asked with [Prov. 23.29] *Solomon, Cui væ?* to whom belongs this woe? I must answer with [1 Cor. 9.16] S. *Paul, Væ mihi,* woe unto me if I doe not tell them to whom it belongs. And therefore since in spirituall things especially charity begins with it selfe, I shall transferre this *Væ* from my selfe, by laying it upon them, whom your owne conscience shall find it to belong unto; *Væ desiderantibus diem Domini; Woe be unto them that desire the day of the Lord, &c.*

But yet if these words can be narrow in respect of persons, it is strange, for in respect of the sins that they are directed upon, they have a great compasse, they reach from that high sin of Presumption, and contempt, and deriding the day of the Lord, the judgements of God, and they passe through the sin of Hypocrisie, when we make shift to make the world, and to make our selves beleeve that we are in good case towards God, and would be glad that the day of the Lord, the day of judgement would come now; and then they come downe to the deepest sin, the sin of Desperation, of an unnaturall valuing of this life, when overwhelmed with the burden of other sins, or with Gods punishment for them; men grow to a murmuring wearinesse of this life, and to an impatient desire, and perchance to a practise of their owne ends: In the first acceptation, the day of the Lord is the day of his Judgements and afflictions in this life; In the second, the day of the Lord is the day of the generall judgement; And in the third, the day of the Lord, is that *Crepusculum* that twilight betweene the two lives, or rather that *Meridies noctis,* as the Poet cals it, that noone of night, the houre of our death and transmigration out of this world. And if any desire any of these daies of the Lord, out of any of these indispositions, out of presumption, out of hypocrisie, out of desperation, he fals within the compasse of this Text, and from him we cannot take off this *Væ desiderantibus.*

First then the Prophet directs himself most literally upon the first sin of Presumption. They were come to say, that in truth whatsoever the Prophet declaimed in the streets, there was no such thing as *Dies Domini,* any purpose in God to bring such heavy judgements upon them; to the Prophets themselves they were come to say, You your selves live parched and macerated in a starved and penurious fortune, and therefore you cry out that all we must die of famine too, you your selves have not a foot of land among all the Tribes, and therfore you cry out that all the Tribes must be carried into another Land in Captivity. That which you call the Day of the Lord is come upon you, beggery, and nakednesse, and hunger, contempt, and affliction, and imprisonment is come upon you, and therefore you will needs extend this day upon the whole State, but *desideramus,* we would fain see any such thing come to passe, we would fain see God goe about to do any such thing, as that the State should not be wise enough to prevent him. To see a Prophet neglected, because he will not flatter, to see him despised below, because he is neglected above, to see him injured, insulted upon, and really damnified, because he is despised, All this is *dies mundi,* and not *dies Domini,* it is the ordinary course of the world, and no extraordinary day of the Lord, but that there should be such a stupor and consternation of minde and conscience as you talk of, and that that should be so expressed in the countenance, that *they which had been purer then snow, whiter then milk, redder then Rubies, smoother then Saphirs,* should not only be, as in other cases, pale with a sudden feare, but *blacker in face then a coale,* as the Prophet sayes there, that they should not be able to set a good face upon their miseries, nor disguise them with a confident countenance, that there should be such a consternation of countenance and conscience, and then such a excommunication of Church and State, as that the whole body of the children of Israel should be *without King, without Sacrifice, without Ephod, without Terafim, Desideramus,* We would fain see such a time, we would fain see such a God as were so much too hard for us.

1 Part

Lam. 4.7 [and 8]

Hos. 3.4

They had seen such a God before, they had known that that God had formerly brought all the people upon the face of the earth so neare to an annihilation, so neare to a new creation, as to be but eight persons in the generall flood, they had seen that God to have brought

[Gen. 7.7]

[Exod. 12.37] [Num. 14.30] their own numerous, and multitudinous Nation, their 600000. men that came out of Ægypt to that paucity, as that but two of them are recorded to enter into the land of promise, And could they doubt what that God could do, or would do upon them? Or as *Ieremy* Jer. 5.12 saith, *Could they belie the Lord, and say it is not he? neither shall evill come upon us, or shall we see sword and famine?* God expressed his anger thrice upon this people, in their State, in their form of government, First he exprest it in giving them a King, for though that be the best form of government in it self, yet for that people at that time, God saw it not to be the fittest, and so it was extorted from him, and he gave them their King in anger. Secondly, he expressed his anger in giving them two Kings in the defection of the ten Tribes, and division of the two Kingdomes. Thirdly, he exprest his anger in leaving them without any King after this Captivity which was prophesied here.

Now of those 6000. yeares, which are vulgarly esteemed to be the age and terme of this world, 3000. were past before the division of the Kingdome, and presently upon the division, they argued *à divisibili ad corruptibile,* whatsover may be broken and divided may come to nothing. It is the devils way to come to destruction by breaking of unions. There was a contract between God and *Iob,* because *Iob* loved and feared him, and there the devill attempts to draw away the head from the union, God from *Iob,* with that suggestion, [Job 1.9] *Doth Iob serve thee for nothing?* Doest thou get any thing by this union? or doth not *Iob* serve himself upon thee? There was a naturall, an essentiall, an eternall union between the Father and the Son in the Trinity, and the devill sought to break that. If he could break the union in the Godhead, he saw not why he might not destroy the Godhead. The devill was Logician good enough, *Omne divisibile corruptibile,* whatsoever may be broken, may be annihilated. And the devill was Papist good enough, *Schisma æquipollet hæresi,* Whosoever is a Schismatick, departed from the obedience of the Romane Church, is easily brought within compasse of heresie too, because it is a matter of faith to affirm a necessity of such an obedience. And therefore the devil attempts to make that Schisme in the Trinity, with that, [Mat. 4.3, 6] *Si filius Dei es, Make these stones bread, If thou beest the Son of God, cast thy self down from this Pinnacle,* that is, do something of thy self, exceed thy commission, and never attend so punctually all thy directions from thy Father. In *Iobs* case he would draw the head from the union; In Christs case he would alienate the Son from the Father, because division is the fore-runner (and alas, but a little way the fore-runner) of destruction. And therefore assoon as that Kingdome was come to a division between ten and two Tribes, between a King of Judah, and a King of Israel, presently upon it, and in the compasse of a very short time arose all those Prophets that prophesied of a destruction; assoon as they saw a division, they foresaw a destruction. And therefore when God had shewed before what he could doe, and declared by his Prophets then what he would doe, *Væ desiderantibus, Woe unto them that say, Let him make speed and hasten his* (Esay 5.18 [and 19]) *work, that we may see it:* That is, that are yet confident that no such thing shall fall upon us, and confident with a scorn, and fulfill that which the Apostle saith, *There shall come in the latter daies scoffers, saying, Where is the promise of his comming? for since the fathers* (2 Pet. 3.[3 and] 4) *fell asleep, all things continue as they were from the beginning at the Creation.* But God shall answer their scorn with scorn, as in *Ezekiel, Son of man, What is that Proverb which you have in the Land of Israel, saying, The dayes are prolonged, and every vision* (Ezek. 12.22 [also 23–25]) *failes?* That is, the Prophets talk of great calamities, but we are safe enough, *Tell them* (sayes the Lord) *I will make their proverb to cease, I will speak and it shall come to passe; in your dayes, O rebellious house, will I say the word, and per-form it.*

And therefore *ut quid vobis?* what should you pretend to desire that day? what can ye get by that day? *Because you have made a covenant with death, and are at an agreement with hell, when that Invadens flagellum,* (as the Prophet with an elegant horror, if they can consist, expresses it) *when that over-flowing scourge shall passe* (Esay 28.15) *through, shall it not come to you?* Why? who are you? have you thought of it before hand, considered it, digested it, and resolved, that in the worst that can fall, your vocall constancy, and your humane valour shall sustaine you from all dejection of spirit? what judgement of God soever shall fall upon you, whensoever this *dies Domini* shall break out upon you, you have light in your selves, and by that light you shall see light, and passe through all incommodities? Be not deceived, this day of the Lord is darknesse and not light, the first blast, the first breath of his indignation blowes out thy candle, extinguishes all thy Wisdome, all thy Counsells, all thy Philosophicall sentences, disorders thy *Seneca,* thy *Plutarch,* thy *Tacitus,* and all thy premeditations; for the sword of the Lord is a two-edged sword, it cuts bodily, and it cuts ghostly, it cuts temporally, and it cuts spiritually, it cuts off all worldly reliefe from others, and it cuts off all Christian patience, and good interpretation of Gods correction in thine owne heart.

Vt quid vobis? what can you get by that day? can you imagine that though you have beene benighted under your owne obduration and security before, yet when this day of the Lord, the day of affliction shall come, *afflictio dabit intellectum,* the day will bring light of it selfe, the affliction will give understanding, and it will be time enough to see the danger and the remedy both at once, and to turne to God by that light, which that affliction shall give? Be not deceived, *dies Domini tenebræ,* this day of the Lord will be darknesse and not light. God hath made two great lights for man, the Sun, and the Moone; God doth manifest himselfe two waies to man, by prosperity, and adversity; but if there were no Sun, there would be no light in the Moone neither; If there be no sense of God in thy greatnesse, in thy abundance, it is a dark time to seek him in the clouds of affliction, and heavinesse of heart. Experience teacheth us, that if we be reading any book in the evening, if the twilight surprise us, and it growes dark, yet we can reade longer in that book which we were in before, then if we took a new book of another subject into our hands: If we have been accustomed to the contemplation of God in the Sunshine of prosperity, we shall see him better in the night of misery, then if we began but then, *Væ desiderantibus.* If you seem to desire that day of the Lord, because you doe not beleeve that that day will come, or because you beleeve that when that day comes, it will be time enough to rectifie your selves, then, *Vt quod vobis?* this day shall be good for nothing to either of you, for to both you it shall be darknesse, and not light.

The dayes which God made for man were darknesse, and then light, still the evening and the morning made up the day. The day which the Lord shall bring upon secure and carnall men, is darknesse without light, judgements without any beames of mercy shining

[Gen. 1.1–5]

through them, such judgements, as if we will consider the vehemency of them, we shall finde them expressed in such an extraordinary heighth, as scarce anywhere else in *Ieremy, Men shall ask one of another if they be in labour, whether they travell with childe. Wherefore do I see every man with his hands on his loines, as a woman in travell? Alas, because that day is great, and none is like it.* This is the unexpected and unconsidered strangenesse of that day, if we consider the vehemency, and if we consider the suddennesse, the speed of bringing that day upon secure man. That is intimated very sufficiently in another story of the same Prophet, that when he had said to the Prophet *Hananiah, That he should die within a year,* when God saith, his judgements shall come shortly, if then we consider the vehemency, or the nearnesse of the day of the Lord, the day of his visitation, we shall be glad to say with that Prophet, *As for me I have not desired that wofull day thou knowest,* that is, I have neither doubted but that there shall be such a day, nor I have not put off my repentance to that day, for what can that do good to either of those dispositions, when to them it shall be darknesse, and not light?

Ier. 30.[6 and] 7

Jer. 28.16

Ier. 17.16

2 Part

Now if this *Woe* of this Prophet thus denounced against contemptuous scorners of the *day of the Lord,* as that day signifies afflictions in this life, have had no subject to work upon in this congregation (as by Gods grace there is none of that distemper here) it is a piece of a Sermon well lost; and God be blessed that it hath had no use, that no body needed it. But as the *Woe* is denounced in the second acceptation against Hypocrites, so it is a chain-shot, and in every congregation takes whole rankes, and here *Dies Domini* is the last day of Judgement, and the desire in the Text is not, as before, a denying that any such day should be, but it is an hypocriticall pretence, that we have so well performed our duties, as that we should be glad if that day would come, and then the darknesse of the Text is everlasting condemnation.

For this day of the Lord then, the last day of judgement, consider only, or reflect only upon these three circumstances: First, there is *Lex violata,* a law given to thee and broken by thee. Secondly, there is *Testis prolatus,* Evidence produced against thee, and confessed by thee. And then there is *Sententia lata,* A judgement given against thee, and executed upon thee.

For the Law first, when that Law is *To love God with all thy power,* not to scatter thy love upon any other creature, when the Law is *not to do, not to covet any ill,* wilt thou say this Law doth not concern me, because it is impossible in it self, for this coveting, this first concupiscence is not in a mans own power? Why, this Law was possible to man, when it was given to man, for it was naturally imprinted in the heart of man, when man was in his state of innocency, and then it was possible, and the impossibility that is grown into it since, is by mans own fault. Man by breaking the Law, hath made the Law impossible, and himself inexcusable; wilt thou say with that man in [Mat. 19.20] the Gospell, *Omnia hæc à juventute,* I have kept all this Law from my youth? From thy youth? remember thy youth well, and what Law thou keptst then, and thou wilt finde it to be another Law, [Rom. 7.23] *Lex in membris, A Law of the flesh warring against the Law of the minde,* nay thou wilt finde that thou didst never maintain a war against that Law of the flesh, but wast glad that thou camest to the obedience of that Law so soon, and art sorry thou canst follow that Law no longer.

This is the Law, and wilt thou put this to triall? Wilt thou say who can prove it? Who comes in to give evidence against me? All those whom thy sollicitations have overcome, and who have overcome thy sollicitations, good and bad, friends and enemies, Wives and Mistresses, persons most incompatible, and contrary, here shall joyne [Phil. 3.4–6] together, and be of the Jury. If S. *Pauls* case were so far thy case, as that thou wert in righteousnesse unblameable, no man, no woman able to testifie against thee, yet when the records of all thoughts shall be laid open, and a retired and obscure man shall appeare to have been as ambitious in his Cloister, as a pretending man at the Court, and a retired woman in her chamber, appeare to be as licentious as a prostitute woman in the Stews, when the heart shall be laid open, and this laid open too, that some sins of the heart are the greatest sins of all (as Infidelity, the greatest sin of all, is rooted in the heart) and sin produced to action, is but a dilatation of that sin, and all dilatation is some degree of extenuation, (The body sometimes grows weary of acting some sin, but the heart never grows weary of contriving of sin.)

When this shall be that Law, and this the Evidence, what can be [Mat. 25.41] the Sentence, but that, *Ite maledicti, Go ye accursed into everlasting fire?* where it is not as in the form of our judgement here, You shall be carried to the place of execution, but *Ite, Goe,* our own consciences shall be our executioners, and precipitate us into that condemnation. It is not a Captivity of Babylon for 70. yeares, (and yet 70. yeares is the time of mans life, and why might not so many yeares punishment, expiate so many yeares sinfull pleasure?) but it is 70. millions of millions of generations, for they shall live so long in hell, as God himself in heaven; It is not an imprisonment during the Kings pleasure, but during the Kings displeasure, whom nothing can please nor reconcile, after he shall have made up that account with his Son, and told him, These be all you dyed for, these be all you purchased, these be all whom I am bound to save for your sake, for the rest, their portion is everlasting destruction.

Under this law, under this evidence, under this sentence, *væ desiderantibus,* woe to them that pretend to desire this day of the Lord, as though by their owne outward righteousnesse, they could stand upright in this judgement. Woe to them that say, Let God come when he will, it shall goe hard, but he shall finde me at Church, I heare three or foure Sermons a week; he shall finde me in my Discipline and Mortification, I fast twice a week; he shall finde me in my Stewardship and Dispensation, I give tithes of all that I possesse. When *Ezechias* shewed the Ambassadors of Babylon all his Treasure and his Armour, the malediction of the Prophet fell upon it, that all that Treasure and Armour which he had so gloriously shewed, should be transported to them, to whom he had shewed it, into Babylon. He that publishes his good works to the world, they are carried into the world, and that is his reward. Not that there is not a good use of letting our light shine before men too; for when S. *Paul* sayes, *If I yet please men, I should not be the servant of Christ;* and when he saith, *I doe please all men in all things:* S. *Austine* found no difficulty in reconciling those two; *Navem quæro,* sayes he, *sed & patriam,* When I goe to the Haven to hire a Ship, it is for the love I have to my Country; When I declare my faith by my works to men, it is for the love I beare to the glory of God; but if I desire the Lords day upon confidence in these works, *væ scirpo,* as *Iob* expresses it, *woe unto me poore rush, for* (sayes he) *the rush is greene till the Sun come,* that is, sayes *Gregory* upon that place, *donec divina districtio in judicio candeat,* till the fire of the judgement examine our works, they may

[2 Kings 20.12–17]

Gal. 1.10

[1 Cor. 10.33]

Job 8.[11 and] 16

have some verdure, some colour, but *væ desiderantibus,* wo unto them that put themselves unto that judgement for their works sake.

For *ut quid vobis?* to what end is it for you? If your hypocriticall security could hold out to the last, if you could delude the world at the last gasp, if those that stand about you then could be brought to say, he went away like a Lambe, alas the Lambe of God went not away so, the Lamb of God had his colluctations, disputations, expostulations, apprehensions of Gods indignation upon him then: This security, call it by a worse name, stupidity, is not a lying down like [Gen. 49.14] a Lamb, but a lying down like *Issachers* Asse between two burdens, for two greater burdens cannot be, then sin, and the senslesnesse of sin. *Vt quid vobis?* what will ye doe at that day, which shall be dark- 1 Tim. 6.16 nesse and not light? God dwels *in luce inaccessibili,* in such light as no man by the light of nature can comprehend here, but when that light of grace which was shed upon thee here, should have brought Mat. 8.12 thee at last to that inaccessible light, then thou must be cast *in tenebras exteriores,* into darknesse, and darknesse without the Kingdome of heaven. And if the darknesse of this world, which was but a dark- [John 1.5] nesse of our making, could not comprehend the light, when Christ in his person, brought the light and offered repentance, certainly in that outward darknesse of the next world, the darknesse which God hath made for punishment, they shall see nothing, neither *intramittendo,* nor *extramittendo,* neither by receiving offer of grace from heaven, nor in the disposition to pray for grace in hell. For as at our inanimation in our Mothers womb, our immortall soule when it comes, swallowes up the other soules of vegetation, and of sense, which were in us before; so at this our regeneration in the next world, the light of glory shall swallow up the light of grace. To as many as shall be within, there will need no grace to supply defects, nor eschew dangers, Apoc. 22.5 because there we shall have neither defects nor dangers. *There shall be no night, no need of candle, nor of Sun, for the Lord shall give them light, and they shall raigne for ever and ever.* There shall be no such light of grace, as shall work repentance to them that are in the light of glory; neither could they that are in outward darknesse, com- Rom. 13.12 prehend the light of grace, if it could flow out upon them. First, you Iohn 3. [19–21] did the works of darknesse, sayes the Apostle, and then that custome, that practice brought you to love darknesse better then light; and then as the *Prince of darknesse* delights to transforme himselfe *into an Angell of light;* [2 Cor. 11.14] so by your hypocrisie you pretend a light of grace, when you are darknesse it selfe, [Ephes. 5.8] and therefore, *ut quid vobis?* what will you get by that day which is darknesse and not light?

3. Part

Now as this Woe and commination of our Prophet had one aime, to beat down their scorne which derided the judgements of God in this world, and a second aime to beat downe their confidence, that thought themselves of themselves able to stand in Gods judgements in the next world; so it hath a third mark between these two, it hath an aime upon them in whom a wearinesse of this life, when Gods corrections are upon them, or some other mistaking of their owne estate and case, works an over-hasty and impatient desire of death, and in this sense and acceptation, the day of the Lord is the day of our death and transmigration out of this world, and the darknesse is still everlasting darknesse. Now for this we take our lesson in *Iob, Vita militia, mans life is a warfare;* Iob 7.1 man might have lived at peace, he himselfe chose a rebellious warre, and now *quod volens expetiit nolens portat,* Greg. that warre which he willingly embarked himselfe in at first, though it be against his will now, he must goe through with. In *Iob* we have our lesson, and in S. *Paul* we have our Law, *Take ye the whole armour of God, that ye may be able having done all to stand;* Eph. 6.11 that is, that having overcome one temptation, you may stand in battle against the next, for it is not *adolescentia militia,* but *vita;* that we should think to triumph if we had overcome the heat and intemperance of youth, but we must fight it out to our lives end. And then we have the reward of this lesson, and of this law limited, *nemo coronatur, no man is crowned, except he fight according to this law,* 2 Tim. 2.5 that is, he persever to the end. And as we have our lesson in *Iob,* our rule and reward in the Apostle, who were both great Commanders in the warfare; so we have our example in our great Generall, Christ Jesus, *Who though his soul were heavy, and heavy unto death,* Mat. 26.38 *though he had a baptisme to be baptised with, & coarctabatur, he was straightned, and in paine till it were accomplished,* [Luke 12.50] *and though he had power to lay down his soul, and take it up againe, and no man else could take it from him,* Iohn 10.18 *yet he fought it out to the last houre, and till his houre came, he would not prevent it, nor lay downe his soule. Væ desiderantibus,* woe unto them that desire any other end of Gods correction, but what he hath ordained and appointed, for *ut quid vobis?* what shall you get by choosing your owne wayes? *Tenebræ & non lux;* They shall passe out of this world, in this inward darknesse of melancholy, and dejection of spirit, into the outward darknesse, which is an everlasting exclusion from the Father of lights, and from the Kingdome of joy; their case is well expressed in the next verse to our Text, *they shall flie from a Lyon, and a Beare shall meet them, they shall leane on a wall, and a Serpent shall bite them;* they shall end this life by a miserable and hasty death, and out of that death shall grow an immortall life in torments, which no wearinesse, nor desire, nor practice can ever bring to an end.

Scribanius

And here in this acceptation of these words, this *væ* falls directly upon them who colouring and apparelling treason in martyrdome, expose their lives to the danger of the Law, and embrace death; these of whom one of their own society saith, that the Scevolaes, the Cato's, the Porciaes, the Cleopatraes of the old time, were nothing to the Jesuites, for saith he, they could dye once, but they lacked courage *ad multas mortes;* perchance hee meanes, that after those men were once in danger of the Law, and forfeited their lives by one comming, they could come again and again, as often as the plentifull mercy of their King would send them away, *Rapiunt mortem spontanea irruptione,* sayes he to their glory, they are voluntary and violent pursuers of their own death, and as he expresses it, *Crederes morbo adesos,* you would think that the desire of death is a disease in them;

Baron. Martyrol. 29. Decemb.

A graver man then he mistakes their case and cause of death as much, you are (saith he, incouraging those of our Nation to the pursuit of death) *in sacris septis ad martyrium saginati,* fed up and fatned here for martyrdome, *& Sacramento sanguinem spopondisti,* they have taken an oath that they will be hanged, but that he in whom (as his great patterne God himselfe) mercy is above all his works, out of his abundant sweetnesse makes them perjured when they have so sworne and vowed their owne ruine. But those that send them, give not the lives of these men so freely, so cheaply as they pretend. But as in dry Pumps, men poure in a little water, that they may pump up more; so they are content to drop in a little blood of imaginary, but traiterous Martyrs, that, by that at last they may draw up at last the royall blood of Princes, and the loyall blood of Subjects; *væ desiderantibus,* woe to them that are made thus ambitious of their owne ruine, *ut quid vobis? Tenebræ & non lux,* you are kept in darknesse in this world, and sent into darknesse from heaven into the next, and so your ambition, *ad multas mortes,* shall be satisfied, you dye more then one death, *morte moriemini,* this death delivers you to another, from which you shall never be delivered.

Conclusion

We have now past through these three acceptations of these words, which have falne into the contemplation, and meditation of the Ancients in their Expositions of this Text; as this dark day of the Lord, signifies his judgements upon Atheisticall scorners in this world, as it signifies his last irrevocable, and irremediable judgements upon hypocriticall relyers upon their own righteousnesse in the next world, and between both, as it signifies their uncomfortable passage out of this life, who bring their death inordinately upon themselves; and we shall shut up all with one signification more of the Lords day, That, that is the Lords day, of which the whole Lent is the Vigil, and the Eve. All this time of mortification, and our often meeting in this place to heare of our mortality, and our immortality, which are the two reall Texts, and Subjects of all our Sermons; All this time is the Eve of the Resurrection of our Lord and Saviour Jesus Christ. That is the Lords day, when all our mortification, and dejection of spirit, and humbling of our soules, shall be abundantly exalted in his resurrection, and when all our fasts and abstinence shall be abundantly recompenced in the participation of his body and his bloud in the Sacrament; Gods Chancery is alwayes open, and his seale works alwaies; at all times remission of sins may be sealed to a penitent soule in the Sacrament. That clause which the Chancellors had in their Patents under the Romane Emperours, *Vt prærogativam gerat conscientiæ nostræ,* is in our commission too, for God hath put his conscience into his Church, and whose sins are remitted there, are remitted in heaven at all times; but yet *dies Domini,* the Lords resurrection is as the full Terme, a more generall application of this seale of reconciliation: But *væ desiderantibus,* woe unto them that desire that day, only because they would have these dayes of preaching, and prayer, and fasting, and troublesome preparation past and gone. *Væ desiderantibus,* woe unto them who desire that day, onely, that by receiving the Sacrament that day, they might de-

Cassiodorus

lude the world, as though they were not of a contrary religion in their heart; *væ desiderantibus,* woe unto them who present themselves that day without such a preparation as becomes so fearful and mysterious an action, upon any carnall or collaterall respects. Before that day of the Lord comes, comes the day of his crucifying; before you come to that day, if you come not to a crucifying of your selves to the world, and the world to you, *ut quid vobis?* what shall you get by that day? you shall prophane that day, and the Author of it, as to make that day of Christs triumph, the triumph of Satan, and to make even that body and bloud of Christ Jesus, *Vehiculum Satanæ,* his Chariot to enter into you, as he did into *Iudas.* That day of the Lord will be darknesse and not light, and that darknesse will be, that you shall not discerne the Lords body, you shall scatter all your thoughts upon wrangling and controversies, *de modo,* how the Lords body can be there, and you shall not discerne by the effects, nor in your owne conscience, that the Lords body is there at all. But you shall take it to be onely an obedience to civill or Ecclesiasticall constitutions, or onely a testimony of outward conformity, which should be *signaculum & viaticum,* a seale of pardon for past sins, and a provision of grace against future. But he that is well prepared for this, strips himselfe of all these *væ desiderantibus,* of all these comminations that belong
[Dan. 10.11] to carnall desires, and he shall be as *Daniel* was, *vir desideriorum,* a man of chast and heavenly desires onely; hee shall desire that *day of*
Psal. 119.71 *the Lord,* as that day signifies *affliction* here, with *David, Bonum est mihi quòd humiliasti me,* I am mended by my sicknesse, enriched by my poverty, and strengthened by my weaknesse; and with S. *Bernard* desire, *Irascaris mihi Domine,* O Lord be angry with me, for if thou chidest me not, thou considerest me not, if I taste no bitternesse, I have no Physick; If thou correct me not, I am not thy son: And he shall desire that *day of the Lord,* as that day signifies, *the last judge-*
[Apoc. 6.9, 10] *ment,* with the desire of the Martyrs under the Altar, *Vsquequo Domine? How long, O Lord, ere thou execute judgement?* And he shall desire this *day of the Lord,* as this day is the *day of his own*
[Phil 1.23] *death,* with S. *Pauls* desire, *Cupio dissolvi, I desire to be dissolved, and to be with Christ.* And when this *day of the Lord,* as it is *the day*
[Psal. 63.5] *of the Lords resurrection* shall come, his soule shall be satified as with marrow, and with fatnesse, in the body and bloud of his Saviour,

and in the participation of all his merits, as intirely, as if all that Christ Jesus hath said, and done, and suffered, had beene said, and done, and suffered for his soule alone. Enlarge our daies, O Lord, to that blessed day, prepare us before that day, seale to us at that day, ratifie to us after that day, all the daies of our life, an assurance in that Kingdome, which thy Son our Saviour hath purchased for us, with the inestimable price of his incorruptible bloud, To which glorious Son of God &c.

DEATH'S DUEL

PSALM LXVIII. 20,.

And unto God the Lord belong the issues of death (i.e. from death).

BUILDINGS stand by the benefit of their foundations that sustain and support them, and of their buttresses that comprehend and embrace them, and of their contignations that knit and unite them. The foundations suffer them not to sink, the buttresses suffer them not to swerve, and the contignation and knitting suffers them not to cleave. The body of our building is in the former part of this verse. It is this: He that is our God is the God of salvation; ad salutes, of salvations in the plural, so it is in the original; the God that gives us spiritual and temporal salvation too. But of this building, the foundation, the buttresses, the contignations, are in this part of the verse which constitutes our text, and in the three divers acceptations of the words amongst our expositors: Unto God the Lord belong the issues from death, for, first, the foundation of this building (that our God is the God of all salvation) is laid in this, that unto this God the Lord belong the issues of death; that is, it is in his power to give us an issue and deliverance, even then when we are brought to the jaws and teeth of death, and to the lips of that whirlpool, the grave. And so in this acceptation, this exitus mortis, this issue of death is liberatio á morte, a deliverance from death, and this is the most obvious and most ordinary acceptation of these words, and that upon which our translation lays hold, the issues from death. And then, secondly, the buttresses that comprehend and settle this building, that he that is our God is the God of all salvation, are thus raised; unto God the Lord belong the issues of death, that is, the disposition and manner of our death; what kind of issue and transmigration we shall have out of this world, whether prepared or sudden, whether violent or natural, whether in our perfect senses or shaken and disordered by sickness, there is no condemnation to be argued out of that, no judgment to be made upon that, for, howsoever they die, precious in his sight is the death of his saints, and with him are the issues of death; the ways of our departing out of this life are in his hands. And so in this sense of the words, this exitus mortis, the issues of death, is liberatio in morte, a deliverance in death; not that God will deliver us from dying, but that he will have a care of us in the hour of death, of what kind soever our passage be. And in this sense and acceptation of the words, the natural frame and contexture doth well and pregnantly administer unto us. And then, lastly, the contignation and knitting of this building, that he that is our God is the God of all salvations, consists in this, Unto this God the Lord belong the issues of death; that is, that this God the Lord having united and knit both natures in one, and being God, having also come into this world in our flesh, he could have no other means to save us, he could have no other issue out of this world, nor return to his former glory, but by death. And so in this sense, this exitus mortis, this issue of death, is liberatio per mortem, a deliverance by death, by the death of this God, our Lord Christ Jesus. And this is Saint Augustine's acceptation of the words, and those many and great persons that have adhered to him. In all these three lines, then, we shall look upon these words, first, as the God of power, the Almighty Father rescues his servants from the jaws of death; and then as the God of mercy, the glorious Son rescued us by taking upon himself this issue of death; and then, between these two, as the God of comfort, the Holy Ghost rescues us from all discomfort by his blessed impressions beforehand, that what manner of death soever be ordained for us, yet this exitus mortis shall be introitus in vitam, our issue in death shall be an entrance into everlasting life. And these three considerations: our deliverance à morte, in morte, per mortem, from death, in death, and by death, will abundantly do all the offices of the foundations, of the buttresses, of the contignation, of this our building; that he that is our God is the God of all salvation, because unto this God the Lord belong the issues of death.

First, then, we consider this exitus mortis to be liberatio à morte, that with God the Lord are the issues of death; and therefore in all our death, and deadly calamities of this life, we may justly hope of a good issue from him. In all our periods and transitions in this life, are so many passages from death to death; our very birth and entrance into this life is exitus à morte, an issue from death, for in our mother's womb we are dead, so as that we do not know we live, not so much as we do in our sleep, neither is there any grave so close or so putrid a prison, as the womb would be unto us if we stayed in it beyond our time, or died there before our time. In the grave the worms do not kill us; we breed, and feed, and then kill those worms which we ourselves produced. In the womb the dead child kills the mother that conceived it, and is a murderer, nay, a parricide, even after it is dead. And if we be not dead so in the womb, so as that being dead we kill her that gave us our first life, our life of vegetation, yet we are dead so as David's idols are dead. In the womb we have eyes and see not, ears and hear not. There in the womb we are fitted for works of darkness, all the while deprived of light; and there in the womb we are taught cruelty, by being fed with blood, and may be damned, though we be never born. Of our very making in the womb, David says, I am wonderfully and fearfully made, and such knowledge is too excellent for me, [1] for even that is the Lord's doing, and it is wonderful in our eyes; [2] ipse fecit nos, it is he that made us, and not we ourselves, [3] nor our parents neither. Thy hands have made and fashioned me round about, saith Job, and (as the original word is) thou hast taken pains about me, and yet (says he) thou dost destroy me. Though I be the masterpiece of the greatest master (man is so), yet if thou do no more for me, if thou leave me where thou madest me, destruction will follow. The womb, which should be the house of life, becomes death itself if God leave us there. That which God threatens so often, the shutting of a womb, is not so heavy nor so discomfortable a curse in the first as in the latter shutting, nor in the shutting of barrenness as in the shutting of weakness, when children are come to the birth, and no strength to bring forth. [4]

It is the exaltation of misery to fall from a near hope of happiness. And in that vehement imprecation, the prophet expresses the highest of God's anger, Give them, O Lord, what wilt thou give them? give them a miscarrying womb. Therefore as soon as we are men (that is, inanimated, quickened in the womb), though we cannot ourselves, our parents have to say in our behalf, Wretched man that he is, who shall deliver him from this body of death? [5] if there be no deliverer. It must be he that said to Jeremiah, Before I formed thee I knew thee, and before thou camest out of the womb I sanctified thee. We are not sure that there was no kind of ship nor boat to fish in, nor to pass by, till God prescribed Noah that absolute form of the ark. [6] That word which the Holy Ghost, by Moses, useth for the ark, is common to all kind of boats, thebah; and is the same word that Moses useth for the boat that he was exposed in, that his mother laid him in an ark of bulrushes. But we are sure that Eve had no midwife when she was delivered of Cain, therefore she might well say, Possedi virum à Domino, I have gotten a man from the Lord, [7] wholly, entirely from the Lord; it is the Lord that enabled me to conceive, the Lord that infused a quickening soul into that conception, the Lord that brought into the world that which himself had quickened; without all this might Eve say, my body had been but the house of death, and Domini Domini sunt exitus mortis, To God the Lord belong the issues of death. But then this exitus à morte is but introitus in mortem; this issue, this deliverance, from that death, the death of the womb, is an entrance, a delivering over to another death, the manifold deaths of this world; we have a winding-sheet in our mother's womb which grows with us from our conception, and we come into the world wound up in that winding-sheet, for we come to seek a grave. And as prisoners discharged of actions may lie for fees, so when the womb hath discharged us, yet we are bound to it by cords of hestae, by such a string as that we cannot go thence, nor stay there; we celebrate our own funerals with cries even at our birth; as though our threescore and ten years' life were spent in our mother's labour, and our circle made up in the first point thereof; we beg our baptism with another sacrament, with tears; and we come into a world that lasts many ages, but we last not. In domo Patris, says our Saviour, speaking of heaven, multae mansiones, divers and durable; so that if a man cannot possess a martyr's house (he hath shed no blood for Christ), yet he may have a confessor's, he hath been ready to glorify God in the shedding of his blood. And if a woman cannot possess a virgin's house (she hath embraced the holy state of marriage), yet she may have a matron's house, she hath brought forth and brought up children in the fear of God. In domo Patris, in my Father's house, in heaven, there are many mansions; [8] but here, upon earth, the Son of man hath not where to lay his head, [9] saith he himself. Nonne terram dedit filiis hominum? How then hath God given this earth to the sons of men? He hath given them earth for their materials to be made of earth, and he hath given them earth for their grave and sepulchre, to return and resolve to earth, but not for their possession. Here we have no continuing city, [10] nay, no cottage that continues, nay, no persons, no bodies, that continue. Whatsoever moved Saint Jerome to call the journeys of the Israelites in the wilderness, [11] mansions; the word (the word is nasang) signifies but a journey, but a peregrination. Even the Israel of God hath no mansions, but journeys, pilgrimages in this life. By what measure did Jacob measure his life to Pharaoh? The days of the years of my pilgrimage. [12] And though the apostle would not say morimur, that whilst we are in the body we are dead, yet he says, perigrinamur, whilst we are in the body we are but in a pilgrimage, and we are absent from the Lord: [13] he might have said dead, for this whole world is but an universal churchyard, but our common grave, and the life and motion that the greatest persons have in it is but as the shaking of buried bodies in their grave, by an earthquake. That which we call life is but hebdomada mortium, a week of death, seven days, seven periods of our life spent in dying, a dying seven times over; and there is an end. Our birth dies in infancy, and our infancy dies in youth, and youth and the rest die in age, and age also dies and determines all. Nor do all these, youth out of infancy, or age out of youth, arise so, as the phoenix out of the ashes of another phoenix formerly dead, but as a wasp or a serpent out of a carrion, or as a snake out of dung. Our youth is worse than our infancy, and our age worse than our youth. Our youth is hungry and thirsty after those sins which our infancy knew not; and our age is sorry and angry, that it cannot pursue those sins which our youth did; and besides, all the way, so many deaths, that is, so many deadly calamities accompany every condition and every period of this life, as that death itself would be an ease to them that suffer them. Upon this sense doth Job wish that God had not given him an issue from the first death, from the womb, Wherefore thou hast brought me forth out of the womb? Oh that I had given up the ghost, and no eye seen me! I should have been as though I had not been. [14] And not only the impatient Israelites in their murmuring (would to God we had died by the hand of the Lord in the land of Egypt), [15] but Elijah himself, when he fled from Jezebel, and went for his life, as that text says, under the juniper tree, requested that he might die, and said, It is enough now, O Lord, take away my life. [16] So Jonah justifies his impatience, nay, his anger, towards God himself: Now, O Lord, take, I beseech thee, my life from me, for it is better to die than to live. [17] And when God asked him, Dost thou well to be angry for this? he replies, I do well to be angry, even unto death. How much worse a death than death is this life, which so good men would so often change for death! But if my case be as Saint Paul's case, quotidiè morior, that I die daily, that something heavier than death fall upon me every day; if my case be

David's case, tota die mortificamur; all the day long we are killed, that not only every day, but every hour of the day, something heavier than death fall upon me; though that be true of me, Conceptus in peccatis, I was shapen in iniquity, and in sin did my mother conceive me (there I died one death); though that be true of me, Natus filius irae, I was born not only the child of sin, but the child of wrath, of the wrath of God for sin, which is a heavier death: yet Domini Domini sunt exitus mortis, with God the Lord are the issues of death; and after a Job, and a Joseph, and a Jeremiah, and a Daniel, I cannot doubt of a deliverance. And if no other deliverance conduce more to his glory and my good, yet he hath the keys of death, [18] and he can let me out at that door, that is, deliver me from the manifold deaths of this world, the omni die, and the tota die, the every day's death and every hour's death, by that one death, the final dissolution of body and soul, the end of all. But then is that the end of all? Is that dissolution of body and soul the last death that the body shall suffer (for of spiritual death we speak not now). It is not, though this be exitus à morte: it is introitus in mortem; though it be an issue from manifold deaths of this world, yet it is an entrance into the death of corruption and putrefaction, and vermiculation, and incineration, and dispersion in and from the grave, in which every dead man dies over again. It was a prerogative peculiar to Christ, not to die this death, not to see corruption. What gave him this privilege? Not Joseph's great proportion of gums and spices, that might have preserved his body from corruption and incineration longer than he needed it, longer than three days, but it would not have done it for ever. What preserved him then? Did his exemption and freedom from original sin preserve him from this corruption and incineration? It is true that original sin hath induced this corruption and incineration upon us; if we had not sinned in Adam, mortality had not put on immortality [19] (as the apostle speaks), nor corruption had not put on incorruption, but we had had our transmigration from this to the other world without any mortality, any corruption at all. But yet since Christ took sin upon him, so far as made him mortal, he had it so far too as might have made him see this corruption and incineration, though he had no original sin in himself; what preserved him then? Did the hypostatical union of both natures, God and man, preserve him from this corruption and incineration? It is true that this was a most powerful embalming, to be embalmed with the Divine Nature itself, to be embalmed with eternity, was able to preserve him from corruption and incineration for ever. And he was embalmed so, embalmed with the Divine Nature itself, even in his body as well as in his soul; for the

Godhead, the Divine Nature, did not depart, but remained still united to his dead body in the grave; but yet for all this powerful embalming, his hypostatical union of both natures, we see Christ did die; and for all his union which made him God and man, he became no man (for the union of the body and soul makes the man, and he whose soul and body are separated by death as long as that state lasts, is properly no man). And therefore as in him the dissolution of body and soul was no dissolution of the hypostatical union, so there is nothing that constrains us to say, that though the flesh of Christ had seen corruption and incineration in the grave, this had not been any dissolution of the hypostatical union, for the Divine nature, the Godhead, might have remained with all the elements and principles of Christ's body, as well as it did with the two constitutive parts of his person, his body and his soul. This incorruption then was not in Joseph's gums and spices, nor was it in Christ's innocency, and exemption from original sin, nor was it (that is, it is not necessary to say it was) in the hypostatical union. But this incorruptibleness of his flesh is most conveniently placed in that; Non dabis, thou wilt not suffer thy Holy One to see corruption; we look no further for causes or reasons in the mysteries of religion, but to the will and pleasure of God; Christ himself limited his inquisition in that ita est, even so, Father, for so it seemeth good in thy sight. Christ's body did not see corruption, therefore, because God had decreed it should not. The humble soul (and only the humble soul is the religious soul) rests himself upon God's purposes and the decrees of God which he hath declared and manifested, not such as are conceived and imagined in ourselves, though upon some probability, some verisimilitude; so in our present case Peter proceeds in his sermon at Jerusalem, and so Paul in his at Antioch. [20] They preached Christ to have been risen without seeing corruption, not only because God had decreed it, but because he had manifested that decree in his prophet, therefore doth Saint Paul cite by special number the second Psalm for that decree, and therefore both Saint Peter and Saint Paul cite for it that place in the sixteenth Psalm; [21] for when God declares his decree and purpose in the express words of his prophet, or when he declares it in the real execution of the decree, then he makes it ours, then he manifests it to us. And therefore, as the mysteries of our religion are not the objects of our reason, but by faith we rest on God's decree and purpose--(it is so, O God, because it is thy will it should be so)--so God's decrees are ever to be considered in the manifestation thereof. All manifestation is either in the word of God, or in the execution of the decree; and when these two concur and meet it is the strongest demonstration that can be: when therefore I find those marks of adoption and spiritual filiation which are delivered in the word of God to be upon me; when I find that real execution of his good purpose upon me, as that actually I do live under the obedience and under the conditions which are evidences of adoption and spiritual filiation; then, so long as I see these marks and live so, I may safely comfort myself in a holy certitude and a modest infallibility of my adoption. Christ determines himself in that, the purpose of God was manifest to him; Saint Peter and Saint Paul determine themselves in those two ways of knowing the purpose of God, the word of God before the execution of the decree in the fulness of time. It was prophesied before, said they, and it is performed now, Christ is risen without seeing corruption. Now, this which is so singularly peculiar to him, that his flesh should not see corruption, at his second coming, his coming to judgment, shall extend to all that are then alive; their hestae shall not see corruption, because, as the apostle says, and says as a secret, as a mystery, Behold I shew you a mystery, we shall not all sleep (that is, not continue in the state of the dead in the grave), but we shall all be changed in an instant, we shall have a dissolution, and in the same instant a redintegration, a recompacting of body and soul, and that shall be truly a death and truly a resurrection, but no sleeping in corruption; but for us that die now and sleep in the state of the dead, we must all pass this posthume death, this death after death, nay, this death after burial, this dissolution after dissolution, this death of corruption and putrefaction, of vermiculation and incineration, of dissolution and dispersion in and from the grave, when these bodies that have been the children of royal parents, and the parents of royal children, must say with Job, Corruption, thou art my father, and to the worm, Thou art my mother and my sister. Miserable riddle, when the same worm must be my mother, and my sister and myself! Miserable incest, when I must be married to my mother and my sister, and be both father and mother to my own mother and sister, beget and bear that worm which is all that miserable penury; when my mouth shall be filled with dust, and the worm shall feed, and feed sweetly[369] [22] upon me; when the ambitious man shall have no satisfaction, if the poorest alive tread upon him, nor the poorest receive any contentment in being made equal to princes, for they shall be equal but in dust. One dieth at his full strength, being wholly at ease and in quiet; and another dies in the bitterness of his soul, and never eats with pleasure; but they lie down alike in the dust, and the worm covers them. [23] In Job and in Isaiah, [24] it covers them and is spread under them, the worm is spread under thee, and the worm covers thee. There are the mats and the carpets that lie under, and there are the state and the canopy that hang over the greatest of the sons of men. Even those bodies that were the temples of the Holy Ghost come to this dilapidation, to ruin, to rubbish, to dust; even the Israel of the Lord, and Jacob himself, hath no other specification, no other denomination, but that vermis Jacob, thou worm of Jacob. Truly the consideration of this posthume death, this death after burial, that after God (with whom are the issues of death) hath delivered me from the death of the womb, by bringing me into the world, and from the manifold deaths of the world, by laying me in the grave, I must die again in an incineration of this flesh, and in a dispersion of that dust. That that monarch, who spread over many nations alive, must in his dust lie in a corner of that sheet of lead, and there but so long as that lead will last; and that private and retired man, that thought himself his own for ever, and never came forth, must in his dust of the grave be published, and (such are the revolutions of the grave) be mingled with the dust of every highway and of every dunghill, and swallowed in every puddle and pond. This is the most inglorious and contemptible vilification, the most deadly and peremptory nullification of man, that we can consider. God seems to have carried the declaration of his power to a great height, when he sets the prophet Ezekiel in the valley of dry bones, and says, Son of man, can these bones live? as though it had been impossible, and yet they did; the Lord laid sinews upon them, and flesh, and breathed into them, and they did live. But in that case there were bones to be seen, something visible, of which it might be said, Can this thing live? But in this death of incineration and dispersion of dust, we see nothing that we call that man's. If we say, Can this dust live? Perchance it cannot; it may be the mere dust of the earth, which never did live, never shall. It may be the dust of that man's worm, which did live, but shall no more. It may be the dust of another man, that concerns not him of whom it was asked. This death of incineration and dispersion is, to natural reason, the most irrecoverable death of all; and yet Domini Domini sunt exitus mortis, unto God the Lord belong the issues of death; and by recompacting this dust into the same body, and remaining the same body with the same soul, he shall in a blessed and glorious resurrection give me such an issue from this death as shall never pass into any other death, but establish me into a life that shall last as long as the Lord of Life himself.

And so have you that that belongs to the first acceptation of these words (unto God the Lord belong the issues of death); That though from the womb to the grave, and in the grave itself, we pass from death to death, yet, as Daniel speaks, the Lord our God is able to deliver us, and he will deliver us.

And so we pass unto our second accommodation of these words (unto God the Lord belong the issues of death); that it belongs to God, and not to man, to pass a judgment upon us at our death, or to conclude a dereliction on God's part upon the manner thereof.

Those indications which the physicians receive, and those presagitions which they give for death or recovery in the patient, they receive and they give out of the grounds and the rules of their art, but we have no such rule or art to give a presagition of spiritual death and damnation upon any such indication as we see in any dying man; we see often enough to be sorry, but not to despair; we may be deceived both ways: we use to comfort ourself in the death of a friend, if it be testified that he went away like a lamb, that is, without any reluctation; but God knows that may be accompanied with a dangerous damp and stupefaction, and insensibility of his present state. Our blessed Saviour suffered colluctations with death, and a sadness even in his soul to death, and an agony even to a bloody sweat in his body, and expostulations with God, and exclamations upon the cross. He was a devout man who said upon his death-bed, or death-turf (for he was a hermit), Septuaginta annos Domino servivisti, et mori times? Hast thou served a good master threescore and ten years, and now art thou loth to go into his presence? Yet Hilarion was loth. Barlaam was a devout man (a hermit too) that said that day he died, Cogita te hodie caepisse servire Domino, et hodie finiturum, Consider this to be the first day's service that ever thou didst thy Master, to glorify him in a Christianly and a constant death, and if thy first day be thy last day too, how soon dost thou come to receive thy wages! Yet Barlaam could have been content to have stayed longer forth. Make no ill conclusions upon any man's lothness to die, for the mercies of God work momentarily in minutes, and many times insensibly to bystanders, or any other than the party departing. And then upon violent deaths inflicted as upon malefactors, Christ himself hath forbidden us by his own death to make any ill conclusion; for his own death had those impressions in it; he was reputed, he was executed as a malefactor, and no doubt many of them who concurred to his death did believe him to be so. Of sudden death there are scarce examples be found in the Scriptures upon good men, for death in battle cannot be called sudden death; but God governs not by examples but by rules, and therefore make no ill conclusion upon sudden death nor upon distempers neither, though perchance accompanied with some words of diffidence and distrust in the mercies of God. The tree lies as it falls, it is true, but it is not the last stroke that fells the tree, nor the last word nor gasp that qualifies the soul. Still pray we for a peaceable life against violent death, and for time of repentance against sudden death, and for sober and modest assurance against distempered and diffident death, but never make ill conclusions upon persons overtaken with such deaths; Domini Domini sunt exitus mortis, to God the Lord belong the issues of death. And he received Samson, who went out of this world in such a manner (consider it actively, consider it passively in his own death, and in those whom he slew with himself) as was subject to interpretation hard enough. Yet the Holy Ghost hath moved Saint Paul to celebrate Samson in his great catalogue, [25] and so doth all the church. Our critical day is not the very day of our death, but the whole course of our life. I thank him that prays for me when the bell tolls, but I thank him much more that catechises me, or preaches to me, or instructs me how to live. Fac hoc et vive, there is my security, the mouth of the Lord hath said it, do this and thou shalt live. But though I do it, yet I shall die too, die a bodily, a natural death. But God never mentions, never seems to consider that death, the bodily, the natural death. God doth not say, Live well, and thou shalt die well, that is, an easy, a quiet death; but, Live well here, and thou shalt live well for ever. As the first part of a sentence pieces well with the last, and never respects, never hearkens after the parenthesis that comes between, so doth a good life here flow into an eternal life, without any consideration what so manner of death we die. But whether the gate of my prison be opened with an oiled key (by a gentle and preparing sickness), or the gate be hewn down by a violent death, or the gate be burnt down by a raging and frantic fever, a gate into heaven I shall have, for from the Lord is the cause of my life, and with God the Lord are the issues of death. And further we carry not this second acceptation of the words, as this issue of death is liberatio in morte, God's care that the soul be safe, what agonies soever the body suffers in the hour of death.

But pass to our third part and last part: As this issue of death is liberatio per mortem, a deliverance by the death of another. Sufferentiam Job audiisti, et vidisti finem Domini, says Saint James (v. 11), You have heard of the patience of Job, says he: all this while you have done that, for in every man, calamitous, miserable man, a Job speaks. Now, see the end of the Lord, sayeth that apostle, which is not that end that the Lord proposed to himself (salvation to us), nor the end which he proposes to us (conformity to him), but see the end of the Lord, says he, the end that the Lord himself came to, death, and a painful and a shameful death. But why did he die? and why die so? Quia Domini Domini sunt exitus mortis (as Saint Augustine, interpreting this text, answers that question), [26] because to this God our Lord belonged the issues of death. Quid apertius diceretur? says he there, what can be more obvious, more manifest than this sense of these words? In the former part of this verse it is said, He that is our God is the God of salvation; Deus salvos faciendi, so he reads it, the God that must save us. Who can that be, says he, but Jesus? For therefore that name was given him because he was to save us. And to this Jesus, says he, this Saviour, [27] belong the issues of death; Nec oportuit eum de hac vita alios exitus habere quam mortis: being come into this life in our mortal nature, he could not go out of this life any other way but by death. Ideo dictum, says he, therefore it is said, to God the Lord belonged the issues of death; ut ostenderetur moriendo nos salvos facturum, to show that his way to save us was to die. And from this text doth Saint Isidore prove that Christ was truly man (which as many sects of heretics denied, as that he was truly God), because to him, though he were Dominus Dominus (as the text doubles it), God the Lord, yet to him, to God the Lord belonged the issues of death; oportuit eum pati; more cannot be said than Christ himself says of himself; These things Christ ought to suffer; [28] he had no other way but death: so then this part of our sermon must needs be a passion sermon, since all his life was a continual passion, all our Lent may well be a continual Good Friday. Christ's painful life took off none of the pains of his death, he felt not the less then for having felt so much before. Nor will any thing that shall be said before lessen, but rather enlarge the devotion, to that which shall be said of his passion at the time of due solemnization thereof. Christ bled not a drop the less at the last for having bled at his circumcision before, nor will you a tear the less then if you shed some now. And therefore be now content to consider with me how to this God the Lord belonged the issues of death. That God, this Lord, the Lord of life, could die, is a strange contemplation; that the Red Sea could be dry, that the sun could stand still, that an oven could be seven times heat and not burn, that lions could be hungry and not bite, is strange, miraculously strange, but super-miraculous that God could die; but that God would die is an exaltation of that. But even of that also it is a super-exaltation, that God should die, must die, and non exitus (said Saint Augustine), God the Lord had no issue but by death, and oportuit pati (says Christ himself), all this Christ ought to suffer, was bound to suffer; Deus ultimo Deus, says David, God is the God of revenges, he would not pass over the son of man unrevenged, unpunished. But then Deus ultionum libere egit (says that place), the God of revenges works freely, he punishes, he spares whom he will. And would he not spare himself? he would not: Dilectio fortis ut mors, love is strong as death; [29] stronger, it drew in death, that naturally is not welcome. Si possibile, says Christ, if it be possible, let this cup pass, when his love, expressed in a former decree with his Father, had made it impossible. Many waters quench not love. [30] Christ tried many: he was baptised out of his love, and his love determined not there; he mingled blood with water in his agony, and that determined not his love; he wept pure blood, all his blood at all his eyes, at all his pores, in his flagellation and thorns (to the Lord our God belonged the issues of blood), and these expressed, but these did not quench his love. He would not spare, nay, he could not spare himself. There was nothing more free, more voluntary, more spontaneous than the death of Christ. It is true, libere egit, he died voluntarily; but yet when we consider the contract that had passed between his Father and him, there was an oportuit, a kind of necessity upon him: all this Christ ought to suffer. And when shall we date this obligation, this oportuit, this necessity? When shall we say that began? Certainly this decree by which Christ was to suffer all this was an eternal decree, and was there any thing before that that was eternal? Infinite love, eternal love; be pleased to follow this home, and to consider it seriously, that what liberty soever we can conceive in Christ to die or not to die; this necessity of dying, this decree is as eternal as that liberty; and yet how small a matter made he of this necessity and this dying? His Father calls it but a bruise, and but a bruising of his heel [31] (the serpent shall bruise his heel), and yet that was, that the serpent should practise and compass his death. Himself calls it but a baptism, as though he were to be the better for it. I have a baptism to be baptized with, [32] and he was in pain till it was accomplished, and yet this baptism was his death. The Holy Ghost calls it joy (for the joy which was set before him he endured the cross), [33] which was not a joy of his reward after his passion, but a joy that filled him even in the midst of his torments, and arose from him; when Christ calls his calicem a cup, and no worse (Can ye drink of my cup) [34] , he speaks not odiously, not with detestation of it. Indeed it was a cup, salus mundo, a health to all the world. And quid retribuam, says David, What shall I render to the Lord? [35] Answer you with David, Accipiam calicem, I will take the cup of salvation; take it, that cup is salvation, his passion, if not into your present imitation, yet into your present contemplation. And behold how that Lord that was God, yet could die, would die, must die for our salvation. That Moses and Elias talked with Christ in the transfiguration, both Saint Matthew and Saint Mark [36] tells us, but what they talked of, only Saint Luke; Dicebant excessum ejus, says he, They talked of his disease, of his death, which was to be accomplished at Jerusalem. [37] The word is of his exodus, the very word of our text, exitus, his issue by death. Moses, who in his exodus had prefigured this issue of our Lord, and in passing Israel out of Egypt through the Red Sea, had foretold in that actual prophecy, Christ passing of mankind through the sea of his blood; and Elias, whose exodus and issue of this world was a figure of Christ's ascension; had no doubt a great satisfaction in talking with our blessed Lord, de excessu ejus, of the full consummation of all this in his death, which was to be accomplished at Jerusalem. Our meditation of his death should be more visceral, and affect us more, because it is of a thing already done. The ancient Romans had a certain tenderness and detestation of the name of death; they could not name death, no, not in their wills; there they could not say, Si mori contigerit, but si quid humanitas contingat, not if or when I die, but when the course of nature is accomplished upon me. To us that speak daily of the death of Christ (he was crucified, dead, and buried), can the memory or the mention of our own death be irksome or bitter? There are in these latter times amongst us that name death freely enough, and the death of God, but in blasphemous oaths and execrations. Miserable men, who shall therefore be said never to have named Jesus, because they have named him too often; and therefore hear Jesus say, Nescivi vos, I never knew you, because they made themselves too familiar with him. Moses and Elias talked with Christ of his death only in a holy and joyful sense, of the benefit which they and all the world were to receive by that. Discourses of religion should not be out of curiosity, but to edification. And then they talked with Christ of his death at that time when he was in the greatest height of glory, that ever he admitted in this world, that is, his transfiguration. And we are afraid to speak to the great men of this world of their death, but nourish in them a vain imagination of immortality and immutability. But bonum est nobis esse hic (as Saint Peter said there), It is good to dwell here, in this consideration of his death, and therefore transfer we our tabernacle (our devotions) through some of those steps which God the Lord made to his issue of death that day. Take in the whole day from the hour that Christ received the passover upon Thursday unto the hour in which he died the next day. Make this present day that day in thy devotion, and consider what he did, and remember what you have done. Before he instituted and celebrated the sacrament (which was after the eating of the passover), he proceeded to that act of humility, to wash his disciples' feet, even Peter's, who for a while resisted him. In thy preparation to the holy and blessed sacrament, hast thou with a sincere humility sought a reconciliation with all the world, even with those that have been averse from it, and refused that reconciliation from thee? If so, and not else, thou hast spent that first part of his last day in a conformity with him. After the sacrament he spent the time till night in prayer, in preaching, in psalms: hast thou considered that a worthy receiving of the sacrament consists in a continuation of holiness after, as well as in a preparation before? If so, thou hast therein also conformed thyself to him; so Christ spent his time till night. At night he went into the garden to pray, and he prayed prolixious, he spent much time in prayer, how much? Because it is literally expressed, that he prayed there three several times, [38] and that returning to his disciples after his first prayer, and finding them asleep, said, Could ye not watch with me one hour, [39] it is collected that he spent three hours in prayer. I dare scarce ask thee whither thou wentest, or how thou disposedst of thyself, when it grew dark and after last night. If that time were spent in a holy recommendation of thyself to God, and a submission of thy will to his, it was spent in a conformity to him. In that time, and in those prayers, was his agony and bloody sweat. I will hope that thou didst pray; but not every ordinary and customary prayer, but prayer actually accompanied with shedding of tears and dispositively in a readiness to shed blood for his glory in necessary cases, puts thee into a conformity with him. About midnight he was taken and bound with a kiss, art thou not too conformable to him in that? Is not that too literally, too exactly thy case, at midnight to have been taken and bound with a kiss? From thence he was carried back to Jerusalem, first to Annas, then to Caiaphas, and (as late as it was) then he was examined and buffered, and delivered over to the custody of those officers from whom he received all those irrisions, and violences, the covering of his face, the spitting upon his face, the blasphemies of words, and the smartness of blows, which that gospel mentions: in which compass fell that gallicinium, that crowing of the cock which called up Peter to his repentance. How thou passedst all that time thou knowest. If thou didst any thing that needest Peter's tears, and hast not shed them, let me be thy cock, do it now. Now, thy Master (in the unworthiest of his servants) looks back upon thee, do it now. Betimes, in the morning, so soon as it was day, the Jews held a council in the high priest's hall, and agreed upon their evidence against him, and then carried him to Pilate, who was to be his judge; didst thou accuse thyself when thou wakedst this morning, and wast thou content even with false accusations, that is, rather to suspect actions to have been sin, which were not, than to smother and justify such as were truly sins? Then thou spentest that hour in conformity to him; Pilate found no evidence against him, and therefore to ease himself, and to pass a compliment upon Herod, tetrarch of Galilee, who was at that time at Jerusalem (because Christ, being a Galilean, was of Herod's jurisdiction), Pilate sent him to Herod, and rather as a madman than a malefactor; Herod remanded him (with scorn) to Pilate, to proceed against him; and this was about eight of the clock. Hast thou been content to come to this inquisition, this examination, this agitation, this cribration, this pursuit of thy conscience; to sift it, to follow it from the sins of thy youth to thy present sins, from the sins of thy bed to the sins of thy board, and from the substance to the circumstance of thy sins? That is time spent like thy Saviour's. Pilate would have saved Christ, by using the privilege of the day in his behalf, because that day one prisoner was to be delivered, but they choose Barabbas; he would have saved him from death, by satisfying their fury with inflicting other torments upon him, scourging and crowning with thorns, and loading him with many scornful and ignominious contumelies, but they regarded him not, they pressed a crucifying. Hast thou gone about to redeem thy sin, by fasting, by alms, by disciplines and mortifications, in way of satisfaction to the justice of God? That will not serve that is not the right way; we press an utter crucifying of that sin that governs thee: and that conforms thee to Christ. Towards noon Pilate gave judgment, and they made such haste to execution as that by noon he was upon the cross. There now hangs that sacred body upon the cross, rebaptized in his own tears, and sweat, and embalmed in his own blood alive. There are those bowels of compassion which are so conspicuous, so manifested, as that you may see them through his wounds. There those glorious eyes grew faint in their sight, so as the sun, ashamed to survive them, departed with his light too. And then that Son of God, who was never from us, and yet had now come a new way unto us in assuming our nature, delivers that soul (which was never out of his Father's hands) by a new way, a voluntary emission of it into his Father's hands; for though to this God our Lord belonged these issues of death, so that considered in his own contract, he must necessarily die, yet at no breach or battery which they had made upon his sacred body issued his soul; but emisit, he gave up the ghost; and as God breathed a soul into the first Adam, so this second Adam breathed his soul into God, into the hands of God.

There we leave you in that blessed dependency, to hang upon him that hangs upon the cross, there bathe in his tears, there suck at his wounds, and lie down in peace in his grave, till he vouchsafe you a resurrection, and an ascension into that kingdom which He hath prepared for you with the inestimable price of his incorruptible blood. Amen.

Scripture References

[1] Psalm 139:6.

[2] Psalm 118:23

[3] Psalm 100:3.

[4] Isaiah 37:3.

[5] Rom. 7:24.

[6] Gen. 6:14.

[7] Gen. 4:1.

[8] John 14:2.

[9] Matt. 8:20.

[10] Heb. 13:14.

[11] Exod. 17:1.

[12] Gen. 47:9.

[13] 2 Cor. 5:6.

[14] Job 10:18, 19.

[15] Exod. 16:3.

[16] 1 Kings 19:4

[17] Jonah 4:3.

[18] Rev. 1:18.

[19] 1 Cor. 15:33.

[20] Acts 2:31; 13:35.

[21] Ver. 10.

[22] Job 24:20.

[23] Job 21:23, 25, 26.

[24] Isaiah 14:11.

[25] Heb. 11.

[26] De Civitate Dei, lib. 17.

[27] Matt. 1:21.

[28] Luke 24:26.

[29] Cant. 8:6.

[30] Cant. 8:7.

[31] Gen. 3:15.

[32] Luke 12:50.

[33] Heb. 12:2.

[34] Matt. 20:22.

[35] Psalm 116:12.

[36] Matt. 17:3; Mark 9:4.

[37] Luke 9:31.

[38] Luke 22:41.

[39] Matt. 26:40.

A Sermon upon the fift of November 1622. being the Anniversary celebration of our Deliverance from the Powder Treason.

Intended for Pauls Crosse, but by reason of the weather, Preached in the Church.

THE PRAYER BEFORE THE SERMON

O LORD open thou my lips, and my mouth shall shew forth thy praise; *for* thou, O Lord, didst make haste to help us, *Thou, O Lord, didst* make speed to save us. *Thou that sittest in heaven, didst not onely looke down, to see what was done* upon *the Earth, but what was done* in *the Earth; and when the bowels of the Earth, were, with a* key of fire, *ready to open and swallow us, the bowels of thy compassion, were, with a* key of love, *opened to succour us; This is the day, and these are the houres, wherein that should have been acted: In this our Day, and in these houres,* We praise thee, O God, we acknowledge thee, to bee the Lord; All our Earth doth worship thee; The holy Church throughout all this Land, doth knowledge thee, *with commemorations of that great mercy, now in these houres. Now, in these houres, it is thus commemorated, in the* Kings House, *where the Head and Members praise thee; Thus, in that place, where it should have been perpetrated, where the Reverend* Judges *of the Land doe now praise thee; Thus, in the* Universities, *where the tender youth of this Land, is brought up to praise thee, in a detestation of their Doctrines, that plotted this; Thus it is commemorated in many severall Societies, in many severall* Parishes, *and thus, here, in this* Mother

Church, *in this great Congregation of thy Children, where, all, of all sorts, from the Lievtenant of thy Lievtenant, to the meanest sonne of thy sonne, in this Assembly, come with hearts, and lippes, full of thankesgiving:* Thou Lord, openest their lippes, that their mouth may shew forth thy prayse, for, Thou, O Lord, diddest make haste to helpe them, Thou diddest make speede to save them. *Accept, O Lord, this Sacrifice, to which thy Spirit giveth fire; This of* Praise, *for thy great Mercies already afforded to us, and this of* Prayer, *for the continuance, and enlargement of them, upon the* Catholick Church, *by them, who pretend themselves the onely sonnes thereof, dishonoured this Day; upon these Churches of* England, Scotland, *and* Ireland, *shaked and threatned dangerously this Day; upon thy servant, our Soveraigne, for his Defence of the true Faith, designed to ruine this day; upon the* Prince, *and others derived from the same roote, some but Infants, some not yet Infants, enwrapped in dust, and annihilation, this day; upon all the deliberations of the* Counsell, *That in all their Consultations, they may have before their eyes, the Record and Registers of this Day; upon all the* Clergie, *That all their Preaching, and their Governement, may preclude, in their severall Jurisdictions, all re-entrances of that Religion, which, by the Confession of the Actours themselves, was the onely ground of the Treason of this day; upon the whole* Nobilitie, *and* Commons, *all involved in one Common Destruction, this Day; upon both our* Universities, *which though they lacke no Arguments out of thy* Word, *against the Enemies of thy Truth, shall never leave out this Argument out of thy* Works, *The Historie of this Day; And upon all those, who are any wayes afflicted, That our afflictions bee not multiplyed upon us, by seeing them multiplyed amongst us, who would have diminished thee, and annihilated us, this Day; And lastly, upon this Auditory assembled here, That till they turne to ashes in the Grave, they may remember, that thou tookest them,* as fire-brands out of the fire, *this Day.*

Heare us, O Lord, and hearken to us, Receive our Prayers, *and returne them with Effect, for his sake, in whose Name and words, wee make them:*

Our Father which art, *&c.*

THE SERMON

Lament. 4.20. *THE BREATH OF OUR NOSTRILS, THE ANOINTED OF THE LORD, WAS TAKEN IN THEIR PITS.*

Of the *Authour* of *this Booke,* I thinke there was never doubt made; but yet, that is scarce safely done, which the *Councell of Trent* doth, in that Canon, which numbers the Books of Canonicall Scriptures, to leave out this Book of Lamentations. For, though I make no doubt, but that they had a purpose to comprehend, and involve it, in the name of *Jeremy,* yet that was not enough; for so they might have comprehended and involved, *Genesis,* and *Deuteronomie,* and all between those two, in one name of *Moses;* and so they might have comprehended, and involved, the *Apocalypse,* and some *Epistles* in the name of *John,* and have left out the Book it selfe in the number. But one of their own *Jesuits,* though some, (whom in that Canon they seeme to follow) make this Booke of *Lamentations,* but an Appendix to the Prophecy of *Jeremy,* determines, for all that Canon, that it is a *distinct Book*. Indeed, if it were not, the first Chapter would have been called, the 53 of *Ieremy,* and not the *first of the Lamentations.* But that which gives most assurednesse, is, That in divers *Hebrew Bibles,* it is placed otherwise, then wee place it, and not presently, and immediately after the Prophecy of *Ieremy,* but discontinued from him, though hee were never doubted to be the Author thereof.

The Booke is certainly the *Prophet Jeremies,* and certainly a *distinct booke;* But whether the Book be a *history,* or a *Prophecy,* whether *Jeremy* lament that which hee had *seen,* or that which he *foresees,* calamities past, or future calamities, things done, or things to be done, is a question which hath exercised, and busied divers Expositors. But, as we say of the *Parable of Dives,* and *Lazarus,* that it is a *Historicall parable,* and a *Parabolicall history,* some such persons there were, and some such things were really done, but some other things were figuratively, symbolically, parabolically added: So wee say of *Jeremies Lamentation,* It is a *Propheticall history,* and a *Historicall prophecy;* Some of the sad occasions of these Lamentations were past, when he writ, and some were to come after: for, we may not despise the testimony of the *Chalde Paraphrasts,* who were the first that illustrated the Bible, in that Nation, nor of S. *Hierome,* who was much conversant with the Bible, and with that Nation, nor of *Josephus,* who had justly so much estimation in that Nation, nor of those later *Rabbins,* who were the learnedest of that Nation; who are all of opinion, that *Jeremy* writ these Lamentations, after hee saw some declinations in that State, in the *death of Josiah,* and so the Book is *Historicall,* but when he onely foresaw their transportation into *Babylon,* before that calamity fell upon them, and so it is *Propheticall.* Or, if we take the exposition of the others, That the whole Booke was written after their transportation into *Babylon,* and to be, in all parts, Historicall, yet it is Propheticall still; for the Prophet laments a greater Desolation then that, in the utter ruine, and devastation of the City, and Nation, which was to fall upon them, after the death of *Christ Jesus.* Neither is any peece of this Booke, the lesse fit to be our Text, this day, because it is both Historicall, and Propheticall, for, they, from whom, God, in his mercy, gave us a Deliverance, this day, are our *Historicall Enemies,* and our *Propheticall Enemies;* historically wee know, they *have* attempted our ruine heretofore, and prophetically wee may bee sure, they *will doe so againe,* whensoever any new occasion provokes them, or sufficient power enables them.

The Text then is as the Booke presented to *Ezekiel;* In it are written *Lamentations,* and *Mournings,* and *Woe;* and all they are written *within,* and *without,* says the Text there; *within,* as they concern the *Jews, without,* as they are appliable to *us:* And they concern the *Jews, Historically* (attempts upon that State *Jeremy* had certainly *seen,*) and they concern them *prophetically,* for farther attempts *Jeremy* did certainly *foresee.* They are appliable to us both ways too: *Historically,* because wee have seen, what they *would have done,* And *Prophetically,* because wee foresee what they *would doe.* So that here is but a difference of the Computation; here is *stilo veteri,* and *stilo novo;* here is the *Jews Calendar,* and the *Papists Calendar;* In the Jews Calendar, *one Babylon* wrought upon the people of God, and in the Papists Calendar, *another Babylon: Stilo veteri,* in the Jews Calendar, 700 yeare before Christ came, there were *pits made, and the breath of their nostrils, The anointed of the Lord, was taken in their pits: Stilo novo,* in the Papists Calendar, 1600 yeare after Christ came in all fulnesse, in all clearnesse, *There were pits made* againe, and *The breath of our nostrils, The anointed of the Lord, was almost taken in those pits.*

It is then *Jeremies,* and it is a *distinct* Book; It concernes the *Jews,* and it concerns *us* too; And it concernes us both, *both wayes, Historically,* and *Prophetically.* But whether *Jeremy* lament here the death of a good King, of *Josiah,* (for so Saint *Hierome,* and many of the *Ancients,* and many of the *Jewes* themselves take it, and thinke that those words in the *Chronicles,* have relation to these Lamentations, *And Jeremy lamented for Josiah, and all the people speake of him, in their Lamentations,*) Or whether he lament the transportation and the misery of an ill King, of *Zedekiah,* (as is more ordinarily, and more probably held by the Expositours) we argue not, we dispute not now; we imbrace that which arises from both, That both good Kings, and bad Kings, *Josiah,* and *Zedekiah,* are the *anointed* of the Lord, and the *breath of the nostrills,* that is, The life of the people; and therefore both to be lamented, when they fall into dangers, and consequently both to be preserved by all means, by *Prayer* from them who are private persons, by *counsell* from them, who have that great honour and that great charge, to be near them in that kinde, and by *support* and *supply,* from all, of all sorts, from falling into such dangers.

These considerations will, I thinke, have the better impression in you, if we proceed in the handling of them thus: First, the main cause of the Lamentation was the Ruine, or the dangerous declination of the Kingdome, of that great and glorious State, *The Kingdome;* But then they did not seditiously sever the King, and the Kingdome, as though the Kingdome could doe well, and the King ill, *That* safe, and *he* in danger, for they see cause to lament, because misery was fallen upon *the Person* of *the King;* perchance upon *Josiah,* a good, a religious King; perchance but upon *Zedekiah,* a worse King; yet, whichsoever it be, they acknowledge him to be *Vnctus Domini, The anointed of the Lord,* and to be *Spiritus narium, The breath of their nostrills:* When this person therefore, was fallen into the pits of the Enemy, the Subject laments; but this lamenting because he *was fallen,* implies a deliverance, a restitution, he was *fallen,* but he did *not ly* there: so the Text, which is as yet but of *Lamentation,* will grow an houre hence to be of *Congratulation;* and then we shall see, That whosoever, in rectified affections, hath lamented a *danger,* and then congratulated a *deliverance,* he will provide against a *relapse,* a falling again into that or any other danger, by all means of sustaining the Kingdome and the King, in safety and in honour.

Our first step then in this Royall progresse, is, That the cause of this Lamentation, was, the declination, the diminution of the *Kingdome.* If the Center of the world should be moved but one inch out of the place, it cannot be reckoned, how many miles, this Island, or any building in it, would be thrown out of their places; A declination in the Kingdome of the Jewes, in the body of the Kingdome, in the soul of the State, in the *form of Government,* was such an Earth-quake, as could leave nothing standing. Of all things that are, there *was* an *Idea* in God; there was a modell, a platform, an examplar of every thing, which God produced and created in Time, in the mind and purpose of God before: Of all things God *had* an *Idea,* a preconception; but of Monarchy, of Kingdome, God, who is but one, *is* the *Idea;* God himselfe, in his Unity, *is* the Modell, He *is* the Type of *Monarchy.* He made but one World; for, this, and the next, are not *two Worlds;* This is but the *Morning,* and that the *everlasting Noon,* of one and the same Day, which shall have no Night: They are not *two Houses;* This is the *Gallery,* and that the *Bed-chamber* of one, and the same Palace, which shall feel no ruine. He made this one World, but *one Eye, The Sunne;* The *Moone* is not another Eye, but a Glasse, upon which, the Sunne reflects. He made this one World, but *one Eare, The Church;* He tells not us, that he heares by a left Eare, by Saints, but by that right Eare, the Church he doth. There is *One God, One Faith, One Baptisme,* and these lead us to the love of one Soveraign, of Monarchy, of Kingdome. In that Name, God hath convayed to us the state of *Grace,* and the state of *Glory* too; and he hath promised both, in injoining that Petition, *Adveniat Regnum, Thy Kingdome Come,* Thy Kingdome of *Grace* here, Thy Kingdome of *Glory* hereafter. All forms of Government have one and the same *Soul,* that is, *Soveraignty;* That resides somewhere in every form; and this Soveraignty is in them all, from one and the same *Root,* from the *Lord of Lords,* from *God* himself, for *all Power is of God:* But yet this form of a *Monarchy,* of a *Kingdome,* is a more lively, and a more *masculin Organe,* and Instrument of this Soul of Soveraigntie, then the other forms are: Wee are sure *Women* have Soules as well as *Men,* but yet it is not so expressed, *that God breathed a Soule into Woman,* as hee did into Man; All formes of Governement have this Soule, but yet God infuseth it more manifestly, and more effectually, in that forme, in a *Kingdome:* All places are alike neare to Heaven, yet Christ would take a *Hill,* for his Ascension; All governments may justly represent God to mee, who is the God of Order, and fountaine of all government, but yet I am more eased, and more accustomed to the contemplation of *Heaven,* in that *notion,* as *Heaven is a kingdome,* by having been borne, and bred in a Monarchy: God is a Type of that, and that is a Type of Heaven.

This form then, in nature the noblest, in use the profitablest of all others, God always intended to his best-beloved people, God always meant that the Jews should have a King, though he prepared them in other forms before; As hee meant them *peace* at last, though he exercised them in *Warre,* and meant them the *land of promise,* though he led them *through the Wildernesse;* so he meant them a *King,* though he prepared them by *Judges.* God intended it in himselfe, and he declared it to them, 400 yeares before he gave them a King, he instructed them, what kinde of King they should set over them, when they came to that kinde of government: And long before that he made a promise, by *Jacob* to *Judah* of a Kingdome, and *that the Scepter should not depart from him, till Siloh came.* And when God came neare the time, in which he intended to them that government, in the time of *Samuel,* who was the immediate predecessor to their first King, *Saul,* God made way for a Monarchy; for *Samuel* had a much more absolute authority, in that State, then any of the Judges had; *Samuel judged* them, and in their petition for a King, they ask but that, *Make us a King to judge us; Samuel* was little lesse then a King; and *Sauls* reign, and *his,* are reckoned both in one number, and made as the reign of one man; when it is said in the *Acts,* that

Saul reigned 40 *yeares, Samuels* time is included in that number, for all the yeares, from the death of *Eli,* to the beginning of *David,* are but 40 years. God *meant* them a Kingdome in himselfe, *promised* them a kingdome in *Judah,* made *Laws* for their kingdome in *Deuteronomy,* made *way* for the kingdome in *Samuel,* and why then was God displeased with their petition for a Kingdome?

It was a greater fault in them, then it could have been in any other people, to ask a King; not that it was not the most desirable form of government, but that God governed them, so immediately, so presentially *himselfe,* as that it was an ingratefull intemperance in them, to turn upon any other meanes; God had ever performed that which he promised them, in that which comprehended all, *Ye shall be a peculiar treasure unto me, above all people;* And therefore *Josephus* hath expressed it well; All other people are under the forme of Democratie, or Aristocratie, or such other formes, composed of men; *Sed noster Legislator, Theocratiam instituit,* the Jews were onely under a *Theocratie,* an immediate government of God, he judged them himselfe, and hee himselfe fought their battels: And therefore God says to *Samuel, They have not rejected thee,* Thou wast not King, *But they have rejected mee,* I was. To bee weary of God, is it enough to call it a levity? But if they did onely compare forme with forme, and not God himselfe with any forme, if they did onely thinke Monarchy best, and beleeve that God intended a Monarchy to them, yet *to limit God his time,* and to make God performe his promise *before his day,* was a fault, and inexcusable. *Daniel* saw, that the Messiah should come within *seventy weekes: Daniel* did not say, Lord, let it bee within fifty weekes, or let it bee this weeke: The Martyrs under the Altar, cry *Vsquequo Domine, How long Lord,* but then, they leave it there, Even as long as pleaseth thee: Their petition should have been, *Adveniat regnum tuum,* Let us have that Kingdome, which because thou knowest it is good for us, thou hast promised to us; But yet *Fiat voluntas tua,* Let us have it then, when thy Wisdome sees it best for us: You said to mee (says *Samuel,* by way of Reproofe and Increpation) *You said, Nay but a King shall reigne over us;* Now, that was not their fault; but that which followes, The unseasonablenesse and inconsideration of their clamorous Petition, *You said a King shall reigne over us, when the Lord your God, was your King;* They would not trust *Gods meanes,* there was their first fault: And then, though they desired a thing good in it selfe, and a good intended to them, yet they *fixed God his time,* and they would not stay his leisure; And either of these, To aske *other things* then God would give, or at *other times,* then God would give them, is displeasing to him: Use his meanes, and stay his leisure.

But yet, though God were displeased with them, he executed his own purpose; he was angry with their manner of asking a King, but yet he gave them a King: Howsoever God be displeased with them, who prevaricate in his cause, who should sustaine it, and doe not, Gods cause shall be sustained, though they doe it not. We may distinguish the period of the Jewish State well enough, thus, that they had *Infantiam,* or *pueritiam,* their infancy, their minority, in *Adam,* and the first Patriarchs till the flood: that they had *Adolescentiam, A growing time,* from *Noah,* through the other Patriarchs, till *Moses:* amd that they had *Juventutem,* a youth and strength from *Moses,* through the Judges, to *Saul:* but then they had *Virilitatem, virilem ætatem,* their established vigor, under their Kings; and after them, they fell *in senectutem,* into a wretched and miserable decay of old age, and decrepitnesse: their kingdome was their best State; and so much, God in the *Prophet,* intimates pregnantly, when refreshing to their memories, in a particular Inventory, and Catalogue, all his former benefits to them, how he *clothed Jerusalem,* how he *fed* her, how he *adorned* her, he summed up all, in this one, *Et profecisti in regnum, I have advanced thee, to be a kingdome:* there was the *Tropique,* there was the *Solstice,* farther then that, in this world, we know not how God could goe; a kingdome was *really* the best State upon *Earth,* and *Symbolically,* the best *figure,* and *Type* of *Heaven.* And therefore, when the Prophet *Jeremy,* historically beheld the declination of this kingdome, in the death of *Josiah,* and prophetically foresaw the ruines thereof, in the transportation of *Zedekiah,* or, if he had seen that historically too, yet prophetically he foresaw the utter devastation, and depopulation, and extermination, which scattered that nation, soon after Christ, to this day, (and God and no man knows, for how long,) when they, who *were a kingdome,* are now no where a *village,* and they who had such Kings, have now no where a *Constable* of their owne, historically, prophetically, *Jeremy* had just cause of lamentation for the danger of that kingdome.

We had so also, for this our kingdome, this day; God hath given us a kingdome, not as other kingdomes, made up of divers Cities, but of divers kingdomes, and all those kingdomes were destined to desolation, in one minute. It was not onely the destruction of the *persons present,* but of the *kingdom,* for to submit the kingdome to the government of a *forein Prelate,* was to destroy the Monarchy, to annihilate the Supremacy, to ruine the very forme of a kingdome; a kingdome under another head, besides the King, is not a kingdome, as ours is. *The oath* that the *Emperour* takes *to the Pope,* is by their authours called *Juramentum fidelitatis,* an oath of Allegiance; and if they had brought our Kings, to take an oath of Allegiance so, this were no kingdome. *Pope Nicolas the second,* went about to create two kingdomes, that of *Tuscany,* and that of *Lombardy;* his successors have gone about to destroy more; for to make it depend upon him, were to destroy our kingdome. That they have attempted historically; and as long as these Axiomes, and Aphorismes remaine in their Authors, that one shall say, that *De jure,* by right all Christian kingdomes doe hold of the Pope, and *De facto,* are forfeited to the Pope, and another shall say, that Christendome would be better governed if the Pope would take the forfeiture, and so bring all these Royall farmes, into his owne *demesne,* we see also, their propheticall desire, their propheticall intention, against this kingdome, what they would doe: In their *Actions* we have their history, in their *Axioms* we have their prophecy.

Jeremy lamented the desolation of *the kingdome,* but that, expressed in the death, and destruction of *the King.* Hee did not divide the King and the kingdome, as if the kingdome could do well, and the King in distresse: *Omnipotentia Dei, Asylum hæreticorum;* it is well said, by more then one of the ancients, that the Omnipotence of God, is the Sanctuary of Heretiques: when they would establish any heresie, they flye to Gods Almightinesse. God can doe *all,* therefore he can doe *this.* So, in the *Roman Church,* they establish their heresie of *Transubstantiation;* And so, their deliverance of soules not from *Purgatory* onely, but from *Hell* it selfe. They think to stop all mouths with that, *God can do it,* no man dares deny that; when as, if that were granted, (which, in such things, as naturally imply contradiction in themselves, or contradiction to Gods word, cannot be granted, for God cannot do that, God cannot lye,) yet though God *can* do it, concludes not that God *will* do it, or *hath* done it: *Omnipotentia Dei Asylum hæreticorum,* The omnipotency of God, is the Sanctuary of Heretiques, and so, *Salus Regni,* is *Asylum proditorum,* Greater Treasons, and Seditions, and Rebellions have never been set on foote, then upon colour, and pretence, of a care of the State, and of the good of the Kingdome. Every where, the King is *Sponsus Regni,* the husband of the Kingdome; and to make love to the Kings wife, and undervalue *him,* must necessarily make any King *jealous:* The King is *Anima Regni,* The soule of the Kingdome; and to provide for the health of the body, with the detriment of the soule, is perverse physick: The King is *Caput Regni,* The head of the Kingdome; and to cure a Member, by cutting off the head, is ill surgery: Man and wife, soule and body, head and members, God hath joyned, and those whom God hath joyned, let no man sever. *Salus Regni, Asylum Proditorum,* To pretend to uphold the Kingdome, and overthrow the King, hath ever been the *tentation* before, and the *excuse* after, in the greatest Treasons. In that action of the *Jews,* which we insisted upon before, in their pressing for a King, *The Elders of Israel* were *gathered together,* and so far they were in their way, for this was no popular, no seditious Assembly of light and turbulent men, but *The Elders;* And then, *they came* to *Samuel,* And so farre they were in their right way too, for they held no counsels apart, but came to the right place, for redresse of grievances, to their then highest Governour, to *Samuel:* When they were thus lawfully met, they forbeare not to lay open unto him, the injustice of his greatest Officers, though it concerned the very *Sonnes of Samuel;* and thus farre they kept within their convenient limits; But when they would presse *Samuel* to a new way of remedy, to an inconvenient way, to a present way, to their own way, and referre nothing to him, what care soever they pretended of the good of the State, it is evident, that they had no good opinion of *Samuel* himself, and even that displeased God, That they were ill affected to that person, whom he had set over them. To sever the King, and the Kingdome, and pretend the weale of the one, without the other, is to shake and discompose Gods building.

Historically this was the Jewes case, when *Jeremy* lamented here, if he lamented the declination of the State, in the death of the King

Josiah, And if he lamented the transportation of *Zedekiah,* and that that crosse were not yet come upon them; Or if he lamented the future devastation of that Nation, occasioned by the death of the King of Kings Christ Jesus, when he came into the world, this was their case *prophetically:* Either way, historically, or prophetically, *Jeremy* looks upon the Kingdome, but yet through that glasse, through the King.

The duty of the Day, and the order of the Text, invites us to an application of this branch too. Our adversaries did not come to say to themselves, *Nolumus Regnum hoc,* we will not have this Kingdome stand, the *materiall Kingdome,* the plenty of the Land, they would have been content to have, but the *formall Kingdome,* that is, *This forme of Government,* by a Soveraigne King, that depends upon none but God, they would not have. So that they came *implicitely* to *Nolumus Regnum hoc,* we will not have this Kingdome governed thus, and they came *explicitely* to a *Nolumus Regem hunc* (as the Jewes were resolved of Christ) We will not have this King to governe at all. *Non hunc?* Will you not have him? you were at your *Nolumus hanc* long before; Her, whom God had set over you, before him, you would not have. Your, not *Anniversary,* but *Hebdomadary* Treasons, cast upon *her* a necessity of *drawing blood* often, and so your *Nolumus hanc,* your desire that she were gone, might have some kinde of ground, or colour: But for your *Nolumus hunc,* for this King who had made no *Inquisition* for *blood,* who had forborne your very *pecuniary penalties,* who had (as himself witnesses of himself) made you partakers with his Subjects of his own Religion, in matters of *grace,* and in *reall benefits,* and in *Titles of Honour, Quare fremuerunt,* Why did these men rage, and imagine a vaine thing? What they did historically, we know; They made that house, which is *the hive* of the Kingdome, from whence all her *honey* comes; that house where *Justice* her self is conceived, in their preparing of *Laws,* and inanimated, and quickned and borne by the Royall Assent, there given; they made that whole house *one Murdring peece,* and charged that peece with Peers, with People, with Princes, with the King, and meant to discharge it upward at the face of heaven, to shoot God at the face of God, Him, of whom God hath said, *Dii estis,* You are Gods, at the face of God, that had said so, as though they would have reproached the God of heaven, and not have been beholden to him for such a King, but shoot him up to him, and bid him take his King again, with a *nolumus hunc regnare,* we will not have this King to reign over us. This was our case Historically, and what it is Prophetically, as long as that remains to bee their doctrine, which he, against whom that attempt was principally made, found by their examination, to be their doctrine, That they, and no Sect in the world, but they, did make *Treason an article of Religion,* That their Religion bound them to those attempts, so long they are never at an end; Till they dis-avow those Doctrines, that conduce to that, prophetically they *wish,* prophetically they *hope* for better successe in as ill attempts.

It is then the *kingdome* that *Jeremy* laments; but his nearest object is the *King;* Hee laments him. First, let it be, (as with S. *Hierome,* many of the *Ancients,* and with them, many of the *later Rabbins* will have it) for *Josiah,* for *a good King,* in whose death, the honour, and the strength of the kingdome took that deadly wound, to become tributary to a forain Prince: for, to this lamentation they refer those words of the Prophet, which describe a great sorrow, *In that day shall there be a great mourning in Jerusalem, as the mourning of Hadadrimmon, in the valley of Megiddon;* which was the place, where *Josiah* was slain; There shall be such a lamentation (says the Prophet, in this interpretation) as was for the death of *Josiah.* This then was for him; for a good King. Wherein have we his goodnesse expressed? Abundantly. *Hee did that which was right in Gods sight;* (And whose Eye need he fear, that is right in the Eye of God?) But how long did he so? *To the end;* for, *Nero,* who had his *Quinquennium,* and was a good Emperour for his first five years, was one of the worst of all: Hee that is ill all the way, is but *a Tyran,* Hee that is good at first, and after ill, *an Angels face,* and *a Serpents taile* make him *a Monster; Josiah* began well, and persevered so, *He turned not aside to the right hand, nor to the left;* That is, (if we apply it to the *Josiah* of our times) neither to the *fugitive,* that leaves our Church, and goes to the *Roman,* nor to the *Separatist,* that leaves our Church, and goes to *none.* In the eighteenth year of his reign, *Josiah* undertook the *reparation* of *Gods house;* If we apply this to the *Josiah* of *our* times, I think, in *that* year of *his* reign, he *visited this Church,* and these wals, and meditated, and perswaded the reparation thereof.

In one word, *Like unto Josiah, there was no King before, nor after.* And therefore there was just cause of lamentation for this King, for *Josiah; historically* for the very loss of his *person, prophetically* for the misery of the *State,* after his death.

Our errand is to day, to apply all these branches to the day; Those men who intended us, this cause of lamentation this day, in the destruction of *our Josiah,* spared him not, because he was so, because he was a *Josiah,* because he was *good;* no, not because he was *good to them,* his benefits to them, had not mollified them, towards him: for that is not their way; Both the *French Henries* were their own, and good to them; but did that rescue either of them, from the *knife?* And was not that *Emperour,* whom they *poisoned* in the *Sacrament,* their own, and good to them? and yet was that, any *Antidote* against their poison? To so reprobate a sense hath God given them over herein, as that, though in their *Books,* they ly heaviest upon Princes of our Religion, yet truly they have destroyed more of their own, then of ours. Thus it is Historically in their proceedings past: And Prophetically it can be but thus, since no King is good, in their sense, if he agree not to *all points of Doctrine* with them: And when that is done, not good yet, except he agree in *all points of Jurisdiction too;* and that, no King can doe, that will not be their Farmer of his Kingdome. Their Authours have disputed *Auferibilitatem Papæ,* whether the Church of God might not be without a *Pope,* they have made a problematicall, a disputable matter, and some of their Authours have diverted towards an affirmation of it; but *Auferibilitas potestatis,* to imagine a King without Kingly Soveraignty, never came into probleme, into disputation. We all lamented, and bitterly, and justly, the losse of our *Deborah,* though then we saw a *Iosiah* succeeding: but if they had removed our *Iosiah,* and his *Royall children,* and so, this form of government, *where,* or *who,* or *what* had been an object of Consolation to us?

The cause of lamentation in the losse of a *good King,* is certainly great, and so it was, if *Ieremy* lamented *Iosiah;* but if it were but for *Zedekiah,* an *ill King,* (as the greater part of Expositors take it) yet the lamentation you see, is the same. How ill a King was *Zedekiah?* As ill, as *Iosiah* was good, that's his measure. *He did evill in the sight of the Lord, according to all that Iehoiakim had done;* Here is his sinne, sinne by precedent; and what had *Jehoiakim* done? *He had done evill in the sight of the Lord, according to all that his Fathers had done.* It is a great, and a dangerous wickednesse, which is done upon pretext of *Antiquity;* The *Religion* of our *Fathers,* the *Church* of our *Fathers,* the *Worship* of our *Fathers,* is a pretext that colours a great deale of Superstition. He did evill, as his Fathers; there was his comparative evill: And his positive evill, (I meane, his particular sinne) was, *That he humbled not himself to Gods Prophets,* to *Jeremy* speaking from the mouth of the Lord; there was *irreligiousnesse;* And then, *He broke the Oath which he had sworne by God,* there was *perfidiousnesse,* faithlesnesse; And lastly, *He stiffned his neck, and hardned his heart, from turning to the Lord of Israel,* there was *impenitiblenesse:* Thus evill was *Zedekiah,* irreligious to God, treacherous to man, impenitible to himself, and yet the State, and men truly religious in the State, the Prophet, lamented him; not his spirituall defections, by sinne; for, they did not make themselves Judges of that; but they lamented the calamities of the Kingdome, in the losse even of an evill King.

That man must have a large comprehension, that shall adventure to say of any King, *He is an ill King;* he must know his *Office* well, and his *actions* well, and the actions of *other Princes* too, who have correspondence with him, before he can say so. When Christ sayes, *Let your communication be yea, yea, and nay, nay, for whatsoever is more then this,* (that is, when it comes to *swearing*) *that cometh of evill,* Saint *Augustine* does not understand that, of the evill disposition of that man that sweares, but of them, who will not beleeve him, without swearing; Many times a Prince departs from the exact rule of his duty, not out of his own indisposition to truth, and clearnesse, but to countermine underminers. That which *David* sayes in the eighteenth Psalme, *David* speaks, not of man, but of *God* himself; *Cum perverso pervertêris, With the froward, thou wilt show thy self froward;* God, who is of no froward nature, may be made froward; with crafty neighbours, a Prince will be crafty, and perchance false with the false. Alas, (to looke into no other profession but our owne) how often do we excuse *Dispensations,* and *pluralities,* and *non-residencies,* with an *Omnes faciunt,* I do, but as other men of my profession, do? Allow a King but that, *That he does but as other Kings do,*

Nay, but this, *He does but as other Kings put him to a necessity to do,* and you will not hastily call a King an ill King. When *God gives his people for old shoes,* and *sells them for nothing,* and, at the same time, gives his and their enemies abundance, when God commands *Abraham,* to sacrifice his own and onely Sonne, and his enemies have *Children at their pleasure,* as *David* speaks, To give your selves the liberty of humane affection, you would think God an ill God; but yet, for all this, his children are to him, a *Royall Priesthood,* and *a holy Nation;* and all *their tears* are *in his bottles,* and *registred in his booke,* for all this. When Princes pretermit in some things, the present benefit of their Subjects, and confer favours upon others, give your selves the liberty to judge of Princes actions, with the affections of private men, and you may think a King an ill King: But yet, we are to him, as *David* sayes, *His brethren, his bone, his flesh,* and so reputed by him. God himselfe cannot stand upright in a *naturall* mans interpretation, nor any King in a *private* mans. But then, how soone our adversaries come to call Kings, ill Kings, we see historically, when they boast of having deposed Kings, *Quia minus utiles,* Because some other hath seemed to them, fitter for the Government; and we see it prophetically, by their allowing those Indictments, and Attainders of Kings, which stand in their books *De Syndicatu,* That that King which neglects the duties of his place (and they must prescribe the duty, and judge the negligence too) That King, that exercises his Prerogative, without just cause (and they must prescribe the Prerogative, and judge the cause,) That that King that vexes his Subjects, That that King that gives himselfe to *intemperate hunting* (for in that very particular they instance) that in such cases, (and they multiply these cases infinitely) Kings are in their mercy, and subject to their censures, and corrections. We proceed not so, in censuring the actions of Kings; we say, with St. *Cyrill, Impium est dicere Regi, Iniquè agis; It is an impious thing,* (in him, who is onely a private man, and hath no other obligations upon him) *to say to the King,* or *of the King, He governs not as a King is bound to do:* we remit the judgement of those their actions, which are secret to God; and when they are evident, and bad, yet we must endevour to preserve their persons; for there is a danger in the losse, and a lamentation due to the losse, even of *Zedekiah,* for even such are *uncti Domini, The anoynted of the Lord, and the breath of our nostrils.*

First, (as it lies in our Text) The King is *Spiritus narium, the breath of our nostrills.* First, *Spiritus,* is a name, most peculiarly belonging to that blessed Person of the glorious Trinity, whose Office it is to convay, to insinuate, to apply to us the Mercies of the Father, and the Merits of the Sonne: He is called by this Name, by the word of this Text, *Ruach,* even in the beginning of the Creation, God had created Heaven and Earth, and then *The Spirit of God, sufflabat,* saith *Pagnins* translation, (and so saith the *Chalde Paraphrase* too) it *breathed upon the waters,* and so induced, or deduced particular formes. So God hath made us, a little World of our own, This *Iland;* He hath given us *Heaven* and *Earth,* The truth of his Gospel, which is our earnest of Heaven, and the abundance of the Earth, a fruitfull Land; but then he, who is the Spirit of the Lord, he who is the breath of our nostrills, *Incubat aquis,* (as it is said there in the Creation) he moves upon *the waters,* by his royall and warlike *Navy at Sea,* (in which he hath expressed a speciall and particular care) And by the breath and influence of his providence throughout the Land, he preserves, he applies, he makes usefull those blessings unto us.

If this breath, that is, this power, be at any time sourd in the passage, and contract an il favor by the pipes that convay it, so, as that his good intentions are ill executed by inferiour Ministers, this must not be imputed to him; That breath that comes from the East, the bed and the garden of spices, when it is breathed out there, is a perfume, but by passing over the beds of Serpents and putrefied Lakes, it may be a breath of poyson in the West: Princes purpose some things for ease to the people, (and as such, they are sometimes presented to them) and if they prove grievances, they tooke their putrefaction in the way, that is, their corruption, from corrupt executors of good and wholesome intentions; The thing was good in the roote, and the ill cannot be removed in an instant.

But then, we carry not this word *Ruach,* Spirit, so high; though since God hath said that Kings are Gods, the Attribute of the Holy Ghost and his Office, which is, to apply to man the goodnesse of God, belongs to Kings also; for, God gives, but they apply all blessings to us. But here, we take the word literally, as it is in the Text; *Ruach, spirit,* is *the Breath* that *we breathe,* the *Life* that *we live;* The King is that *Breath,* that *Life,* and therefore that belongs to him. First our

Breath, that is, *sermo,* our *speech* belongs to him; *Be faithfull unto him, and speake good of his Name,* is commanded by *David* of God. To Gods Anointed, we are not *faithfull,* if we doe not speake good of his Name. First, there is an *internall* speech in the *heart,* and God lookes to that; *The foole hath said in his heart, there is no God;* though he say it but in his heart, yet he is a foole: for, as wise as a Politician would thinke him, for saying it in his heart, and comming no further, yet even that is an overt act with God, for God seeth the heart. It is the foole that saith in his heart, there is no God, and it is the foole that saith in his heart, I would there were no *King.* That enormous, that infamous Tragedy of the *Levites* Concubine, and her murder, of which it is said there, *There was no such thing seen, nor done before,* (and many things are done, which are never seen) with that emphaticall addition, *Consider of it, advise, and say your minde,* hath this addition too, *In those dayes there was no King in Israel;* If there had beene any King, but a *Zedekiah,* it could not have been so: *Curse not the King, not in thy thoughts:* for, they are sinnes that tread upon the heels of one another, and that induce one another to conceive ill of Gods Lievtenant, and of God himselfe; for so the Prophet joyneth them, *They shall fret themselves, and curse their King, and their God:* He that beginneth with the one, will proceed to the other.

Thus then he is our Breath; *our Breath is his; our speech* must be contained, not expressed in his dishonour; not in misinterpretations of his Actions; jealousies have often made women ill; incredulitie, suspiciousnesse, jealousie in the Subject, hath wrought ill effects upon Princes, otherwise not ill. We must *not speake ill;* but our duty is not accomplished in that abstinence, we must *speake well:* And in those things, which will not admit a good interpretation, we must be apt to remove the perversenesse and obliquity of the act from him, who is the first mover to those who are *inferiour instruments.* In these divers opinions which are ventilated in the Schoole, *how God concurreth to the working of second and subordinate causes,* that opinion is I think, the most antient, that denies that God *workes in* the second cause, but hath onely *communicated* to it, a power of working, and rests himselfe. This is not true; God does work in every Organ, and in every particular action; but yet though he doe work in all, yet hee is no cause of the obliquity, of the perversenesse of any action. Now, earthly Princes are not equall to God; They doe not so much as work in particular actions of instruments; many times, they communicate power to others, and rest wholly themselves; and then, the *power* is from them, but the *perversenesse* of the action is not. God does work in ill actions, and yet is not guilty, but Princes doe not so much as worke therein, and so may bee excusable; at least, for any cooperation in the evill of the action, though not for countenancing, and authorising an evill instrument; but that is another case.

They are our breath then; *Our breath is theirs,* in good *interpretations* of their actions; and it is theirs especially, *in our prayers* to Almighty God, for them. The Apostle exhorts us to pray; for whom? first, *for all men* in generall; but in the first particular, that hee descends to, *for Kings.* And both *Theodoret,* and *Theophylact,* make that the onely reason, why the Apostle did not name Kings first, *Vt non videatur adulari,* lest hee should seeme to flatter Kings: Whether mankinde it selfe, or Kings, by whom mankinde is happy here, be to be preferred in prayer, you see both *Theodoret,* and *Theophylact,* make it a probleme. And those prayers, there enjoyned, were for *Infidel Kings,* and for *persecuting Kings;* for even such Kings, were the breath of their nostrils; their breath, their speech, their prayers were due to them. But then, beloved, a man may convey a *Satir* into a *Prayer;* a man may make a prayer a *Libell;* If the intention of the prayer be not so much, to incline God to give those graces to the King, as to tell the world, that the King wants those graces, it is a Libell. We say sometimes in scorn to a man, *God help you,* and *God send you wit;* and therein, though it have the sound of a prayer, wee call him foole. So wee have seen of late, some in obscure Conventicles, institute certain prayers, *That God would keep the King, and the Prince in the true Religion;* The prayer is always good, always usefull; but when that prayer is accompanied with circumstances, as though the King and the Prince were declining from that Religion, then even the prayer it selfe is libellous, and seditious; Saint *Paul,* in that former place, apparels a Subjects prayer well, when hee sayes, *Let prayers bee given with thanks;* Let our prayers bee for continuance of the blessings, which wee have, and let our acknowledgement of present blessings, bee an inducement for future: pray, and praise together; pray thankfully, pray not suspiciously: for, beloved in the bowels of Christ Jesus, before whose face I stand now, and before whose face, I shall not be able to stand amongst the righteous, at the last day, if I lie now, and make this Pulpit my Shop, to vent sophisticate Wares, In the presence of you, a holy part, I hope, of the Militant Church, of which I am, In the presence of the whole Triumphant Church, of which, by him, by whom I am that I am, I hope to bee, In the presence of the Head of the whole Church, who is All in all, I, (*and I thinke I have the Spirit of God,*) (I am sure, I have not resisted it in this point) I, (and I may bee allowed to know something in Civill affaires) (I am sure I have not been stupefied in this point) doe deliver that, which upon the truth of a Morall man, and a Christian man, and a Church man, beleeve to be true, That hee, who is *the Breath of our nostrils,* is in his heart, as farre from submitting us to that Idolatry, and superstition, which did heretofore oppresse us, as his immediate Predecessor, whose memory is justly precious to you, was: Their wayes may bee divers, and yet their end the same, that is, The glory of God; And to a higher Comparison, then to her, I know not how to carry it.

As then the Breath of our nostrils, our breath, is his, that is, *our speech,* first, in *containing* it, not to speak in his diminution; then in *uttering* it *amongst men;* to interpret fairly, and loially, his proceedings; and then in uttering it *to God,* in such prayers for the continuing thereof, as imply a thankfull acknowledgement of the present blessings, spirituall and temporall, which we enjoy now by him; So farre, *Breath is speech;* but *Breath is life too,* and so *our life is his.* How willingly his Subjects would give their lives for him, I make no doubt, but hee doubts not. This is argument enough for their propensenesse and readinesse, to give their lives, for his honour, or for the *possessions of his children;* That though not *Contra voluntatem,* not against his will, yet *Præter voluntatem,* without any Declaration of his will, or pleasure, by any Command, they have been as ready voluntarily, as if a *Presse* had commanded them. But these ways, which his wisdome hath chosen for the procuring of peace, have kept off much occasion of triall, of that, how willingly his Subjects would have given their lives for him. Yet, their lives are his, who is the breath of their nostrils: And therefore, though they doe not *leave* them for him, let them *lead* them for him; though they bee not called to die for him, let them live so, as that may bee for him; to live *peaceably,* to live *honestly,* to live *industriously,* is to live for him; for, the sinnes of the people endanger the Prince, as much as his owne. When that shall bee required at your hand, then die for him; In the meane time, live for him; live so, as your living doe not kindle Gods anger against him, and that is a good Confession, and acknowledgement, That *hee is the breath of your nostrils,* That your life is his.

As then the breath of our nostrils, is expressed by this word in this Text, *Ruach, spiritus, speech,* and *life,* so it is his. When the breath of life was first breathed into man, there it is called by another word, *Neshamah,* and that is the *soule,* the immortall soule: And is the King the breath of that life? Is hee the soule of his Subjects so, as that their *soules* are *his;* so, as that they must sinne *towards men,* in doing unjust actions, or sinne *towards God,* in forsaking, and dishonouring him, if the King will have them? If I had the honour to aske this question, in his royall presence, I know he would bee the first man, that would say *No, No;* your souls are not mine, so. And, as hee is a most perfect Text-man, in the Booke of God, (and by the way, I should not easily feare his being a *Papist,* that is a good *Text-man*) I know hee would cite *Daniel,* saying, *Though our God doe not deliver us, yet know, O King, that we will not worship thy Gods;* And I know hee would cite S. *Peter, We ought to obey God, rather then men;* And he would cite *Christ* himself, *Feare not them,* (for the soule) *that cannot hurt the soule.* He claimes not your souls so: It is *Ruach* here, it is not *Neshamah;* your life is his, your soule is not his, in that sense. But yet, beloved, these two words are promiscuously used in the Scriptures; *Ruach* is often the *soule; Neshamah* is often the temporall life; And thus farre, the one, as well as the other, is the Kings, That hee must *answer for your soules;* so *they are his;* for hee is not a King of *bodies,* but a King of *men,* bodies and soules; nor a King of men onely, but of *Christian men;* so your *Religion,* so your soules are *his;* his, that is, appertaining to *his care, and his account.* And therefore, though you owe no obedience to any power under heaven, so as to decline you from the true God, or the true worship of that God, and the fundamentall things thereof, yet in those things, which are, in their nature but circumstantiall, and may therefore, according to times, and places, and persons, admit alterations, in those things, though they bee things appertaining to Religion, submit your selves to his directions; for here, the two words meet, *Ruach,* and *Neshamah,* your lives are his, and your souls are his too; His end being to advance Gods truth, he is to be trusted much, in matters of *indifferent* nature, by the way.

He is the word of our Text, *Spiritus,* as *Spiritus* is the Holy Ghost, so farre, by accommodation, as that he is Gods instrument to convey blessings upon us; and as *spiritus* is our *breath,* or *speech,* and as it is *our life,* and as it is *our soule* too, so farre, as that in those temporall things which concern spirituall, (as *Times* of meeting, and much of the *manner* of proceeding when we are met) we are to receive directions from him: So he is the *breath* of our *nostrils,* our *speech,* our *lives,* our *soules,* in that limited sense, are his.

But then, did those subjects of his (And I charge none but his *Subjects,* with this plot, for, *I judge not them who are without*) from whom God delivered us this day, did they think so of him, That he was the breath of our nostrils? If the breath be soure, if it bee tainted and corrupt, (as they would needs thinke, in this case) is it good Physick for an ill breath, to cut off the head, or to suffocate it, to smother, to strangle, to murder that man? Hee is the breath of their nostrils; They owe him their *speech,* their *thanks,* their *prayers,* and how have these *children of fooles made him their song, and their byword?* How have these Drunkards, (men drunke with the Babylonian Cup) made Libels against him? How have those *Seminatores verborum, word-scatterers,* defamed him, even with contrary defamations. Heretofore, that he *persecuted their* Religion, when he did not; now, that he hath *left his own* Religion. He is their breath, they owe him their *tongues,* and how foully do they speak; and they owe him their *lives,* and how prodigally do they give away their lives to others, that they might take away His? He is their breath, (as breath is the soule) that is, *Accomptant for their soules,* and how have they raised themselves out of his Audit, and withdrawne themselves from his Allegiance? This they have done historically, and to say prophetically, what they would do, first, their *Extenuation* of this fact, when they call it an enterprise of a few unfortunate Gentlemen. And then their *Exaltation* of this fact, when they make the principall person in it, a *Martyr,* this is prophecy enough, that since they are not ashamed of the Originall, they will not be afraid to copy it often, and pursue the same practises, to the same end.

Let it be *Josiah* then, let it be *Zedekiah,* he was the Breath, the life of his Subjects, (and that was the first attribute) and he was *The Anoynted of the Lord,* which is the other. Vnction it self alwayes separated that which was anoynted from prophane, and secular use; unction was a religious distinction. It had that signification in practise, before any Law was given for it; when *Jacob* had had that vision upon the stone, which made him see, that *that place was the house of God, and the gate of heaven*, then he tooke up that stone which he had slept upon, and set it up for a pillar, and anoynted it. This was the *practise in nature;* and then the *precept in the Law,* was, as for the Altar it self, so for many other things, belonging to the service of God in the Temple, *Thou shalt anoynt them, to sanctifie them.* Thus it was for *things;* and then, if we consider *persons,* we see the dignity that anoynting gave; for it was given but to three *sorts* of persons, to *Kings,* to *Priests,* and to *Prophets: Kings,* and *Priests* had it, to testifie their ordinary, and permanent, and indelible jurisdiction, their power is laid on *in Oyle;* And *Prophets* had it, because they were extraordinarily raised to denounce, and to execute Gods Judgements, upon persons that were anoynted, upon Priests, and upon Kings too, in those cases, for which, they were then particularly imployed. Thus then it is, anoynted things could not be touched, but by anoynted persons, and then anoynted persons could not be touched, but by persons anoynted; The *Priest* not directed, but by the *King;* The King, as King, not corrected, but by the *Prophet:* And this was the State, that they lamented so compassionately, That their King, thus *anoynted,* thus *exempted,* was taken prisoner, saw his Sonnes slaine in his presence, and then had his owne eyes pulled out, was bound in chains, and carried to *Babell.*

And lesse then this, in himself, and in his Sonne, and in all, was not intended this day, against our, not *Zedekiah,* but *Josiah:* for death (speaking in nature) hath all particular miseries in it. An anoynted King (and *many Kings* anoynted there are *not*) and he that is anoynted *præ Consortibus suis,* above his fellow Kings, (*for, I think, no other King of his Religion,* is *anoynted*) The anoynted of the Lord, who in this Text hath both those great names, *Meshiach Jehovah, Christus Domini,* as though he had been but *the Bramble anoynted for King of the Trees,* and so made the fitter fuell for their fire, as though (as *Davids* lamentation is for *Saul*) *He had not been anoynted with Oyle,* This *eye* of God, he by whom God looks upon us, This *hand* of God, he by whom God protects us, This *foote* of God, he by whom, in his due time, (and *Vsquequo Domine,* How long, O Lord, before that time come?) God shall tread downe, his owne, and our enemies, was swallowed and devoured by them, in their confidence of their owne plot, and their infallible assurance of his perishing. So it was historically; And how it stands prophetically, that is, What such as they were, would do for the future; as long as they write, (not in Libels clandestinely and subreptitiously stollen out, but avowed by publique Authority) *That our Priests are no Priests,* but *the Priests of Baal,* for so they write, *That the conspiracy of this day, being against him, who oppressed Religion, was as just, as that against* Cæsar, who did but oppresse the State, And that they write, *That those who were the actors herein, are therefore saved,* because at their execution, they submitted all to the Romane Church, and were content, if the Church condemned it, then to repent the Fact, for so they write also, *That the Religion of our present King, is no better, then the Religion of Jeroboam,* or of *Numa Pompilius,* for so they write too, that the last *Queene,* though an *Heretique,* yet because she was *Anointed,* did cure that disease, *The Kings evill,* but because, in scorne thereof, the King refused to be anointed at his Coronation, therefore hee cannot cure that disease, and so *non dicendus unctus Domini,* he is not to be called the Anointed of the Lord, says that Author, (for all these are the words of one man, and one, who had no other provocation to say all this but onely *the Kings Apology for the oath of Allegiance*) by retaining in their avowed books, and by relying upon such Authors, and Authorities as these, which remaine for their future instruction, we see their dispositions for the future, and judge of them prophetically, as well as historically.

Now the misery which is here lamented, the declination of the kingdome, in the person of the King, is thus expressed, *He was taken in their pits; taken,* and taken in *pits,* and taken in *their pits,* are so many staires, so many descents, so many gradations (rather degradations) in this calamity. Let it bee *Josiah,* let it bee *Zedekiah; They were taken;* taken, and never returned; Let it bee our *Josiah,* and will it hold in that application? Was hee taken? Hee was plotted for, but was hee *Taken?* When hee himselfe takes publique knowledge, that both at home and abroad, those of the Romane persuasion, assured themselves, of some especiall worke, for the advancement of their cause, at that time, when they had taken that assurance, hee was so taken, taken in that their assurance, infallibly taken in their opinion; so, as this kingdome was taken in their opinion, who thought their *Navy invincible;* so this King was taken in their assurance, who thought this plot infallible.

Hee was taken, and *in fovea, in a pit,* says the Text; If our first translation would serve, the sorrow were the lesse, for there it is, he was taken in *their net;* now, a man that *flattereth,* spreadeth a net, and a Prince that discerns not a flatterer, from a Counsellor, is taken in *a net;* but that's not so desperate, as in a pit: In *Josiahs* case, it was a pit, a *Grave;* in *Zedekiahs* case, it was a pit, a *Prison:* in our *Josiahs* case, it was fully, as it is in the Text, not in *fovea,* but *in foveis,* plurally, in their *pits,* in their *divers* pits; death in the mine where they beganne, death in the Cellar where they pursued their mischiefe.

And then it was *in foveis Illorum,* in *their pits,* says the Text; but the Text does not tell us, in whose; in the verse before, it is said, *Our persecutors did this,* and this, then it followes, *Hee was taken in their pits;* In the persecutors pits certainely; but yet, who are they? If it were *Josiah* that was taken, the persecutor was *Necho,* King of *Egypt,* for from his army, *Josiah* received his deaths wound: If it were *Zedekiah,* the persecutor was *Nebuchadnezzar* King of *Babylon,* for hee carried *Zedekiah* into captivity. Certainly the holy Ghost knew well enough, and could have spoken plaine, whose these pits were, but it pleased him to forbeare *names.* Certainly *our Josiah* knowes well enough, whose, those pits, which were digged for him, were; but, according to his naturall sweetnesse, to decline the drawing of more bloud, then necessarily hee must, or the laying of imputations and aspersions upon more, then necessarily hee must, hee hath forborne names. The holy Ghost knowes better then all the expositors, in all our Libraries, who digged those pits, our *Josiah* knowes, better then all wee, who come but to celebrate, and solemnize the deliverance, whose hands, and whose counsails were in the digging of these pits too. *Hee was taken,* says our Text: *fuit,* hee *Was.* Fix that in *Josiah,* who was taken, and never taken back: fix it in *Zedekiah,* who was taken, and never taken back; they both perished; in both them, there is just cause, of perpetuall, and permanent lamentation, and no roome left, for the exercise of any other affection. But transfer it *to our Josiah,* and then, *Hee was taken,* is, *Hee was but taken; God did not suffer his holy one to see Corruption,* nor God did not suffer his Anointed, to perish in this taking; And so the *lamentation* is become (as wee said at first) a *Congratulation,* so our *Væ* is an *Euge,* our exclamation turned to acclamation; and so our *De profundis,* is a *Gloria in excelsis,* The pit, the vault is become a hill, from whence we may behold the power of our great God; this *Sepher kinoth,* the book of Lamentations, is become *Sepher tehillim,* the book of Psalmes, and thanksgivings; And *Davids Bonus es omnibus, Lord thou art good to all,* is come to *Moses non taliter, Lord thou hast not done so well, with any nation,* as with us; for when we might have fear'd a *dereliquisti,* that God had forsaken us, we had S. *Augustines appropinquavi & nesciebam,* we came nearer and nearer to God, and knew it not, we knew not our danger, and therefore knew not his speciall Protection. It was one particular degree of his mercy, to proceed so: As it is an ease to a man, not to heare of his friends sicknesse, till he heare it, by hearing of his recovery, so God did not shake us, with the knowledge of the danger, till he established us, with the deliverance: And by making his servant, and our Soveraigne, the blessed means of that discovery, and that deliverance, he hath directed us, in all apprehensions of dangers, to rely upon that *Wisdome,* in civill affaires, affaires of State, and upon that *Zeale,* in causes of Religion, which he hath imprinted in that soule. Historically, God hath done great things for us, by him; Prophetically, God hath great things to doe for us, and all the Christian world, and will make him, his Instrument to doe them.

Now, we reserved at first, for the last gaspe, and for the knot to tie up all, this Consideration: That he that was truely affected in the sad sense of such a danger, and the pious sense of such a deliverance, would also use all means in his power, to secure the future, that that Kingdome, in that King, might alwayes bee safe, from the like dangers. No doubt, our *Josiah* doth that, in that which appertaineth unto him; and *all,* that is, The *care of all,* appertaineth unto him. If God had made him his *Rod,* to scourge others with Warres and Armies, we might be affraid, that when God had done his worke by him, he would *cast the rod in the fire;* God doth not alwayes blesse those Instruments, who love blood, though they pretend his Glory. But since God hath made him *his Dove,* to flie over the world, with the Olive branch, with indevours of Peace, in all places, as the Dove did, so he shall ever bring his Olive branch to the Arke, that is, endevour onely such peace, as may advance the Church of God, and establish peace of Conscience in himself.

That care, on his part, shall preserve him: And for his preservation, and ours in him, these things are to be done on our part: First, let us returne to God, so, as God may looke upon us, clothed in the righteousnesse of Christ; who will not be put on, as a fair gowne, to cover course clothes; but first put off your sinnes, and then put on him; sinnes of the *Time,* sinnes of your *Age,* sinnes of your *Sex,* sinnes of your *Complexion,* sinnes of your *Profession;* put off all; for your Time, your Age, your Sex, your Complexion, your Profession, shall not be damned; but you, you your selves shall. Doe not thinke that your *Sundayes zeale* once a weeke, can burn out all your extortions, and oppressions, and usury, and butchery, and simony, and chambering and wantonnesse practised from Monday to Saterday. Doe not thinke it to bee so with the Spirituall man, as with the Naturall: In a Naturall body, a great proportion of Choler will rectifie a cold, or old, or flegmatique man; he is the better, for having so much choler; but a vehement zeale on Sunday, doth not rectifie the sixe dayes sinner: To cry out then, I am sterved for want of an *afternoon Sermon,* and to fast all the weeke long, so as never to taste how sweet the Lord is, in thy cleansing thy heart, and withdrawing thy hand from sinne, this is no good diet; Not onely upon your Allegiance to God, but upon your Allegiance to the King, be good: No Prince can have a better guard, then Subjects truly religious. *Quantus murus patriæ est vir justus,* is S. *Ambrose* his holy exclamation, What a wall to a City, what a Sea, what a Navy to an Iland, is a holy man? The sins of former times, the sins and provocations of *Manasseh,* lay heavy upon *Josiah,* as well as God loved him. The sins of our daies, our sins, may open any Prince to Gods anger. This is the first way of preserving our *Josiah,* to turn away the wrath of God, by our abstinence from future sinnes, after our repentance of former.

A second is, to uphold his honour and estimation with other men; especially amongst *strangers* that live with us, who for the most part, value Princes so, as they finde their subjects to value them. *Ambassadors* have ever been sacred persons, and partakers of great priviledges. A Prince, that lives as ours, in the eye of many Ambassadors, is not as the *children of Israel,* in the midst of *Canaanites,* and *Jebusites,* and *Ammonites,* who all watched the destruction of *Israel;* but he is in the midst of *Tutelar Angels, Nationall Angels,* who study (by Gods grace, and as it becomes us to hope) the peace and welfare of the *Christian State.* But then all strangers in the land, are not noble, and candid, and ingenuous *Ambassadors;* and even *Ambassadors* themselves may be misled to an undervalue of the Prince, by rumours, and by disloyal, and by negligent speaches, from the Subject; we have not yet felt *Solomons whippes;* but our whinings and repinings, and discontents may bring us to *Rehoboams Scorpions.* This way hath a part, in the Kings safetie, and in our safety, to hold in our selves, and to convay to strangers, a good estimation of that happy government, which is truly good in it self.

And then a third, and very important way towards his preservation, is, a cheerfull disposition, to supply, and to support, and to assist him, with such things as are necessary for his outward dignity. When God himselfe was the immediate King of the Israelites, and governed them, by himself, he took it ill, that they would depart from him, who needed nothing of theirs, for there could be no other King, but must necessarily be supplyed by them: And yet, consider, Beloved, what God, who needed nothing, took: The *sacrifices* of the Jews, were such, as would have kept divers Royall houses: Take a bill of them, but in one Passeover, that *Iosiah* kept, and compare that and other the like, with the smalness of the land, that they possessed, and you will see, that that they gave, was a very great proportion. Now, it is the service of God, to contribute to *the King,* as well as to *the Priest:* He that gives to a Prophet, shall have a Prophets reward; he that gives to the King, shall have a Kings reward, a Crown, in those cases, where to give to your King, is to give to *God,* that is, where the peace of the State, and the glory of God in his Gospel depends much, upon the sustentation of the estimation, and outward honour and splendour of the King: preserve him so, and he shall the lesse be subject to these dangers, of such falling into their pits.

But lastly, and especially, let us preserve him, by preserving God amongst us, in the true, and sincere profession of our Religion. Let not a mis-grounded, and disloyall imagination of coolness in him, cool you, in your own families. *Omnis spiritus, qui solvit Iesum,* says the Apostle, in the *Vulgat,* every spirit that *dissolves* Jesus, that *embraces not Iesus intirely, All Iesus,* and *All his, All his Truth,* and *all that suffer for that Truth, is not of God.* Doe not say, I will hold as much of Jesus, as shall be necessary, so much as shall distinguish me from a *Turk,* or a *Iew,* but if I may be the better, for parting with some of the rest, why should I not? Doe not say, I will hold All, my self, but let my wife, or my son, or one of my sons, goe the other way, as though *Protestant,* and Papist were two severall callings; and, as you would make one son a Lawyer, another a Merchant, you will make one son a Papist, another a Protestant. Excuse not your own levity, with so high a dishonor to the Prince; when have you heard, that ever he thanked any man, for becoming a Papist? Leave his dores to himselfe; The dores into his kingdome, *The Ports,* and the dores in his kingdome, The *prisons;* Let him open and shut his dores, as God shall put into his minde: look thou seriously to thine own dores, to thine own family, and keep all right there. A Thief that is let out of New-gate is not therefore let into thy house; A Priest that is let out of prison, is not therefore let into thy house neither: still it may be felony, to harbour him, though there were mercy in letting him out. Cities are built of families, and so are Churches too; Every man keeps his owne family, and then every Pastor shall keep his flock, and so the Church shall be free from schisme, and the State from sedition, and our *Josiah* preserved, Prophetically for ever, as he was Historically this day, from them, in whose pits, the breath of our nostrils, the anointed of the Lord, was taken. *Amen.*

Also from Benediction Books ...

Wandering Between Two Worlds: Essays on Faith and Art
Anita Mathias
Benediction Books, 2007
152 pages
ISBN: 0955373700

Available from www.amazon.com, www.amazon.co.uk
www.wanderingbetweentwoworlds.com

In these wide-ranging lyrical essays, Anita Mathias writes, in lush, lovely prose, of her naughty Catholic childhood in Jamshedpur, India; her large, eccentric family in Mangalore, a sea-coast town converted by the Portuguese in the sixteenth century; her rebellion and atheism as a teenager in her Himalayan boarding school, run by German missionary nuns, St. Mary's Convent, Nainital; and her abrupt religious conversion after which she entered Mother Teresa's convent in Calcutta as a novice. Later rich, elegant essays explore the dualities of her life as a writer, mother, and Christian in the United States--Domesticity and Art, Writing and Prayer, and the experience of being "an alien and stranger" as an immigrant in America, sensing the need for roots.

About the Author

Anita Mathias was born in India, has a B.A. and M.A. in English from Somerville College, Oxford University and an M.A. in Creative Writing from the Ohio State University. Her essays have been published in The Washington Post, The London Magazine, The Virginia Quarterly Review, Commonweal, Notre Dame Magazine, America, The Christian Century, Religion Online, The Southwest Review, Contemporary Literary Criticism, New Letters, The Journal, and two of HarperSanFrancisco's The Best Spiritual Writing anthologies. Her non-fiction has won fellowships from The National Endowment for the Arts; The Minnesota State Arts Board; The Jerome Foundation, The Vermont Studio Center; The Virginia Centre for the Creative Arts, and the First Prize for the Best General Interest Article from the Catholic Press Association of the United States and Canada. Anita has taught Creative Writing at the College of William and Mary, and now lives and writes in Oxford, England.

"Yesterday's Treasures for Today's Readers"

Titles by Benediction Classics available from Amazon.co.uk

Religio Medici, Hydriotaphia, Letter to a Friend, Thomas Browne

Pseudodoxia Epidemica: Or, Enquiries into Commonly Presumed Truths, Thomas Browne

The Maid's Tragedy, Beaumont and Fletcher

The Custom of the Country, Beaumont and Fletcher

Philaster Or Love Lies a Bleeding, Beaumont and Fletcher

A Treatise of Fishing with an Angle, Dame Juliana Berners.

Pamphilia to Amphilanthus, Lady Mary Wroth

The Compleat Angler, Izaak Walton

The Magnetic Lady, Ben Jonson

Every Man Out of His Humour, Ben Jonson

The Masque of Blacknesse. The Masque of Beauty,. Ben Jonson

The Life of St. Thomas More, William Roper

Pendennis, William Makepeace Thackeray

Salmacis and Hermaphroditus attributed to Francis Beaumont

Friar Bacon and Friar Bungay Robert Greene

Holy Wisdom, Augustine Baker

The Jew of Malta and the Massacre at Paris, Christopher Marlowe

Tamburlaine the Great, Parts 1 & 2 AND Massacre at Paris, Christopher Marlowe

All Ovids Elegies, Lucans First Booke, Dido Queene of Carthage, Hero and Leander, Christopher Marlowe

The Titan, Theodore Dreiser

Scapegoats of the Empire: The true story of the Bushveldt Carbineers, George Witton

All Hallows' Eve, Charles Williams

My Apprenticeship: Volumes I and II, Beatrice Webb

Last and First Men / Star Maker, Olaf Stapledon

Darkness and the Light, Olaf Stapledon

The Worst Journey in the World, Apsley Cherry-Garrard

The Schoole of Abuse, Containing a Pleasaunt Invective Against Poets, Pipers, Plaiers, Iesters and Such Like Catepillers of the Commonwelth, Stephen Gosson

Russia in the Shadows, H. G. Wells

Wild Swans at Coole, W. B. Yeats

A hundreth good pointes of husbandrie, Thomas Tusser

The Collected Works of Nathanael West: "The Day of the Locust", "The Dream Life of Balso Snell", "Miss Lonelyhearts", "A Cool Million", Nathanael West

Miss Lonelyhearts & The Day of the Locust, Nathaniel West

The Worst Journey in the World, Apsley Cherry-Garrard

Scott's Last Expedition, V1, R. F. Scott

The Dream of Gerontius, John Henry Newman

The Brother of Daphne, Dornford Yates

The Poetry of Architecture: Or the Architecture of the Nations of Europe Considered in Its Association with Natural Scenery and National Character, John Ruskin

The Downfall of Robert Earl of Huntington, Anthony Munday

Clayhanger, Arnold Bennett

South: The Story of Shackleton's Last Expedition 1914-1917, Sir Ernest Shackketon

Greene's Groatsworth of Wit: Bought With a Million of Repentance, Robert Greene

Beau Sabreur, Percival Christopher Wren

The Hekatompathia, or Passionate Centurie of Love, Thomas Watson

The Art of Rhetoric, Thomas Wilson

Stepping Heavenward, Elizabeth Prentiss

Barker's Delight, or The Art of Angling, Thomas Barker
The Napoleon of Notting Hill, G.K. Chesterton

The Douay-Rheims Bible (The Challoner Revision)

Endimion - The Man in the Moone, John Lyly

Gallathea and Midas, John Lyly,

Manners, Custom and Dress During the Middle Ages and During the Renaissance Period, Paul Lacroix

Obedience of a Christian Man, William Tyndale

St. Patrick for Ireland, James Shirley

The Wrongs of Woman; Or Maria/Memoirs of the Author of a Vindication of the Rights of Woman, Mary Wollstonecraft and William Godwin

www.ingramcontent.com/pod-product-compliance
Lightning Source LLC
Chambersburg PA
CBHW030522100426
42813CB00001B/122
* 9 7 8 1 8 4 9 0 2 0 4 0 4 *